PLAN "Z"
TOP SECRET
OPERATION RIMAU

EASTERN ANCHORAGE

FLEET

THE HEROES OF
RIMAU

Unravelling the mystery of one of World War II's most daring raids

by LYNETTE RAMSAY SILVER
from the research of Major Tom Hall

LEO COOPER
London

This book is dedicated to the twenty-three.

First published in 1990 by
Sally Milner Publishing Pty Ltd
17 Wharf Road
Birchgrove NSW 2041 Australia

First published in Great Britain in 1991 by Leo Cooper
190 Shaftsbury Avenue, London WC2H 8JL
an imprint of Pen & Sword Books Ltd.
47 Church Street, Barnsley, S. Yorks S70 2AS

© Major Tom Hall & Lynette Ramsay Silver

Design by Doric Order
Cover design by David Constable
Production by Sylvana Scannapiego,
Island Graphics
Typeset in Australia by Asset Typesetting Pty Ltd
Printed in Malaysia by SRM Production Services Sdn. Bhd.

A CIP catalogue record for this book is available from
The British Library

ISBN 0 85052 334 6

Contents

Foreword
by Colonel The Lord Langford, OBE, DL

The Heroes of Rimau is a factual historical record, telling of profound determination and dedication to duty which ended in the ultimate in courage – facing execution by the sword.

Lieutenant-Colonel Ivan Lyon, Gordon Highlanders, led two expeditions against Japanese-held Singapore. Operation Jaywick in 1943 was resoundingly successful, with no Allied casualities and 37 000 tons of Japanese shipping sunk. Operation Rimau in 1944 was equally successful regarding Japanese shipping losses but this time, by the greatest mischance, the Japanese were alerted. There was a running fire fight through the islands south of Singapore in which Ivan Lyon and twelve of his companions were killed. The remaining ten were taken prisoner and executed only six weeks before the Japanese surrender in August 1945.

There have been at least three attempts to distort or prevent the true facts of Operation Rimau becoming widely known.

The Japanese could not believe that the sinkings of their ships were carried out by other than internal resistance groups and they therefore executed hundreds, if not thousands, of Chinese and Malays in Singapore, together with a substantial number of Allied internees. The Japanese were also understandably sensitive about the legality of the trial which resulted in the deaths of the ten captured Rimau men.

A Royal Navy submarine commander failed to keep a rendezvous on the right date, arriving no less than two weeks late and for no adequate operational reason.

Following a superficial Allied investigation into the fate of the Rimau men, the Australian government also played its part in general post-war secrecy. Three days after the Japanese surrender, the Allied Intelligence Services received a derisive message from the Japanese, from which it became obvious that a large part of our Allied special operations within Japanese-held territories had been seriously compromised since mid 1943, with usually fatal results to the field operatives involved.

Such were the face-saving cover ups by the Japanese and the Allies at the highest levels that it has taken thirty years for Major Tom Hall to uncover the truth. Using his research, Lynette Ramsay Silver has now written the definitive account of Operations Jaywick and Rimau – two of the most remarkable expeditions of World War II.

Rhuddlan, North Wales, May 1991.

Editor's note: Lord Langford, who appears in this book as Major Geoffrey Rowley-Conwy, was a colleague and close friend of Ivan Lyon.

Maps

Glossary of Malay terms

attap   woven palm-leaf
kampong   a village
kolek   a small two-three man boat
               for fishing in sheltered waters
pagar   a large fish-trap on stilts
prahu   an ocean-going sailing vessel
pulau   an island
tandjung   a cape (geographical feature)
tonga   a two-wheeled, horse drawn vehicle
tonkan   any wooden boat or ship

Acknowledgements

We gratefully acknowledge the trustees of the Australian War Memorial for permission to reproduce photographic material from the collection; the families, friends and colleagues of the Jaywick and Rimau men who supplied information and photographic material from their private collections, particularly Moss Berryman, Commander Geoffrey Brooke, Harry Browne, Muriel Buie, the late K. P. 'Cobber' Cain, Sir Walter Campbell, Professor Sam Carey, Rae Chambers, the late Ron Croton, Rose David, John Grimwade, Biddy and Gordon Kurtz, Lord Langford (Colonel Geoffrey Rowley-Conwy), Mary Lennox, Clive Lyon, Commander Hubert Marsham, Vice-Admiral Sir Hugh Mackenzie, Major Francis Moir-Byres, Major Ron Morris, Roma Page, Brian Passmore, Bettina Reid, Margaret Reynolds, Peter and Tom Sachs, Noel Wynyard, and Horrie Young; the people of the Indonesian Islands of Kasu, Merapas, Bintan and the Lingga Archipelago, particularly Abdul Rachman Achap, Arafin Bin Akup, Batjuk, Karta, Abdul and Mrs Latif, Mahat Kunil, Raja Mohammad and the late Sidek Bin Safar; Yoshi Tosa for his translation of Japanese documents; Marlene von Bornemann and David Reeve for checking Indonesian translations; Ursula Davidson, Ron Gilchrist, Liz Nathan, and Joy Wheatley for particular assistance with research material; Drs Kenneth Brown and Godfrey Oettle for forensic analysis; the many who gave assistance and support to Tom Hall during his research, particularly Major Mike Askey, Charles Buttrose, Tip Carty, Colonel George Cardy, Joy and Norm Craig, M. G. Eussen-Mrëyen, the late Tony Wykeham-Fiennes, Mavis Hedrick, Ian Headrick, Alf Henricksen, the late Major Rich Hertz, Alan Johnson, Caroline Jones, Alan Morris, Colonel Henk Mrëyen, Elanora Poullos, Captain John Stevenson, Jim Sloggett, Fred Spring, Bruce Stracey, Leigh Sydenham and Jim Walpole; and our immediate families and friends, particularly Marie Hall, Neil Silver and Suzy Baldwin, for their unstinting encouragement and support during the researching and writing of this book.

Prologue

Lieutenant Tom Hall was in a distinctly foul mood as he waited on the small beach beneath the sea wall at Chowder Bay. Beyond the beach, the waters of Sydney Harbour had none of their usual sparkle, for the winter of 1958 had been cold, wet and miserable. He thought of his diggers, by now enjoying a scheduled parachute jump at Williamtown Airbase. 'Everyone in the platoon is having a great time except me,' he fumed. Trust the Commanding Officer of One Commando Company to lumber him with this ridiculous assignment, ostensibly in the name of good public relations. Since when had the army ever bothered itself with PR and why pick on him in particular? Not that he hadn't put on quite a turn when it was announced that he had been pulled out of the parachute exercise and placed on special duty. Of course, this voluble outburst hadn't done him the slightest bit of good and the CO had finally been obliged to tell him, in very plain language, to get on with it.

Well he had got on with it. His two-man canoe was drawn up on the damp, gritty sand beside him, the truck was ready for the return trip to the barracks and he was spick and span in army fatigues, his green commando beret clamped firmly on his head in defiance of the blustery wind. And now he was waiting for a journalist who, for some unknown reason, wanted to learn all about two-man canoes. At the harsh sound of an army utility, scrunching suddenly to a stop in the gravel of the road above, he turned to focus his attention upon the source of his discontent. 'About bloody time too,' he thought.

Hall figured that the civilian was aged about forty, which seemed so far removed from his own youthful twenty-four years that it bordered on the decrepit. But it was not the advanced years of the visitor that stopped Hall momentarily in his tracks — it was his clothing. With the utmost self control, his resolve undoubtedly bolstered by the proximity of his superior officer, the lieutenant suppressed his mirth. Never, on any of his army assignments, had he seen anything quite like it. The gentleman looked as if he had just emerged from one of the tailoring establishments so favoured by Prime Minister Bob Menzies, for he was immaculately clad, dapper even, in a dark, three-piece, pinstriped suit, double-breasted at that. 'It's a wonder,' thought Hall, 'that he didn't bring a bloody bowler hat and umbrella as well.'

With great difficulty Hall managed to keep a perfectly straight face as he greeted the newcomer, farewelled the CO and led the way over the sea wall and down to the beach. It seemed that the journalist was writing a book and wanted the lowdown on operational army canoes — the collapsible, lightweight variety used in commando work. As the visitor inspected the rubberised canvas craft sitting high and dry on the coarse sand, Hall decided on his line of action. He looked at his guest and said, with the most disarming smile, 'There's only one way to learn about paddling canoes, Sir, and that is to get in.'

Without the slightest protest, the gentleman removed his shoes and coat, placed them in the truck for safekeeping, and climbed gingerly aboard while Hall selected the route. With the wind roaring in from the Heads, there was no question of their paddling towards the Harbour Bridge, for they would stand little chance of getting back. Instead, he chose a destination on the other side of the harbour, a small cove on the southern shore known as Nielsen Park.

Since the wind had created quite a chop on the normally smooth harbour waters, the ride was far from enjoyable. Spray beat into their faces and salty water slopped over the sides of the low-profile craft. The continuous drip of the paddle, as Hall, who had three years' experience of canoe paddling, cut expertly through the waves, did little to alleviate the discomfort of the journalist, perched stoically in the rear. By the time they reached Nielsen Park they were both soaking wet and the passenger was looking more than bedraggled. The return journey was worse, for their saturated clothing was now uncomfortably cold in a wind that whistled around Middle Head and hit them broadside as Hall manoeuvred the small boat back to Chowder Bay.

However, his frustration at having been ordered to carry out this exercise had not been mitigated in the slightest by the return trip across the harbour so, with nothing to lose and a great deal of satisfaction to gain, he capsized the canoe in deep water. The fact that he was as wet as his victim was of small consequence, for he was used to such discomfort. His passenger, quite clearly, was not. With as much dignity as he could muster, he emerged from the icy harbour waters looking very much like a drowned rat and shivering uncontrollably.

The lieutenant bundled him into the truck and returned to the barracks. Here they were met by the CO. On his viewing the dishevelled state of the formerly impeccably dressed journalist, it was obvious that Lieutenant Hall's popularity had taken yet another dive. Realising that a quick exit was in order, Hall grabbed his unfortunate guest and made for the safety of the Officers' Mess. There, still feeling far from contrite, Hall handed him a generous tot of rum and said, without much conviction, 'I'm sorry you got so wet.'

The journalist uttered no word of complaint as he responded to the proffered apology. But his reply sent Hall on a search that was to last thirty-one years.

'You couldn't have given me a better introduction to canoeing,' he said, between sips of the life-restoring rum. 'I know of three soldiers who paddled a canoe just like yours over a distance of more than two thousand five hundred miles from Singapore to Timor during the Second World War.'

Hall, for once, was speechless. It wasn't possible, he thought. During his training he had paddled one of these craft for fifty miles (eighty kilometres) down the peaceful Hawkesbury River. Apart from wanting to rip apart the bloke in the rear cockpit who had dripped cold water from his paddle down Hall's neck for the entire journey, he recalled that, although very fit, they had both been potential candidates for the intensive care ward at the end of the exercise. So, to paddle over two thousand five hundred miles (four thousand kilometres)? In a two-man canoe? With Japs after you? Existing on hard rations at best? It just wasn't possible.

'Who were these blokes?' Hall quizzed his informant, his annoyance at missing the parachute exercise now temporarily forgotten. 'I know the name of only one,' the journalist said, 'and he was executed before the end of the war. The names of the other two men have, unfortunately, not been recorded.' 'That's not bloody fair,' retorted Hall with some heat. 'You can't know what they did and not know who they are.'

But, to the officer's dismay, the journalist insisted that, fair or not, it was true. No one knew their identities, only that somehow they had managed to paddle from Singapore to Romang Island near Timor. Then they had apparently vanished into thin air.

The young commando's imagination was fired. He had spent six years in and around army barracks and had never heard the slightest whisper of anything remotely resembling this story. He had to know who had accomplished this apparently impossible feat.

So began a quest that was to dominate Tom Hall's life for the next three decades. For five years he made little headway. All official documents were closed until 1975 and a brief account that was published in 1960, later to prove a mixture of fiction and fact, raised more questions than it answered. In desperation, in 1963, Hall wrote a letter to the Minister for the Army, requesting the names of the mysterious paddlers and the details of their mission, only to find his request for information was met with answers that told him nothing and evaded the issue. Why? he wondered. What was such a big deal about two canoe paddlers? Undeterred, he tried elsewhere. During the next four years he wrote a total of seventeen letters to every government department he could think of, asking the same question. But it was not until he wrote to Prime Minister Robert Menzies that he finally received some action. Hall was summoned to Victoria Barracks where he was ordered to cease asking any more questions on the subject. Although threatened with a court martial, he refused to obey the order, a decision that ultimately cost him his career in the army.

In 1978, having spent the intervening years gleaning a little information here, another snippet there, the breakthrough finally came. Many of the documents that were to help him in his search had finally been released after the lifting of a thirty-year, post-war secrecy ban.

His research gained momentum and in the process of his lengthy investigation a story far greater than that of two canoeists emerged — a story of bravery, of unbelievable tenacity, of tragedy and despair. It was the story of Operation Rimau, in which his two unnamed heroes had been engaged. This operation involved not three but twenty-three gallant men, none of whom survived. It was an operation shrouded in mystery and hopelessly complicated by misinformation that reached far beyond the mission itself.

Finally, in 1983, after a lifetime of running up against brick walls, of being confronted by evasiveness, bureaucratic red tape and false trails, of being fed almost pure fiction through which ran thin threads of truth, Hall at last achieved what he had initially set out to do on that cold July day.

He discovered the names of the two men.

Fired with even greater enthusiasm, and realising that the true story had not yet fully emerged, he set about filling in the details until, after a six-year search, the last piece of the vast, complicated jigsaw fell into place. Hall had uncovered a saga beyond his wildest imagination, a story that both frightened and overawed him, and which vindicated his determination to arrive at the truth. After thirty-one years Tom Hall knew what had happened to every person engaged in Operation Rimau.

This, then, is their story.

Chapter 1
A Fool's Paradise

Along the entire length of Sumatra's Indragiri River the silence of the heavy, moisture-laden air was palpable. From the village of Prigi Radja on the mangrove-clustered rivermouth to the upper reaches above Rengat the jungle was still. Waiting.

The occasional ripple from a crocodile, disturbed from its somnolence on the muddy banks by monkeys chattering in the trees overhead, was the only movement perceptible on the sluggish water. Beyond the river's edge, the craggy, jungle-clad mountains reared almost vertically, thrusting cloud-shrouded peaks to the pale equatorial sky. In the small scattered villages, hidden behind palm groves and lush rainforest, the native people went about their daily business with typical languor, undisturbed and unaware that events about to happen in Singapore, 300 kilometres beyond the horizon, would reshape history.

Singapore, a small emerald isle in a milky jade sea, hung like a precious jewel at the end of Britain's rich, far-eastern necklace. This valuable crossroad between East and West, handling and monopolising the vast tin and rubber resources of Malaya, had served the Empire well. Although a bare forty-two kilometres by twenty-three kilometres in size, the tiny, roughly diamond-shaped island was the centrepiece of the oriental trade routes; a tropical colonial outpost whose trade and commerce, centred around a bustling, busy port, had swelled the coffers of the Motherland for decades.

Life for the privileged white community was slow paced, carefree and terribly British. Despite the heat, cricket was played in the time-honoured way on the lushly green, picturesque fields of the Cricket Club, a mere stone's throw from the colonnaded City Hall and the domed Supreme Court whose architecture was so reminiscent of many of London's public buildings. Nearby, Saint Andrew's Cathedral, traditional in line but clad in bright tropical white, called the faithful to Matins and Evensong each Sunday, adding to the illusion that here was a little slice of England.

How easy it was to forget about the hundreds of thousands of Asians who lived in the cluttered slums of Chinatown, on the sampan-choked waterways and in palm-thatched native kampongs. Fortunately for the illusion, these less desirable aspects of the Singapore scene were kept well out of sight, way beyond the walls of the good, solid British bungalows with their neatly clipped lawns and hedges.

With servants galore, social clubs abounded, staffed by battalions of acquiescing Chinese ready to fulfil the slightest wish at the snap of two well-manicured white fingers. At the very exclusive Tanglin Club, which was barred to all non-Europeans, the sign 'No Chinese or Dogs Allowed' left the Chinese in no doubt whatever as to their status. The cheap and plentiful workforce created by them, and the even less acceptable Malays and Indians, enabled the most lowly paid expatriate to have at least one servant at his beck and call. From their position of privilege and power, the Europeans, who made up less than one per cent of the population, had absolute control of the social scene, the government and the purse strings. Apart from the usual shortcomings of bureaucratic civil servants, things were run more or less efficiently, with the local people doing the bulk of the real work and the British reaping the benefits.[1]

But it was not trade and government alone that bound the British to their small colonial empire. The island was also the site of the world's most up-to-date naval base. Nearing completion in 1941 after more than twenty years of stop-start delays and at a cost of over sixty million pounds sterling, it was the pride of the British Empire. Protected by a seaward-facing armament of twenty-seven fixed guns, ranging up to fifteen inches (thirty-eight cm) in calibre, the island and its base were considered to be a fortress, impregnable to attack — a citadel that could withstand a siege for months. This was a widely held belief, reinforced by the fact that, to the rear of the island, sheltering it from any land-based attack, lay Malaya — mountainous, jungle-covered, inhospitable, impenetrable Malaya.[2]

Although the war in Europe had been in progress for over two years, the events in the northern hemisphere in late 1941 were of little consequence in Singapore. If the aggressive and land-hungry Japanese left their bases in Indo-China and came too close, heavily defended Singapore would be a safe haven, protected by the might of the British Far Eastern Fleet and ably assisted by the air force (actually at its lowest strength ever), according to propaganda that appeared in the London newspapers and the local *Straits Times*. With Air Vice-Marshall Brooke-Popham, Commander-in-Chief of the Far East, stating that the Japanese were neither air minded nor properly trained,[3] it is little wonder that the civilians believed the nonsense that they read over breakfast on 27 October 1941, in a newspaper item which declared:

I bring you good news — there is no need to worry about the strength of the Air Force that will oppose the Japanese should they send their army and navy southward . . . The Air Force is on the spot, and is waiting for the enemy — clouds of bombers and fighters are hidden in the jungle, and are ready to move out on to camouflaged tarmacs of our secret landing fields and roar into action at the first move of the Japanese towards this part of the world . . . The planes consist of the most modern planes Britain, Australia and America are producing.[4]

Consequently, air raid drills were deemed to be unnecessary and, since it was a well-known fact that Japanese pilots were unable to fly in the dark, so were blackouts. In any case, it was reasoned, how could a nation like Japan be a threat to a powerful stronghold like Singapore? Consequently, while Europe tore itself apart and Nazi terror spread like a bloodstain across the occupied countries, life in Singapore went on much the same as usual.[5]

On the morning of 8 December 1941, everything changed.

As the younger set danced the night away at Raffles Hotel, and society's more mature members sipped on their chilled Singapore Slings at the Singapore Club, the Imperial Japanese Army invaded Malaya — on bicycles. As the Defence Chiefs in Britain had paid scant attention to warnings that Japan might just do what a handful of far-seeing military personnel had long ago suggested, the invaders pedalled down the fine bitumen roads virtually unopposed.[6]

As far back as 1924 it had been reported that invasion of Malaya could be achieved by landing on the north-eastern coast and then pushing southwards on the excellent roads that cut a swathe through the jungle. This report had elicited no response whatever from the army hierarchy. Fourteen years later another report by Colonel Hayley Bell, the Chief Intelligence Officer based in Singapore, was virtually ignored, as was a similar report sent by Major-General Dobbie, General Officer Commanding Singapore, the previous year. Bell, who had been raised in Japan, spoke perfect Japanese and understood the Japanese mind, had been keeping a watchful eye on Japanese movements and had been investigating their espionage activities in his area since October 1936. He pin-pointed the most likely place for a land-based invasion as the north-eastern coastal beaches near Kota Bharu, in the Kalatan area of Malaya, and those of southern Siam (now Thailand), during the period of the north-east monsoon, a time previously thought to be unlikely.[7] When this perceptive analysis had been independently confirmed by exercises, the complete report was dispatched to England in 1938, advising that the security of the naval base depended entirely upon holding northern Malaya and Johore.[8] In the light of what followed, it can only be assumed that these papers, along with the earlier analyses, were neatly filed away in the correct bureaucratic manner, never again to see the light of day.

In spite of the general apathy of the Defence Ministry in England and the hostility of the local administration, who would have much preferred that Bell's frightening document never existed, Dobbie's request for extra fortifications did result in limited funds being made available and some work being carried out.[9] Unfortunately, when General Dobbie, one of the few to realise the precarious defensive state of Malaya and Singapore, was recalled to England, the work stopped with only one-third of the paltry £60 000 allocated having been spent.[10] The disturbing assessment by the brilliantly percipient Bell was so unwanted by the local civil administration that he too was recalled to England in 1939 at the special request of the Governor, whose word was almost law. With Bell out of the way, the excellent counter-espionage organisation that he had set up with the Malay States Chief of Police was disbanded, giving the Japanese spy network a completely free reign.[11]

Sadly, internal faction fighting was as much a threat to the stability of Malaya as that posed by the Japanese. Despite fierce protests from the army that airstrips were in positions impossible to defend, construction work by the air force continued willy-nilly.[12] When it was suspected that Japan might enter the war, no proper air raid shelters were built, nor were the defensive works completed. The fragile egos of the local administration and the bitter dissension between the military and the Colonial Office hierarchy as to who was in charge ensured that there was a minimum amount of co-operation and a maximum amount of delay for any decision.[13]

The lesser government servants, and indeed the private sector, were no better, not even when it became obvious that Singapore was in serious trouble. When Major Angus Rose of the Argyll and Sutherland High-landers wanted to cut down a row of banana palms to improve his field of fire, he was told that before he could do so he needed written permission from 'the competent authority'. The secretary of the strategically placed Singapore Golf Club, on being informed that the club was to be turned into a strongpoint, declared that before such a thing could be contemplated a special committee meeting would have to be convened.[14] As no one, from the defence chiefs to the humblest clerk, could perceive any real danger, the 'fortress' myth, reinforced in the popular mind by the press, became an unshakeable 'fact'.[15]

As a result, by 1940 the air force was severely under strength, as was the number of garrisoned troops, while the naval base was almost devoid of ships since the fleet was elsewhere, fighting battles in the Mediterranean and Atlantic. The 'alarmists' were shouted down and Winston Churchill, the British Prime Minister, expounded his belief again and again that the fortress of Singapore was impregnable, safe from invasion by the awesome firepower of its guns and the 'splendid, broad moat' that surrounded it.[16]

Australia and New Zealand were not as complacent. Vulnerable to attack, since almost all their trained troops had been dispatched to the Middle East, they had voiced their anxiety on many occasions, only to be reassured by Churchill that war with the Japanese was almost beyond the realms of possibility. In December 1939 he had written:

Singapore is a fortress armed with five fifteen-inch guns and garrisoned by almost 20 000 men. It could only be taken after a siege by an enemy of at least 50 000 men . . . such a siege would be liable to be interrupted if at any time Britain chose to send a superior fleet to the scene . . . It is not considered that the Japanese . . . would embark on such a mad enterprise.[17]

His wildly extravagant promises that Britain would neither allow Singapore to fall nor permit a serious attack on either Australia or New Zealand should never have been made. As Churchill later confided to US President Roosevelt 'any threat of major invasion . . . would, of course, force us to withdraw our Fleet from the Eastern Mediterranean with disastrous military possibilities there'.[18]

Five months later, singularly unimpressed by Churchill's fine sentiments, the General Officer Commanding Malaya submitted a new appraisal of the situation, requesting an extra four divisions, including two tank regiments. Not a single tank ever appeared.[19] Neither would the much vaunted Eastern Fleet ever arrive, for by August 1940 the defence chiefs had conceded that this was a pipe dream and that if it came to all-out war the whole of Malaya would have to be held.[20] While they acknowledged that this would require more troops and a minimum of 336 aircraft to supplement the eighty-eight obsolete machines already in Malaya, they also decided that none could be spared for the time being.[21]

This policy paper, along with other top secret documents, was handed over to Japan after the German Raider *Atlantis* intercepted SS *Autonedan* on her way to Malaya. On receipt of this priceless information the Japanese, who had long assumed that there was an integrated plan for the defence of the area, knew that the vision of Singapore the fortress was an illusion. Consequently, they began to plan in earnest.[22]

In November 1940, shortly after the generals in Malaya had advised Churchill that without a massive injection of planes and equipment it was not thought that 'a Japanese invasion could be defeated',[23] the Australian Defence Minister was horrified to discover that Singapore's capacity to withstand any attack from the land was almost nil.[24] Once again Churchill and Brooke-Popham made assurances that Singapore was strong enough to hold off any attack for six months until the fleet arrived — a period of time euphemistically called 'the Period before Relief', which had progressively climbed from seventy days at the beginning of the war to one hundred and eighty.[25]

By April 1941, when Churchill made his high-handed decision to start an ill-fated campaign in Greece, twenty-six years after Gallipoli, another Churchillian disaster that had almost wiped out a generation of Australian youth, Prime Minister Menzies began to have doubts about Churchill's 'unilateral rhetoric'. Completely disillusioned, Menzies considered the British War Cabinet to be 'deplorable — dumb men most of whom disagree with Winston but none of whom dare to say so . . . The Chiefs of Staff are without exception Yes men, and a politician runs the services'. About Churchill's dictatorial style he was especially scathing, reporting that 'the people have set him up as something little less than God, and his power is therefore terrific'.

When this assessment of the capabilities of the leaders of the Mother Country, and of Churchill in particular, became known, Menzies found himself even less popular in England. Constantly treated like a poor relation and repeatedly fobbed off by Chiefs-of-Staff, his request for Hurricane fighters to be dispatched to the Far East was turned down with the argument that the Middle East had priority and, in any case, the Buffalo aircraft already there would 'probably prove more than a match for any Japanese aircraft'.[26]

Plans had been put into operation the previous year to strengthen the garrison in Malaya and Singapore. British regiments transferred from Shanghai in August were supplemented by hastily formed, partially trained Indian troops who arrived in October and November.[27] As the Indian brigades did not provide nearly enough manpower, pressure was put on Australia, which had already sent three divisions to the Middle East. It was only after much hesitation that three battalions of the Eighth Division were detached to Malaya in February 1941, on the condition that, as soon as more Indian troops were ready, the Australians would join their comrades in the Middle East.[28] Apart from the officers serving in the Indian Army and the regiments from Shanghai, no British-born troops were diverted or conscripted for the reinforcement of Malaya. It was simply a case of the subjects of one colonised part of the British Empire being sent to the defence of another.

Five months later, three more Australian battalions arrived. The Australians, known as the AIF Malaya,[29] were placed under the command of Major-General Gordon Bennett, a brilliant and highly decorated citizen soldier from the First World War who had seen action in Gallipoli and France and who had gained the distinction of becoming the British Empire's youngest general at the age of twenty-nine.[30]

Although his Commanding Officer was British Lieutenant-General Percival, Bennett was unique in that he had direct access to the Australian Government, to whom he was answerable for the troops' well being. The fiascos of the First World War, when Australians were used as shock troops by British generals, had made the government very wary the second time around. This accountability, coupled with Bennett's somewhat tempestuous nature and his inability to suffer fools gladly, was inevitably to generate friction with General Percival.[31]

Back in London's War Office, there was concern in some quarters that the predictions made by so-called scaremongers might perhaps come to fruition. After much delay, Chief Engineer Brigadier Ivan Simson arrived in Malaya in August 1941 with orders to install the most modern types of defences, particularly in areas vulnerable to beach landings, tank and air attack. With Allied sanctions severing supplies of oil, rubber and iron ore, forcing Japan to cast envious eyes towards the resource-rich Far East, Simson's work should have assumed top priority. Unfortunately, a long-standing enmity between the Engineer's Office and the General Staff ensured that any co-operation he received from military and civil chiefs was minimal.[32]

Simson's greatest opposition came from Percival who, while being an excellent staff officer, had no experience of command in war. Described as being 'good on paper but no leader' and thought to be a former schoolmaster who perhaps should have remained so, Percival was evidently a colourless personality, a 'nice, good man', who appeared to consider the entire situation as being nothing more than 'a field day at Aldershot'.[33] He took no interest in Simson's mission,[34] even though he had himself prepared the 1937 report for General Dobbie, stating that the threat to Malaya would be from the north.[35] Undeterred by Percival's attitude, Simson set off on a six-week tour of the area, visiting every beach head and travelling every road. He was appalled by what he saw.

There was no way that Malaya could fight off a full scale attack, either in the air, on the land, or from the sea. Apart from a sickening lack of equipment, including planes, tanks and naval craft, the troops were not in a state of readiness. Softened by months or even years of leisurely garrison living, all were, with the notable exception of the 2nd Battalion Argyll and Sutherland Highlanders and General Bennett's Australians, unfit to engage in jungle warfare.[36]

Almost as soon as he arrived in Malaya, Bennett had taken his Eighth Division into the jungle. It was just as well, for the European residents in town were less than welcoming to the soldiers from down under. Professing on the one hand that their love of the British Empire was almost equal to their love of God, King and Country, they looked down their noses with disdain when the 'colonials' — who inhabited, and were there to defend, that Empire — actually arrived on the scene. Barred from the clubs and better restaurants, the Australians were forced to patronise the sleazy back street establishments. The locals then explained away their ostracism by declaring that it had been difficult for them to be hospitable as the Australians were always hanging about the red light district.[37]

However, there was little time to fret over such matters. Before they had left home, Bennett's men had been issued with pamphlets warning that the jungle-wise Japanese were experienced, ruthless, highly trained, had few physical requirements and, unencumbered by non-essential paraphernalia, were able to move across country at great speed — a viewpoint quite opposite to that held by the Malayan Command.[38]

Trained and outfitted for a conventional war, the Australians, like the Argylls, found the jungle a new and terrifying experience. Bennett and the Argyll's Lieutenant-Colonel Stewart realised that retraining in tactics to suit the difficult terrain and enervating climate was essential. Clothing and equipment were modified or discarded and long-range weapons rejected in favour of short-range. The troops learned to ignore the discomfort of being constantly wet and to cope with energy-sapping heat, exotic animals, and the vast population of insects and reptiles. They learned to make the jungle work for, rather than against, them and, above all, they learned to adapt to conditions at a moment's notice.[39]

No one at headquarters took the slightest notice of the work being done by these two leaders and when Stewart passed on his information, Brigadier Torrence went so far as to declare that his ideas on jungle training were 'those of a crank'.[40] It was a view obviously shared by others for when one junior officer based in Singapore was enterprising enough to organise a training exercise in Johore, his Commanding Officer took no interest. He did not even turn up to observe, much less lead the exercise. He was occupied with something far more important on the day — playing cricket.[41]

While the British continued to indulge themselves in such frivolity, the Japanese were poised, ready to strike. Not only had they spent months in training, they had also been engaged in mock exercises designed to simulate conditions in Malaya. Years of preparation and planning had ensured that all soldiers knew what to expect and, to make certain that they had every angle covered, the Japanese commanders had issued all troops with a brilliantly thought-out publication entitled *Read This Alone — And The War Can Be Won*. This jungle fighting manual covered everything from the political situation in South-East Asia to care of weapons, from movement through plantations, jungle and bamboo groves to personal hygiene. There was nothing with which to compare it in the entire Allied army.[42]

While Bennett and Stewart were doing their utmost to prepare their men for action, Simson was applying himself to the task of putting the defensive works in order. Using Dobbie's unused equipment as a basis, he worked out a five-point comprehensive defence plan that involved use of anti-tank devices, booby traps, pill boxes, field defences, barbed wire barricades, minefields and finally, trained Malay and Chinese guerilla bands to operate behind enemy spearheads. He then went immediately to headquarters where he informed his superiors of the unpalatable defence position, the remedy, and the disturbing fact that the water supply for Singapore, coming via an exposed pipeline from Malaya, could not be protected from a direct hit. As the only other source of water was the old original rainwater reservoirs which, with careful rationing, might last for a protracted period, a scheme to sink supplementary wells was begun but later abandoned when the water was found to be contaminated.[43]

Simson's carefully thought out defence plans and recommendations achieved absolutely nothing. Percival ignored his persistent entreaties with a curt 'Defences are bad for morale — for both troops and civilians'.[44] He was obviously taking the same line to which, as late as November 1941, Churchill and General Wavell, Commander-in-Chief India, were still sticking — Japan would not make war. The Japanese might 'shout and threaten', Churchill had said, 'but would not move'. Wavell, full of bluff good cheer, had told Brooke-Popham, 'Personally, I should be most doubtful if the Japs ever tried to make an attack on Malaya, and I am sure they will get [it] in the neck if they do'.[45]

Despite troops being placed on a second degree of readiness, the feeling that nothing would happen was evidently so great that a cable was sent to Bennett in Cairo, telling him not to hurry back to Malaya as 'things are quiet and there is no prospect of hostilities'. Bennett, who had been visiting Australian troops engaged in a campaign in the Western Desert, decided to return to Malaya as planned. He had a gut feeling that something would happen, soon.[46] It is a pity that no one else felt the same way. According to the experts — Churchill, Wavell and Percival — the Japanese would not go to war with the British. Furthermore, the fortress would not fall. While the high command, ostrich like, ignored all the warning signals, and other observers wondered what the 'horrid little Japs' would do next,[47] Japan massed its military strength — an invasion army of 125 000 troops, many of whom had seen action in China, supported by tanks and the Japanese Navy and Air Force.

By December 7, the Allies had only managed to raise 88 600 men. The British garrisoned troops numbered 19 391, half of whom would not venture from the safety of Singapore. The Australians accounted for 15 279, while the Chinese and Malay volunteers totalled almost 12 000. Except for two thousand-odd British civilian volunteers, the rest, a staggering 37 000, was composed of Indian troops. Apart from the Argylls and the Australians, almost all the troops had no knowledge of jungle warfare. The Indians in particular, raised in such a hurry, were poorly trained and led for the most part by British Indian Army Officers whose main qualification was an ability to converse with their men in their mother tongue. As one senior commander so bluntly put it, 'the quality went quickly from cream to sour milk'.[48]

If quality was lacking, so too was quantity. Seventeen more infantry battalions, four light anti-aircraft regiments and two tank regiments were still needed, as well as the Hurricanes that had finally been promised — when and if the Japanese attacked. After four years of begging, there was still not a single tank to be had.[49] For poor, neglected Malaya, the outpost too far, it was the beginning of the end. No defences, no equipment, not enough trained troops, no fleet, no planes and no hope.

With lightning efficiency the Japanese struck on the morning of 8 December 1941. Without any declaration of war they bombed the

American Fleet at Pearl Harbour, the Philippine capital of Manila, the British Crown Colony of Hong Kong, Midway, Guam and Wake Islands and, just as had been predicted, landed on the beaches of southern Siam and at Kota Bharu, on the north-east coast of Malaya.[50] Despite the protestations of Winston Churchill, Britain, as well as the United States, was now at war with Japan.

It was a situation that elated, rather than deflated, Churchill. Although he admitted that he had misjudged the might of Japan and expected 'terrible forfeits in the East' he was ecstatic that Pearl Harbour had forced the United States to enter the war. 'So we had won after all!' he exalted.

> England would live. Britain would live; the Commonwealth of Nations and the Empire would live. Once again in our long Island history we should emerge, however mauled or mutilated, safe and victorious . . . there was no doubt about the end.[51]

Little did he realise that not only did the attacks herald a period of almost unsurpassed horror, producing some of the darkest days of the war, but that the death knell of the British Empire was already sounding.

Quite incredibly, the British Command, alerted by three Australian pilots on December 6 that an invasion fleet was off the Malayan coast, had done nothing except place troops in that area on a first degree of readiness. The following day, when these sightings were confirmed and a cruiser opened fire on one of the planes[52] Brooke-Popham was still not convinced that an invasion was imminent. Had he and Percival come to this conclusion he could have put into effect an operation code-named 'Matador'. It involved, in part, the deployment of troops into Siam to a place called The Ledge, a perfect defensive position for repelling an invasion from the coast. Having been given the go ahead to make the decision, but terrified that he might be the first to break the neutrality of Siam and so cause a serious diplomatic row — or worse, actual hostilities — Brooke-Popham dilly-dallied.

Evidently he did not consider the Japanese's having fired upon the aeroplane as a sufficiently aggressive act. He wanted more evidence. Were the Japanese, as the intelligence indicated, bound for Malaya or were they up to something else? He took the latter viewpoint.[53] Although the air force was alerted, there was 'no undue alarm owing to GHQ's view that the Japanese expedition was directed against Siam'.[54] While Brooke-Popham vacillated about whether or not to implement 'Matador', the Japanese invaded, leaving no doubt as to their intentions. By the time this became known at headquarters, it was far too late to do anything.

While the defence chiefs were discussing the 1.30 am landings on the Malayan coast, the Japanese turned their attention to Singapore. Quite amazingly, three hours after the invasion at Kota Bharu, Singapore city was still ablaze with lights. Squadrons of enemy planes, piloted by Japanese who obviously had no trouble flying in the dark, released their deadly hardware upon the sleeping city below. As the bombs rained down on Chinatown, officially killing sixty people, many of the white civilians watched the show from their living-room windows, believing that it was a rather spectacular and very realistic air force exercise.[55]

Awakened by the noise, Gunner Major Geoffrey Rowley-Conwy went out onto his lawn to investigate, believing initially that the coastal defence artillerymen were having a party. Realising that something might be up, he reported to one of his anti-aircraft batteries where he found that no order had been given to open fire and that the only thing engaging the Japanese bombers was very inadequate search lights.[56]

Although the seventeen enemy aircraft had been detected by radar when still fifty-five minutes distant, no warning had been sounded in Singapore on the orders of the Governor, Sir Shenton Thomas, who was worried about frightening the population. By the time he had made up his mind to raise the alarm, thirty-five precious minutes had passed by. RAF radar operator Harry Grumber, who had detected the unidentified aircraft on his screen, alleged that, 'I telephoned ARP Headquarters, which *was* manned, on my direct line', only to be told that 'they were powerless to sound the air raid sirens because their Chief Warden was at the late night cinema . . . and only he had the keys that controlled the alarm switch'. While Grumber unsuccessfully tried to have the city lights extinguished as a matter of urgent priority, the remaining twenty-five minutes were wasted in a fruitless search for the warden and his keys.[57] Three Australian Buffalo fighters, on alert and with their engines warmed in readiness, were not sent up to attack the bombers, despite the perfect moonlit conditions, since Air Vice-Marshall Pulford was afraid that the incompetent anti-aircraft gunners would shoot them down.[58]

Amazingly, the early morning raid did not seem to perturb the population of Singapore too much, particularly as the city was not bombed again for three weeks. After the initial shock of the attack had worn off, life went back to normal. It was almost as if they believed that, by ignoring the whole thing, the air raid had never happened and the Japanese did not exist. The War Communique issued in Singapore simply added to the general air of complacency. It informed the population that the Japanese had been repulsed at Kota Bharu, where only a few bombs had fallen harmlessly on the airfield, that 'the few [enemy] troops on the beach had been machine gunned' and that all Japanese surface craft were 'retiring at high speed'.[59]

Perhaps the only official honest enough to admit the truth was Mr V. Bowden, Australia's Official Representative in Singapore. In a lengthy and forthright cable he informed his government on December 23 that Singapore could only be saved by the dispatch of powerful reinforcements from the Middle East and large numbers of the latest aircraft, complete with trained personnel. He emphasised that the reinforcements must be divisions, not brigades, and that it was a waste of time sending anything that was not powerful, modern and immediate. Without this aid, he declared, the fall of Singapore would be 'only a matter of weeks'.[60]

Although the British Army was taking a relaxed view of the invasion, the Navy had decided, on the morning of December 8, that it could not let the Japanese landings in Malaya go unchallenged. The newly arrived battleship *Prince of Wales* and the battle cruiser *Repulse* were ordered to sail to the Gulf of Siam to show the enemy that the British meant business. Ignoring Admiralty advice that they would be 'more of a bait than a deterrent' and that their dispatch was a 'major strategical blunder fraught with the gravest of risks', these ships, the pride of the British Fleet, had been sent from England on November 17, on Churchill's insistence, as a show of strength. As their aircraft carrier escort had run aground in Jamaica, they were without any air cover.[61]

The Japanese, quite aware of the arrival of the ships, which had been a well-publicised event, were ready. By the time the British realised that the element of surprise had been lost and turned for Singapore, thirty-four high level bombers and fifty-one torpedo bombers were on their way from Saigon, now controlled by the Vichy-French. The ships did not stand a chance. Five torpedoes struck *Repulse*, which sank shortly after noon on December 10, while less than an hour later *Prince of Wales* succumbed to torpedoes and a well-placed bomb. The destroyers accompanying the ships were powerless to do anything but rescue the survivors. As the great grey goliaths slid to their watery graves, taking 845 men with them, a stunned world learned that the Japanese were storming their way across the mainland of Malaya almost unchecked.[62]

There were some brave pockets of determined resistance. In particular, the Argyll and Sutherland Highlanders, the Australian battalions and the legendary Ghurkas from Nepal put up a fierce fight, losing many men in the process.[63] For some inexplicable reason, the jungle-toughened Australian troops had been deployed too far down the peninsula. Although well trained and itching to fight, most were forced to wait five weeks until the front line of less able Indian brigades collapsed under the Japanese onslaught and the fighting finally reached them.[64] By this stage the Japanese army was on a roll and battles were fierce as the enemy encountered its first really protracted opposition.

At Gemas, the Japanese suffered enormous losses from the 27th Australian Brigade which, in using Bennett's 'attack and ambush' methods, held up the Japanese advance for an entire week, before being forced to succumb by the sheer weight of numbers and superior arms. But at the Muar River, the scene of fierce and protracted fighting, the outcome was disastrous. Here the 2/19 Battalion was all but wiped out in a bitter battle, fought with tenacity and great courage, which saw a Victoria Cross awarded to its commanding officer. When the survivors finally withdrew near Parit Sulong they were forced to leave behind the wounded —

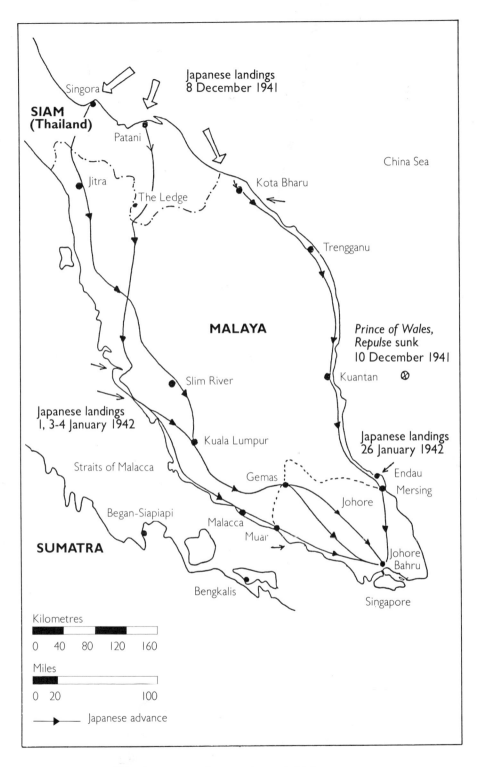

Map I. Route of the Japanese advance through Malaya.

110 Australians and forty Indians who, tragically, were machine-gunned by an enraged enemy before being doused with petrol and set alight.[65]

But the Japanese did not always react in this manner. Soon after dawn on January 27, after a brilliantly executed ambush along the Jemaluang-Mersing road, between one hundred and two hundred Australian soldiers, members of the rearguard and some engineers, entered the tiny mining town of Jemaluang. Here they ran up against a large Japanese force, including a tank regiment, which had recently landed at Endau. Before the small Australian force was overcome in a ferocious battle which left few survivors, it accounted for a great number of the enemy, either killed or wounded. This bravery in the face of overwhelming odds so impressed the Japanese that they erected a huge wooden cross with the words 'To our Gallant Enemies, the Australians'. This gesture was so unusual that the cross and the details of the confrontation were long remembered by Mamoru Shinozaki, a former Japanese consular official who was sent to Endau to organise schooling under Japanese occupation.[66]

But these relatively small groups of well-disciplined and gallant men were the exception rather than the rule. Gordon Bennett was under no illusions about the almost impossible task he faced when he cabled Australia on January 19, advising:

> Whole situation most serious. MERSING GEMAS MUAR fronts each held by 2 Australian Battalions with very FLIMSY support by Indian troops who have not stood firm and by new English units inexperienced in local conditions. Even Malaya command expressed doubts as to their reliability. We cannot plug up SEGAMAT [inland Malaya] holes and are finding it difficult to hold present positions against overwhelming numbers. So far our companies have to meet attacks by whole battalions, and face all ways, a situation that cannot continue for long. Further withdrawals contemplated . . . could have been avoided if all the units here fought as our men have done. They have been wonderful meeting all cunning methods used by Japanese with SKILL and determination. Their courage is beyond words. It would be a pity if all their efforts had been in vain.

Although Bennett's confidence in his men was supreme, it was a lost cause. With no reinforcements, and an apparent unwillingness by Percival to release the three battalions of British troops from the Singapore garrison, even the best soldiers to hand could not have hoped to save Malaya.[67]

As the army fled down the Malayan peninsula, it was easily overtaken. As one Japanese colonel crowed:

> Even the long legged Englishmen could not escape our troops on bicycles. This was the reason why they were continually driven off the road into the jungle, where, with their retreat cut off, they were forced to surrender.

Thanks to Britain's dear money spent on the excellent paved roads, and to the cheap Japanese bicycles, the assault on Malaya was easy.[68]

Not only could the Japanese cyclists move faster than the Allies could run, they were not hindered by roadblocks or stopped by streams whose bridges, almost without exception, had been demolished. The Japanese estimated that, had they used conventional forms of transport, Malaya would have taken twelve months to conquer. Not even the inconvenience of flat tyres stopped the remorseless advance, for the bicycles ran perfectly well on the wheel rims[69] — an aspect that had an unexpected bonus for the Japanese when the noise made by the metallic rims running over the hard paved roads tricked an Allied commander into ordering his troops to retreat in the face of what was believed to be a tank attack.[70]

Freddy Spencer Chapman, a British special operations officer involved with inserting trained guerilla parties behind the lines, lay concealed in the jungle at the side of the road as the Japanese rode past his hiding place. Wide eyed with amazement Spencer Chapman watched:

> . . . hundreds and hundreds of them, pouring eastwards towards the Perak River. The majority of them were on bicycles in parties of forty or fifty, riding three or four abreast . . . travelling as light as they possibly could . . . in marked contrast to our own front line soldiers, who were at this time equipped like Christmas trees with heavy boots, web equipment, packs, haversacks, waterbottles, blankets, groundsheets and even great coats and respirators, so they could hardly walk, much less fight.[71]

Finally, the Allies, with their units cut off and their lines of communication severed, were reduced to a fighting retreat. As the Japanese continued to ride easily down the well-sealed roads, their transports which followed gathered the booty left behind by the retreating army — ammunition, weapons, vehicles, fuel, and food.[72] With their supply lines stretched to the limit, the equipment, and the food in particular, were as manna from heaven to the lightly equipped Japanese troops, enabling their commanding officer to report to the Emperor, a bare seven weeks after landing on the north-eastern coast, that Japanese domination of Malaya was all but complete.

On 30 January 1942, the remnants of the shattered Allied army could retreat no more. Battered and confused, their units either almost wiped out or scattered and lost, they struggled to Johore Bahru, on the most southerly tip of Malaya, some having to fight every inch of the way.

The battle for Malaya was over. Less than one and a half kilometres away, across the narrow Straits of Johore, lay Singapore — their last hope and their last bastion.

Chapter 2
The Fortress Falls

While the army had been fighting its way backwards down the Malayan peninsula, the people of Singapore had been jolted from their lethargy. The unexpectedly aggressive actions of the invaders, the constant air attacks and the tales of terror from fleeing refugees were now contradicting the long-accepted views on Singapore's security. In spite of ridicule and active discouragement from officials who insisted that there was no danger, a sense of purpose filled the civilian population as they organised themselves into fire watching, firefighting and air-raid teams. Unfortunately, because of the military and civilian authorities' failure to face reality in time, they were not put to work on the one thing that may have repelled the enemy — defence works.[1]

It was not until January 16 that Wavell, now Supreme Commander American, British, Dutch and Australian Forces in the Far East, discovered that, since 'little or nothing' had been done to construct defences, there was nothing to safeguard the northern shore and that Singapore, the fortress, was an illusion. When Churchill learned of this, he was aghast.

> I ought to have known. My advisors ought to have known and I ought to have been told, and I ought to have asked . . . The possibility of Singapore having no landward defences no more entered my mind than that of a battleship being launched without a bottom.[2]

This protestation that he had been kept in the dark was a position from which Churchill never wavered. Aware of the political repercussions, he composed a long memo on January 19 for the benefit of the Chiefs-of-Staff in which he said:

> I must confess to being staggered by Wavell's telegram of the sixteenth . . . Merely to have seaward defences and no forts or fixed defences to protect their rear is not to be excused on any ground . . . I warn you that this could be one of the greatest scandals that could possibly be exposed.[3]

His recuperative powers were amazing. The next day, in typically Churchillian style, he cabled Wavell:

I want to make it absolutely clear that I expect every inch of ground to be defended, every scrap of material or defences blown to pieces to prevent capture by the enemy, and no question of surrender to be entertained until after protracted resistance in the ruins of Singapore city.

He had also sent a ten point memo to the Chiefs-of-Staff on how it should be done.[4]

Within hours he was having second thoughts. Perhaps, he pondered, they should abandon the island, 'blow the docks and batteries and workshops to pieces and concentrate everything on the defence of Burma'.[5] When this information was secretly leaked to the Australian Government, it declared that any abandonment of the island would be regarded as 'an inexcusable betrayal', forcing Churchill to revert to his previous stance.[6] The defence of Singapore would be sustained.

Ten days later, despite exhortations from Churchill that Singapore 'should be converted to a citadel and defended to the death', Wavell was ordering the removal of one of his 'essentials' — his air force, now in a very sorry state. Only twenty of the fifty-one long-awaited Hurricanes, which had taken to the skies on January 20, were left. When fourteen of these were ordered to the safety of Sumatra ten days later, eight remained to defend the island with the help of six outdated Brewster Buffaloes. All non-essential airfields and open spaces were rendered useless, while another eighty-six Hurricanes, many of them still in packing cases, were diverted to Sumatra and the East Indies.[7]

It was a rather mixed blessing that Japanese planes decided to concentrate their attention on convoys moving out of, rather than into, Singapore. While all but one ship reached the island safely, many trying to flee south to safety were sunk, with the loss of much valuable equipment.[8] On January 24 one of these incoming convoys had brought the first Australian reinforcements. Although sorely needed to bolster the greatly depleted battalions, almost all of them should have stayed at home. Of the 3000 that arrived, almost 2000 were raw recruits. Not only had some never seen a Bren gun, not one of them had ever handled a sub-machine-gun or anti-tank rifle, been instructed in small arms fire, or taught bayonet fighting.[9]

Although there were 87 000 trained militia men in Australia,[10] the Australian Constitution specifically prohibited citizen soldiers from being used on active service in any location other than Australia or its mandated territories. To ensure that enough trained men were left for the defence of the country, only a small percentage was permitted to volunteer for overseas duty. The reinforcements for Singapore were therefore largely composed of young men described by Gordon Bennett as being 'recruited in Martin Place, Sydney on a Friday and put on a boat to Malaya the following week'.[11] The 7000 Indian troops who had arrived two days before were no better, and the British 18th Division, on whom Percival pinned all his hopes, disembarked on January 29, unfit from the long sea voyage and untrained for war in close country. Of the troops recruited closer to home, the Malay battalions had not been in action and the Straits Settlement Volunteers were only sketchily trained.[12] These soldiers, with the remnants of the army from Malaya, were expected to hold Singapore against a better equipped, better prepared, better trained enemy. It was to be a hopelessly one-sided contest.

On January 30, the retreating army withdrew across the 1200 metre long, twenty-one metre wide causeway that stretched like an umbilicus from Johore to Singapore. They were protected in the rear by those troops who had proved themselves in battle and who could be expected to make a last ditch stand if the need arose — the remaining 250 Argylls, part of the Australian Eighth Division, and the 2nd Battalion Gordon Highlanders who had been sent from the Singapore garrison late in the campaign.[13]

So began the final withdrawal. The 30 000 weary soldiers, accompanied by thousands of frightened and bewildered refugees who were to push Singapore's native population to above the million mark, straggled to safety, followed by the rearguard. Incongruously, as the engineers waited for the last of the troops to cross so that they could blow the causeway, the haunting notes of bagpipes were heard, floating thinly on the still, early morning air. Along the road, with heads held high and backs erect and looking anything but defeated, came the Australians and the Gordons, followed by the Argylls, marching to the stirring strains of 'Hielan' Laddie' and 'A Hundred Pipes'.[14]

There were now 85 000 troops crammed into Singapore. Of the 75 000 classified as combat troops many, because of their poor training, were completely useless as a fighting force, while the experienced soldiers were battle fatigued from weeks of fighting in Malaya. With this force, Percival planned to hold the island.[15]

Contrary to General Wavell's opinion that the main Japanese thrust would be to the west of the causeway, Percival believed that it would be to the east.[16] Yet, instead of concentrating his troops at this point, he elected to form an outer perimeter of 115 kilometres in length. Pre-war statistics recommended one battalion for every 455 metres of front line. In Singapore it was one battalion for every 4800 metres. Moreover, the only section that could be considered to be well fortified was the area around the naval guns.[17]

It is a complete misconception that one of the reasons Singapore fell was because its guns pointed in the wrong direction. Although they faced out to sea and had a rather flat trajectory, most were able to traverse a full 360 degrees and could have been put to good use against invaders from the north, had someone thought to obtain anti-personnel ammunition. Armour-piercing shells, while devastating against warships, were entirely ineffective against troops, artillery or land targets, as they simply buried themselves harmlessly in the soft ground without detonating. There were about thirty rounds apiece of handy, high explosive shells for the 9.2 inch (twenty-three cm) guns but, if Singapore was supposed to hold out for six months, this meant only one round per week could be fired.[18] With the guns virtually useless, Singapore's very existence, in nineteenth-century British military jargon, depended entirely upon an extremely 'thin red line'.

While the military and the soldiers who had seen action in Malaya may have been well aware of the imminent danger that all now faced, the civilian authorities were still living in a fool's paradise. There was a complete censorship of all war news by Sir Shenton Thomas who, on the grounds that the population might become demoralised, refused permission for details of any of the fighting to be released or the massive casualty statistics published. Bodies of the hundreds that were being killed in daily air raids were quickly buried in mass graves, many of them unidentified. While this may have been mandatory to avoid an outbreak of disease in Singapore's sauna-like heat, it also served to hide the truth about the number of casualties. Although people could insert newspaper notices enquiring as to the whereabouts of missing persons, death notices were not permitted on the grounds that long lists of them would make depressing reading. With the Governor saving everyone from feelings of gloom and doom it is little wonder that the majority of the locals believed that the war with Japan was nothing more than an inconvenient skirmish. Indeed, the propaganda was so effective that many of the citizens were lulled into thinking that the withdrawal over the causeway had been a ploy to lure the Japanese into Singapore and so allow the Allies to fight on their own patch.[19]

Even the bombing was not taken seriously by many for a long time. Although air raids had become heavy during January, the civilians had taken a rather cavalier attitude to the entire proceedings, standing in the open to watch aerial dog fights and swarming in great numbers to view the damage done by the frequent bombing raids. In any case, since scarcely any public shelters had been constructed there were few places where one could take cover, apart from some air raid shelters that had been built in the gardens of the rich, mainly for their novelty value.[20] While the solidly built European bungalows may have afforded some shelter, for the large Malay and Chinese population there was almost no protection whatever. Their flimsy, often makeshift houses were useless against the Japanese bombs that fell with impunity, killing thousands whose bodies were never recovered from the rubble.[21]

Although many of the factories and workshops had closed down because of the bombing raids, the milk was still delivered and, as soon as the all clear was sounded, stores re-opened, inviting housewives into brightly lit interiors to indulge in merchandise such as 'Snappy American frocks for day and afternoon wear'. In Government House, Sir Shenton Thomas was still insisting that his guests wear collar and tie and observe all the niceties of gracious living.[22] For the whole of December and January and even into the first fortnight of February, the Governor pretended that no emergency existed. Refusing to carry out instructions to evacuate 'all useless mouths', he neglected to inform the civilians in Singapore that evacuation had been recommended and that all evacuees would be transported free of charge. For two months, therefore, ships bringing supplies and troops into Singapore returned to their home ports virtually empty.

With no public announcement about free passage, many who had sensibly decided to leave Singapore paid large sums to shipping companies who were still issuing tickets. Burns Philp optimistically advertised that their first class tickets (priced at £1000 to Melbourne) were 'interchangeable for the return voyage'. Other civilians, who knew about the free ride, turned down the offer of a free berth on the grounds that they wanted to go to England, not to less desirable Australia or India or New Zealand.[23] Consequently, when February 8, the day of the Japanese assault across the Straits of Johore dawned, instead of being practically free of civilians, Singapore was full of defenceless women and children.

The Japanese had been preparing since January 31. From their excellent position in the glassed-in room atop the tower of the Johore Bahru Administration Building, adjoining the Sultan's Palace, they had a fine view of everything that was going on in Singapore. When Australians on the other side of the causeway finally detected that the stately, square-sided tower was being used as a command post it took twenty-four hours and a violent argument from Bennett to obtain permission from Percival to fire upon it. An incredulous Bennett reported to his officers that Percival was reluctant to fire upon the tower in case the Sultan was upset.[24] Their subsequent eviction from their observation deck did not deter the Japanese. They simply took to the skies in a balloon, floating frustratingly out of reach of the small arms fire while observing everything that they wished.[25]

On the other side of the strait was an anti-aircraft battery to which, in a last frantic effort to improve the northern defences, had recently been added sixteen 40mm Bofors guns. It was to this particular battery, manned by the affable Major Rowley-Conwy and his gunnery crew, that a very unmilitary figure, mounted on a grime-encrusted Triumph motorcycle, arrived. Douglas Fraser — Malayan planter, ex-pilot, and compulsive volunteer — informed the major that he wanted to join up there and then, without any further ado. When Rowley-Conwy established that Fraser didn't expect to be paid he decided to ignore military regulations. Suitably outfitted, 'gunner' Fraser was soon taking great delight in giving the Japanese some of their own medicine.[26]

In spite of intelligence reports to the contrary,[27] Percival stuck to his theory that the Japanese would attack to the east of the causeway. He ordered engineers to put huge supply dumps on that side of the road, which was to be defended by those perceived to be the strongest troops — the fresh, recently arrived British 18th Division. On discovering that the ever resourceful Simson had installed defensive devices (petrol barrels that could be set alight by tracer bullets to turn the surface of the water ablaze with burning fuel, underwater obstacles, floating logs festooned with loops of murderous barbed wire, and car lamps to illuminate the shoreline) on the western side, Percival ordered their immediate removal to the east.[28]

Relegated to the western side of the causeway, Gordon Bennett and his Australians[29] were under no misapprehension of the job that was ahead of them. On arrival from Malaya, they had looked in vain for the fortifications and defences that they had been hearing about for so long. As one horrified infantryman lamented,

We thought we were coming back to an island fortress where there would be barbed wire and weapon pits and all the paraphernalia of a defended position and there wasn't a damn thing. Flat beaches and swampy ground and nothing — not even a strand of barbed wire.[30]

A British engineer, who had been blowing up bridges in Malaya, also noticed the lack of barbed wire and trenches. He went at once to the Base Ordinance Depot in Singapore city to collect some of the tonnes of wire that were in storage, only to be thwarted in his errand. The Depot was locked up and deserted. He had arrived on a half holiday.[31]

Between the British and Australian forces, defending the roadway itself, was a newly formed company of 2000 Chinese irregulars, organised by Chinese Tan Kah Kee, with the backing and under the overall command of Englishman Colonel John Dalley.[32] After years of trying to break down opposition to form such a group, Dalley, dubbed 'Dalley Sin Sang' by his hero-worshipping followers, had been given the go-ahead at the eleventh hour. His men, a bare two weeks out of training camp, were disadvantaged in that all the arms intended to supply this unit, known as Dalforce, were sitting on the bottom of the sea in the bombed *Empress of Asia*, which had been attacked just before it reached the safety of the harbour.[33] With no proper weapons, Dalley's band was armed with Martini Henry rifles, some of which had been converted to shotguns, that had apparently been unearthed from some forgotten corner of Fort Canning. Ammunition for these single shot weapons, which had not been used by the British Army since the nineteenth century, amounted to exactly five rounds apiece.[34]

While Percival was deploying his army, the Japanese began an elaborate feint. After clearing a twenty kilometre radius around Johore Bahru of

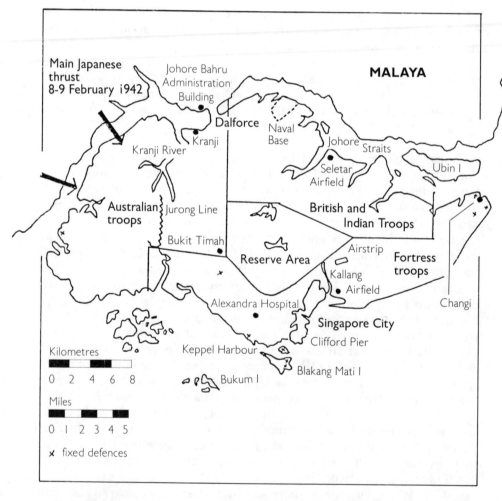

Main Japanese
thrust
8-9 February 1942

Johore Bahru
Administration
Building

MALAYA

Dalforce

Naval
Base

Kranji

Johore
Straits

Kranji River

Ubin I

Seletar
Airfield

Australian
troops

Jurong Line

British and
Indian Troops

Reserve Area

Airstrip

Fortress
troops

Bukit Timah

Kallang
Airfield

Changi

Alexandra Hospital

Singapore City

Keppel Harbour

Clifford Pier

Blakang Mati I

Bukum I

Kilometres

0   2   4   6   8

Miles

0   1   2   3   4   5

✗ fixed defences

Map II. Disposition of troops in Singapore on 8 February 1942.

all civilians, they ostentatiously set up a dummy camp on the eastern shoreline while the thousands of assault troops and a massive flotilla of landing craft were secretly moved into position on the western shore.[35] Percival was totally confused. His recce parties had not been able to detect the big troop concentrations or the large numbers of landing craft so carefully hidden. Although an Australian party had crossed the strait on February 7 and had seen troops massed on the opposite side, this news was not given priority. On the available information it appeared that any attack was a few days off at the least.[36]

At 10 o'clock the following morning the enemy barrage began, reaching such intensity by nightfall that General Percival likened the roar of the guns and the crash of the shells to the bombardments of World War I. Over at Government House, on the other side of the island, Sir Shenton Thomas was most put out to find that the shelling disturbed his bath.[37]

At about 10.45 pm, on February 8, the first of 23 000 Japanese troops swarmed across Churchill's 'splendid moat', concentrating their attack on the over-extended Australian forces on the western side of the causeway. With the vitally important supply dumps out of reach on the eastern side and with none of the dismantled booby traps able to be activated, it was an uphill task for the Australians. For some reason the searchlights did not come on and the defenders could hardly see where or what they were shooting. Although artillery fire sank or damaged a number of assault craft and the forward defence posts fought hand to hand, accounting for a considerable number of the enemy, many of the Australians were eventually overwhelmed.[38] But while some were forced to retreat in the confusion, others stood magnificently, fighting the enemy to a standstill. A large number of Japanese, having crossed the straits, were incinerated in the mangrove swamps when the defenders released oil from the tanks of the Kranji oil depot and set fire to it. The river of flame that enveloped the invaders filled the straits from shore to shore. The enemy was stopped in its tracks and, had the resistance been able to be maintained, would have been forced to abandon its attack and attempt to land at another point the following day. But, although these defenders held their ground with outstanding ferocity they were overcome by sheer weight of numbers.[39] By 9.30 am on February 9, one battalion had lost half its men, 330 of them killed.[40]

The company of Dalforce Chinese, positioned in the creeks and mudflats between the Australians and Kranji, found itself up against a Japanese machine-gun battalion whose objective was to seize the end of the causeway. When their five bullets per man had been fired from their shotguns and rifles, the Chinese fought hand to hand. The wounded, propped up with rifles, fought until they died. Not one of these volunteer fighters, rejected for so long by the British Army, gave an inch. And not one of them survived.[41]

It was left to one British officer and five British other ranks to report the fearless courage of the Chinese soldiers in what must be one of the greatest acts of bravery under fire, equal to that displayed by the British Army at Rorke's Drift in the Zulu War of 1879, when a record number of Victoria Crosses was won.

With the Australians and the Chinese overwhelmed, the Japanese stormed ashore, infiltrating the widely scattered defended areas, which were too extended to be plugged quickly. Slowly but surely the Japanese increased their foothold, forcing the Allies to retreat in an ever-decreasing circle. The causeway, which Bennett had wanted completely destroyed, was soon repaired. Since the water across the mere twenty-one metre breach to which Percival had agreed was little more than a metre deep at low tide, the first of the enemy troops had been able to wade across.[42] With the causeway mended, Japanese tanks and heavy vehicles soon followed. Enemy aeroplanes kept up a constant attack, bombing and strafing while the land assault continued.

With the constant artillery barrage, the almost uninterrupted air raids, the stench from the growing number of corpses lying bloated and unburied in the streets and the terrifying sound of gunfire clearly audible, Singapore's civilians, at long last, had received the message loud and clear. They now attempted to leave Singapore in droves.[43]

After February 8 the panic became more frantic each day. Chinese and Malays, who had no hope of evacuation, ran in every direction, mingling with army stragglers and deserters who were looking for booty and a chance to leave the island. There was wholesale looting in the streets and housewives scuttled for cover loaded with foodstuffs and anything else that they thought might come in handy.[44] The scene at Clifford Pier was chaotic, with terrified men, women and children fighting tooth and nail for a place aboard a ship. Incredibly, the P and O shipping line was still selling tickets — from the manager's house since the office had been bombed. Those trying to board without tickets were sent back down the crowded gangplanks, jostling with those who were clawing their way on board. On the orders of the Royal Navy, loyal Malay and Chinese shipping staff found their employment suddenly terminated and their jobs given instead to Europeans, some of whom were completely unqualified to hold the positions. Travel passes were only issued to selected civil servants and families of defence personnel, and to some Eurasians who had sufficient documentation to hand to prove part-British parentage. The Chinese, Malays and Indians did not rate at all, while the Oriental and Eurasian wives of British citizens were cast aside like unwanted toys.[45]

Inexorably the noose tightened around the city of Singapore until all the military, plus the million or so civilians, were confined to a very small area. On February 10 Percival ordered the destruction of the large oil storage tank at Bukit Timah. The blaze was spectacular, sending black smoke hurtling into the air for three days. The previous day the tanks at Kranji had been set ablaze, covering everyone with oily sludge when heavy rain set in.[46] The burning of the oil was followed by destruction of other oil reserves, supplies, ammunition, guns and equipment. Huge bonfires of banknotes were just as startling as the sight of monsoon drains awash with thousands of litres of liquor when bond stores and hotel cellars were emptied of their contents. [47]

By the time General Wavell arrived on February 10 it was obvious that Singapore would not be able to hold out. After ordering the RAF to plough up the airfields, destroy all bombs and petrol supplies and leave at once for the Dutch East Indies, Wavell informed Churchill merely that the 'battle was not going well'. He was more forthcoming in a later dispatch in which he wrote, 'I left Singapore on the morning of 11th February without much confidence of any prolonged resistance'.[48]

That evening, while the Bukit Timah blaze cast a glow over the island, Wavell received Churchill's answer to his latest message. Unable to comprehend that Singapore was fighting with its back to the wall, the Prime Minister sent the following stirring communication:

> Defenders must outnumber Japanese forces who have crossed the Straits and in a well-contested battle they should destroy them. There now must be at this stage no thought of saving the troops or sparing the population. The battle must be fought to the bitter end at all costs. The 18th Division must make its name in history. Commanders and senior officers should die with their troops. The honour of the British Empire and the British Army is at stake. I rely on you to show no mercy to weakness in any form. With the Russians fighting as they are and the Americans so stubborn in Luzon the whole reputation of our country and our race is involved.[49]

Wavell paraphrased Churchill's message into an equally wounding exhortation for Percival to distribute to the battle-weary officers and men, ate his dinner and flew back to the safety of Java.[50] Australian Colonel Kent Hughes, having been instructed by Percival to deliver Wavell's message to his troops, decided it was an order he could not obey. Rather than pass on what he regarded as being a 'slur on the troops in Malaya', he threw the message away.[51]

On February 12 the situation was very grave. The previous evening the Japanese had dropped twenty-nine wooden boxes containing copies of a letter from Japan's General Yamashita, urging Percival to surrender. Had the British surrendered on this particular date the Japanese would have been ecstatic as it was the anniversary of the accession to the throne of the first Emperor and therefore the greatest patriotic festival of the year.[52] But Percival was not about to co-operate. He ignored the proposal for the time being, but it was clear from his orders to destroy as much military equipment as possible that the end was in sight. He also ordered the cruiser *Durban* and three other naval vessels to sail for Batavia (now Jakarta), escorting a flotilla of evacuation craft. The convoy carried women and children, the remaining aircraft ground personnel, selected staff officers and technicians, a number of nursing sisters and the balance of the shore-based naval staff. It was to be the last convoy to escape safely from Singapore.[53]

Civilians scrabbling for a place on the evacuation fleet met with fierce competition from a growing number of army deserters — mainly green, undisciplined troops. Although they came from both British and Australian ranks, the fact that all troops had been given permission to wear the easily recognisable Australian slouch hat tended to make identification nigh on impossible and earned for the Australians a reputation that they did not wholly deserve. General Bennett, aware of rumours that were circulating about the behaviour of slouch-hatted soldiers, made sure that his troops, particularly the raw recruits, were constantly rounded up, therefore making the pool of potential troublemakers very small.[54] But panic stricken or not, there was no excuse for some of the acts committed by undisciplined men intent on survival. In one particularly ugly incident a group of soldiers, described as 'felt hatted' and said to be Australian, shot dead Dockyard Captain T.K. Atkinson, who asked to see their orders as they boarded the evacuation ship *Empire Star*. After levelling their weapons at the crew and onlookers on deck, they continued up the gangway unmolested.[55] Yet even this dreadful deed paled into insignificance when compared with a band of English army deserters who, in their determination to survive in a drifting lifeboat, murdered and then cannibalised other castaways.[56]

The following day, Friday February 13, while a large number of civilians and non-combatant personnel was being loaded onto a variety of ships and small craft, the harbour and wharves were heavily bombed, killing and drowning many. Absolute pandemonium followed. People who were allocated passage on particular ships boarded others, some did not turn up at all, while others with valid passes tried vainly for admittance. Some, including senior civil servants who had been ordered to remain behind, took advantage of the berths now left vacant by the dead and injured.[57]

As the refugees left the harbour, bound for the Bangka Straits, the smoke from the burning oil reserves at Pulau Bukum and Pulau Samboe hung in the sky like twin palls of a great funeral pyre. The billowing black columns would indeed prove to be an omen of death. Although the Dutch had sent warnings on February 10 that Japanese shipping would rendezvous in the straits on February 13 for an attack on Palembang, the messages had not been decoded as the code books had been destroyed with unnecessary and inexplicable haste. Consequently, almost all the convoy ships, plus many others that had tried to flee to Java or Sumatra, were intercepted. Australia's Mr Bowden was one of many who, having survived the onslaught of the guns and the sinking of the ships, was taken ashore and massacred.[58]

On the afternoon of the 13th, Percival and his generals held a conference. Although a message had just been received from Wavell that they 'must all fight it out to the end', it was unanimously agreed that Percival should seek wider discretionary powers, for 'there must come a stage when in the interests of the troops and civil population further bloodshed will serve no useful purpose'.[59] As Bennett drove back from the meeting, he witnessed a scene that reinforced his belief that, although the Chinese were withstanding the destruction of their city with the same stoicism as their English brethren in London, immediate capitulation was the only course possible if they were to be saved.

There was devastation everywhere. There were holes in the road, churned up rubble lying in great clods all round, tangled masses of telephone, telegraph and electric cables strewn across the street, here and there smashed cars, trucks, electric trams and buses that once carried loads of passengers to and from their peaceful toil. The shops were shut and deserted. There were hundreds of Chinese civilians who refused to leave their homes. Bombs were falling in a nearby street. On reaching the spot one saw the side of a building had fallen on an air raid shelter, the bomb penetrating deep into the ground, the explosion forcing in the sides of the shelter. A group of Chinese, Malays, Europeans and Australian soldiers were already at work, shovelling and dragging the debris away. Soon there emerged from the shelter a Chinese boy, scratched and bleeding, who immediately turned to help in the rescue work. He said 'My sister is under there'. The rescuers dug furiously among the fallen masonry, one little wiry old Chinese doing twice as much as the others, the sweat streaming from his body. At last the top of the shelter was uncovered. Beneath was a crushed mass of old men, women, young and old, and young children, some still living — the rest dead. The little Oriental never stopped with his work, his sallow face showing the strain of anguish. His wife and four children were there. Gradually he unearthed them — dead. He was later seen holding his only surviving daughter, aged ten, by the hand, watching them move away his family and the other unfortunates. This was going on hour after hour, day after day, the same stolidity and steadfastness among the civilians was evident in every quarter of the city.[60]

The fighting this night was fierce and bitter. The following day the Japanese, unable to break through the Australian sector, moved on to make an assault parallel to the coast near the Alexandra Barracks and hospital. For some time the defending Indian troops resisted, inflicting casualties upon the enemy with machine guns mounted in the hospital grounds. When they eventually retreated through the hospital, the Japanese, infuriated that the Indians had breached the traditional neutrality of areas under the protection of the Red Cross, followed, massacring everyone in sight — soldiers, patients and the medical staff alike, including the sisters who had elected to remain behind when the evacuation fleet sailed. Padre Wearne, who escaped, watched in horror as Squadron Leader Griffith, an English ear, nose and throat specialist, was bayonetted to death in the operating theatre, along with his patient.[61] Thirty-six hours later, on the fifteenth of February, the Japanese were on the outskirts of the city itself.

Percival, now considered by many officials who had been urging his replacement to be quite incapable of rational thought, had received further orders to 'continue to inflict maximum damage on the enemy for as long as possible, by house to house fighting if necessary'.[62] In defiance of this order and the ridiculous edict which had appeared in the single sheet edition of the *Straits Times* of February 14, declaring that 'Singapore must stand; it SHALL stand. H.E. The Governor', Percival made a vital and, under the circumstances, clear-headed decision.

Although the Japanese had not turned off the water supply at the pumping station, water was down to a trickle or not running at all because of heavy damage sustained to the distribution system. There was an adequate supply of ammunition and food for civilians, but garrison food supplies were down to seven days and petrol was scarce.[63] There would have been more than sufficient food for all had the city authorities not stored tonnes of flour, rice and other staples in warehouses by the docks. As the docks were bombed at least four times a day, forty-six of the sixty-four sheds, along with their contents, had been completely destroyed, while the remainder had been seriously damaged.[64]

There were only two possible alternatives for Percival to consider — launch a counter-attack and drive the Japanese back far enough to regain control of the water supply, fuel and food dumps, or capitulate.[65] With the enormous number of defenceless civilians in the city, the troops in a state of utter exhaustion and no hope of any fresh reinforcements, he really had no choice. Fortunately for everyone concerned, Churchill had also reached the conclusion that the man on the spot must make the ultimate decision. Percival, on the morning of the fifteenth day of February, and with the blessing of both Churchill and Wavell,[66] decided to surrender.

The air of gloom that accompanied this decision was lightened somewhat by the contents of the telegram that had been sent by Wavell, sanctioning capitulation:

> So long as you are in position to inflict losses to enemy and your troops are physically capable of doing so you must fight on.
> Time gained and damage to enemy vital importance at this crisis. When you are fully satisfied that this is no longer possible I give you discretion

to cease resistance. Before doing so all arms, equipment and transport of value to the enemy must of course be rendered useless.

The message then continued with the following order:

Also just before final cessation of fighting opportunity should be given to any determined bodies of men or individuals to try and effect an escape by any means possible. They must be armed. Inform me of intentions. Whatever happens I thank you and all troops for your gallant efforts of last few days.[67]

General Percival read the message and then censored it, editing out all reference to Wavell's order to escape. This latest instruction reconfirmed an order sent on February 13, when Wavell had said, 'When everything humanly possible has been done, some bold and determined personnel may be able to escape by small craft and find their way to Sumatra through the islands'.[68]

Percival told no one about these escape orders, not even his Generals Bennett and Heath, and most certainly none of the tens of thousands of troops who were soon to become prisoners of the Japanese. But Bennett, for one, had no intention of spending the rest of the war in captivity, particularly as he was one of the few senior officers alive who knew anything about jungle fighting. He waited until almost two hours after the ceasefire before he left,[69] unaware that his escape had been urged, nay ordered, by his supreme commander. (See Appendix 1.)

The ceasefire, for which Bennett had waited before escaping, had been set for 8.30 on the evening of February 15, Singapore Time.[70] Troops were informed that the Allies had surrendered and that once they had witnessed the humiliating sight of a Japanese victory parade the following morning, all would be marched away to captivity. Such was the feeling of shame that several senior officers refused to sign the orders giving the troops their instructions. The documents were passed down the ranks and finally signed by Major Waller, a very junior officer attached to Percival's staff.[71]

Rather than face the prospect of spending the rest of the war in prison, many chose to take the perilous journey across the sea to Sumatra, the only escape route now open. Colonels and brigadiers, civilians and civil servants, battle-hardened warriors and army deserters intent on escape at any price, left in launches, junks, rowing boats, naval craft, in fact in anything that floated.[72]

One civilian, who had left on February 12 in a boat which he had appropriated, was an enterprising, immensely tall, tough-as-nails Australian by the name of William Roy Reynolds. His ship, a smelly, run-down ex-Japanese fishing vessel, was decidedly unglamorous. Until the outbreak of the war it had been chugging backwards and forwards from fishing fleet to home base, ferrying out supplies and returning with a load of fish. Taken over immediately after the outbreak of hostilities on December 8, the lowly *Kofuku Maru*, merely one fishing boat among many, was destined to achieve notoriety in the mistaken belief that she was the first Japanese ship captured by the Royal Australian Navy in the Pacific Zone.

When Bill Reynolds — master mariner, First World War naval officer, and now mining engineer — entered Singapore from Malaya he had already given the Japanese a run for their money. Before quitting Perak, Malaya, he and a group of Royal Engineers had armed themselves with an ample supply of dynamite and blown up a telegraph station, followed by a power station, telephone exchange and finally Reynolds's own mining plant. Fired with enthusiasm, the Australian had arrived in Singapore, where he had volunteered to help blow up the naval base, left almost intact by the hurriedly departing navy. Impressed by his expertise, the harbour master had asked Reynolds on February 10 if he could assist in the rescue of 262 Dutch civilians requiring evacuation from Tandjung Pinang on Bintan Island, 128 kilometres away.

The harbour master could not have picked a better man. A skilled engineer and brilliant navigator and sailor, the forty-nine-year-old Reynolds had spent almost twenty years in Malaya, Burma and the islands of the Dutch East Indies. When he spied the *Kofuku Maru*, one of a number of rather battered captured fishing vessels tied up at the wharf, Reynolds told the harbour master that that vessel, provided she was in working order, would do nicely. With the help of a crew of eight Chinese rounded up from a local boarding house, he spent February 10 and 11 reconditioning, fuelling and provisioning the ship, before setting off at 10 am the following day. After dodging bombs as the ship entered the Singapore Strait, he reached Tandjung Pinang where he squeezed fifty refugees into *Kofuku Maru* and took the rest in tow on board *Silver Gull*. When he finally delivered his human cargo to the Dutch Administrator at Rengat, on the upper reaches of the Indragiri River, he found the once peaceful village bursting at the seams. As by this stage there were many others who required transportation from surrounding islands to the safety of Sumatra, Reynolds assisted in the rescue work.[73]

He had just finished one of his trips and tied up at Rengat's rickety wharf when a small boat nudged the timbers of *Kofoku Maru*, rocking her on her mooring lines. Those in the small craft were treated to the intimidating sight of an enraged Bill Reynolds emerging from the wheelhouse. His tall, rugged frame, deeply tanned by prolonged exposure to the sun, was clad in a tattered shirt and scruffy pair of shorts. Above a square, determined jaw covered in stubble sat a pair of horn-rimmed spectacles, framing eyes that glared with a ferocity that could scarcely have been called welcoming.

After a lifetime of practice Bill Reynolds was a master of the Australian vernacular. Without any preliminaries he let forth a stream of colourful abuse which made clear to the occupants of the boat his opinion of their seamanship. When he had finished, he glanced down to see what, and who, had dared to bump his ship.

It was just a small, ordinary, diesel-driven boat. Standing in the prow was an army medical orderly and at the tiller, staring back at Reynolds with a look of utter astonishment, sat an English Army officer — a captain in the Gordon Highlanders. His name was Ivan Lyon.[74]

Chapter 3
Escape from Singapore

The tawny eyes that looked up to meet Bill Reynolds's furious glare sparkled with barely suppressed amusement. Flecked with indeterminate shades of green and brown they were, as Reynolds would come to discover, Lyon's emotional barometer. In moments of joy or excitement they would suddenly lighten, only to darken just as quickly in times of profound thought. These rapid shifts made it difficult for the ordinary observer to determine their precise colour, for they appeared to be quite definitely a pale greenish-hazel one minute and just as definitely a dark brown the next.

The enquiring face that Reynolds now viewed from his superior perch was in some ways not unlike that of a fox — finely boned, sharp and alert — with close-cropped, reddish-brown curls hugging the neat skull. Not, for the moment, in evidence was the ready, gap-toothed smile that transformed an often pensive expression.

Although he was well over one hundred and eighty centimetres tall, the muscular spareness of the build, at first glance, suggested frailty — an impression reinforced by slender fingers and the quick, bird-like movements often found in those possessed by restless, nervous energy. But any illusion of frailty was deceptive. Lyon had a mind like fine tempered steel and resolution to match: his sense of purpose and determination were quite capable of forcing the whippet-like body well beyond its own, or any other body's, normal limits of endurance.[1]

This was not the first time that Lyon and Reynolds had come across each other, and it would not be the last.

Ivan Lyon was descended from a long line of distinguished military men whose roots extended back into Scottish history. Born in 1915 while his father, a general in the British Army, was away at the Great War, Ivan had spent a childhood immersed in tales of the family's military exploits. As he grew to adulthood, he developed a taste for all things military, particularly history, an interest encouraged by his father who was keen for his eldest surviving son to follow in the footsteps of his forebears.

This natural inclination, coupled with the spirit of family tradition, had developed in Ivan a keen sense of duty, a love of Empire, a deep patriotism and, above all, an adherence to a quite rigid code of gentlemanly behaviour.[2]

When he announced that he intended to join the Royal Navy upon leaving school, it came as no surprise. While a schoolboy at Harrow, Ivan had learn to sail, developing such a passion for it that he had become an exceptionally skilled, single-handed yachtsman.[3] Ultimately, he was thwarted in his quest for a life on the high seas, not because of any intellectual or physical deficiency but because Ivan, by this time a rather individual thinker, did not deliver the expected answers to questions posed by a conventional Navy Board.[4]

Francis Lyon, Ivan's father, now took the initiative. He offered his son the choice of entering the artillery, thereby following in the footsteps of his father and grandfather, or of joining the Gordon Highlanders, whose bravery in 'going over the top' in the 1914-18 War had impressed the General greatly. After weighing up the prestige of intellectual superiority, universally associated with the exacting science of the artillery, against the snappily immaculate image projected by the kilt-swinging Gordons, Ivan opted for the latter, informing his mother that he had decided it was 'easier to be smart than clever'. Having made his choice, an apt one for a man who came from such an old Scots family (although this had no bearing on his decision), Ivan, already a gentleman, marched off to the Royal Military College at Sandhurst in order to learn to be an officer.[5]

His military training over by the end of 1935, he was posted to Redford Barracks in Edinburgh, where soldiering for the next twelve months consisted of guard duty, ceremonial parades and courses on how to handle a cantankerous Lewis gun, and where spare time was filled with cross-country running — a sport often suited to lean, wiry people and one in which Ivan excelled. It was here, in the comfortably old-fashioned Redford Barracks, that Ivan found a soul mate — Francis Moir-Byres, a self-sufficient officer whose passion for sailing matched his own.

When the time came to choose between spending the next six years in the safe, familiar confines of the Barracks or somewhere overseas, both Ivan and Francis jumped at the chance to extend their limited horizons. In the winter of 1936-37 they left England on the troop ship *Dorchester*, bound for Singapore, where European society was still enjoying the last halcyon pre-war days of Empire.

Francis found in the weeks that followed that, although Ivan was a man of boundless enthusiasm, able to make snap decisions, he was not a superficial thinker. Indeed, quite the opposite was true, for Ivan had the ability to tackle a problem or approach a new idea from many angles. At the same time, his agile mind was able to skip far ahead to the crux of the matter while others were still plodding along. When he was confident that a solution had been found, he delivered it succinctly, quietly and calmly, his well-modulated tones more powerful and impressive than louder, more insistent voices.[6]

This soldier by default could never resist the lure of the sea. Almost as soon as they arrived in Singapore, Ivan and Francis purchased a three tonne, five and a half metre sloop named *Vinette*. Experienced sailors though they were, they quickly discovered that sailing in Singaporian waters was a whole new ball game. Consequently, in order to avoid being carried off by a strong rip tide in the direction of the South China Sea, they learned the intricacies of the capricious wind patterns and ferocious tidal movements that swirled around the straits. From sheer necessity they also became expert meteorologists, reading the weather with uncanny accuracy and developing an ability to detect the often sudden approach of the fierce tropical storms, commonly known as 'Sumatras'. By August of 1937 they felt confident enough to undertake a voyage of adventure, selecting Kota Bharu, on the eastern coast of Malaya, as their destination. Not deterred in the slightest by the fact that few Europeans had ever sailed in that area, they set off as planned, *Vinette* setting a cracking pace as she ran before the south-west monsoon. As they travelled from one small village to the next, the pair had no trouble making friends with the locals, practising their Malay at every opportunity and slaking their thirst with the juice from freshly cut green coconuts, for which Ivan had an absolute passion.

Aided by fair weather, they penetrated one hundred illegal kilometres beyond Malaya, into Siam, before turning homewards, calling at Trengannau to renew an acquaintance with a European whom they had met on the way up. He was John Dalley, the unconventional-minded head of the local police, who was, even at that stage, trying to convince his superiors that the Chinese could play a vital part in the defence of Malaya, an idea which eventually became a reality four years later with the formation of Dalforce. Dalley, being cast in a mould not usually found among Europeans of that period, appealed to Ivan enormously.

Although the trip had ostensibly been one of pure pleasure, they submitted on their return a comprehensive intelligence report to Colonel Hayley Bell. As Bell was at this time collecting evidence to try to convince the British High Command of the need for defensive action, he was most interested to learn that his junior officers' opinion about possible Japanese invasion coincided with his own. Unfortunately, this report suffered the fate of all warnings submitted to London. But Colonel Bell, who also recognised men not cast in the usual mould, was to find other work for Ivan Lyon before the fall that, Cassandra-like, he kept prophesying to unreceptive ears.

In the meantime, while crewing a ketch to Australia, Ivan arrived in Darwin, where he fell instantly in love with a daughter of the famous Durack pastoral family. The feeling must have been reciprocated, for Ivan returned to Singapore informing Francis that he was now engaged —

unofficially at least. The relationship was apparently sufficiently intense for the powerful and wealthy Duracks to dispatch a family envoy to Singapore with instructions to give the impoverished army officer the once over. Although he and Ivan got on famously, the visit was to prove less successful in the question of assessing Ivan's marriageability. However, at this stage the would-be suitor considered himself still to be betrothed and farewelled the Durack uncle cordially.

Although sailing occupied the bulk of his spare time Ivan continued to star as a distance runner, became accomplished in the art of ju-jitsu, and even had a stab at learning to fly when the army offered to pay for the tuition of any officer who gained an 'A' rated pilot's licence. While he did not succeed in his quest to become an airborne officer, owing to his propensity for trying to land the plane when still fifteen metres above the ground, he did manage to leave an indelible mark upon Singapore's social scene when he chose the swanky Singapore Swimming Club, the busy hub of young Singaporian colonial society, as the venue for a rather spectacular prank.[7]

In a fit of exuberance one evening, after consuming a large curry tiffin washed down by copious amounts of Tiger beer, Ivan emerged from a tattooist on Serangoon road sporting a large tiger's head emblazoned in brilliant red, blue and yellow upon his chest. Francis considered it to be a real work of art, as did Ivan himself and, believing that such a masterpiece should not go unnoticed, they decided to try it out on the unsuspecting public at Singapore Swimming Club. After grabbing the attention of the onlookers by anchoring *Vinette* directly in front of the club, they swam ashore. Their entrance was nothing less than spectacular. As they emerged, bare torsoed, from the water, there was not a single eye that was not focussed upon Ivan's magnificent tiger, snarling at them as he flexed the muscles of his chest.[8]

Ivan enjoyed indoor partying in Singapore almost as much as he enjoyed his outdoor sport, attacking both with equal enthusiasm. No saint when it came to the fairer sex, he pursued the ladies with great vigour. And he loved to dance. An exponent of the art of sword dancing as well as the energetic Highland Fling, he did not require any encouragement other than a glass or two of his favourite drop to entice him onto the floor. On one occasion, when Ivan's natural high spirits had received rather more encouragement than usual from the more liquid variety, he discarded his clothing and cavorted stark naked on the immaculately manicured lawn of the Air Force Base, demonstrating his dancing skill in a manner which would long be remembered.

It was the mixture of pink gins, sailing and an eye for the ladies which led Ivan in August 1938 to a woman who was to change his life irrevocably. He learned, over a congenial tipple with the regiment's colonel, that an exceptionally beautiful French girl lived on the prison island of Poulo Condore, where her father was governor. Without further ado Ivan was off for the coast of Indo-China, the current love of his life, the Durack lady, quite forgotten. Although he had learned a considerable amount about navigating on his trip to Australia, Ivan's navigational skill was still, as Francis succinctly put it, 'bloody awful'. Unfazed by the fact that he was unable to establish his exact longitude by making a star fix, Ivan sailed away with a watch, compass and charts as his only navigational aids, confident that he could find Poulo Condore, a mere speck in the ocean.

Blessed with the luck normally attributed to the Irish, he found that his lack of navigational skill was no handicap whatever. After sailing for a number of days in the right general direction he decided, by dead reckoning, that he was in the vicinity of the island. A floating grapefruit box told him he was on a shipping route and from the presence of a butterfly he deduced that he was quite close to land. By taking a cross bearing from the nearest point in Indo-China and the known shipping route, Ivan, with more good luck than good management, plotted and found Poulo Condore.[9] He immediately went ashore, introduced himself to the governor and, being a British officer on an island where visitors were few and far between, found himself invited to dinner.[10]

He stayed five days, supposedly effecting repairs to *Vinette's* hatch cover and falling head over heels in love with Gabrielle Bouvier, the lady he had sailed so far to meet. For Ivan, completely bewitched by the dark-haired, dark-eyed beauty from the moment he set eyes on her, it was love at first sight.[11] The feeling was not initially reciprocated by the charming Frenchwoman. Although attracted by Ivan's good looks and ready wit, attributes that had melted the heart of many a fair lady, she considered that he drank too much and was far too wild. She was also extremely wary of any romantic involvement. Married at the tender age of seventeen, she had produced a daughter and been divorced before her nineteenth birthday, a harrowing experience which made her view Ivan's overtures with great caution.[12]

She had not, however, reckoned with the Lyon charm. Ivan returned to Singapore determined to marry her and characteristically set about achieving his aim with the same dedication and purpose with which he tackled everything else in life. Fortunately, he had been let off the hook in his engagement to his Australian fiancée when she wrote to say she could no longer wait for him and was going to marry someone else. Following a cleverly orchestrated plan, which even involved his giving up drinking, he wooed his new-found love relentlessly, by letter and in person, until she finally capitulated. By February Gabrielle had agreed to become Ivan's wife.[13] On 27 July 1939, after the prospective bridegroom threatened to sack the church of a priest who refused to conduct the service on the grounds that the Roman Catholic Gabrielle was divorced, they were married in Saigon.[14]

On his return to Singapore the regiment saw even less of Ivan than previously. Since August 1938, when he had been seconded from his normal duties, he had been undertaking special missions for Colonel Hayley Bell, who had shifted his attention from analysing the precarious defence position to the establishment of his secret intelligence network. Lyon sailed to normally inaccessible areas of Malaya and Siam in *Vinette* to make forays into the jungle. The variety of the job and the odd hours suited him down to the ground, as laying traps for Japanese agents had far more appeal than irksome garrison duties and regimental life in Singapore, which he had grown to loathe.[15] After Bell was banished to England in 1939 and the intelligence network subsequently disbanded, Ivan, who spoke fluent French, was appointed to a new job organising Free Frenchmen operating as fifth columnists in Japanese-controlled Indo-China. When the threat of outright hostilities with Japan became more distinct, Ivan and a small group of men, including his friend John (Dalforce) Dalley, formed a secret counter espionage cell at the request of MI-5 which worked in close association with the recently established (1940) wartime intelligence organisation known as Special Operations Executive. The group, whose main aim was to eliminate enemy agents, was headed by Royal Marine Lieutenant-Colonel Alan Warren, who was so impressed with Ivan's ability to get on with the job that he informed Malaya Command that 'they could keep everybody else provided he had Ivan to work for him'. This band of extremely tough individuals was given a completely free hand in manner of dress, weapons and modus operandi, allowing them to account for the assassination of a large number of Japanese spies.[16]

Once Malaya was invaded, the group turned its attention to establishing a fifth column. Consequently, while his battalion was safely ensconced on Singapore Island, venturing across the causeway only when the battle for Malaya was all but over, Ivan was busy assisting Chinese Communists infiltrate behind enemy lines in Malaya. Such was the urgency and importance of the work that he was still in Johore Bahru on 30 January 1942, attempting to secrete a supply dump. The Japanese were so close that he compelled his terrified labour force to complete the work at gun point, only allowing the party to join the crocodile of troops retreating across the causeway when the Japanese presence could no longer be ignored.[17]

While Ivan had been scuttling about Johore caching supplies for the 'stay behind parties', it had become obvious to Colonel Alan Warren that, unless something was done to provide a safe route, movement in and out of Singapore would soon be extremely difficult. Ignoring the increasing cacophony of sound from without, he clamped his steel helmet firmly on his head and formulated a plan. Like all good ideas it was relatively simple. The secret lay with Sumatra, the back door to both Singapore and Malaya.

He would set up three bases to move men and equipment in and out — two in Sumatra and the other at a suitable point midway between Singapore and the most southerly Sumatran base. The first would be across the Straits of Malacca on the east coast of Sumatra, where there was an old pirate haunt known by the melodious name of Began-Siapiapi. From this small fishing village, Warren believed, he could infiltrate men and supplies across the narrow straits into Malaya, where they could operate behind the Japanese lines. The Indragiri River, whose navigable waters led upstream for over two hundred kilometres to Rengat, would be the second base. With the co-operation of Dutch administrators, equipment and troops could be ferried from the deep water anchorage near Padang on Sumatra's west coast, over the mountains to Rengat, and then on to Singapore. The purpose of the third base, its location as yet to be determined, would be to provide a point between Singapore and the Indragiri where food could be distributed and personnel redirected. Should the unthinkable indeed occur and Singapore fall into enemy hands, Warren envisaged that the route could be reversed to move men, stage by stage, to safety.[18]

With the idea fast becoming concrete, Warren turned his attention to selecting personnel capable of organising such a scheme. Having already earmarked undercover agents John Davis and Richard Broome for the behind-the-lines operations from Began-Siapiapi, the names of Ivan Lyon and SOE naval officer Brian Passmore sprang to mind. However, Passmore had already been snapped up by Davis and Broome, who wanted him to find a diesel-engined junk, victual it and take them to Sumatra where, apart from infiltrating enemy territory, the pair also had high hopes of bribing local fishermen to rescue Argylls, reportedly stranded on some islands.

Passmore considered the two offers. When he decided that rescuing marooned Argylls and infiltrating guerillas sounded far more exciting than setting up food bases on palm-fringed islands, Warren was forced to cast about for an alternate recruit.[19] He settled on Major H.A. Campbell, a bustling, bullet-headed King's Own Scottish Borderer with bright blue eyes and a sandy moustache, who had managed a large rubber estate in Johore before the war. When hostilities had broken out Campbell, commonly known as Jock, had re-enlisted with his old unit, a distinctive regiment whose members wore trews, or tartan trousers, in place of the more traditional kilt.

When Ivan Lyon arrived at the Cathay Building to answer Warren's summons on January 31, the morning after his return from Johore, the plan was almost finalised. Campbell was to organise the Sumatran end of the route, leaving Lyon, with his excellent knowledge of the local waters and his ability to speak Malay, to take charge of setting up the island-hopping route to the Indragiri. He was to select a conveniently situated island as a base and then stock it with food, weapons and medical supplies. As the latter would be more use in the hands of someone with some medical knowledge, Lyon suggested Ron 'Taffy' Morris, a chirpy, good-humoured, Welsh ex-miner from the Royal Army Medical Corps, whom he had met at SOE's 101 Special Training School.[20]

Hurriedly organised in late 1941 in the palatial, west coast home of an Armenian millionaire mining speculator, this establishment had been training European and Chinese volunteers in the art of sabotage and clandestine warfare. When officialdom, at the urging of Dalley and others, had finally realised that the Chinese, well versed in undercover work through dealings with their many secret societies, were the ideal candidates for sabotage work, SOE had been granted permission to put them through an intensive, two-week course.[21] One of the instructors was Englishman Freddy Spencer Chapman, a daredevil and completely fearless individual who, after spying on the Japanese as they cycled down the Malayan peninsula, disappeared into the jungle from where he was to create havoc for the entire duration of the war.[22]

On 1 February 1942, the day after their meeting with Warren, Lyon and Campbell sounded out Morris and engineer Lance Corporal Baker. With the school about to close, the pair were keen to join the operation and reported to Lyon on SOE's recently acquired *Hong Chuan*, a small coastal trader. With the harbour the target for frequent bombing attacks, the four Chinese-Malay crew members loaded the provisions for the supply dumps in record time. Designed to provide twenty-four hour sustenance for twelve men, the sealed, four-gallon (eighteen litre) tubular tin cans contained a supply of corned beef, ship's biscuits and a 'for medicinal purposes only' bottle of whisky.

For the next day or two the small ship cruised through the islands of the Riouw Archipelago, while Lyon and Campbell made contact with inland villages, or kampongs, and fishing communities, or pagars, which were essentially houses surrounded by fish traps built out over the sea. At each centre they talked with village headmen and at the village of Moro on Sugibawah Island and other strategic spots they laid down many emergency ration tins and instructions on how to reach the next rendezvous. Using some of the apparently unlimited amount of cash carried by Campbell, they were able to form a network of fishermen who promised to collect and ferry refugees to Lyon's halfway house, which he decided to set up on uninhabited Pulau Durian (near Sugibawah Island), at the northern end of the wide, cliff-lined Durian Strait. With its inconspicuous approaches, a precipitous overhang to give protection from bombers, and a rather steep, jungle-covered hill that provided an excellent vantage point, Durian was perfect for their needs.

After anchoring in the shadow of the cliffs Lyon and the others began the backbreaking task of transferring the supplies up a narrow dirt track to the summit of the hill, a job that was not made any easier by heavy rain squalls that swept the island without warning. When the stores were safely stowed in a small attap hut, built by *Hong Chuan*'s crew, the SOE team moved on to Prigi Radja, on the mouth of the Indragiri. Realising that the two breast-like hills, jutting up from behind the village, were a useful landmark from the sea, Lyon and Campbell persuaded the local headman to look after a supply dump and redirect escape parties upriver to Tambilahan, where they established more contacts. From here they chugged upstream to Rengat, which proved to be quite a sizeable centre, with docks, a quayside and some rather large warehouses. It was here, 140 kilometres from the river mouth, that most of the escape vessels would have to terminate, since beyond this point the river was navigable only to small craft.[23]

By the time the party returned to Singapore, late on February 5, the situation had deteriorated alarmingly. It was now obvious to Warren that his route would be used only for escapes. He ordered Lyon, Campbell, Morris and Baker to board SS *Krain* on the afternoon of February 6 to return to their respective escape route bases. Once ashore and installed in the little hut on Pulau Durian, Lyon spent most of the daylight hours weaving in and out of the islands in a five metre sailing dinghy, informing all the headmen that, as the 'army' (that is, himself) was now in occupation on Durian, all vessels from Singapore should be directed there. When night fell he and Morris, the chores complete, shared a bottle of medicinal purposes whisky while they listened to the crump of the heavy artillery barrage and watched the reflection of the explosions lighting the dark tropical sky over Singapore. For the rest of the night they both took turns at watch, lest the Japanese attempt to infiltrate Singapore from the south via the Durian Straits.

When a black oily haze from ruptured fuel tanks at Bukit Timah spread across the horizon they realised that they might soon see some activity. Within thirty-six hours, ships which had taken the risk of leaving in daylight were running the gauntlet of waves of Japanese bombers. On February 12 the *Durban* convoy raced through the Durian Strait, fighting off attack after attack from bombers which seemed to be focussing attention on the *Kedah* and *Empire Star*, the ship chosen by Captain Atkinson's murderers for their escape.[24]

The slower, smaller ships that had fled independently had to cope as best they could, using passengers' rifles and the occasional deck-mounted gun to stave off the enemy's determined assault. These smaller craft, which supplied Lyon with his first customers, were soon followed by survivors from boats that had run aground. As many of the arrivals were injured, Morris was kept on his toes, extracting chunks of splintered wood and sewing up jagged wounds. As he moved about the camp, he dispensed words of comfort in his soft Welsh lilt, particularly to the small, frightened children left orphaned by the sinkings or gunfire. For those who were beyond earthly help he could do nothing, save bury them in a small clearing nearby.

On February 17 two ships and a launch named *Joan* arrived, bringing news that Singapore had surrendered. This information coincided with a marked increase in the amount of traffic and news from the Bangka Straits survivors that ships had been sunk, not by aircraft, but by the enemy surface vessels which had massed on February 13 to attack Palembang.[25]

Three ships, the *Kuala, Tien Kwang* and *Kung Wo*, had not even made it that far. They had just passed the island of Pompong, to the south-east of Durian, when they were caught by enemy bombers.[26] Some of those who made dry land were taken further south to Dabo on Singkep Island in tonkans dispatched by Silahili, the Amir of Selengad,[27] while the rest were picked up by the growing number of vessels now part of Warren's escape operation. When news of the sinking of the three ships at Pompong reached Major Campbell on February 15, the irrepressible Bill Reynolds, captain of the *Kofuku Maru*, having already delivered his 262 Dutch civilian passengers from Tandjung Pinang to safety, immediately volunteered to cross the 100 kilometres of enemy-held sea to help effect a rescue.[28]

The *Kofuku Maru* was followed by *Numbing*, a sixty-six tonne coastal launch skippered by Major Rowley-Conwy who, along with the members of his battery, including the civilian 'gunner' Fraser, had high-tailed it out of Singapore immediately after the surrender. The Dutch Controller at Prigi Radja had given *Numbing* to Rowley-Conwy in order to assist in the rescue operations. No sailor, the artilleryman ran the boat aground so often that he was subsequently given *Plover*, a nine metre, wood-burning steam launch. Being a much smaller craft with less powerful engines, this was able to spend more time in the water and less time on the mud.[29]

While these and other rescues were taking place in the south, at the northern end of Sumatra there had been a few changes to the rest of Warren's plan. Shortly after Lyon had left Singapore on February 6, updated intelligence had prompted Warren to broaden the scope of the operation. It was decided to infiltrate armed Chinese guerilla parties from Began-Siapiapi into Malaya and try to contact Freddy Spencer Chapman, who was still somewhere in the jungle. Brian Passmore had managed to find a suitable boat — an eighty tonne motor tonkan called *Hin Leong*, requisitioned in such a hurry that its cargo of sugar, soy sauce and rice was still on board. On February 8 the vessel, with part of its original cargo replaced by arms, ammunition, explosives and a great deal of tinned provisions, was ready for sea.

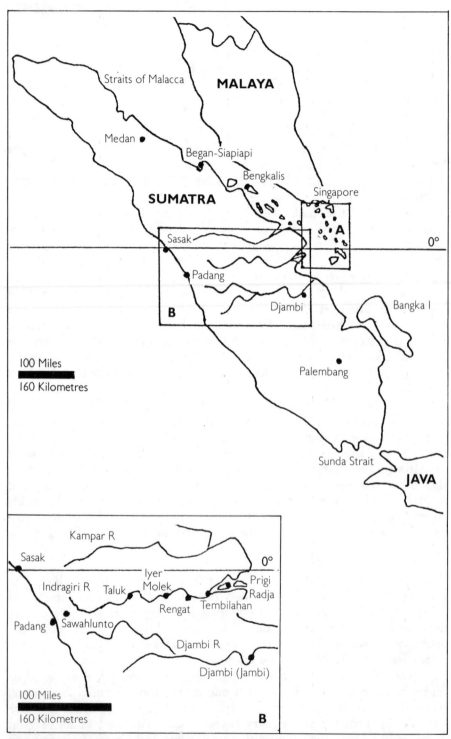

Map III. Escape route from Singapore to Padang on the west coast of Sumatra. A and B are enlargements of corresponding areas on Map III.

46

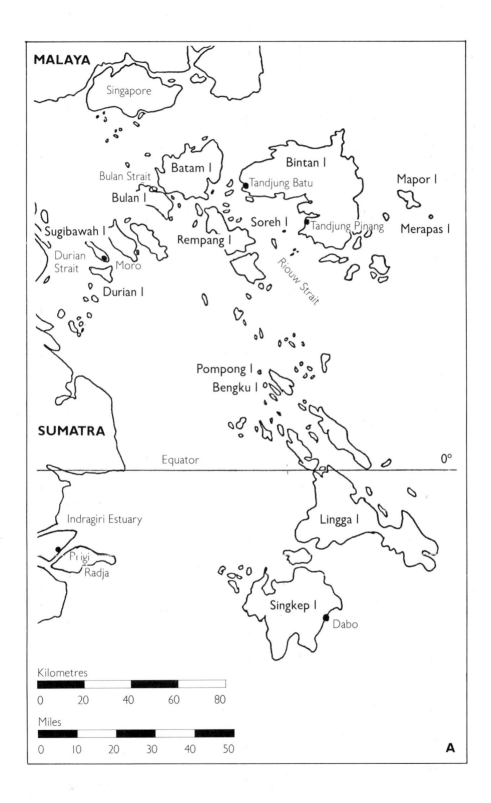

MALAYA

Singapore

Bulan Strait

Batam I

Bintan I

Tandjung Batu

Mapor I

Bulan I

Sugibawah I

Soreh I

Merapas I

Rempang I

Tandjung Pinang

Durian
Strait

Moro

Rempang I

Riouw Strait

Durian I

Pompong I

Bengku I

SUMATRA

Equator   0°

Indragiri Estuary

Lingga I

Prigi
Radja

Singkep I

Dabo

Kilometres

0   20   40   60   80

Miles

0   10   20   30   40   50

A

47

Besides the crew of four — two huge Irish stokers, an engine room assistant (survivors from the *Repulse*) and a corporal in the Gordon Highlanders named Boyle — there were two lorry loads of Chinese guerillas; two ex-planters/SOE men named Vanrennan and Graham; Broome, who brought his Chinese cook, and Davis, who was accompanied by Jamal, his orderly from the Malayan Police Force. Also included was a naval reservist of equal rank with Passmore, a Lieutenant Lind, who had been recruited for the operation by Warren on February 5 as he spoke Dutch fluently.[30]

When all the passengers had been packed on board, Lind took the ship out into Singapore Harbour, only to return some hours later when he could not find the entrance to the safe passage through the minefield. Back in port they picked up an additional, rather unexpected passenger. While *Hin Leong* had been going nowhere fast, the situation in Singapore had deteriorated to such an extent that, when the ship returned to Singapore, Colonel Warren, who now wanted to liaise with the Dutch on secret matters, decided to go with them.[31]

Having cleared the minefield successfully on the second attempt, they arrived in Began-Siapiapi, where Warren sold the cargo of sugar and, with the money, he and Passmore hired three junks and their Malayan crews. Everyone then took off in various directions for Malaya. One junk began a search for the stranded Argylls, Vanrennan and Graham headed for Port Selangor to look for Spencer Chapman while the thirty Chinese guerillas made their way to Sapang, south of Port Swettenham, with Davis and Broome, who were disguised as Malays.[32]

When the junk dispatched to rescue the Argylls returned empty with the news that there was no trace of them,[33] the rest of the party moved to the small seaport of Labuanbilik, where the Dutch informed Warren that Singapore had fallen.[34] With the Japanese expected to land on the eastern coast of Sumatra in the near future, Warren decided to investigate the possibility of setting up another operation on the western side. As this required the purchase of additional supplies and a ship of some kind, Passmore was dispatched in a taxi to Medan, about four hundred kilometres further north, where there was a branch of an English bank. There he hit the jackpot. The bank manager was so happy to get rid of his cash before the Japanese arrived that he handed over 14 000 guilders to Passmore without batting an eyelid.[35]

While Passmore was away, Warren received a signal from GHQ Java ordering him to assess the situation at Padang, where large numbers of British and Australians were reportedly arriving. Taking Lind to act as interpreter, he journeyed to the west coast on a twofold mission — to sort out the problem at Padang and investigate the possibility of setting up a new base. After crossing the mountains without incident, they arrived in Padang on February 26,[36] having left Passmore and his companions to wait for the other two junks to return from their missions in Malaya.

In the meantime, word had reached the Dutch Resident in Medan that a party of British officers was down the coast. Feeling that the matter required his personal attention, he turned up in full diplomatic regalia, cocked hat, oakleaf-encrusted uniform and all, accompanied by the Police Commandant. As a result of a conference, in which Jamal acted as interpreter, Passmore was given a letter instructing all Dutchmen to assist the party and it was agreed to swap *Hin Leong* for two lorries, four police drivers, a police corporal and two accumulator batteries for the radio set. The fact that the boat was in such a poor state that it was incapable of sailing any distance did not worry the Dutch, who only wanted to scuttle the vessel to blockade the river against the Japanese. Before handing it over, Passmore stripped *Hin Leong* of everything possible, including the tinned food, radio, mattresses, compass, and the swags of explosives for which Warren had an absolute passion.[37]

When Broome and Davis finally arrived from Began-Siapiapi it was with the worrying news that Vanrennan's and Graham's junk had returned without them. Apparently, the vessel had anchored off the Malayan coast while the two men went ashore. The following day a Japanese launch had become so suspicious that the junk's crew had taken fright and fled, leaving the SOE men stranded. It was not until after the war that their fate became known. Finding that the junk had gone without them they had turned inland, blowing up everything in sight and leaving such a trail of devastation in their wake that the Japanese took entire villages hostage. Believing that local guerillas must be reponsible, the Japanese threatened to execute the lot unless the saboteurs surrendered. Wishing to avoid further bloodshed, Graham and Vanrennan gave themselves up on March 25. Not long afterwards they, and six other like-minded individuals, were executed in the cemetery at Kuala Lumpur.[38]

When it was realised that the chances of Vanrennan and Graham returning were slim, the party was ordered to abandon the base and join Warren in Padang, with Passmore's letter of introduction ensuring that they enjoyed VIP treatment all the way.[39]

While the survivors of the Pompong sinkings were being rescued and Passmore was riding around northern Sumatra in a taxi, Lyon and Morris were still at Pulau Durian receiving the now dwindling numbers of survivors, who were fed and rested before being transported the 112 kilometres across the sea to Major Campbell at Prigi Radja. As the numbers slackened off to a mere trickle towards the end of February, Lyon and Morris decided that enough was enough. After making arrangements with the fishermen to take any stragglers to the Indragiri River, Lyon pinned a map and detailed instructions on how to reach Prigi Radja to the wall of the hut. Leaving the now vacant camp site with its lonely rows of graves, they scrambled down the steep path to the shore, climbed into the sailing boat and set off in a south-westerly direction for Sumatra.[40]

At about midnight, when quietly drifting down the straits, they were startled to see the silhouette of an enemy destroyer, anchored off their port bow. On veering immediately to starboard, they were further alarmed to find another great shadow looming out of the darkness, its glaring searchlight sweeping the shoreline in an enormous arc. Hurriedly ripping down the sail, Lyon and Morris lay down on the bottom of the boat which, to their relief, floated past the destroyers undetected.

For Morris, relief was short lived as they were soon caught in the tail of a storm that lashed the frail craft, sending it rollercoasting over the crests and down the troughs of mountainous waves. This helter-skelter ride in pitch darkness, which so terrified the formerly land-based Morris, did not perturb Lyon at all. He simply sat in the stern, hand on the rudder, casually glancing at the dial of his luminous compass from time to time. Morris, who was amazed by Lyon's display of sang-froid, was flabbergasted when Lyon announced that he felt rather tired and was going to sleep. To contemplate rest in these circumstances astounded the Welshman, but even as he spoke, Lyon was busy taking up the rudder bar and rudder and tucking them away under the stern sheets. He then curled up like a cat and, despite the pitching of the boat, was fast asleep within minutes. Morris, who was warily watching the still-raging waters, could scarcely believe either his ears or his eyes. However, Lyon's quietly slumbering form so inspired him with confidence that he too followed suit. Like his unflappable superior officer he was soon sleeping soundly while the storm blew itself out.

They awoke the following morning to find themselves tossed in heavy seas beneath scudding grey clouds and with not a skerrick of land in sight. Indeed, they saw nothing but empty stretches of ocean until midday when, with aim as true as an archer sending an arrow through the centre of a target, Lyon steered the boat through the mouth of the Indragiri River.

It was while sailing across the wide, many-channelled estuary, that they first came across Bill Reynolds, who was making for Prigi Radja with a load of evacuees. On seeing that they were in a small boat, Reynolds altered course to enquire if they required assistance. Unfortunately, he chose to come alongside just as Morris was changing into a pair of shorts. The bow wave created by *Kofuku Maru* rocked the much smaller boat so violently that Morris was pitched over the side. Splashing furiously, he kicked off his shorts and, before a rather interested audience, was forced to scramble back on board minus his trousers. Reassured by Lyon that he and Morris, apart from being completely soaked, were indeed able to fend for themselves, Reynolds chugged off up river.

At Prigi Radja, Lyon and Morris had a well-earned rest before making their way to Rengat by a variety of motorised craft. It was at the end of their journey, while they were putting along in a small, nondescript boat, that they scraped alongside the *Kofuku Maru* and renewed their passing acquaintance with Bill Reynolds. His extended and colourful enquiry as to who had taught them to sail amused both Morris and Lyon, who decided that he would like to become more closely acquainted with the gutsy Australian. With his taste for unorthodox and flamboyant characters, Lyon was fascinated by Reynolds, a man larger than life who obviously feared neither man nor beast.[41]

With Lyon's and Reynolds's rescue work almost completed, the time had now come for them to consider the future. Technically, there were two ways open for escape. One was across Sumatra on the established route to Padang, the route that Lyon and Morris planned to take. The other was by ship to India, via the very risky, Japanese-infested Straits of Malacca. On paper, the Malaccan route seemed suicidal, but Reynolds told Lyon that he believed it was possible. For this very reason, he had been stockpiling fuel for days, always taking on more than he had expended in his rescue work.[42] His boat, to all intents and purposes, appeared to be nothing more than a simple Japanese fishing vessel. On the basis that the best way to hide was to be one of the crowd, Reynolds reasoned that he could run the Japanese blockade by simply sailing through it. When he learned that the Australian had so far eluded the enemy in his scruffy fishing boat without the slightest trouble, Ivan Lyon was also convinced. He suggested to Reynolds that if *Kofuku Maru* could get *out* of Japanese waters unchallenged, it could surely get back *in*. Provided the ship and its motley crew could make India in one piece, they might yet live to fight another day. Fired with the confidence of the fearless, Lyon and Reynolds made a pact. Provided both survived, they would meet again in Bombay.[43]

As Reynolds's dilapidated little boat disappeared down the muddy waters of the Indragiri to Prigi Radja in search of more customers, Lyon and Morris applied themselves to the urgent and pressing problem of crossing the mountain range to Padang, before the Japanese arrived.

They were now following a well-worn path. When Campbell had arrived with Baker at Rengat on February 7, he had immediately sought the co-operation of the Dutch administration to transport refugees across Sumatra to the west coast. With this arranged, they had set up a staging post at Tambilahan, before moving downstream to Prigi Radja. Here Campbell had directed operations until it was decided at the end of

February, with the Japanese drawing near, that Prigi Radja, like Tambilahan, should be evacuated. Before he left, Campbell posted instructions directing all escapers to press on upriver and then make for Padang, and asked the village headman to help any latecomers so that they too could make their way to Rengat.

The headman did a fine job. But the number of refugees using the escape route caught the organisers unawares. With the sudden fall of Singapore, civilians, soldiers and deserters had fled before the Japanese in such huge numbers that the camps along the river were soon bursting at the seams. As more and more evacuees streamed into Sumatra, the COs were hard pressed to provide food, shelter and transportation. Yet, despite the hundreds, or indeed thousands, that were passed from camp to camp, the escape route worked.

When they were disgorged from the larger craft at Rengat, the evacuees moved further upstream to Iyer Molek on *Faith, Hope* and *Charity* — two flat-bottomed barges drawn by an old steam-driven, wood-fired launch. From here they proceeded inland, climbing over the tall mountain peaks in whatever vehicles could be provided, some completing the final stage of the journey to Padang from Sawahlunto in the comparative comfort of a mountain train, for which there was no shortage of passengers. As well as the hundreds of refugees who had wound their way upstream from Prigi Radja, there were those who had used an alternate route along the Djambi River valley — mainly evacuees who had either been passed on by Amir Silahili from Singkep Island, or who had found their way to the river after eluding the Japanese in the Bangka Straits.[44]

When the time had come for Morris and Lyon to quit Rengat, they were more than ready to go. The mosquitoes were so thick that the pair had spent the entire night strolling along the quayside, puffing profusely on cigarettes and pipe in an effort to make enough smoke to discourage the voracious creatures, before continuing their journey in the back of an open tourer that Campbell had managed to acquire. As the vehicle groaned its way over mountainous terrain at an altitude of almost two thousand metres, they huddled beneath a groundsheet in a futile effort to ward off the chilling rain. At every hairpin bend, the twin shafts of light from the headlamps shone alarmingly into inky nothingness as the vehicle negotiated the precipitous road. Having made their tortuous way slowly towards a coastal rendezvous, they were shattered to find that a submarine, arranged to take them to safety, had not turned up, necessitating their having to backtrack a considerable distance before finally, on March 2, they too reached Padang.[45]

For Lyon and Morris, like all those who had weathered the bombs, the strafing, the sea and the jungle, their arrival at this place marked the completion of one journey and the beginning of another — a journey that would lead them variously to freedom, captivity or death.

Chapter 4
The Incredible Voyage of the *Sederhana Djohanes*

The quiet, usually sleepy seaside town was, on the morning of 5 March, crowded with soldiers and civilians. About five kilometres away, at the port of Emmahaven, one of two ships tied up alongside the remnants of the heavily bombed wharves had space for fifty evacuees — men only, as the ship's captain flatly refused to carry any women. Taking advantage of the captain's bias, Warren ordered all his SOE other ranks, including Morris, to leave. As the ship threaded its way between the superstructures of sunken ships, Morris wondered if he would ever see Lyon and Campbell again.[1]

A continuous stream of refugees had passed through the small port, grabbing every inch of space on a variety of vessels from fast naval destroyers to rusty cargo boats and flimsy native traders. The day before, a group of Rowley-Conwy's gunners had been among 102 officers and men who had left on a 1200 tonne cargo boat carrying 900 tonnes of bombs. Existing on rations intended to last three and a half days, they were destined to arrive safely in Colombo after a ten-day voyage, with nothing to guide the captain other than a compass and a school atlas.[2]

Both the Australian commander, General Gordon Bennett, and English Brigadier Paris had also arrived in Padang in late February after a hair-raising escape from Singapore, which saw only four boats out of a possible forty-four reach safety. Bennett had been evacuated by flying boat to Java, where he delivered a request for arms and wireless sets from Warren before being airlifted to Australia. Within days he and five survivors of the 2/19 Battalion had begun working on a jungle warfare manual which was put to good use during the bitter fighting to regain control of New Guinea, turning the retreat along the Kokoda Track (commonly called 'Trail') into an advance to Buna and Gona.[3] Shortly after Bennett had left, Brigadier Paris and a large number of civilians and military personnel were evacuated on the *Rooseboom*, a small coastal boat that usually plied the waters between Java and Sumatra.[4]

The Allied troops that remained at Padang had little chance of escape and the general air of nervousness was not improved by rumours of the relentless Japanese advance. At his headquarters at the Eendracht Club Colonel Warren, pressured by the Dutch into taking command, was forced to monitor news broadcasts from Ceylon for information, as the Consul had rather prematurely destroyed all the cipher books. The news that he received on March 7 was not encouraging. It was feared that the last boat to leave, bound for Java, had been torpedoed and a ship, dispatched from Colombo to evacuate more survivors, was two days overdue.[5] He would have been even more dispirited had he known the fate of the *Rooseboom*, torpedoed and sunk when three days out of Padang. At first it was believed that the two Javanese picked up by Morris's ship were the sole survivors.[6] However, another 135 people, packed chin to chin in, or clinging to the sides of, a lifeboat built to hold twenty-eight persons, had also survived the sinking. As it drifted aimlessly, many, including Brigadier Paris, died from the combined effects of exhaustion, thirst and starvation. These victims were among the more fortunate, for a number of others were callously murdered by a group of British Army deserters from Liverpool, who had indulged in unspeakable acts of cannibilism before being forced over the side. After twenty-eight days adrift, enduring unimaginable privation, only four people were left alive — two mad Javanese, Chinese/British agent Doris Lim and an English soldier, Sergeant Walter Gibson, the last of the Argyll and Southern Highlanders. A short time after staggering ashore on an island off the Sumatran coast, Lim and Gibson were captured by the Japanese.[7]

It was as well that such news had not reached Padang to demoralise the refugees further for, on the evening of March 7, it was confirmed that the Japanese were a mere ninety-six kilometres up the road. The Dutch, who were now hoping to negotiate, were anxious to appear neutral so all aid for transportation ceased, a boom was placed across the harbour and a close eye was kept on all vessels lest any be misappropriated. For those who may have been flush with funds, the purchase of a boat was still technically a possibility, but prices were exorbitant and well beyond the means of men who, for the most part, owned only the clothes they stood up in.[8]

There was, however, one boat available — a native coastal boat or prahu, fully provisioned and lying a short distance up the coast where it was less likely to attract attention. When Warren had crossed to the west coast, looking for suitable bases to bring in supplies from India, he had spied the craft anchored near a fishing village.[9] Named the *Sederhana Djohanes* or *Lucky John,* it had been purchased with what remained of the 14 000 guilders obtained by Passmore from the generous Medan bank manager. When Passmore, Davis and Broome arrived from the east coast, Warren had taken them straight to the boat, tied up on the river at Padang, to unload their lorry loads of supplies and equipment taken from the *Hin Leong.* On viewing the threadbare sails, Broome and Passmore had gone on a shopping spree, purchasing 144 packets of needles, a similar quantity of thread and a roll of canvas. Warren then produced papers that allowed the boom to be raised and the vessel to sail to its hiding place up the coast.[10]

As the Japanese drew near, Warren had realised that seaborne raids behind enemy lines were no longer feasible and that *Sederhana Djohanes* could be used as an escape boat for anyone unlucky enough to miss out on evacuation. However, when the numbers of people waiting at Padang far outnumbered Warren's expectations, he realised that the boat could provide a means of escape for only a select few. There was no question of his leaving, for he was regularly receiving disturbing reports from the Dutch of rape and theft, and of soldiers selling their weapons to raise cash. In addition, some of the officers had 'done a bunk', leading to a growing feeling of disrespect for authority among the rank and file. The non-arrival of Colonel Dillon, whom it had been hoped would assume command, and the outright refusal of several more senior officers to take over, meant that Warren himself must stay to keep law and order.[11]

With Warren remaining behind, there was room on the ship for eighteen. As all the SOE lesser ranks had already been evacuated and only six places were required for the officers, there was room for twelve others. Warren chose those whom he believed could be of special value to the war effort. There was need for great caution and absolute secrecy. Not only might the Dutch consul put a stop to the plans but there would be wholesale panic should the hundreds of men and women left behind learn that this was definitely the last boat to freedom. Furtively, on Warren's instructions, the chosen men assembled at the Eendracht Club, where they were told to proceed up the coast, board the prahu and sail 2400 kilometres across the Indian Ocean to Ceylon (now Sri Lanka).

Having finished this alarmingly short briefing, Warren impressed on them the need for secrecy at all costs. No one was permitted to return to his billet to collect even a few possessions in case it aroused suspicion. Under cover of darkness the small band left Padang, any noise made by the departure of their convoy of two-wheeled, horse-drawn tongas effectively masked by the sound of intermittent rain squalls. As the Malay drivers peered through the inky blackness of the moonless night, their passengers' apprehension was heightened by the driving rain and the knowledge that if they lost sight of the barely visible red oil lamps of the vehicle in front, they were likely to become hopelessly lost in the jungle.

The journey ended finally at about two am at Panjalanan, a small, palm-fringed fishing village. By this time it had stopped raining and the moon had risen, bathing the scene in the kind of silvery light that under different circumstances, would have been regarded as highly romantic. Moored about eight hundred metres offshore was the native prahu.

A nondescript vessel of about twenty-five tonnes, the twenty metre *Sederhana Djohanes* was a trader built purely for sailing the waters along the Sumatran coast. Almost the entire deck space, except for a small strip along the sides and at each end, was covered by a steeply pitched roof, made of planks coated with sheet copper then a layer of attap, providing an excellent and quite waterproof shelter. The bowsprit was extraordinarily long, as was the tiller, and above the deck towered two masts, one of about eight metres in height, the other about fifteen metres, supporting sails which were so thin and worn that the stars could actually be seen through them. There was no keel and the copper-clad hull was so broad that the overall effect was not unlike that of a sailing saucer. It may have been an ideal craft for localised trading voyages but whether it could sail vast distances through open seas, whipped up by roaring monsoon winds and treacherous tropical squalls, was, thought the sailors among them, quite another matter.

It was 3 o'clock on the morning of March 9 before they were ferried out to join those already on board. When they awoke, some hours later, they found to their astonishment that the prahu was well under way, with Ivan Lyon at the helm. On the mast he had pinned a pendulum and a small piece of lined paper with the comment, 'If the pendulum goes past that line, we'll turn over'. With daylight now flooding the boat and everyone properly awake, the eighteen passengers took stock of one another. Besides Lyon there were the five other SOE men — Richard Broome, who had been on the *Hin Leong* and who was in overall command, Jock Campbell, controller of the ship's provisions, and Brian Passmore, Allen Lind and John Davis, also from the *Hin Leong*. Present as well, to the annoyance of several people who believed that their places could have been better filled by 'more useful' white personnel, were Davis's orderly, Jamal Bin Diam, and Broome's Chinese cook, Lo Gnap Soon.

Also on board was the other man who, with Ivan Lyon, was essential to their escape. He was Garth Gorham, a swarthy-skinned Merchant Navy man with a magnificent black beard, a fiery eye and an oft-voiced contempt for all things pertaining to the Royal Navy. Gorham, the ill-fated *Kung Wo*'s second officer, had been at Padang, about to board a ship for India, when Warren grabbed him to navigate the *Sederhana Djohanes*. He knew it would be a tough job as his only navigational aids were an unreliable wristwatch, a dog-eared Sumatran Pilot Book, some hurriedly copied navigational tables, a chart of the coast of Sumatra, and a wind map of the Indian Ocean, torn from a pocket dictionary. He also had a sextant, whose usefulness would depend on whether the dilapidated radio and two batteries, procured by Passmore as part exchange for the *Hin Leong*, could hold out long enough to give accurate time signals.

The other nine men were Major 'Doc' Davies, an RAMC doctor; two Naval Lieutenants, 'Holly' Holwell and Richard Cox, who had survived the grounding of the minesweeper *Trang*; Lieutenant Geoffrey Brooke who, like Gorham, had been on the *Kung Wo*; a cheery, freckle-faced, immaculately turned out captain in the 1st Manchesters named

Spanton who had joined forces with the rather pessimistic Bill Waller (the unfortunate army major who had been obliged to sign the surrender orders) to row part of the way to Sumatra in a flat-bottomed boat given to them by a Chinese waiter at Raffles Hotel. The last four mentioned had been picked up in the Indragiri River by two men who were also on board — Major Rowley-Conwy, now sporting a rakish Trilby hat, and his civilian friend Douglas Fraser, whom 'Rowley', as he was always called, had lately 'promoted' to the rank of lieutenant. The last passenger was an Intelligence Corps Lieutenant named Clarke who, because of his mixed Japanese parentage and fluency with that language, was nicknamed 'Tojo'.

It was this very diverse band whom Broome now summoned together. They were split into two watches and informed of the provisions that had been stowed on board. Food included cases of bully beef, potatoes, carrots, condensed milk, tinned fruit, coffee, butter, biscuits, porridge, sugar, rice, coconuts and a small quantity of limes and bananas. Water was contained in two forty-four gallon (200 litre) drums prepared by the Irish stokers, while 360 litres more were stored in earthenware jars and petrol tins. Boredom was to be staved off by two tatty copies of *Esquire* magazine and a copy of Daphne du Maurier's thriller *Rebecca*. Stray Japanese were to be kept at bay by two Lewis guns, a few rifles and some revolvers, all of which had adequate supplies of ammunition. Should anyone require medical attention there were good stocks of morphine, drugs, bandages and castor oil. Cigarettes, cigars and pipe tobacco were on hand for the nicotine addicts, while the recently purchased supplies of sailcloth, needles and twine, as well as sundry amounts of hardware, were available for running repairs. Naturally, the five bottles of whisky were designated 'for medicinal use only'.

These provisions may have seemed, to the uninitiated landlubber, quite adequate for a voyage across the Indian Ocean. However, as Broome outlined the plans it became evident that great caution would have to be exercised and the supplies, particularly the water, carefully rationed. He announced that they were to work their way more than three hundred kilometres up the coast of Sumatra, to a latitude that was about equal with that of Ceylon, where they should be able to pick up the north-east monsoon. Aided by this steady wind, they hoped to sail directly across the ocean to make the expected landfall. If everything went to plan and the winds were favourable, the voyage should take about three weeks.

However, the treacherous western coast of Sumatra and the change of direction of the monsoon, which occurred in April, were unknown factors — factors upon which success or failure depended. To lessen the danger of the first, the prahu's former Malayan crew, composed of an old man and two boys, had agreed to sail with them for some distance up the coast, until the worst part of the shoreline had been negotiated and the new crew had learned to handle the rather tricky boat. While the others enjoyed the sea air, Lyon conducted an animated conversation in Malay with the elderly sailor. Although some of those on board the prahu had sailing experience, none except Lyon had any idea of how to handle a small boat in ocean conditions. The more astute among those who watched him talk happily with the Malays suspected that it might be on his strength and resourcefulness alone that they would soon have to rely.

For the time being, however, the Sederhana Djohanes fairly bowled along the Sumatran coast under fair skies and before a stiff breeze. By the afternoon of the first day, before the appearance of many small islands forced them to anchor for the night, they had covered more than sixty kilometres. At dawn the following morning they weighed anchor in a strong easterly wind only to have the worn mainsail rip asunder and the boom crack under the strain. As the wind freshened so did the anxiety, but the Malays were old hands at this caper. While the wind howled and the seas heaved beneath the prahu's protesting timbers, the native crew bound up the boom and manoeuvred the boat through murderously sharp coral reefs towards the sheltered waters of a small island.[12]

After the local fishermen had supplied two lengths of bamboo suitable for a new boom, the Malays announced that this was as far as they were prepared to go. As they took their leave, there were handshakes all round and the old man intoned in Malay, 'Tuan, good luck for your journey. I shall be praying to Allah that you will arrive at your destination'. The blessing having been dispensed, he got down to business, extorting another fortnight's wages plus enough extra money to pay for a hire car home in exchange for his silence. Despite this, the mariners actually felt a bit lost when they saw the old rascal and his two boys paddling away, for it suddenly hit them that they were now really on their own.[13]

At this point the leadership shifted unobtrusively from Broome to Lyon, for it had become obvious to all that their ultimate fate depended solely on this immensely capable man. Saying little, he missed nothing, preferring to keep out of the sometimes spirited discussions until asked his opinion, when he would give a wry smile and say, 'I always try to keep an open mind'. This calm attitude was greatly reassuring. Those who might have grown apprehensive during the long and often terrifying voyage had only to look at Lyon to have their spirits restored as he sat comfortably in the stern, tiller in hand, apparently unconcerned by the danger around him, exuding that quietly confident air of one who has been born to the sea.

Lyon needed all the skill that he had acquired on his long single-handed voyages, for the Sederhana Djohanes was a difficult boat to sail, exhibiting a tendency to sail backwards when the wind was not in the right quarter. More often than not, when the breeze was finally propelling them along in the right direction, there would be the sound of a sickening rip as the sails tore once again from top to bottom. When this happened there was nothing for it but to heave to and take out the needles and twine. With many pricked fingers and much swearing from the very unskilled amateur sailmakers, the sail would be mended, more or less, until hit by the next strong gust.

On about the fifth night out they were hit by a violent storm, the second in as many nights. Tired bodies that had battled the fury of a Sumatra not twenty-four hours previously now had to muster renewed strength to keep the boat afloat. With the mainsail and jib in imminent danger of ripping yet again, Broome undertook the hazardous job of climbing the mainmast while Rowley tackled the bowsprit. As the deck bucked alarmingly beneath the mountainously heaving seas, and the waves and wind-driven rain saturated everything and everyone on board, the pair inched their way up and out, until the sails were retrieved intact, much to the relief of those watching the procedure from the shelter of the covered area. Only one man was outside on deck. At the helm of the pitching, rocking boat Ivan Lyon was completely in control. Wrapped in a groundsheet, water streaming from every pore, he was in his element, enjoying every minute of this absorbing contest between man and nature.

The sounds of the tempest were just subsiding when there came a new noise — the alarming sound of waves pounding on rocks — a sound that most certainly did not belong out there, so far away from land. Lyon pulled hard on the tiller. With agonising slowness, her every timber straining under the load, the *Sederhana Djohanes* responded as a reef of cruelly jagged coral slid past. The boat had scarcely righted itself when they heard once more the chilling sound of waves on coral, this time dead ahead. As Lyon again averted an impaling on rocks that threatened to tear the bottom from the boat, he realised that they were trapped, completely encircled in the darkness by a reef. Giving orders to secure the anchor, he wrapped his arms around his legs under the groundsheet and, with his head upon his knees, fell instantly asleep.

By morning all signs of the storm had passed and the men woke to a bright sun shining from a clear blue sky and confirmation that they were indeed entrapped within a reef. The most pressing problem was how to get out. Every time they edged the boat towards what appeared to be a channel, they found the way blocked by razor-sharp coral ready to convert the craft to matchwood. Lyon finally announced that there was only one way out — to pole the boat like a gondola, inch by inch, until they were clear of the danger. After hours of backbreaking work, the *Sederhana Djohanes* was once again in clear water.

They had barely made it into the open sea when a squall hit. Hands still raw and bleeding from the poling exercise were not nimble enough to furl the mainsail in time. Predictably, it tore along the full length of its recently mended seam before it could be hauled in. However, the wind was of such intensity that the boat moved along without any sails at a record speed of seven knots, while sore and blistered fingers grappled with yet another bout of sewing. These periods of favourable wind were punctuated all too often by spells of intense calm on glassy seas, when the heat radiated in great waves from the deck and water was rationed to one small tin cup per man. The monotony at such times was filled by singing, by discussing every topic imaginable and by much eye boggling over the contents of *Esquire* magazine. It was not, however, the luscious lovelies, portrayed in various titillating poses, that were the focus of all the attention. Rather, the subject of the long drawn out sighs was a photograph — a full page, living colour print — that evoked memories of those far off, carefree days before the war, before the fall of Singapore. It was a tantalising, lifesize picture of polished glass tumblers holding tinkling ice, bubbling thirst-quenching tonic water . . . and gin.[14]

There was, however, one period of dark despair, a time of utter hopelessness, when the morale of some fell to its lowest possible level. They were becalmed during a spell of intensely hot weather, without a whisper of air and only a few drops of severely rationed water to moisten parched lips. With no sign of rain and the sails hanging limply in air so heavy that it seemed to press the very breath from their bodies, some of the men wanted to give up, believing that surrender, even to the Japanese, could be no worse than the torture of floating aimlessly on the ocean with no apparent hope of salvation.

Ivan Lyon had other ideas. There was no way known that he was going to allow any one to quit. With the same powerful determination exhibited by another great sailor, the castaway Captain Bligh, one hundred and fifty years before, Lyon exerted his will. While Campbell continued to dole out the meagre water ration, Lyon, his revolver cocked and ready, made it quite clear that he was not going to tolerate the thought of surrender. This outstanding display of absolute, if ruthless, determination later prompted Bill Waller, one of those whose morale had dissolved, to declare, 'Ivan Lyon is one of the most courageous men I have ever known'.[15]

There was nothing to break the monotony or the heat until March 28, when a steady breeze and a Japanese fighter plane arrived almost simultaneously. The boat's company went into a well-rehearsed drill. In the hope of the vessel being mistaken for a native trader, Jamal took the tiller, Soon made himself conspicuous and the rest dived for cover as the air was rent with the sound of machine-gun fire. Bullets sprayed across the deck, thudding into the sides of the hull and the planking on the shelter. Up on deck, Jamal and Soon held their positions until Davis remembered them and told them to take cover. Even then, Jamal was not going to be rushed. It was probably his typical islander's gesture of calmly standing up and adjusting his sarong before moving below that finally convinced the enemy pilot that the boat was manned by harmless Malayan fishermen.[16]

In all, the plane had emptied five long bursts of machine-gun fire into the vessel. Drained by the ordeal, eighteen shaken men crawled from their hiding places to find that although the sails were distinctly perforated, not a single person had suffered any injury, the hull had not been punctured below the water line and the water containers were wholly intact. It was nothing short of miraculous. Their luck held, for the following morning, when the plane returned to check them out, *Sederhana Djohanes* was safely concealed beneath low cloud cover. While the men waited, expecting every moment to be their last, the plane flew back and forth in frustration overhead, heard but unseen, unable to find a gap in the cloud.

Although the monsoon blew in their favour, its benevolent winds continued to be interspersed with severe rain squalls and periods of depressing calm. Spirits plummeted somewhat when a time check, on the rapidly fading, battery-powered wireless, revealed that Gorham's old watch, on which he had been forced to rely for his navigation, was out, making their real position 176 kilometres further from safety than they had thought. But this was nothing compared to the fright they received only 320 kilometres from the coast of Ceylon, when a curious plane, thought to be friendly, came down for a closer look. As it banked, the sun caught the unmistakeable glint of the menacing red circle of the Imperial Japanese Air Force. Luckily all it did was look, but the incident prompted the men to reject their western clothing in favour of sarongs.

As the days dragged on, fickle winds alternately filled and deflated sails that were now a mosaic of patches upon patches, held down by fraying ropes that had been spliced and respliced. The *Sederhana Djohanes*, never a smart-looking vessel at any stage, began to look very tatty indeed. Not that the condition of the voyagers was much better. After more than a month on a reduced diet with no green vegetables or fruit, all had lost weight and many were suffering from a variety of complaints, mostly skin-related ailments. Their mental state was on the whole quite good, but morale fluctuated according to the whims of the capricious breeze that seemed to be intent on doing all it could to hinder their progress.[17] Then, quite suddenly, on April 12, the waiting was over.[18]

It was Gorham who first confirmed it, but Lyon who first saw it.[19] Afraid to raise hopes that might be then dashed, he waited until he was certain before announcing, 'There is a cloud over there which might be land'.[20] When Gorham's field glasses confirmed that the mauve triangle was Ceylon's Friar's Hood Mountain, just visible in the mist, the boat reverberated with whoops of delight that the ordeal was almost over. Only one man was totally unmoved by the sighting. It was, predictably, Lyon. Of all those on board, he was the only one to feel sorry that the voyage was almost at an end.

Two tankers were sighted the next morning. As the signal lamp was on the blink, a makeshift distress signal was raised but, to the disappointment of all, particularly the pro-Merchant Navy Gorham, the vessels took absolutely no notice. It was only later that they learned how narrowly they had avoided disaster. These same ships, which were part of a Japanese convoy, intercepted and captured an escape party headed by Colonel Dillon shortly afterwards.[21] For the next two days they saw no more ships other than a far-off tanker which failed to respond to their frantic signalling. Worse, the land disappeared. When Gorham announced that they would make for the Great Bases Light, which was somewhere over the horizon, there was a serious breach in the otherwise harmonious relationship. The ship's company split into two distinct camps, based more or less on the ability to swim. The non-swimmers wanted to sail on to find a proper landing place, while the swimmers were willing to go over the side if it meant reaching terra firma more quickly. As the swimmers outnumbered the rest, Ivan Lyon headed for the nearest land.[22]

Late that afternoon they sighted the coast again. Cliffs and palm trees were clearly visible and once more an argument erupted as to the advisability of trying to make a landing. The closer they came the less desirable the longed-for land appeared. Scrubby dunes and wild-looking, bush-covered mountains lent a backdrop to breakers that crashed upon the beach. As rocks started to appear quite alarmingly from beneath the surface of the water, everyone moved towards the bow for a better view. As the boat inched closer to the menacing surf, Lyon ignored the looks of great anxiety appearing on the faces of all, including those of the terra firma faction. Since he had advocated finding a more suitable landfall, he was now enjoying the discomfiture of those who had refused to listen to reason. When the *Sederhana Djohanes* came to within two hundred metres of the shore, the would-be landlubbers called a halt. At the shout of 'You win, for God's sake let's get out of it', Lyon swung on the tiller and the boat set about, thereby saving them all from a disastrous landing at an uninhabited game reserve.

Their luck had definitely changed. Almost immediately a ship was sighted, coming straight towards them. The distress signal was again hoisted and the ensign flown upside down. Brooke, his signal lamp having died in one last attempt, climbed onto the roof of the shelter where, with classic British understatement, he semaphored, 'Sixteen British officers from Singapore request assistance please', while everyone else waved and shouted. At first it seemed as if the ship would pass them by, but then it turned and made in their direction, a large gun covering them from the stern as the prahu came alongside.

The inquisitive faces lining the railings of the towering *Anglo-Canadian* must have thought them a very odd sight. They certainly were a motley lot. Some were clad in identifiable, carefully preserved uniforms, others in tattered rags or sarongs. All were burnt nut brown by five weeks at sea and to top it off, they were sailing a native prahu that looked as if it might break up at any minute.

The eighteen were soon scrambling up the Jacob's ladders. There was general hilarity when Waller fell into the sea and Gorham lost his sarong on the climb to the top, necessitating his greeting his rescuers completely starkers. With all safely on board, the ship's telegraph clanged the engines to action and the *Sederhana Djohanes* slipped astern. After a voyage of 2656 kilometres, it was a poignant moment to see the battered old hull, still carrying the sails aloft like a decrepit banner, floating alone on the open sea. The death knell came when the captain decided that the unmanned craft might constitute a danger to shipping. When the smoke from the twelve-pounder gun cleared, the watchers at the rail saw a pathetic, stricken thing, the mast in tatters, the hull holed, but still afloat. In the end, no one saw her demise, for the range was opening fast. Last sighted, she was still bobbing along, fading away into the Ceylonese sunset, a brave tribute to a most amazing voyage.

The mariners were in fine spirits when the *Anglo-Canadian* docked in Bombay, where they revelled in the luxury of the Taj Mahal Hotel for four days before going their separate ways. Broome and Davis disappeared to an ancient fort in India to prepare for clandestine operations which would return them to Malaya by submarine. Fraser, still technically a civilian, was sent on an Officer's Field Gunnery course before being attached to a special forces unit. He returned to Malaya by parachute to operate with the resistance movement, his 'army' status never being questioned. Rowley went off to active service in the jungles of Burma, while the naval officers returned to England for further commissioning.[23]

For almost all of them, the days of terror spent crossing the Indian Ocean were now a memory, a series of reminiscences to bring out and examine from time to time, like faded photographs in an album.

Not so for Ivan Lyon. From the time that they had been strafed by the Japanese plane, Lyon's agile mind had been working overtime. His sense of outrage at the attack was matched only by his fury at the ineptitude of the British High Command, whose refusal to face facts had resulted in the loss of Singapore, and by an overwhelming sense of guilt. Although he had saved the lives of hundreds who had fled along the escape route, he nevertheless felt guilty. Guilty that so many of his fellow Gordons were dead or in Japanese hands. Guilty that, in its hour of need, he had not been there to fight the battle which had brought the mighty British Empire to its knees. Fuelled by this guilt, by an ice-cold inner rage at the stupidity of those responsible for the fall of Malaya and Singapore, and by the memory of the bullets thudding into the deck, he sought for a way to strike back. For hour upon hour, alone at the tiller, he had searched for the answer.[24]

By the time he reached Ceylon his anger was no longer impotent. An idea, germinated on the far off Indragiri River, had grown to fruition

— a plan for a daring operation that could be carried out provided he had the help of one particular man and his ship.

Aided by Bill Reynolds and his down-at-heel Japanese fishing boat, *Kofuku Maru*, Lyon would hit back at the Japanese in a place where they would least expect it — Singapore.

Chapter 5
Jaywick Begins

When Lyon arrived in India, he found Bill Reynolds waiting for him. In the weeks that had passed since their farewell on the Indragiri, the lanky Australian had been busy. Besides undertaking an espionage trip on March 6 for the Dutch administration to the Riouw Straits, where he had come off best in an altercation with a Japanese patrol vessel near Tandjung Pinang, Reynolds had continued with his rescue work. Ten times in all he had returned to the islands, rescuing a total of 1100 people, until Japanese bombs, and damage to *Kofuku Maru*'s stern by an inopportune ramming, forced him to put into Rengat. When he learned that the Japanese were expected within forty-eight hours, Reynolds decided that the time had come to call it quits.

As soon as repairs had been effected, Reynolds was off, but not before he renamed the ship *British Privateer Suey Sin Fah* (a Narcissus bloom). This rather swashbuckling title was no doubt popular with the Chinese members of the ship's company, for although *Kofuku Maru* meant 'Happiness', it was a Japanese name and, under the circumstances, would have been regarded as very bad 'joss'. When Reynolds wrote the new name in bold, firm printing on the first of three exercise books that were to serve as the ship's log, *Kofuku Maru* officially became the blockade-running *Suey Sin Fah*.

After obtaining sailing clearance from Military Headquarters in India, Reynolds took on British sailor Frank McNeil, who swelled *Suey Sin Fah*'s crew to a total of six — three Chinese, including a young stewardess who doubled as a cook and helmsperson, and three Europeans. Also on board was Looi Lam Kwai, the stewardess's three-year-old daughter. They were a scant seventy-five minutes out of Rengat when McNeil had second thoughts, putting on such a convincing performance of having badly injured his pelvis that Reynolds put in at Tambilahan. The patient was carted off to hospital on a stretcher, only to reappear a short time later, walking perfectly well under his own steam. After a cross examination by Reynolds, McNeil admitted he had feigned illness as he considered that they were all lunatics to attempt such a voyage. As it turned out, he should have stayed with the madmen. Within twenty-four hours of his return to Rengat, the Japanese arrived.[1]

On the morning of March 15, with the news that enemy troops were advancing down the river, Reynolds left Tambilahan for Prigi Radja, where he turned north for Bengkalis, threading his way through the narrow straits and channels between Sumatra and the offshore islands. On reaching Bengkalis, he ignored the suggestion from the Dutch Controller that the ship should make for Began-Siapiapi, where it could be hidden among the Chinese fishing junks, electing instead to rest the crew, clean the engine and check that the Lewis guns, machine guns and rifles were in order.[2]

Apparently the size of *Suey Sin Fah*'s arsenal worried the Controller, for at four in the afternoon of March 17 he sent for Reynolds. When asked outright what he intended to do if Japanese craft entered the harbour, Reynolds, commanding officer of an armed British trawler in the First World War[3] and fresh from his recent skirmish in the Riouw Straits, replied that he 'would engage the enemy in action'. This was definitely not what the Controller, who was wary of compromising his position with the Japanese, wanted to hear. After some 'heated discussion' Reynolds agreed that if he wanted to shoot at the enemy he would do so in the Brouwer Strait — a narrow strip of water that separated the island from Sumatra and was apparently sufficiently removed from the Dutchman's territory to be regarded as international waters. Although it went much against the grain, Reynolds also had to promise not to fire at Japanese aircraft while in port.[4]

At 8 pm the following day, the Controller learned that the enemy was moving down the Siak River to take Bengkalis. Alarmed by the prospect of an armed British merchant ship being found in his harbour, he ordered Reynolds to leave by midnight 'in order to avoid capture in a Dutch port'.

As the ship's Chinese motormen had deserted the previous day, this presented something of a problem until Reynolds struck a deal with the captain of the motor launch *Rasak*, agreeing to tow him to Began-Siapiapi in return for the loan of two Malays to fill the position temporarily.

Hiding in a creek by day and sailing by night, they managed to avoid attracting the attention of low-flying reconnaissance aircraft, arriving safely in Began-Siapiapi, where Reynolds hired a new motorman. The sight of the armed ship did not rest easy with this Controller either, for he politely suggested that they leave as soon as it was convenient. They were preparing to do so when the police inspector arrived and forcibly removed the motorman, wanted by his wife for desertion. With the husband restored to his matrimonial abode, Reynolds was back to square one until the police, anxious to be rid of the ship, supplied a mechanic to start the engine — a complicated procedure that required the use of compressed air.

On leaving Began-Siapiapi, Reynolds and his crew were forced by the continuous presence of low-flying aircraft to exercise extreme caution. Sailing only under the cover of darkness, they nevertheless made excellent time, aided by the strong current that flowed through the straits. With the sail hoisted, they anchored during the day near one of the many fishing villages, looking for all the world like innocent fishermen going about their normal business. The fishermen, whose traps they had temporarily borrowed, kept them up to date with the movements of the Japanese, who were by this time in occupation at every large centre.

On March 27, assisted by fine weather and calm seas, *Suey Sin Fah* had left Sumatran waters and was steaming towards Nagapattinam in southern India, at a rate of about eight knots. For the next four days they saw no sign of the enemy, nor indeed of anyone at all, apart from the glow of fishermen's fires as they passed to the north of the Nicobar Islands. At 3.40 on the afternoon of March 31, sixteen days after leaving the Indragiri, they dropped anchor in the Nagapattinam Roads. By the time Ivan Lyon arrived on the *Anglo-Canadian* almost three weeks later, Reynolds had reported to the Navy and had sailed the ship 290 kilometres north to Madras, where it was to be slipped and the engine overhauled.[5]

With Reynolds and his boat safe and sound, Lyon put forward his plan. Basically, it involved sneaking back to Singapore with a select group of men who were to blow up shore installations and place delayed action, magnetic limpet mines upon ships anchored in the harbour. Reynolds's ship, in the guise of a Japanese fishing boat, would provide the undercover transport to the islands near Singapore, where it would hide among the mangroves while the final assault was carried out with the aid of small, two-men kayaks. Lyon was confident that a well-trained, well-disciplined team could carry out the attack, and furthermore, get away with it.[6] Unfortunately, apart from Bill Reynolds, Lyon was the only one who thought so.

He had no trouble convincing Reynolds that such a dare-devil stunt was feasible. In 1925, when in the merchant marine, Reynolds had gone to Mecca disguised as an Arab. Totally ignoring the fact that this holy Islamic city was absolutely forbidden to Arab non-believers, let alone Anglo-Saxons of Church of England persuasion, Reynolds had risked his life in what he regarded as an interesting excursion. Knowing that it was possible to enter Mecca in the guise of a Muslim, Reynolds was convinced that the penetration of Japanese-held Singapore in a Japanese fishing boat was perfectly feasible.[7] The problem was that no one believed either him or Lyon.

In early May, after knocking on unresponsive doors for the best part of a fortnight, Lyon walked into the Delhi office of Bernard Fergusson, an old sailing friend who had recently been appointed to Wavell's Planning Staff. When Lyon outlined his plans for attacking Singapore, Fergusson pricked up his ears. It sounded like something that Wavell, who liked offbeat ideas, might go for.[8]

He did. With the full support of SOE and General Wavell, who gave him a letter of introduction, Lyon was told to go to Australia and see

America's General Douglas MacArthur, Supreme Allied Commander for the South-West Pacific Area. If the Americans sanctioned the idea, Lyon's attack on Singapore, which lay just inside Britain's patch, could easily be launched from Australia.[9]

On learning that he must travel to Australia, Ivan immediately telegraphed his wife, telling her to remain there. Lyon, who had not seen either Gabrielle or his small son Clive since their evacuation from Singapore five months before, had only just arranged to have them join him in India. Unfortunately, his message was far too late. By the time it arrived Gabrielle and Clive had sailed for Bombay.[10] The *Nankin* had departed Fremantle at 8 am on May 5, carrying general cargo and 162 passengers, of whom thirty-eight were women and children. Five days out of Fremantle, the ship had disappeared without a trace, evidently the victim of an attack by an enemy submarine or surface raider. In India, Lyon heard the devastating news that there were no survivors.[11] The stiff upper lip of the Lyon family, who for generations had shown a brave face to pain and adversity, prevailed. Although grief stricken, Ivan's only public comment was, 'War is a grim business, isn't it'.[12]

Pushing aside his personal sorrow, Ivan threw himself into the tough job of turning his plan into reality. His first task was to recruit his old comrade Ron Morris, who had reached Ceylon safely and was now working in a Colombo military hospital. Although he had no idea of what Lyon's mission entailed, the irrepressible Welshman accepted the offer of a new job immediately, more than pleased to be rescued from the humdrum life of bedpan duty. When his CO, who did not share Morris's enthusiasm, refused to relinquish him, Lyon told Morris to be of good cheer and went back to Delhi. Within days, General Wavell had issued a direct order, which saw Morris on board *Athlone Castle* at the end of June, bound for Australia with Lyon's other hand-picked man, Jock Campbell.[13]

Before he left for Australia, leaving Reynolds to supervise a complete overhaul of *Suey Sin Fah*'s engines, Lyon had two things to finalise. He needed a name for the mission and another name for the boat. *Suey Sin Fah* was now old hat. What was required was something with a bit more punch. Reynolds came up with a suggestion that was brilliant — 'Krait', the name of a skinny, innocuous-looking snake whose appearance was so ordinary that it was barely noticeable until it attacked.[14] It then delivered a bite of such venom that the victim was dead within minutes. The analogy was perfect. Like the cunning little reptile, the motor vessel *Krait* would sneak up upon its Japanese victims and deliver a blow of such potency that the enemy would not know what had hit it.

With Reynolds bagging the limelight in the ship's christening stakes, it was up to Lyon to come up with a name for the operation. What, he mulled, would be a suitable title for a mission designed to remove the smell of ignominious defeat which had humbled Britain and its Empire?

In a sudden flash of inspiration, he had the answer — 'Jay Wick'. The powerful, locally made deodoriser was a common sight in Singapore, particularly in public lavatories, where the combination of high temperatures and poor sanitation made it an indispensable item. If the magical Jay Wick could sweeten the noisome air of Singapore's public conveniences, Lyon was convinced that operation Jaywick could surely obliterate the stench of one of the most humiliating defeats in British military history.[15] With that, Operation Jaywick was born.

At about the same time that Lyon arrived in Fremantle, a new intelligence organisation, destined to be the instrument by which Jaywick would be achieved, was also developing. Known as the Allied Intelligence Bureau (AIB), and financed by the Australian, American and Dutch governments, it was to absorb all the existing intelligence agencies into one properly co-ordinated bureau, to make efficient use of personnel, equipment and information. Covering many areas, AIB was to draw together four separate entities — the Royal Australian Navy's well-developed coastwatching organisation; a propaganda unit to operate in enemy-occupied territory, known as Far East Liaison Office or FELO; an ultra-secret intelligence group known as 'M Special' and, finally, the Australian version of Britain's SOE, which would recruit both civilians and military personnel, train them in the art of sabotage and send them behind enemy lines.[16]

The preliminary stages for the formation of this organisation based along SOE lines, Special Operations Australia, had been under way for some weeks. Under the cover name Inter-Allied Services Department (ISD), two Englishmen, Majors Mott and Trappes-Lomax (former head of Singapore's 101 Special School), had set up headquarters in 'Airlie', a magnificent mansion in Melbourne's South Yarra.

Potential operatives for ISD's covert missions were initially dispatched to a guerilla warfare school at Foster, near Melbourne. When the cold Victorian climate proved unsuitable for training men who were expected to operate in tropical zones, operatives were transferred to 'Fairview', a large hillside property located on the outskirts of Cairns in Queensland's far north. From July 1942, a small wireless relay station, known as 'Z Experimental Station', set up by ISD's Signals Officer Israel, had occupied the site, providing a wireless link between Melbourne and New Guinea, where Dutch personnel were operating. However, Z station's role had soon been expanded to provide a jumping off point for New Guinea operations. Later, in April 1943, when a new wireless link was developed in the Northern Territory, the Cairns station was taken over completely by ISD as a training ground for Special Operations. Situated far from prying eyes, the colloquially known 'House on the Hill' (originally owned by the grandfather of pioneer aviator Charles Kingsford Smith), laboured under its original title of Z Experimental Station. When the importance of Special Operations grew, an administrative support unit was organised, known, in deference to its wireless station origins, as Z Special Unit. Under the intelligence umbrella of ISD, Z Special handled a wide range of personnel — servicemen who volunteered for special duty, specialist civilians, indigenous peoples from all over the Pacific and South-East Asia, and Europeans such as planters, geologists, timber growers and civil servants who had intimate knowledge of enemy-held territory. Typical of this group was Australian geologist Sam Carey, who was recruited by ISD and sent to New Guinea — his pre-war stamping ground. While carrying out his 'official' job of supplying information on tides, volcanoes, native population, terrain conditions and the like, Carey received and transmitted encoded messages, arranged contact with Coastwatchers and men from the M intelligence bureau and found suitable recruits for ISD, FELO and M sections.[17]

When passed as being suitable, all ISD recruits were transferred (in the case of the AIF) or seconded to Z Special. Since this unit did not actually carry out operations, special missions were autonomously organised and given code names such as 'Lizard', 'Lagarto' and 'Jaywick', while personnel were identified by officially designated secret numbers. Those prefixed by 'AK' (Also Known), were civilian or army operatives, 'AKN' were naval, 'AKR' air force and 'AKS' were signallers. All other AK combinations belonged to either headquarters or camp staff, which formed the bulk of the unit. In this way, the high command knew precisely who was who. When secret plans had to be committed to paper, the operatives were referred to by their special numbers and their mission by code name.[18]

The order that reorganised the existing intelligence groups into AIB came into effect on 6 July 1942, coinciding with the arrival in Western Australia of Ivan Lyon, who carried a letter from Wavell in his hand and his ambitious sabotage plan in his head. In Fremantle, Lyon having conferred with General Bennett, now banished to Western Australia, it was decided that Jaywick should be an army commitment. Consequently, Lyon was ordered to liaise with ISD's Major Mott, who arranged a meeting with two senior United States Intelligence officers.

To Lyon's dismay, the letter from Wavell to General MacArthur scored no points with the Americans, whose plans for the future did not include Singapore. The Australian Army's reaction was only marginally better. The AIF, although keen to use the Jaywick concept in Timor, was not prepared to back a venture so far behind enemy lines. Never a man to let official indifference stand in his way, Lyon discarded his service contacts and moved on to more personal avenues.

Since his arrival in Melbourne, Lyon had been staying as guest of Governor Sir Winston Duggan at Government House, where he succumbed to a bout of malaria. By the time he had recovered he had both the ear of the Governor and the support of Governor-General Lord Gowrie, who arranged a meeting on July 17 with a highly enthusiastic

Director of Naval Intelligence, Commander Long. It was agreed that Jaywick, which would remain essentially an SOE operation, would be carried out under the guidance of Naval Intelligence. The entire cost of the exercise, estimated to be in the region of £11 000, £3 000 of which had already been forwarded, was to be borne by SOE in London. As soon as Morris and Campbell arrived in Melbourne from India on August 2, they set to work spending some of this cash — Morris in his capacity as general factotum and Campbell as administrator.[19]

With Lyon's time fully occupied in planning and strategy, the time had now come to appoint an officer capable of selecting and training volunteers. It was quite a tall order. Besides being physically fit, he had to be skilled in guerilla tactics, at home on the sea and in the jungle, and able to assume command. He also needed to be resourceful, fearless, and, if necessary, quite ruthless. The name of Donald Davidson, a lieutenant in the Royal Naval Reserve, was put forward by his brother-in-law, who happened to be the equerry of Lyon's host, Governor Duggan.[20] Despite the blatant nepotism of the nomination, Davidson was to prove an admirable choice.

The son of a clergyman, Davidson had been raised in England but had forsaken his native land in 1926 to become an Australian jackeroo. Realising, after two years on an outback Queensland property, that the likelihood of owning a sheep station was remote, he had headed for the teak forests of Siam. This job, with the Bombay Burmah Trading Company, was tailor-made for a man like Davidson, who craved variety and activity in his everyday life.

The jungle fascinated him. He rediscovered his boyhood passion for nature, delighting in creatures both great and small and building up such a substantial collection of rare and beautiful butterflies that it was acquired by London's Victoria and Albert museum. He was just as at home with the elephants and other wild animals as he was with the colourful insects, for Donald Davidson simply did not know the meaning of the word fear. Actively seeking situations that would cause his heart to pound and his adrenalin to run, he stalked tigers, often without a gun, simply for the sheer excitement of following their footpads in the dew-soaked grass. For six years he revelled in this exotic wilderness, his only contact with the outside world through letters carried by foot runners to Bangkok.

After Davidson returned from leave in England in 1935 he was sent to Burma, where he took advantage of his new location on the Irrawadi River by building a boat by day and studying navigation by night. By this time he was sharing his campfire with a wife — an old girlfriend who had turned up suddenly and whom he married on the spur of the moment. The outbreak of war was perhaps the only thing at that time that could have enticed Davidson away from the Burmese forests. Unable to resist the lure of active service, he was in Singapore, on his way to join the AIF in Australia, when he became waylaid at the Naval Base, going into the mess to play a game of dice and coming out with a Naval Reserve commission. He stayed in Singapore until evacuated with other naval personnel, finally reaching Australia, where he joined his wife and small daughter, born in the same hospital on the same day as Lyon's son.[21]

Davidson was languishing in Melbourne, bound to a desk job and bored out of his mind, when Ivan offered him Jaywick. Within days he had rounded up eighteen volunteers from Flinders Naval Depot, had put them through a gruelling course and eliminated two of them. The rest were given eight days' leave and ordered to report to Sydney's Garden Island before noon on September 6 to undertake a more specialised type of training at Camp 'X'.[22]

While Davidson had been knocking his men into shape, Lyon, Morris and Campbell had travelled to Sydney. Unhindered by red tape and with the apparently unlimited resources of ISD, Morris, Campbell and a typist had set up headquarters in a flat in Potts Point, while Lyon had undertaken a search of the wilderness around Broken Bay, north of Sydney, in search of a suitable location for Camp X.[23]

He settled on a cliff top high above Refuge Bay. Protected from sight by dense bush and substantial trees, it had a permanently running stream and afforded a 180 degree view from the top of a waterworn sandstone precipice. Accessible only by boat from Coal and Candle Creek or after a three kilometre hike through the bush from the defence road leading to the West Head army post, the area was both well concealed and remote. By the time Davidson was due to arrive from Melbourne the camp, set up by Morris and a team of labourers, was all but ready.[24] He was met at Central Station by Lyon, Campbell and Morris, the last of whom, not having laid eyes on Davidson, was looking forward to the meeting with great interest.

The tall, fit-looking figure that strode down the platform in an immaculate naval uniform was, at first glance, an impressive sight. Morris's critical gaze travelled from the brilliantly polished shoes, past the golden braid of the 'Wavy Navy' (as the Volunteer Reserve was called), to the receding hairline that made Davidson look older than his years. When he reached the eyes, or more correctly, the left eye socket, he stopped dead, for there, firmly tucked between eyebrow and cheekbone was a monocle. While Morris stood transfixed by this incongruous accessory, Davidson missed his footing, thereby making a spectacularly memorable, if undignified, entrance to Sydney — his body shooting in one direction and his briefcase and precious monocle slithering off in another. It was not until some time later that Morris realised that the wearing of the eyepiece was an act of pure theatre by Davidson, whose love of the ridiculous was offset by a dedication to duty that was as single-minded as that of Ivan Lyon.[25]

With *Krait* expected in late November, Davidson had three months in which to train his men at Refuge Bay and bring them to peak physical condition. With explosives expert Sub-Lieutenant Overell and Captain 'Gort' Chester, another SOE graduate, Davidson put them through the most intensive training procedures that he could possibly devise, carried out in all weathers, at all times of day and night.

By trial and error they found solutions to the problems of betrayal by sound or smell. Soft japarra cloth or bare skin ensured that noise from clothing was kept to a minimum. Smelly, tarry ropes were exchanged for cords made of odourless materials and feet were toughened by going barefoot whenever practicable. Soggy, squelching footwear was abandoned for thick woollen socks which, after providing protection on sharp, barnacle-covered rocks, were wrung out and thrust into dry sandshoes that made no noise. Finally, and perhaps most importantly, the art of endless patience and stealth was so ingrained by hours of tactical manoeuvres that it became second nature.

Since noiseless, indetectable movement on the water was just as vital as that on land, intensive training in small two-men craft was an integral part of the programme. Not unlike the kayaks of the Eskimoes, these low-profile 'folboats', made of black rubberised canvas stretched over a lightweight wooden and bamboo frame, were collapsible, portable and highly manoeuvrable. Expertly handled, they were all but impossible to detect upon the water. Finely honed single paddles eliminated tell-tale flashes of light while 'freezing' end-on to the observer reduced the profile to such an extent that they were almost invisible, even at close range. By the end of the training period, each man was so skilled that he was able to paddle undetected past the searchlight battery on nearby Juno Point and the various defence posts placed around Broken Bay.

But to reach the target unobserved was only part of the aim. The real skill came in blowing it up successfully. This was to be achieved with a brand new weapon — delayed action, magnetic limpet mines, designed to adhere to the iron hulls of ships as the limpet shell clings to the rocky seashore. The lightweight folboats were ideal for the job. While the bowman held the craft steady against the tide by attacking a magnetic holdfast to the hull of the ship, the rear man, using a collapsible 183 centimetre rod, clamped the mines in position, well below the water line. When three limpets, connected by detonating cord, had been attached, the boat proceeded to the next target. As each folboat could carry a total of nine limpets, weighing forty-five kilograms in all, three ships could be sabotaged by one team at any one time.

When a reasonable amount of skill in canoeing and limpet placement had been acquired, any naval ship that came into Broken Bay was considered to be fair game. Raids were mounted against the vessels and even when the ships' companies were alerted, the raiders usually succeeded in approaching the target unobserved. They were just as successful in their land-based raids, directed at night against the army post at West Head. After paddling from Refuge Bay and scaling the great cliffs, they crept through the bushland to infiltrate the army camp. Using a series of chalked 'brands' they poisoned the water supply, knocked out the searchlight battery, blew up the guns, demolished the communications centre and captured or disposed of any personnel not a wake-up to their tactics. Sometimes, through stupidity or plain bad luck, a raider would be 'killed' or captured, but the end result was usually the same — overwhelming success.

In order to ensure that these results were duplicated under real conditions, a thorough knowledge of the Bren, rifle, pistol, Oerlikon, Lewis and the new-fangled Owen gun was mandatory. Apart from being required to fire all with extreme accuracy from any position, the men also had to strip down and reassemble weapons in the dark. Should less noisy methods of killing be required, they became experts in the use of the knife — stiletto, sheath, parang and an ingenious knuckleduster variety supplied to Davidson's specific order.

Ivan Lyon, who flitted in and out of the camp like a will o'the wisp, was delighted with the progress. So too were the top brass, mostly naval, who often dropped in for an inspection. When Lord Gowrie and an impressive retinue turned up, he acceded to a request to launch an experimental canoe, designed and built by Davidson, with the help of one of the recruits, apprentice cabinetmaker Freddie Marsh. Perhaps the smallest and most lowly craft ever to be launched by such an illustrious personage, it was christened HMAS *Lyon*.[26]

Towards the end of the training period, all those involved in the operational side, including Lyon, Overell and Chester, were sent on three-day endurance tests. Sustained only by iron rations, the men were required to cover distances in excess of one hundred kilometres, hiking, paddling and carrying the folboats where necessary. It was at the end of one of these endurance tests, in an attempt to save some energy, that Davidson unexpectedly met his match.

It had been decided that instead of returning to camp by folboat, his endurance team would come ashore at the Hawkesbury River Bridge for transportation back to camp by army truck. As requested, army headquarters supplied a three tonne truck, driven by a young soldier who, having been wounded in fierce fighting along New Guinea's Kokoda Track, was very experienced in the ways of soldiering. As the weary canoe teams approached the bridge just on dusk, they were relieved to see through the gloom the truck and the young soldier, rifle in hand, waiting at the correct rendezvous point. As they left the river and made their way across the mudflats, he called loudly, 'Halt. Password'.

When the canoeists took absolutely no notice of his challenge, the soldier issued a sterner warning, firing over their heads and clipping a branch of a nearby tree in the process. To say that the sailors were startled is putting it mildly. Not one, Davidson included, had been in action. Moreover, no-one had ever fired at them with live ammunition. To a man they dropped to the ground. After recovering his composure, Davidson informed the sentry in his most authoritative tone that he was 'an officer of the Royal Navy on exercise', a statement that was met with the re-cocking of the rifle and a no-nonsense, 'You'll be a bloody dead one unless I get a password'.

Clearly, since this was no time to argue the toss, Davidson gave the magic word, 'Snake'. 'Gully,' echoed the soldier, followed by, 'Pass, friend'. Their credentials proven beyond all doubt, the team returned to camp, considerably wiser in the ways of military procedure.[27]

The only people in camp who were excused from these fearsome physical exercises were telegraphist Sharples, whose excellence in signalling made up somewhat for his aversion to rigid discipline, and Morris, whose role as medical orderly and general dogsbody did not require him to meet Davidson's exacting standards. One of his chores had, however, unexpectedly resulted in some improvised physical jerks for another member of the company. On being instructed to find suitable places for both an incinerator and latrine, Morris had decided to combine the two by utilising a deep, narrow cleft between two sandstone rocks. At the top he erected a toilet seat, while at the bottom he placed all the rubbish that had to be burned. This arrangement worked perfectly until the day that Freddie Marsh decided to make use of the topside facilities at the same moment that Morris stoked up his fire underneath, aided by a judicious application of kerosene. It was not until the blaze was roaring along, sending a column of searing heat skywards that Morris became aware that someone was in residence above. The yelps of fright and alarm, emanating from the enthroned and somewhat singed occupant, and the war jig that followed, were the source of great amusement for some time to come.[28]

Any smiles of amusement were quickly wiped from the senior officers' faces when they learned that *Krait*'s ancient engine needed more than just a basic overhaul. The news that the ship had been moved to Mandapam to have the bearings and big end remetalled, cracks rewelded and the recirculating pump repaired, and the follow-up information that it needed to travel to Bombay for repairs to the clutch, put an end to the plan to carry out the raid on February 15, the anniversary of the fall of Singapore and a date dear to Lyon's heart. A series of frantic signals went back and forth across the Indian Ocean between Lyon, Campbell and Reynolds during October and November, trying to ascertain if and when *Krait* would arrive. At the end of October, Campbell was so desperate that he was advocating the transfer of the operation to a pearling lugger or fishing trawler. A few days later hopes soared when it was arranged for *Krait* to be transported to Australia on board the steamer

Shillong Shillong, only to plummet once more when sailing was put back a further fifteen days, until November 24.[29]

The delay had one advantage in that everyone, except Morris and Sharples, who remained behind to guard the camp, was able to take four days' leave over Christmas. Davidson also took the opportunity of the break to rid himself of one of the trainees whom he considered would be a disruptive influence on board a small ship. As he had already blotted his copy book by placing a mortar bomb upside down in the firing tube, Davidson had no qualms about instructing ISD 'to ship him off to some far place where he could do us no harm through talking too much'. As for the rest, Davidson was satisfied enough with their individual performances, although some naturally rated much better than others, particularly the two who, apart from himself, were the only non-smokers.[30]

While they were enjoying their festive dinners, *Krait* finally made her appearance in Sydney. However, owing to the holiday break and a shortage of labour, she sat on the deck of the steamer until January 4. For the next eight days the RAN engineers worked overtime, repairing the damage to the hull that had occurred during the transit and refitting the interior to accommodate eighteen men.[31] Finally, on January 13, having been victualled by the naval depot at Balmoral, *Krait* was ready to sail. But before she had made any headway, the engine was stopped dead by a cracked cylinder head. When this was fixed, she was further held up by poor engine timing.[32]

Back at the camp, packed up and raring to go, Davidson and the men scanned the entrance of the bay for the first sight of the ship that was to take them to their as yet unknown destination. At 9.15 on the morning of January 17, to the sounds of undisguised shouts of joy, *Krait* rounded Challenger Head and entered the sheltered waters of Refuge Bay, fully six weeks late. After loading the gear, the officers and the twelve chosen operatives boarded the ship.[33] They were followed by Morris, who also had tucked under his arm a beautiful white Persian cat by the name of Cleopatra. She had arrived at the camp one day, quite out of the blue, to give birth to a litter of kittens on Morris's pyjamas. Although her offspring had been found good homes on visiting warships, Cleopatra had remained, becoming Morris's inseparable companion.[34]

When *Krait* slipped her moorings at six the following morning, the operation, after months of planning and preparation, was at last underway.[35] As the early morning sun spilt golden light across the craggy cliffs of Broken Bay, the small ship turned her bows to the north. For all but three on board, it was a voyage to the unknown.

Chapter 6
Singapore Bound

It all too soon became evident why Lyon had dubbed *Krait* 'The Reluctant Dragon'. A bare five hours out of Refuge Bay, engine failure and an overheated clutch forced Reynolds to make for Newcastle partly under tow. When reports of enemy submarine activity caused a further delay, Lyon returned to Sydney and settled one or two matters before catching up to the ship by train. There was no need for him to have hurried, for *Krait*'s troubles were far from over. Hiccupping its way along the New South Wales coast, the Reluctant Dragon made unscheduled stops at Trial Bay and Coffs Harbour with problems as diverse as blocked bilge pumps, a faulty generator and a seized front-end bearing.[1]

As *Krait* was only twenty-one metres long and a mere three and a half metres at maximum breadth, conditions on board were little better than tolerable. Apart from a few minor alterations, the vessel was still the same grubby little craft that had plied up and down the Indragiri. From the back of the compact wheelhouse, into which a combination bunk/chart table had been squeezed, now stretched a tar and paper awning which all but covered the deck. In the enclosed engine room below decks, tucked away in the roof space in a type of mezzanine arrangement and almost on top of the hot, noisy engine, was another bunk where Manson the stoker slept. Immediately behind the wheelhouse, bolted firmly to the roof of the engine room, was a large box, filled with weapons for easy access.

Right in the stern and partially protected by awnings fastened around the sides was a pokey little galley and a primitive 'head' that made the average Australian outback lavatory appear positively luxurious by comparison. Next to the engine room, in a small space euphemistically called the Officers' Mess, was the combined radio room, store room, sick bay and officers' quarters, into which were crammed three bunks, a wireless desk, transmitter and receiver, chart table, batteries, medical equipment and anything else which did not have a particular home, including a copy of *The Sheik*, a racy novel chosen to alleviate possible boredom. The forward hold was filled with a veritable arsenal of arms and ammunition, stores for six months, oil drums and the remainder of the equipment, including the folboats. More drums of oil, kerosene and petrol were lashed to the teakwood deck, above which the men's hammocks were strung. To complete the ship's overloaded, rather gypsy-like look, Krait's wheelhouse roof was stacked with miscellaneous items, shrouded under lumpily shaped tarpaulins.[2]

As the seas rose to a nauseating swell off the northern coast of New South Wales, seasickness added to the general discomfort. Morale, which was becoming difficult to maintain under the circumstances, was lowered even further when Cleopatra, much to Morris's distress, disappeared over the side as Reynolds changed course in the heavy seas. It was not until the end of January, after this less than pleasant passage up the coast, that a rather waterlogged Krait and some very seedy passengers finally reached Brisbane. With the ship docked for repairs that engineers predicted would take at least a month, the men were sent to Southport Beach for further fitness training while Lyon endured the accommodation provided by Brisbane's Anne Hathaway Hotel, described by him as being 'fully representative of truth, temperance and bad sanitation'. Although chafed by the constant delays, his disappointment was alleviated by the wealth of intelligence information that he had been able to put together and, above all, by the joyous news that Gabrielle and Clive were, in fact, alive.[3]

Their ship, Nankin, had indeed been attacked — by the German raider Thor — but, contrary to expectations, all the passengers had survived. When the ship's captain had surrendered to prevent loss of life, the Germans had taken everyone prisoner and sailed Nankin to Japan. Although the details that had so far filtered back to Australia were sketchy, there was no doubt at all that, although behind barbed wire in Japan's Fukushima Internment Camp, Gabrielle and Clive were safe. Furthermore, steps were already underway in the hope of securing their release in a prisoner exchange. It was a jubilant Lyon who farewelled Jock Campbell at Brisbane on March 2, when, fully three months after the original date of departure, Krait was at last ready to sail.[4]

While the ship had been in dock, there had been a change of personnel and a structural addition. Stoker Manson, who had demonstrated an inability to carry out even minor repairs, had been replaced by engineer Paddy McDowell, a tough old salt from the First World War, and Lyon had ordered the decking to be bullet-proofed with a coating of tough, bituminous marine glue.[5]

They had covered only about one-quarter of the distance to Townsville, when they were hit by a series of calamities. Davidson went down with malaria and was taken off to hospital, the engine completely self-destructed in a mass of molten metal, necessitating a tow to Townsville, and Reynolds had an altercation with one of the crew.[6]

Possibly pushed to the limits of his endurance and surely by now frustrated beyond belief, Reynolds attempted some rather 'unseamanlike methods of coercion' on one of the crew, who had apparently not responded to more acceptable means of persuasion. In the ensuing quarrel, Reynolds had effectively put a stop to the argument by flattening the source of his irritation with a well-aimed blow. Normally, for a naval officer to strike a seaman, no matter how great the provocation, constituted a crime of utmost gravity. Ironically, although Reynolds was preparing himself for some form of retribution, it appears that the state of *Krait*'s engine, rather than his civilian status, let him off the hook.[7]

With the complete collapse of the engine, it was decided, at a special high level meeting called in Melbourne on March 27, that until a new engine could be found, Jaywick would have to be indefinitely postponed. The highly trained naval personnel were dispersed until such time as they might be needed and the useless engine was removed from the ship at Townsville, along with some of the stores. *Krait* and the rest of the equipment then made an ignominious voyage to storage in Cairns, under tow.[8]

With no ship to skipper, at least in the immediately foreseeable future, Reynolds was approached by a section of the American Intelligence network, which recognised that his maritime experience and intimate knowledge of the Far East were too valuable to waste. Fortunately for the Americans, the prospect of sneaking behind Japanese lines and collecting information vital to the war effort appealed very much to Reynolds. With his dream of taking Lyon to Singapore now seeming less of a possibility, Bill Reynolds, Master Mariner, became a secret agent.[9]

While the fifty-year-old Reynolds was undertaking a new career in wartime espionage at an age when most men are thinking of slowing down, Lyon and Campbell were working overtime to find a new engine for *Krait*. They were helped in their search by the unlimited resources of ISD, which had been revamped and renamed Services Reconnaissance Department — SRD. After combing the length and breadth of Australia, a brand new, six-cylinder, 103-horsepower Gardner diesel, complete with spare parts, was finally located and flown from Tasmania. For the next few weeks the engineers at Stratford Bridge slips on Cairns's Barron River fitted the engine that would give a new lease of life to *Krait*'s dilapidated shell and put Jaywick back on the drawing board.[10]

A few kilometres away there had been the usual buzz of activity at Z Experimental Station as various operations were planned and outfitted. By this time the locals were quite accustomed to seeing European and native personnel tearing around the countryside, paddling kayaks and learning seamanship in what was believed to be a strenuous keep-fit programme. One of the Australians engaged in these activities was Sam Carey, the Z liaison officer from New Guinea, who had been in training for some months. In December 1942, when air reconnaissance photographs indicated a heavy buildup of enemy shipping in Rabaul Harbour, General Blamey had sent for Carey to see if he had any bright ideas. Just as Ivan Lyon knew Singapore, so Sam Carey knew Rabaul.

And just as Lyon's fertile mind had conceived Jaywick, so a quarter of a hemisphere away, and eight months later, Carey formulated Scorpion — a plan that was almost identical. Betraying no surprise, Blamey had listened while Carey outlined his plan to enter Rabaul Harbour in submarine-launched folboats, blow up the shipping with limpets and hide in the caves on Vulcan Island until the heat was off.

As he did not wish American-controlled GHQ to know anything about the proposal, Blamey wrote to Australia's Lieutenant-General Northcott informing him that Carey was returning to Australia with 'special instructions personally given him' and ordering Lieutenant-General Berryman to 'assist him any way you can'. Thus armed, Carey had personally selected his team, many of whom were old New Guinea hands. However, there were problems, not the least of which were finding a means of transportation to the operational zone and an upheaval in the upper echelons of ISD, where Major Mott had become most disenchanted by outside interference from GHQ. Its meddling in ISD's affairs had caused ructions, many of which were brought about by an inability to understand the role of ISD and an insistence on knowing details that would best be kept secret. Dealing with Chinese communist guerillas, taking part in clandestine activities in officially neutral Portuguese Timor and 'bumping off [German] missionaries and other undesirable persons' were facets of his organisation which Mott believed the least known about the better. He had pointed out rather forcefully to AIB's Colonel Roberts, who could not grasp that ISD should be left alone to get on with the job, that he merely required 'general direction and backing', thereby ensuring that GHQ was at all times 'in a position to disown, if necessary, any activities which are officially undesirable but unofficially very much required'. Unfortunately, Roberts did not share Mott's point of view and, without telling either Mott or Blamey until it was a fait accompli, replaced him with Mott's 2IC, Australian Major Oldham.

With the top brass playing politics, Carey's strike date schedule for March was so delayed that it was decided to launch Jaywick and Scorpion simultaneously. However, just when Carey's men had attained physical and technical perfection, MacArthur's headquarters advised that, owing to anti-submarine activity in the area, no submarines were available to take Scorpion to Rabaul Harbour. While Carey waited to hear the outcome of a counter proposal to drop his team off in the open sea, he was ordered to report to Oldham in Melbourne. Lyon, who had arrived some time before Carey, had just learned from Oldham that GHQ, from whom Blamey had hoped to keep the details of the Scorpion project secret, had thrown a spanner in the works. Having discovered what Lyon and Carey planned to do, headquarters decided that penetration of the enemy's defences with a limpet attack was impossible. Oldham advised Lyon that unless something could be done to prove otherwise, the whole idea would have to be abandoned. Picking up the very broad hints that his superior was dropping, Lyon volunteered to mount a dummy operation in Australia. His offer was refused. Oldham, aware that with submarine transportation unavailable HQ would sanction only one operation at best, and also aware that whoever mounted a dummy raid would be in extremely hot water, had already decided that Scorpion and Carey were expendable.

It was a decision that only a man still clinging to the idea of Singapore, the British fortress, and still smarting from its inglorious defeat could have made. Ignoring the fact that Rabaul, being the key base to the Japanese offensive through the Solomon Islands, was a far more important target, Jaywick was selected over Scorpion.

Carey was left in no doubt whatever as to what he was supposed to do. Without any orders being given and indeed, without any specific words to that effect being uttered, Carey walked out of Oldham's office knowing that he was to mount a raid that would convince the army hierarchy and put Jaywick back on the rails. Carey also realised that by giving no direct orders Oldham had carefully hedged his bets. If the raid was botched, Oldham would be in the clear, leaving Carey to carry the can. If he pulled it off, Oldham, being in the box seat, would take all the credit. Since less than full commitment to any project had never been Carey's style, he decided to pull out all the stops. Scorpion would raid the ships in Townsville Harbour.

At 11 o'clock on the night of June 19, Carey's team of ten slipped from the southbound train just north of Townsville and, after a strenuous thirty-six hours of non-stop paddling and portage down the almost impassable Black River, reached Magnetic Island. Once rested, they were ready to tackle their target, which lay ten kilometres across the water, guarded by a minefield. After plotting a dozen ships through a powerful telescope, the Scorpion team set off, apprehensive that the bright moonlight would make their task extremely tricky. However, it was all too easy. While one folboat made its way towards the roadstead, the other four, after drifting through the narrow entrance and passing the mine control point unobserved, entered the harbour proper. Once inside, they paddled up to various ships and placed their dummy, sand-filled limpet mines into position. Although the port was busy and well lit, only once was any of them challenged. A sailor hanging over the rail of a ship that had already been limpeted yelled, 'What are youse blokes doing out here?' The answer that they were 'just paddling around' satisfied the sailor's curiosity for he turned away with a cheerful 'good night mate'. By 7 am, with forty-five mines clinging to fifteen ships, Scorpion's men had paddled into Ross Creek, dismantled the folboats in full view of workers passing over a nearby bridge and eaten breakfast. While the rest of the team went off up the river, Carey booked into the Officer's Club, went to bed and waited for the balloon to go up.

Three hours later, all hell broke loose. With its cargo unloaded, the Dutch freighter *Akaba* was now riding high in the water. So high, in fact, that the substituted parachute cord linking the limpets was visible just above the waterline. When it was realised that the chunks of metal just discernible under the water were probably some kind of explosive device, the alarm was raised. Orders were issued for the immediate evacuation of all suspect ships and for a convoy, about to sail to Port Moresby, to remain in port.

Soon the ship-to-shore gangplanks were filled with scurrying sailors as more and more of the strange objects were detected. Rumours circulated like wild fire — Townsville had been invaded by Japanese submarines and all the ships in the harbour would soon blow up! The entire wharf area was evacuated while astounded and worried naval personnel tried to find out what had happened. No one had seen anything and the navy swore that nothing could have possibly entered the harbour. The telegraph wires ran hot with signals passing between Townsville and the Admiralty and to MacArthur's headquarters in Brisbane. When word finally reached the American GHQ-AIB liaison officer, Lieutenant-Colonel Ind, the penny finally dropped. Sam Carey had to be the culprit. The modus operandi for Scorpion and Carey's close proximity to Townsville were just too much of a coincidence. 'Find Captain S.W. Carey,' he suggested, and with that, the hunt was on.

It did not take them long to find and arrest Carey, who had booked his room in his own name. After being paraded in front of a succession of increasingly senior army officers, to whom he would admit nothing, he was passed on to Naval Lieutenant Asher Joel. When Carey declared, 'Sir, my name is Carey and I beg to report that last night, with my raiding party, I sank the following ships', and then proceeded to reel off the names of fifteen destroyers, corvettes and freighter verbatim, Joel was both astonished and impressed. So too was the commander of HMAS *Arunta*, the first of the latest Tribal-class destroyers and the pride of the navy.

With Carey's credentials established by Blamey's authorisation, Scorpion was invited to drinks on board *Arunta* late that afternoon. Overhearing the destroyer's captain teasing Townsville's Naval Officer-In-Command, Commander Wheatley, about the incident, Carey realised that the captain was unaware that *Arunta* had also been limpeted. The tables were now turned. In full view of a vastly interested and highly amused audience, Dick Cardew, Scorpion's 2IC, took a small boat alongside the ship to remove the limpets that had been clinging to the hull, undetected for almost twenty-four hours.

Although many thought that the escapade had been a huge joke, most of the port and naval authorities in Townsville were less than amused and, indeed, highly embarrassed. Under their very noses, ten men had crossed the harbour defences, mined fifteen ships, prevented a convoy from sailing and terrified half of north Queensland. But it was an excellent lesson. In demonstrating the need for far greater security, Carey had also shown that successful raids in enemy ports, probably no better patrolled than those in Australia, had every chance of success. Ironically, when Carey's team carried off the raid that ultimately made them legends in their own lifetime, they also sealed Scorpion's fate. Jaywick was now definitely on.[11]

By the time Lyon was re-assessing the operational plans for Jaywick, he had received the news that he, Morris and Reynolds had been decorated for their rescue work in Sumatra. Ivan Lyon, MBE, now poured over plans that had been substantially altered. As the decision to blow up land installations had been scrapped, explosives expert Overell had been withdrawn and replaced by Gort Chester, whose old position (in charge of Krait while the raiders were gone) was filled by a Lieutenant Watt. There were now to be six canoeists — three officers and three men — with two reservists. Five of the original operational team were assigned for duty along with two appointments in the non-operative field. A young, rather pale-faced and very seriously minded telegraphist named Horrie Young replaced Sharples, while an extremely steady, very experienced, round-faced fellow, Kevin P. Cain, who answered to the name of 'Cobber', replaced Leading Seaman Johnson.[12]

Leading Telegraphist Young, a wireless-mad naval reservist, had been called up for signal training on the outbreak of war. He had been serving in this capacity at HMAS Assault, Nelson's Bay, when he met up with Sharples who, being disenchanted with his job on Krait, for which his temperament was ill suited, had arranged to swap jobs.[13]

The other newcomer, Cain, was a man cast in the mould of Bill Reynolds — a strong, silent type who liked peace and quiet and was quite prepared to use his fists to get it. Not that he had to, for one look at the handsome, dark-haired Cain, with his powerful build and pectoral muscles that would do justice to a weightlifter, was sufficient to reduce even the most belligerent to a state of cautious decorum. Having spent years in and around ships, there wasn't a knot he couldn't tie, a rope he couldn't splice, or a seam he couldn't caulk.[14]

The roles of cook and ship's navigator were less easily filled, with the loss of Reynolds, in particular, a real blow. However, when Operation Scorpion was called off, an RANVR Lieutenant named Ted Carse, who had been assisting with Scorpion's small boat training and trying to turn Indonesian recruits into sailors, had suddenly become available. A contemporary of Commander Long, whom he had known from his early days in the navy, Carse had joined SRD in a pique of ill temper following an argument with his wife.

He had since come to regret his rather hasty decision as the interesting assignment that had lured him to Cairns had not materialised. Instead, he had been relegated to the teaching post that he found most unsatisfactory. When asked to assist with victualling Krait, with the hint that a mission might be in the offing, Carse, who had vowed never to volunteer for anything again, for some reason agreed. Although he had not had command of a vessel other than *Gnair*, his dilapidated old training boat, he was sufficiently skilled in navigation and in handling small ships to guide *Krait* to Singapore.

No spring chicken, Carse had a varied background. At the age of thirteen he had become a naval cadet, graduating as a midshipman just in time to see the end of World War I. By the time he was twenty-one years old and a sub-lieutenant, he had developed a dislike for authority and an almost insatiable appetite for beer. He left the navy in the twenties to follow a brief career as a schoolteacher but within two years was back at sea again, serving as an able seaman and third mate on a merchant ship and then a tramp steamer. In an attempt to break his heavy drinking habits, a job was arranged for him on a pearling lugger in the Torres Straits, hundreds of kilometres from the nearest pub. The pearling was followed by bêche de mer collecting, cleaning in a Sydney factory, unsuccessful gold prospecting in the outback and, finally, selling imitation jewellery. Unsuitable as most of these jobs appeared for one engaged in war work, it was his experience in the northern Australian waters that had made Carse eligible for SRD recruitment.[15]

Although an able navigator, his appearance and demeanour did not make a favourable impression on Morris, who was used to associating with well-turned-out, snappily correct officers. In Morris's opinion, the rather jaded, weather-worn looking Carse, whose face clearly showed the ravages of his intemperance, looked as if he might be better suited to being in charge of some tinpot trading vessel. Lyon, who was running out of options, was in no position to consider whether or not an officer measured up to Morris's exacting standards. He ran the tape over Carse and decided he would do well enough. Besides, finding a navigator who was also an officer allowed him to reduce the number of senior personnel. It did not take two officers to oversee one medical orderly, one cook, one leading seaman and two reserve operatives, who were to remain on *Krait* while the raid took place. As Chester was now an operative, the newly appointed Watt was given his marching orders.[16]

Then, quite suddenly, Chester, who had lived in Borneo for twenty years before the war, was recalled to Melbourne by Oldham, who had decided to make better use of his talents by assigning him to lead Operation Python to Borneo. Since he was to leave on the southbound train on July 19, a new, exceptionally fit officer, conversant with folboats and limpet mines, had to be appointed. By the same twist of fate that had taken Carse to Jaywick, so Australian Army Lieutenant Robert Page, one of Scorpion's men, joined Lyon's team.[17]

Raised in New Guinea, the son of a highly decorated Great War soldier, tall, dark-haired, slim-built Bob Page, blessed with the good looks usually associated with matinee idols, was an instant and overwhelming success. Well educated and cultured, he had an exceptionally charming nature and a well-developed sense of humour. Believing his father, the Assistant Administrator of New Guinea, to be in Japanese hands, Page had given up his medical studies in 1942 to join the AIF, hoping that he might somehow be able to effect a rescue, or at least go partway towards avenging his father's capture. Thwarted by Scorpion's cancellation from realising his dream, he had been more than eager to join Jaywick. Without a doubt, Bob Page was a real find.[18]

With the matter of choosing a new navigator and officer operative out of the way, Lyon and Campbell redoubled their efforts to find a cook. When they had learned that Hobbs, the original cook, was no longer available, they had searched in vain for an Asian to carry out the dual role of decoy-cook, in much the same way as Soon had done on *Sederhana Djohanes*. After calling equally unsuccessfully for unmarried Australian volunteers from the Seventh Division, which was training on the nearby Atherton Tablelands, Lyon was approached by a small, curly-headed corporal — an engineer whose health had deteriorated so badly in New Guinea that he was awaiting medical discharge.

Having established that a cook was required for a special mission, Scots-born Andy Crilley went into miraculous and instantaneous remission, inventing a convincing tale as to the level of his culinary prowess, and conveniently forgetting to tell Lyon about his medical history. As Crilley was keen, unmarried and said he could cook, Lyon signed him on. Unfortunately, another memory lapse caused Crilley to forget to tell his old CO about his new job, so that when he failed to return to his unit he was posted as a deserter. By this time, however, Crilley was beyond the long arms of the military police. Bags packed, he was on board *Krait*, where he had the distinction of being one of the only two members of the team (the other was Bob Page) who belonged to the AIF.[19]

After sailing to Townsville to retrieve the stores, Jaywick quietly slipped out of Cairns as dawn broke on the morning of August 8.[20] They were certainly a mixed bag. Lyon, a highly unorthodox but very professional English soldier and skilled amateur sailor, in command; the monocled Davidson, a former jackeroo cum teak forester as 2 IC; navigator Carse, a reformed alcoholic and former bêche de mer collector; the handsome Page, a partly qualified doctor and now an idealistic army lieutenant; Morris, the Welsh-born medical orderly and one-time coalminer who never stopped singing; Seaman Cain, an exceptionally practical sailor, whose well-developed muscles gave him the appearance of an ocean-going Tarzan; Crilley, an engineer turned cook who should have been invalided out of the army; Young, a quietly intense telegraphist who looked far too pale and introspective to be part of a commando-style operation; Engineer McDowell, an Irish-born Scot who had served in the Royal Navy in the First World War and whose fiercely protective attention lavished on the new engine rivalled that bestowed by a mother on her newborn baby, and the five seamen who had volunteered for special duty twelve months previously.

The only thing these five had in common was that they were fit, young, strong and enthusiastic. The eldest of the group was Wally Falls, who had been raised on a dairy farm in Casino in northern New South Wales. When war broke out Wally's father, a First World War digger, had exhorted his sons to steer clear of the army with its penchant for engaging in suicidal trench warfare. As life in the trenches did not sound at all like fun, the Falls brothers had taken their father's advice and joined the navy. Compared with the much younger sailors in the group, Wally's extreme age of twenty-three years and his independent, mature outlook, had earned him the name 'Poppa'. He was almost 190 centimetres tall, calm, even tempered, infinitely reliable, eminently trustworthy and, from his life of hard work on the farm, built like a mallee bull. With his superb physique, dancing blue eyes, softly waving blond hair and perfect teeth that flashed in a ready smile, Wally reminded Morris of a great Nordic god.[21]

The apprentice cabinetmaker who had helped Davidson build HMAS *Lyon*, eighteen-year-old Freddie Marsh, was one of the youngest in the group. An irrepressible larrikin, not above secreting snakes in the bedding of an unsuspecting victim, Marsh was the acknowledged clown of the party. Although stocky, he was quick on his feet and a natural fighter, so skilled in all sports, particularly unarmed combat, that it was rather demoralising to be his training partner. His rather square-shaped head, covered with thick blond curls and set on powerful shoulders, had earned him the nickname of 'Boof' — an endearment coined by his best mate, Andrew Huston.[22]

A complete opposite to Marsh, this slender, olive-skinned Queenslander had neither smiled much, nor sworn at all, until he had met up with Boof Marsh. On the whole, Andrew's life had not been easy. Raised during the Depression, he had left school at the age of fourteen to work for a banana-wholesaling firm, from where he joined the navy in March 1942. Now aged nineteen but, because of his fresh-faced complexion, looking younger than Marsh, Huston was regarded as the baby of the group. Although not as large as his happy-go-lucky friend, he was about the same height, immensely fit and very strong. His tendency to have a moan in the early part of his training, which had not come easily to him, as well as his rather serious demeanour, had earned him the ironic nickname of 'Happy' — a label which long outlived his temporary grumbles. Yet in Huston there was a maturity that belied his youth and a steel-willed determination to succeed, no matter what obstacles might lie in his path. His insistence that he should not be passed over for selection for Jaywick, for instance, had led to his having to learn to swim and fight.[23]

Another youngster was Mostyn Berryman, commonly known as Moss. Also aged eighteen, Moss came from South Australia where, being blessed with a good brain and a talent for figures, he had been employed by a share broker. Dark, quiet and reserved, he could have been easily overlooked had Davidson not recognised, along with his skill and exceptional fitness, his ability to get things done efficiently and with the minimum of fuss. He believed that, with a little more maturity, Berryman would become an excellent officer — high praise indeed from one as pernickety as Davidson.[24]

The last, but by no means least, of the group was Arthur Jones, commonly known as Joe, who had been given the rank of acting able seaman, making him slightly senior to the other four. With his quite dark complexion and thick black hair, his slightly shorter stature gave him the ability to pass, at a distance, as Japanese. Although intelligent, Jones, like many who had grown up during the Depression years, had left high school at the age of fourteen. After being retrenched from a number of labouring jobs, he landed a position in a grocer's shop where he remained until he joined the navy in January 1941. Having been posted for overseas duty on the armed merchant cruiser *Manoora*, Joe was the only one of the five with any real naval experience. Although the twenty-one-year-old Western Australian was ready to indulge in the lighter side of life, he also had an underlying steadiness which greatly impressed the hard-to-please Morris.[25]

Unlike the passage to Cairns, the journey across Australia's northern waters, via Thursday Island and the Gulf of Carpentaria, was virtually trouble free. Indeed, apart from an incident, later dubbed 'The Battle of Carpentaria', when Cobber Cain accidently discharged a gun, smashing a glass bottle which lacerated Morris's ankle rather badly, the trip was uneventful. Taking advantage of the fair weather and leisurely cruise, Lyon decided to remove the bullet-proof coating in an attempt to cure *Krait*'s top heaviness. In all but the calmest of seas the ship had been behaving like a drunken whale, hard to handle and threatening to capsize at the slightest wave. Since, on the balance of probabilities, they were in greater danger of sinking under their own weight than from strikes by enemy aircraft, the armourlike compound was chipped off and dumped overboard. Once free of her two tonnes of overburden the ship's freeboard rose from twenty-three centimetres to thirty-four centimetres, making her ride infinitely better in the water. With this liability out of the way, *Krait* headed full ahead for her final port of call — Potshot, the United States Naval Base at Exmouth Gulf.[26]

While the men, as guests of the American Navy, gorged themselves on three sumptuous meals a day, and *Krait* was refuelled, restocked and had her deck painted a flat, camouflaging grey, Lyon took off for the interior.[27] Accompanied by US Admiral Christie, he flew to 'Yanrey', the outback cattle station property of the De Pledges who, having looked after Gabrielle and Clive in Perth, were able to give Ivan firsthand news of his family. Admiral Christie, on learning the details of Lyon's mission, was so impressed by the young officer that, even years later, the high-ranking American would be able to recall every detail of the conversation with utmost clarity.[28]

Davidson, on the other hand, had not had such an enjoyable time. On arrival he had unpacked the stores that had been brought from Melbourne by Chester as he passed through on his way to Borneo. In the parcel were spare parts for *Krait*, compasses, anti-glare glasses, mail, a telescope, a pair of binoculars and, most importantly, the four brand new folboats that had been especially made in England. To Davidson's disgust, they were nothing like the ones he had ordered. It was as if his exacting plans, pattern layouts and cutting directions had never existed. The framework fitted poorly, the canvas was shoddily stitched and the refinements and improvements he had asked for had been completely omitted. Since he had no other options, other than the worn-out training folboats, he spent his four days making on-the-spot improvisations and composing a tersely worded report to his superior officers.[29]

Jaywick eventually waved farewell to their magnamous hosts on September 1. However the joy in receiving Admiral Royle's top priority message, 'Bug in. Good Hunting', and the news that Young was the father of a bouncing baby boy, evaporated when, barely ninety metres from the dock, the tail shaft broke. While the American Navy again showered the men with hospitality, mechanics and engineers from USS *Chanticleer* worked all night and half the following day to remedy the problem. With the hope that these temporary repairs would see them through, *Krait* left the coastline of Australia on the afternoon of September 2, setting course, not for the closest shipyard, but for Java's Lombok Strait.[30]

Almost immediately, they ran into mountainous seas that battered their port side, throwing Horrie Young out of his hammock and almost washing him overboard. As the seas swirled around the wheelhouse, where Lyon was fighting desperately to swing the ship around, tonnes of dark green water poured waist deep across the deck, through the open hatches and down the ladders, rendering it nigh on impossible for those below to force their way to the top. Even without her armour, the ship rolled heavily, lunging into the sea as one wave after another hit the hull. Just when it seemed impossible that the vessel could stay afloat, *Krait* righted herself. Within twenty-four hours the swell had abated, allowing all on board to settle down to a routine voyage.[31]

The next day, Lyon divulged Plan Jaywick. When the men recovered from the surprise that the target was Singapore and not Java's Soerabaya (now Surabaya), the odds-on favourite, they listened intently to Lyon's detailed instructions. As soon as they reached enemy-controlled waters, a Japanese flag would be flown, all uniforms would be replaced by sarongs and all exposed skin would be covered with a spirit-based, dark brown makeup. If they came under surveillance, three only were to stay on deck — Lyon, whose light build, brown eyes, darkly waving hair and deeply tanned skin made him so like a Malay that he often joked that one of his ancestors must have had an exotic dalliance somewhere along the line; Carse, whose darkly tanned skin and lined face made it difficult to decide if he was an Arab or a Lascar pirate, and olive-skinned Jones, who had a definitely Japanese look about him. The others were to secrete themselves and take up action stations. With the decoys making themselves conspicuous, it was hoped that the observer would take the ship to be nothing more than a locally crewed Japanese fishing vessel, going about her normal business.[32]

The attempts to convert most of the crew into convincing-looking Malays was spectacularly unsuccessful. For a start, the foul-smelling stain adhered to almost everything except the skin that it was supposed to cover. Used neat, it was far too dark while thinned down it had a tendency to streak. As it stung abominably, the eyelids and those areas of anatomy not usually exposed to the public gaze were left until last.

After donning checked sarongs similar to those worn by Soon and Jamal on *Sederhana Djohanes*, they admired each other's handiwork. Cain, whose generous chest measurements were always the focus of much ribald teasing, had been transformed into a benignly smiling, mahogany coloured heathen god. The redheads and very fair among them looked quite ludicrous as their hair stubbornly refused to take the stain: golden fuzz glinted on streakily blackened limbs while crowning glories were reduced to sweaty yellow or ginger spikes poking defiantly from inky scalps. Those with darker complexions, such as Huston and Berryman, fared a little better as their tanned skins made the streaks less noticeable. But blue eyes looking out from patchily marked faces did not look natural either and the massive frames of men like Falls were a dead give away.[33] However, with all these shortcomings it was hoped that the disguise, and the displaying of the Japanese ensign, sewn in absolute secrecy by Mrs Manderson, wife of an SRD official, would keep Japanese patrol boats from coming too close.[34]

If it did not, Davidson had concocted an amazing contingency plan. Through the bottom of the ship's dinghy, under which had been secured a harness and four limpets clinging to tin plates, he had placed two breathing tubes connected to a modified gas mask. With Davidson secreted beneath the dinghy, Jones was to come alongside the enemy ship, indicating that they needed fresh water. As soon as Davidson had attached the limpets, Jones was to paddle with all speed to the other side of the vessel, thereby putting the hull between himself and the explosive devices. As the charges went off and the ship heeled over, the men on *Krait* would rake the decks with machine-gun fire. The only casualty besides the enemy was expected to be Davidson, who quite cheerfully pointed out that, being underwater, he could be killed by the explosions. Fortunately, this rather hare-brained scheme was never put to the test.[35]

As they neared Lombok Strait, security became absolute. No smoking was allowed lest empty packets, matches or butts float away and betray their presence. All rubbish had to be collected in tins, weighted and sunk. The labels on tinned foods had already been replaced by numbers for easy identification and other stores had been carefully selected to make sure they were of Japanese origin or design. Mirrors that might flash in the sunlight meant that all shaving had to be done below decks while the use of toilet paper was absolutely forbidden. When the authorised replacement, a jar of small smooth pebbles for each man, ran out it would be sea water, native-style.[36]

The passage through the strait, flanked by the towering volcanic peaks of Gunong Agung on the left and Gunong Rinjani on the right, was frustratingly difficult and agonisingly slow. After a twenty-four hour, 272 kilometre detour, caused by a navigational error, which took them to the west of Bali, instead of to the east, Carse, who had been dreading this part of the journey for days, finally located the strait, only to discover that the tidal information supplied was incorrect. Unable to make any headway against the unexpectedly outward-rushing tide, the ship, at times, actually went backwards. For almost three hours, until the tide turned in their favour, the men watched the headlights of enemy vehicles travelling along the same stretch of road. Once clear of Lombok, however, they made good progress, skirting the Kangean Islands and heading towards the Carimata Straits, south of Borneo.

The journey was now so incident free that Lyon reported it as 'almost dull'. However, morale remained high and with good reason. They had encountered no trouble from the Japanese; the weather, though tremendously hot, was not troublesome; they heard on Young's wireless the news that Italy had capitulated; the nicotine addicts had been given permission to smoke below decks in daylight hours, and Andy Crilley's cooking was remarkably good. Besides being able to transform dehydrated food — which closely resembled poultry food pellets — into tasty, hot meals, he was a dab hand at making pancakes — a talent exhibited so often that he was dubbed 'Pancake Andy'.[37]

With the exception of Carse, whose eyes were giving him trouble from the glare, and Morris, whose wound had not quite healed, they all kept fit and healthy. The engine, too, continued to behave itself under the tender ministrations of McDowell, who could hardly bear to tear himself away from its side for a minute. Although Paddy's offsider, Boof Marsh, had shown a surprising aptitude in mastering the intricacies of the internal combustion engine, he was not given many chances to show off his skill. It took something as pressing as a call of nature, or the need to partake of some sustenance, to prise Paddy from the side of his oily, mechanical baby.[38]

On September 14, near the Pelapis, their disguise was put to the test when they passed through a group of native sailing craft. At the sight of the Japanese flag the boats scattered in all directions. The next day they crossed the equator and, for the first time since leaving Exmouth Gulf, struck rain. The first deluge replenished their water supplies and gave them all a much-needed shower as they soaped their bodies and cavorted about the deck. The second, a wild Sumatra which hit about midnight and lasted some hours, struck terror in the hearts of the uninitiated, particularly the middle watch helmsman, who was startled to see a huge tanker bear down out of the gloom and cut across their bows not four hundred metres away. With the storm over, the hours before noon brought the beautiful tropical islands of the Lingga Archipelago with their enticing coconut-fringed beaches, picturesque villages and native tonkans, some of which were so streamlined that, in comparison to the more chunky Chinese junks, they looked almost European.

When they finally reached Lingga's Pompong Island, where they had hoped to make a base while searching for a suitable hide for *Krait*, they were disappointed to find that the presence of visiting fishermen had rendered the island unsuitable. As the ship continued around the point, their disappointment turned to fright when a mast suddenly appeared. However, a closer inspection from *Krait*'s masthead revealed that it was not the enemy patrol boat they expected, but the wreck of *Kuala* — her mast, poking pathetically from the water like a drowned telegraph pole, now marking the place from which Reynolds had rescued so many people such a short time before.[39]

Hoping that Bengku Island might offer better shelter, they sailed eastwards only to find it surrounded by an impassable reef. While checking it out they were spotted by a Japanese float plane, apparently from a base on nearby Tjempa Island, which came down for a better look. However, the sight of the flag and the brown bodies, upon which stain had fortunately been reapplied after the storm, evidently reassured the pilot, who flew away.

With no hide for *Krait* yet found, they spent the night anchored off a deserted bay at Pompong. Next morning they were startled by the appearance of three Malays in a small kolek — an old man and two boys — making their way towards Pompong for some fishing. Worried that the mission might now be compromised, Lyon's first reaction was to shoot them but, as they had not given *Krait* a second glance, he was persuaded simply to upend the anchor and sail away from the area as quickly as possible.[40]

As it was too early in the day to approach Pulau Durian, the old escape route camp that Lyon had selected as Jaywick's canoe base, *Krait* headed north. As they passed the west coast of Rempang Island, they spied small, hilly, jungle-covered Pandjang Island. As it appeared to be uninhabited, and as they had already investigated the immediate area and found it safe, Lyon cancelled the plan to sail to Pulau Durian.[41]

With the newly selected canoe base miles from the original choice, the old plan possibly to hide *Krait* about fifty kilometres from Durian, in Sumatra's Kampar River Estuary, was also scrapped. Furthermore, since Lyon now realised that it was unrealistic to expect that *Krait*, no matter how well concealed, could remain undetected in one place for the best part of two weeks, any idea of finding a permanent hiding place was shelved. As the ship would be less likely to attract attention if she kept moving, it was decided that *Krait* should wander about the waters off Borneo until it was time for the pickup.[42]

At 10 o'clock that night, after spending the day sailing the waters of the Bulan Straits, they were back at Pandjang, Lyon having navigated his way in the dark with the aid of the lights of fishing pagars, the positions of which he had memorised. When a reconnaissance had been completed and the stores ferried ashore, the three canoe teams of Lyon and Huston, Page and Jones, Davidson and Falls, were ready to take their leave. As they were now so close to Singapore that the glow of the city's lights were visible above the horizon, it was a great blow for the reserve team of Berryman and Marsh to see them go. Marsh was bitterly disappointed to be left behind. His frequent and voluble prayers, offered at regular intervals all the way from Australia, in which he had begged the Almighty to strike one of the six operatives with something sufficiently serious to force a replacement, had gone unanswered.[43]

The eight men left on board *Krait* did not expect to see the raiding party until after dusk on October 1. If anything went wrong and the rendezvous was not kept by any or all of them, Carse had been ordered to return to Australia immediately. As *Krait* headed off for fourteen days of aimless wandering, Morris wondered, for the second time in as many years, whether he would ever see Lyon again.[44]

Chapter 7
Mission Accomplished

Before *Krait* had disappeared into the pre-dawn darkness, Lyon and his men had lumped the stores out of sight and set up camp in the jungle behind the beach. For the next two days they rested and relaxed, bathing in the sea with a family of otters for whom they named the bay and exerting themselves only to secrete a supply dump high in the cliff face.[1]

On the night of September 20, after a day which had been spent checking all equipment and stores, they were about to leave on the first leg of their journey when they heard the sound of a patrol vessel making a nightly check of the area. They immediately froze and the folboats, riding low in the water with their 315 kilogram loads, remained undetected. As soon as the sound of the boat's engine had died away, they followed Davidson in a close arrowhead formation, reaching Pulau Bulat, about twenty kilometres away in the Bulan Strait, about midnight. After a rather difficult recce in the darkness, the folboats were dragged clear of the water to the base of a cliff and the men dropped to the sandy beach where they slept until dawn.[2]

How the Japanese, crewing a boat that drifted to within metres of the beach and the great heaps of stores, failed to see them the following morning, remains a mystery. The men were in the process of moving their equipment to a less exposed position when the small boat, flying the unmistakeable red and white flag of Japan, decided that the small bay would be an ideal place for breakfast. For the raiders, stranded between the shore and adequate cover, there was nothing to do but freeze. After what seemed an interminably long meal, during which time not one person on the boat glanced in Jaywick's direction, the engine was restarted and with much noisy chatter from the crew, the boat disappeared.

The men had only just resumed their task when they were surprised to see a lone fisherman heading straight towards them in his small kolek. As Falls and Jones prepared to dispatch him with the minimum of fuss, the intended victim avoided a premature journey to join his ancestors by diverting to a nearby island. They were then left in peace for the rest of the day, resting, swimming, eating their most unappetising rations and observing the procession of vessels passing up and down the straits.[3]

The next night's journey was appalling and they made very poor progress. After making huge detours to skirt fishing pagars and mistaking the lights on a fishing junk for a Japanese patrol boat, they were caught in a tide race which caused a collision between Davidson's and Lyon's folboats, damaging the latter. With dawn approaching and exhausted from lack of sleep and the night's exertions, they were forced to seek refuge in the slimy, sandfly-infested and mosquito-ridden mangroves of Pulau Boyan. They spent a miserable day in the mud, unable to move or speak above a whisper because of the proximity of a nearby village and the constant stream of traffic on the water. In the afternoon they were released from their purgatory by a tremendous thunderstorm which made such a racket and so reduced the visibility that they were able to frolic about, sing, refill their water bottles and generally relieve the tension.[4]

That night, aided by a favourable tide, they were soon free of the straits and rounding the tip of Pulau Batam, from where they could see the lights on Pulau Samboe, the oil storage island only eight kilometres south of Singapore Harbour.[5] From Batam, according to the plan, they were to set up their observation post on 'Hill 120', a small island rising 120 feet (thirty-six metres) into the air. However, it was now 8.30 on the night of September 22, fully five days before the date selected for the attack and at least three days ahead of schedule. Unable to bring forward the attack date, and unwilling to squander five days which could be better spent in gathering intelligence, Lyon decided to undertake a slight diversion.[6]

It was a wise decision. Despite its height and suitable cover, Hill 120 was inhabited and its all-important view was masked by the tiny, but also hilly, island of Subar, which lay a short distance to the north. Although an excellent position from which to observe everything going on in Singapore Harbour, Subar is without water and, being poorly vegetated, is extremely hot and very exposed. Its scrubby bushes, low bracken and ribbon-like grass afford no shade and would have offered scant cover for six men and their equipment for five days. The fortuitous change of plan sent them thirteen kilometres further east, past Samboe and its huge oil tanks, which were illuminated like Christmas trees, to the island of Dongas.[7]

Apart from dozens of yellow-and-black-striped iguanas and a couple of small crocodiles which scuttled away into a mangrove swamp on the southern side of the island, Dongas was deserted. Superbly positioned, the steep, jungle-covered island overlooks the Roads and, in good visibility, Keppel Harbour itself. By night, the lights of cars travelling along Beach Road, past Raffles Hotel, could be seen and by day, wireless masts on the top of the Cathay Building were clearly distinguishable. As there was water aplenty from a disused well and lush foliage in which to hide, Dongas was an ideal observation post.

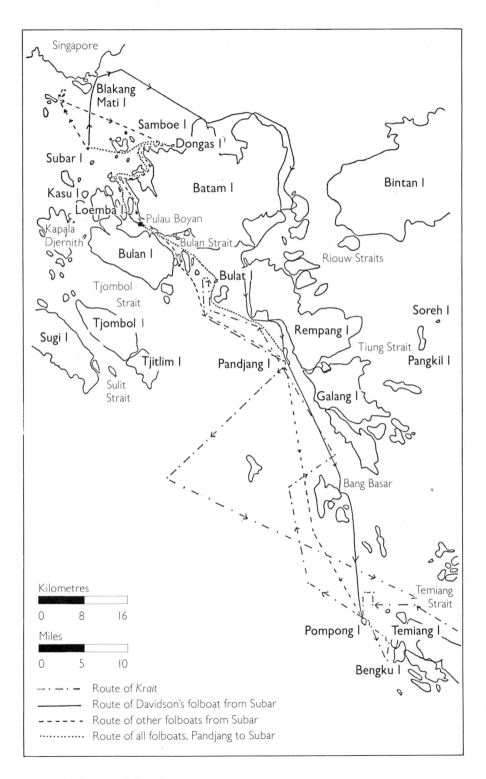

Map IV. Route of Operation Jaywick.

For the next two days the raiders kept a careful watch through a powerful telescope, noting everything that was happening in and to the east of Singapore Harbour. The huge numbers of ships, the absence of patrol vessels and the freedom of movement by medium-draught native craft convinced them that no minefields had been laid. By late afternoon on September 24 they had counted a total of sixty-five thousand tonnes of shipping assembled in the Roads opposite the island.

It was like waving a lollypop in front of a sweet-toothed child. Deciding that the opportunity to blow up the Roads anchorage was too good to miss, they set off at 8 o'clock that night towards the targets. It was useless. Although they had an easy enough start, the strength of the tide made it impossible to reach their objectives. At 1 am they abandoned the attempt, only to find that the return trip was almost as difficult, particularly for Lyon and Huston whose damaged folboat kept diverting to the left. This so reduced Lyon's and Huston's speed that when dawn broke, uncertain of their position, they were forced to seek cover among some boulders on the nearest island. After spending an unpleasant and sleepless day sitting in the rain, they were disgusted to find that they had been on Dongas all the time. When they located the other four at about seven that evening, Lyon agreed that they should move off at once to Hill 120.[8]

When the many drawbacks of Hill 120 were ascertained, the party moved to Subar. The extremely hot day spent trying to snatch some rest in the limited shade and conceal themselves in the low-level shrubbery, was compensated to some extent by the fact that the view of the target area was magnificent. At seven that evening, after a thorough briefing, the three folboat crews slipped silently away from Subar and melted into the darkness. Thirteen kilometres away lay Singapore and the Japanese.[9]

To be captured by the enemy, they had been told, was to court instant disaster, for there was no telling what might be revealed under torture or what might babble forth from the lips of those who were drugged. To preclude any such possibility, each man carried a small, bakelite-coated glass capsule, filled with deadly sodium cyanide. Perfectly harmless in its unbroken state it could be held in the mouth or even swallowed, passing through the body without any ill effects. It was not issued, however, with the instruction that it should be swallowed whole. All persons embarking upon special duties had made an undertaking that they would never allow themselves to be taken alive. If capture was inevitable, everyone knew the drill. Bite the glass and release the cyanide. Death would be almost instantaneous and secrecy, on which the lives of many might depend, would be maintained.[10]

But thoughts of suicide, or even detection, were far from the minds of the Jaywick men as, with each carefully measured stroke of their paddles, they neared their objectives. While Lyon's and Page's teams headed off together, Davidson and Falls struck off towards the boom and Keppel Harbour. On the way they narrowly missed being run down by a steamer, but otherwise reached the boom, which was not only open but unmanned, without any further bother. Finding no targets worthy of their attention along the wharves and noting that the Empire Docks were too well lit, they proceeded to the Roads, where there were still ships in plenty. They settled on three 6000 tonne cargo vessels, two of which were heavily laden. With clockwork precision they approached the first and went into action. They knew it off by heart — holdfast, limpet, contact, fuse, release.

As they were preparing to place the limpets on the final target, the sound of the clock on Victoria Hall, chiming the hour of one, reverberated across the water, a reminder that it was almost time to go. Their work completed, they turned towards the large island of Batam, where Davidson would later fill his notebook with details of the ships and installations they had seen. Like the other two teams, he and Falls would meticulously record the size, shape, tonnage, and appearance of the ships they had mined as well as anything that might be of interest. When added to the information they had already recorded on topography, native habitations, shipping routes, aircraft movements, observation posts and enemy installations, it would amount to a sizeable intelligence report.[11]

While Davidson and Falls had been cruising in and out of the ships in the roadstead, the other two teams had parted company and were at their respective targets — Lyon and Huston at Examination Anchorage and Page and Jones at the island known as Pulau Bukum. At Examination Anchorage Lyon and Huston looked in vain for the ships they had so clearly seen that afternoon from Subar. Completely blacked out, they were now impossible to detect against the inky backdrop of the island. After finding a ship, which he rejected as a target as he thought it was one of those allocated to Page, Lyon decided to place all nine limpets on a tanker — a multi-compartmented target generally considered to be unsuitable because it was extremely difficult to sink — hoping that the blaze would at least cause some damage.

After making a direct approach to the stern, aided by the red lamp doing duty as an anchor light, they were midway through their work when Huston looked up to see a man gazing intently at them from a porthole, not three metres away. He apparently looked with eyes that did not see for, after continuing to stare in their direction, he withdrew his head and lit his bedside lamp, leaving a greatly relieved Lyon and Huston to set off for the safety of Dongas, nineteen kilometres away.[12]

About an hour after leaving Lyon at 9 o'clock, Page and Jones reached the Bukum wharves. Although the entire area was ablaze with light and swarming with Japanese sentries and workmen, they spent over an hour examining various targets without the slightest trouble. After placing their limpets on a freighter, anchored not far from the wharf, they hung onto the anchor chain, taking a breather while they watched the sentries strutting up and down and the welders working on the ship behind them. After a munch on some chocolate they tackled a 4000 tonne freighter tied up alongside the wharf. While its crew leaned over the side, chatting to seamen on the wharf and smoking cigarettes, Page and Jones paddled around to the other side where, in the reflected light from the wharves, they left their deadly calling card. Much encouraged by their success thus far they paddled another 450 metres to victim number three — a rusting, heavily laden cargo ship. It was fortunate that this ship was not illuminated as the first two had been for its hull was so corroded that Jones's holdfast magnets were unable to grip the metal. After some diligent scraping, enough new iron was exposed to hold the folboat steady and set the limpets in place. They then dumped the superfluous equipment over the side and made straight for Dongas, anxious to put as much distance between them and the Japanese before the alarm was raised.[13]

The two folboat teams headed by Lyon and Page arrived at Dongas shortly after five, just as dawn was breaking and just in time to hear the first of the explosions. During the next half-hour another six were heard, confirming that all the limpets had detonated. As the noise had roused the interest of every person within earshot, the four men quickly sought the shelter of the island. Almost immediately, the distinctive wail of ships' sirens was followed by a complete blackout of Samboe and the city.

On nearby Batam, the villagers of Patam were jubilant. They laughed and shouted, prancing around and miming the effect of the explosions, the results of which were now clearly evident. Beyond the thick black smoke belching forth from the bowels of the burning tanker, the raiders could see quite clearly the bows of a second ship pointing skywards. It appeared that Jaywick had achieved 100 per cent success, bagging a total of almost thirty-seven thousand tonnes of shipping and creating absolute chaos.

The Japanese obviously had no idea of what had happened. Some ships quit their anchorages and sailed aimlessly about to the confused cacophony of sound provided by the continuous wail of the sirens. Patrol boats swarmed across the water like angry ants, following no particular pattern and getting nowhere fast, while aircraft quartered the skies above the Malacca Straits, looking for something. What, they were not quite sure.[14]

Davidson and Falls, who were returning to Pompong by way of the Riouw Straits, were skirting the Batam coastline in search of a hiding place when they heard the sound of the explosions but, because of their position, they heard only six.[15] They would not know any details nor learn of the fate of the other raiders until they all met at Pompong in five days' time.

That night, as soon as darkness fell, they left Batam and made for the Riouw Straits. Forty-eight hours later, they were paddling into

Pandjang's Otter Bay, having negotiated a circuitous and tricky path past a large number of fishermen and fishing stakes. Here they rested, swam and tucked with great relish into a gastronomic feast concocted from the supplies left in the food cache. After scribbling a short note to Lyon they left on the last leg of their journey to Pompong.

They had not progressed six kilometres when a violent Sumatra blew up, electrifying the sky and lashing the sea to a fury. For two hours they rode out the storm, until the wind and rain abated sufficiently to allow them to seek shelter on a nearby island. The delay meant that they could not reach Pompong in one hop, but with only a short distance to go they completed the last section of the journey in relative ease, reaching the rendezvous with almost twenty-four hours to spare.

As darkness fell on the night of October 1, Falls and Davidson waited with growing tension for the first sight of *Krait*. Fourteen days had now passed. Fourteen days in which anything might have happened. Had she run into trouble? Had the engine given up the ghost? Would she make Pompong on time? Would she make Pompong at all?

At fifteen minutes after midnight on October 2 the waiting was over. A dark shadow on an already darkened sea, *Krait* slipped into the bay. Silently, the folboat paddled out to the ship, observed by Cobber Cain, who was on lookout. When he was about three metres away Davidson's sense of humour got the better of him. Throwing caution to the wind he called in hideously fractured English that all on board should put up their hands and surrender. The resultant reception was tumultuous, with questions being fired from all directions. But the one question everybody wanted answered was — where were the others?[16]

The other four had in fact a trouble-free run from Dongas, stopping to camp in a Chinese graveyard at the northern end of Bulan Straits, before proceeding back the way they had come. In the early hours of September 30 they reached Otter Bay, where they were lashed by the same violent storm that was giving Falls and Davidson a rough time only a few kilometres away. With another storm appearing imminent they were forced to delay their departure until dawn on October 1, leaving them forty-five kilometres to cover, most of it in daylight, that day. This would have been no problem had Lyon and Huston, lumbered with the damaged folboat, not been forced to expend enormous amounts of energy simply to keep on course. After a day of superhuman effort, all four made Pompong on the morning of October 2, three hours before dawn, the deadline for the rendezvous. Tired as they were, they paddled to and fro in the bay, looking without success for any signs of *Krait*, before falling into an exhausted sleep upon the beach. When they awoke at 6.15 they saw the ship. To their dismay, she was about three kilometres out to sea and heading down the Temiang Strait. While they had been at the southern end of the bay, *Krait* had been anchored at the north. Somehow, in the darkness, they had missed her.[17]

It was evident, judging from the traces of a newly vacated campsite, that Davidson had made it back safely. Unable to count on Davidson's amending the orders and returning at a later date, Lyon organised the men for a lengthy stay on Pompong, telling them that as soon as the monsoon changed he would pirate a native vessel and sail them to India.[18] There was no reason whatever to doubt his word. They all knew he had done it once and, if necessary, he would do it again.

While Page supervised the building of a hut, Ivan made arrangements with an old Malay and his small son, who had paddled up in their kolek, to keep them supplied with food — an excellent arrangement as uninhabited Pompong had no village with which to trade.[19] With the matter of their food supply settled, the men were about to bed down for a second night on the island when, shortly after eight o'clock, Krait returned.

It was, of course, Davidson's doing. Having paddled Lyon's damaged folboat from Dongas to Subar he knew that, even in calm seas, they would have experienced great difficulty in making Pompong on time. Although the orders had been quite definite, Davidson also knew that Lyon himself bent the rules if the occasion warranted it. He put it to the vote. Would they sail away and leave the others to an uncertain fate, or would they return?[20] All except the unstable, and by now very nervous, Carse voted to go back. The problem of Carse's dissension was solved when Davidson, assisted by a well-positioned pistol, persuaded him to change his mind, thereby making the vote unanimous.[21]

Worried that the folboat teams might require extra time, Davidson delayed the pickup by an extra twenty-four hours. If this rendezvous failed, he intended to sail to Pandjang to see whether Lyon had found his note. If there was still no sign of them, then, and only then, would Krait abandon the search.[22] As Lyon and the other three were waiting on the beach when Krait made her second appearance, the alternative plans fell by the wayside. After a joyful reunion, made even more agreeable by tots of medicinal rum, it was time for the raiders to learn what the others had been doing.[23]

It appeared that Krait's crew had spent a boring but tension-filled fortnight sailing in the shallow waters of southern Borneo, wondering when and if the raid had taken place and whether the raiders had survived.[24] The uncertainty of not knowing what was happening had taken its toll on the nerves of some of the crew, particularly those of Carse, who had become 'heartily sick' of 'hanging around the coast of Borneo trying to dodge all comers'. His temper, which had become rather frayed by what he described as the 'worst sixteen days of my life', had evidently not been improved when Berryman and Marsh discovered that he had been sampling the rum supply. Perhaps it may have been better for them to have turned a blind eye, allowing him his crutch in a situation that was obviously getting the better of him. Unable to tipple at will, he had become irritated in the extreme by what he perceived to be the relaxed attitudes to routine duty exhibited by the 'younger members' of the crew, who apparently found such jobs as cleaning rifles and keeping watch very tedious. The atmosphere was apparently so tense that it was only Cain's and Morris's unfailing good humour, coupled with Crilly's talent for producing such tasty morsels as steamed pudding, that had kept the situation from boiling over.[25]

However, with *Krait* now headed for home and the mission obviously an unqualified success, the tensions and petty annoyances were put aside. If the journey up had been boring, the voyage back to Lombok was mind-numbingly so. Apart from a minor engine breakdown and a couple of days of rough weather when the Officers' Mess was flooded, absolutely nothing happened. In fact it was so boring that someone fell asleep while on watch, a crime that invoked a rather draconian sounding 'three days water and dry biscuits besides additional punishment'.[26] The miscreant was just welcoming the return to a normal diet when real trouble struck.

They had spent the entire day of October 11 in anxious anticipation as the boat approached the most dangerous part of the voyage — the passage through Lombok Strait. About midnight, just as they were roaring along with the riptide in their favour and believing that the worst was over, a seventy-six metre Japanese patrol boat came out of the darkness. When Falls and Jones raised the alarm, the crew, roused rudely from their sleep, went to action stations. Grabbing his Bren, Berryman made for the stern where he found Crilley, a devout Catholic, had resorted to the thing he thought best in times of trouble — a fast and fervent prayer to the Almighty.

While Davidson stood poised, ready to detonate the great mass of plastic explosive placed on Young's radio and sufficient to blow them all to kingdom come, and Lyon prepared to hand out the suicide pills, the others waited, breaths held and fingers tensely gripping light machine guns. All on board were only too well aware that they were in a precarious position. To be caught without uniforms on a ship flying a Japanese flag was more than sufficient reason to be declared spies — a charge which, although not against the rules of warfare, would probably result in their execution. If it came to a fight, nothing could save them. To engage in war while flying the enemy's flag was a flagrant breach of international law. For five agonising minutes the ship paced the smaller boat. Then, without warning, she sheered away and turned for Lombok, disappearing as fast as she had come.[27]

Why she let *Krait* go unchallenged is a question that can never be answered. About as close to the truth as any one is ever likely to get is Carse's guess that, being close to midnight and the change of the watch, the officer-in-charge was more attracted to the thought of his bunk than to finding out what a run-down fishing boat was doing in Lombok Strait.[28]

By comparison, the riptides and heavy seas which they encountered soon after were, according to Carse, 'like sitting before a nice fire'. As soon as the sun had shed its last light across the sea, the Japanese ensign was hauled down for the last time, an action that brought great approval from the navigator, who was sick of 'skulking by the byways and corners of the sea'. Considering the obvious nervousness of the man, which manifested itself so often in the remarks in his log from the time they had left Australia, it is rather amazing that he then did something that put all their lives in jeopardy. On the evening of October 13, when still within range of the Japanese air patrols, he ordered Young to break radio silence. Apparently he had arranged with a crony that he would pass on information as to whether Lombok Strait was patrolled. As Lyon sanctioned no such message, it could only have been Carse, hankering to exert his imagined status as 'Officer Commanding *Krait*', who ordered Young to transmit the message. Lyon, always a stickler for security, was enraged.[29]

Although there had been no overt friction between Carse and Lyon, it was apparent that the former was miffed by the fact that he, a naval officer, was subordinate to an army major on a sea-going operation. This attitude became more obvious in later years when Carse carved for himself a far greater slice of the action and, when speaking about his part in the operation, assumed the mantle of overall command, placing Lyon in a subordinate position. Perhaps his inferior role to Lyon and his underlying resentment at being the navigator rather than the captain were the reasons why there was a coolness between them. Always polite, Lyon kept Carse at the same subtle distance that commanding officers normally reserved for other ranks. Aware that unquestioned obedience might easily mean the difference between life and death, Lyon carefully maintained his relationship with his men, his position as commander demanding that, unlike Davidson, he could never overstep the fine line that divided familiarity from authority. It was a successful recipe. Almost all the men under his command both respected and admired him, some to the point of hero worship.[30]

Fortunately the message transmitted by the telegraphist was brief enough not to lead to their detection. In any case, the whole exercise had been futile as the wireless station near Darwin could not be raised. Two days later, with more distance between themselves and Lombok, Young tried the radio again, this time with the full approval of his commanding officer. Typical of Lyon, it was probably one of the most succinct and laconic signals ever received from any leader of a successful wartime operation. It read simply: '*Mission completed*'.[31]

They arrived at Exmouth Gulf on the morning of October 19, after a journey that had taken them over six thousand four hundred kilometres in forty-eight days. For Young, it was a nightmare that was over. For Lyon it was the end of a successful mission in which he had not lost a single man. For Marsh it was the satisfaction of knowing what it was like to 'fly the Rising Sun'. And for the military it was an unprecedented chance to trumpet the news to the entire world that the Japanese were not invincible.[32]

It was an opportunity which they chose not to grasp. By the use of well-controlled propaganda the enemy could have been reduced to a state of absolute panic. The merest suggestion that raiders had infiltrated from the outside would have been sufficient to force hundreds, if not thousands, of troops to be deployed in strengthening garrisons and maintaining round-the-clock watches at every port in Japanese-occupied territory. Had the High Command taken this course, Jaywick would have accomplished far more than the blowing up of five ships and the sinking of two others.[33]

But this was not to be. The Jaywick men returned to a high-level but low-key welcome at Potshot, the details of the mission still secret to all but Admiral Christie, who hosted a small dinner for Lyon and Page. Stunned by their success, the US Admiral recorded:

> Last evening I had the great honour of entertaining Major Lyon of the Gordon Highlanders and Captain Page of the Australian Army upon their return from a dangerous operation against the enemy — almost a single-handed endeavour of extremely bold pattern. My hat is off to them.[34]

Although they were now back on Australian soil, they were not yet free to relax. Morris was taken to Perth to receive treatment for his unhealed ankle, Lyon and Page were flown to Melbourne for a debriefing and the rest of the crew sailed to Darwin, where they were interrogated by intelligence officers. *Krait*, which had served them so well and for so long, was left behind in Darwin, where she would undertake other risky and covert operations. Finally, almost three weeks after their return, all, including Lyon and Page, were put on a plane for Brisbane, where they were reunited with Morris and treated to a well-deserved, slap-up party.[35]

While the toasts were being proposed and the tales were told again and again with varying degrees of jollity, the man who had been Jaywick's catalyst was heading north along the very same route followed by *Krait*. Unaware that his old fishing boat had ever left Australia, let alone carried Lyon and his team to victory, Bill Reynolds had entered a completely alien world. In place of the tang of the salt-laden breeze and the slap of waves against *Krait*'s wooden hull were the distinctively stale odour of recycled air and the purr of almost silent diesel engines. The limitless blue of the sky was now invisible, replaced by confining and constricting walls, streaming constantly with condensation. Bill Reynolds, secret agent, was in the bowels of USS *Tuna*, an American submarine.

The twin peaks of the volcanoes that guarded the Straits of Lombok slid by unseen as the iron monster cut silently through the waters and entered the Java Sea. But instead of turning to the west at the Kangean Islands, as *Krait* had done, the submarine held its course to the north. A short distance from Borneo's south-easterly tip, at the entrance to the Straits of Macassar, it stopped. Somewhere out in the tropical darkness, about three kilometres to the west, lay Pulau Laoet.

From this island, entirely alone, Reynolds was to carry out his secret mission. In the guise of procuring a junk loaded with rubber and quinine, and aided by vast amounts of money provided by his employer (the innocuously entitled United States Bureau of Economic Warfare), he was to collect intelligence of vital importance before making his way back to Exmouth Gulf in the trading vessel. Reynolds had complete confidence that he could do it, undoubtedly figuring that it was no more hazardous than blowing up installations, rescuing castaways, indulging in naval warfare, eluding the Japanese or sailing across the Indian Ocean. On the night of November 13/14, a handful of submariners watched in silence as the middle-aged Australian stepped into his small rowing boat and paddled away, a lone and rapidly fading figure on an inky black sea. Three days later, following a tip off, Captain William Roy Reynolds, MBE, was in Japanese hands.[36]

Back in Australia, Lyon had no idea that his old friend had undertaken a mission potentially more dangerous than that of Jaywick, which was fast becoming a state secret. Towards the end of October, when intercepted and decoded enemy signals revealed that the Japanese 'did not know what had hit them', orders were issued at the highest level to 'take maximum precautions to ensure secrecy' and inform only a 'minimum number of high-ranking officers' that Jaywick had ever taken place.[37] These instructions, carried out to the letter, ensured that it was now impossible for anyone outside the top military echelons, let along the Japanese, to know the truth. Consequently, while military chiefs were slapping each other's backs in smug self congratulation, the anger of the Japanese in Singapore was reaching fever pitch. With all the excitement that had surrounded Jaywick's safe return, who could have envisaged how tragically prophetic would be the words written by Horrie Young in his diary: 'curious to know what the Japs will have to say — probably say it is internal sabotage and shoot a couple of hundred chinks.'[38]

He was appallingly close to the truth. As the champagne flowed in Sydney and Melbourne, the blood of the innocent was running down the gutters of Singapore.

Chapter 8
Lyon's Tigers

The victorious Imperial Japanese Army that had stormed into Singapore a bare eighteen months previously was, by September 1943, not quite as cocksure. The first flush of victory was over and, as progress became more difficult, losses were being encountered. This decrease in momentum was more than just a military blow for it also made their propaganda, promoting a united Asia under benevolent Japanese patronage, far less effective. Aided by BBC broadcasts, picked up on clandestine radio sets, the subjugated people, forced by the Japanese into grudging co-operation, began to suspect that the all-powerful conquerors might have feet of clay after all.

As resentment began to mount, this anti-Japanese feeling had given way to action — acts of sabotage which, although small, lifted the morale of the civilians and made the invaders feel less than easy. Warehouses and factories were inexplicably burnt down, a Japanese transport ship caught fire and sank off the Malayan coast, and telegraph wires were cut, severely disrupting communications. With these niggling acts of sabotage and widely circulated rumours that the British would soon be back, the Japanese, seeing ghosts behind every tree, decided that a highly organised spy ring was operating underground.

Convinced that prominent pre-war Eurasians and Europeans, now in detention at the Changi Civilian Camp, were masterminding the operation, Tokyo appointed Lieutenant Sumida in May 1943 to set up a branch of the Kempei Tai, or secret police, in order to sniff out suspects believed to be responsible for the recent sabotage. With the aid of undercover agents, planted at the Changi Camp and infiltrated into the town population, the Kempei was ordered to amass evidence sufficient to bring about arrests by December and so put an end to the suspected spy network. They had scarcely made any inroads into their secret investigation when, on the morning of 27 September 1943, Ivan Lyon and his men blew up the ships in Singapore Harbour.

Outraged by this unprecedented act of sabotage, the infuriated Japanese hierarchy ordered Sumida to 'clean up the enemy elements in Singapore'. Anxious not to incur the wrath of the high command, the Kempei Tai chief gave top priority to the investigations, now known as

'Dai ichi Kosako' or 'Number One Work'. By the second week of October he was ready. Believing that the existence of a sabotage group had been proven beyond all doubt, the Kempei Tai swooped upon the hapless native population and then upon the civilian internment camp.

So began a bloody reign of terror that would last for months. Civilians and internees were hauled from their beds in the dead of night, never to return. No one was safe, from the humblest coolie to the Bishop of Singapore. The number one work was destined to become a hideous and terrifying monster from which there was no escape. The nightmare that began on October 10 — 'the tenth of the tenth' — was destined to go down in history as the 'Double Tenth Massacre'.

The Kempei Tai, like their Gestapo brothers in Germany, were masters at extracting 'confessions' by whatever means were necessary. Once they had made up their minds that a suspect was guilty, it was the job of the interrogators to ensure that the crime was then admitted. As one prisoner was told, 'it is essential that you make a confession. Under our law you cannot be tried until you confess. For that reason I have the authority to use any degree of force'. In this way, some of the most horrific crimes known to man were perpetrated in the name of Japanese justice.

To the amazement of Lieutenant Sumida, the hideous tortures, starvation diets and barbaric executions achieved nothing. Although the interrogators extracted information about camp organisation and hidden radios, the Europeans stubbornly refused to admit to anything else. Unintimidated by a purge in February the previous year, when 6000 of their community had been machine-gunned to death as part of 'Operation Cleanup', the stoic Chinese were even more unyielding. Every one of them, although subjected to even worse treatment than that meted out to the Europeans, was prepared to die before confessing to 'crimes' that would lead to the punishment of others.

The tortures, the appalling conditions and inhumane treatment took a dreadful toll in the six long months that the Japanese interrogations lasted. Thirty Europeans, tried and found guilty, were either executed or sentenced to varying terms of imprisonment. Fifteen civilians from Changi, along with an untold number of Chinese and Malays whose only crime had been to attract the attention of the Japanese, died as a result of questioning. Yet, at the end of this period, the Japanese were still no closer to solving the mystery. John Long, a former Shell Petroleum employee, remained the prime suspect but as he had not confessed, despite prolonged torture, the Kempei decided to detain him indefinitely. While his bruised and battered body was subjected to even greater punishment and the Japanese continued to scratch their heads over the loss of the shipping, Ivan Lyon, quite oblivious to the suffering that Jaywick had caused, was busily planning another raid.[1]

This time he had all the help he needed. Impressed by Jaywick's success, Louis Mountbatten, Supreme Allied Commander South-East

Asia, now urged SRD to seek American approval for raids to be mounted against targets such as Singapore and Saigon, and the recently repaired Singapore Naval Base.[2]

The chances of the Americans agreeing to special operations organised by SRD in their patch were never good. Keen to maintain superiority over their Allies, and therefore appear to be winning the war single handed in the eyes of the American voting public, the United States was very suspicious of individual organisations such as Britain's SOE and Australia's AIB, which controlled SRD. By the same token, the Australians and British, realising that 'there is no doubt that the main weight of attack on Japan will be delivered by commands that are overwhelmingly American', were anxious to 'increase the representation of the point of view and the interest of the British Commonwealth in this area'. As a result, activities organised by SRD and SOE assumed an importance out of all proportion, their operations and their personnel becoming mere pawns in a massive battle of political wills as the two governments fought to retain their foothold. As part of this struggle, being unable to exert control over the infrastructures of the secret networks, the United States insisted that MacArthur have total power in deciding whether any operation could take place in his zone.[3]

Therein lay the first stumbling block. Before reaching MacArthur, all plans had to be passed by General Willoughby, MacArthur's powerful representative. Willoughby's track record for sanctioning operations was poor and, indeed, it was Willoughby who had rejected Jaywick, forcing Lyon to seek assistance elsewhere. Steering clear of operational areas known to be off limits, such as the Philippines, SRD examined Mountbatten's proposal and, hoping that the Americans would co-operate, came up with a new operation, code named 'Hornbill'.[4]

Hornbill was to be a larger, far more ambitious version of Jaywick, involving the use of folboats, limpets, submarines and a completely new method of transportation known as 'Country Craft', which would operate out of the Natuna Islands, north of Borneo. It was anticipated that these diesel-driven, native-style vessels would be able to enter enemy waters in much the same way as *Krait* had done, to drop off sabotage teams, coastwatching parties and intelligence agents.[5]

Mountbatten had no problem in gaining the co-operation of MacArthur, as he was already on side. By sheer chance, Ivan Lyon, with the assistance of General Blamey, who had been much impressed by Jaywick's results, had sidestepped the all-powerful General Willoughby. It was not hard to do, for Jaywick's success, from which the Americans by their own actions had excluded themselves, ensured that ears that might have been closed were now open. After meeting Lyon and an equally enthusiastic Blamey in Brisbane, shortly after Lyon's return from Singapore, MacArthur pledged his help and his submarines, declaring that raids similar to Jaywick were invaluable as 'opportunities for clandestine military attacks and [the] effect on enemy war effort by such attacks are greater here than any other theatre'. Keen to enter areas out of range of normal military activity, he ordered his Chiefs-of-Staff to pull out all stops to ensure that submarines were made available, a decision which delighted SRD.[6]

Since the first two targets were to be Singapore and Saigon, Lyon, now a Lieutenant-Colonel, was a natural choice as party leader. He was dispatched to England in March 1944 to inspect HMS *Porpoise*, the submarine which had been assigned to Hornbill, and check up on the latest sabotage equipment. Upon arrival in London he headed straight for SOE's Baker Street headquarters, where he met Major Walter Chapman, a Royal Engineer whose talent lay in organising specialised and ingenious devices for clandestine operations. On learning the aims of Operation Hornbill, the tall, bespectacled engineer announced that what Lyon needed was a brand new invention — a miraculous form of underwater transport called a 'Sleeping Beauty'.[7]

Sleeping Beauty, or SB, was the code name of a highly secret, very sophisticated one-man, submersible craft, known officially as a Motor Submersible Canoe and the brainchild of Royal Marine folboat expert, Major 'Blondie' Hasler. Made of mild steel and aluminium, the SBs were almost four metres in length and seventy centimetres in width, and were propelled by four standard six-volt car batteries. The half horsepower produced by the batteries enabled it to travel at four and a half knots on the surface and three and a half when submerged. Range at full speed was nineteen kilometres, or thirty-eight at cruising speed. As it was unaffected by Force 5 winds and was considered to be virtually impossible to capsize, it had a distinct advantage over folboats and canoes. Theoretically, it could be paddled or sailed if the batteries went flat, but because of its weight of 270 kilograms, this was found to be not really practicable.

The craft was operated with a joystick control by one man, wearing an underwater suit and special breathing equipment. There were two ways to approach a target — either completely submerged or with the head only above water until the final approach. As there was no periscope, the driver could 'porpoise' to the surface at fifty to one hundred metre intervals or make use of an underwater compass to obtain his bearings. Buoyancy was controlled by flooding two tanks set alongside the driver's legs, but underwater movement was limited to two hours' duration — the limit of the operator's oxygen supply. With its almost negligible profile, its lack of attention-grabbing paddles and its silent motor to eliminate driver fatigue, the SB seemed superior in every way to the folboat.[8]

Lyon, with an enthusiastic Chapman in tow, went to Staines Reservoir, just outside London, to see this fantastic invention in action. He was so impressed by its outstanding manoeuvrability that he asked for a test drive. After a short period of instruction, he donned the rubber suit and took to the cold waters of the reservoir, being cautioned not to try anything as spectacular as looping the loop, a feat which chief test pilot Sub-Lieutenant Riggs performed with ease. Within an amazingly short space of time, Lyon was handling the SB with great proficiency and envisaging its possibilities. However, it was the follow-up demonstration in Portsmouth, when Riggs showed how easy it was to approach and mine naval ships completely underwater, that convinced Lyon he must have Sleeping Beauties for Hornbill.[9]

Wanting them was one thing, getting them to Australia and out to the Natunas was quite another. Any idea of carrying them inside the submarine was scotched when the Royal Navy's Commander Newton informed Lyon that it was doubtful that any submarine commander would agree to such a plan. Although the SBs would fit, the time taken to unload them in enemy waters would require the submarine to be on the surface, fully buoyant and with the hatches open, for a prolonged period. There was a chance however, that *Porpoise* could carry them externally in its mine-laying casing — a square, tunnel-like structure that ran the full length of the hull. Following a suggestion made by Hubert Marsham, *Porpoise*'s commanding officer, the sub had for some time been successfully carrying supplies to Malta, packed into specialised containers, in this fashion.[10]

Thwarted by 'security' from making contact with Marsham, with whom he had hoped to thrash out details, Lyon was forced to leave the design and manufacture of the specialised SB containers in the hands of others, who were unfortunately adept at theory but short on practical experience. After considerable delay, the first of fifteen very expensive 'J' containers was produced, only to find that it was impossible to eject them from the mine casing without jamming. Additional support and modifications were obviously needed, but as the rest of the containers would not be delivered for some considerable time, Lyon was told that the work would have to be carried out in Australia.[11]

While he was wrestling with the problems of SBs and the submarine, a talented young ex-Malayan Army Lieutenant was trying to talk his way into active service in Room 238 of the Victoria Hotel, on London's Northumberland Avenue. The officer conducting this interview in such unexpected surroundings was Edgerton Mott, the former Director of SRD. Before him stood twenty-six-year-old Harold Robert (Bobby) Ross. Although born in India, the son of a British Army doctor and a coffee plantation owner's daughter, Bobby Ross had been raised in England. A bright lad, good at sport and schoolwork, he had entered Cambridge University in 1936, where he excelled in Natural Sciences and Anthropological Studies, achieving first class honours in both. His studies over, he had sailed for the the Far East to embark upon a career in the Malay Civil Service, arriving just in time to see war break out in Europe. His brief military career — as a gunner in the Federated Malay States Volunteer Force — had ended abruptly on the night of 15 February 1942 but, unlike many, he had avoided the necessity of spending the rest of the war in a POW camp. Six hours after the surrender, he and seven companions had made good their escape, joining General Gordon Bennett's party as it left Singapore. After Bennett's team left the slow moving tonkan in favour of a fast motor launch, Ross's party had continued to Padang where it was evacuated to India. Discharged in June 1942, Ross had returned to civilian life and had been posted to Africa, where he had spent an anthropologically interesting but militarily boring time with the Nigerian Administrative Service. By February 1944 he had had enough. Prompted by his ambition to see some real action, he had returned to England to seek active service with the British Army.

Ross's credentials for the work in which Mott was involved were impressive — a good working knowledge of colloquial and everyday Malay, although not, Ross cheerily admitted, of the standard or type that would enable him to pass formal examinations; a thorough understanding of South-East Asian people; an ability, from his months spent in isolated areas of Nigeria, to find his way across unmapped territory; a fundamental grasp of the principles of road and bridge engineering, suited to tropical climates; and finally, a well-developed passion for adventure. Added to this was a desire totally to avoid administrative work and to take part in field assignments as part of a small team. Although he did not know it at the time, Bobby Ross was tailor-made for Hornbill. Mott, who could no doubt see a great similarity between Ross and Lyon, sent him to SOE's training school in England before assigning him to the operation.[12]

By April 24, Lyon's spirits had risen substantially. Hornbill had gone to GHQ for final approval and he was informed that he had been awarded a DSO for Jaywick. There were no details of course, as Jaywick was still a closely guarded secret, neither was it divulged that Ivan would have received a Victoria Cross had it not been for a technicality in the award structure. Donald Davidson and Bob Page had been similarly honoured, while raiders Jones, Falls, Huston and engineer McDowell (who had been specially singled out by Lyon) received Distinguished Service Medals. Morris and Crilley, also highly praised by Lyon, became the proud holders of the Military Medal.[13]

When it was realised that the engineer, cook and medical orderly had received medals and navigator Carse, the only other officer, had not, there were quite a few raised eyebrows. As there are no adverse written reports by Lyon, it must be assumed that SRD director Chapman-Walker, who made the recommendations, knew of the incident at Pompong and of Lyon's anger when radio silence had been broken. Carse's snide remarks about younger crew members and their light-hearted approach to life, placed on record in *Krait*'s log, also affected Chapman-Walker's recommendations. In the end, he decided that all those who had remained on *Krait* (with the exception of Morris, McDowell and Crilley) should receive a Mention in Despatches.[14]

While Ivan Lyon, now DSO, MBE, visited his family and old friends before returning to Australia by plane on May 1, Major Chapman set about the task of extricating himself from his desk at SOE and attaching himself to Hornbill. As it turned out, Ivan had left England one hour too soon. Immediately after farewelling her son, whom she had not seen for seven years, Mrs Lyon learned from the Red Cross that Gabrielle and Clive, of whom there had been no word for more than fourteen months, were still alive and well.[15]

Much relieved by this news when it finally reached him, Lyon turned his attention to Hornbill, which, because of the SBs, he now found had been substantially altered. On May 30 he was briefed on a very complicated plan to attack Singapore. This involved transporting men and equipment by submarine to the Natunas, where SBs, folboats, assault boats and personnel would be transferred to Country Craft. These would sail to within seventy kilometres of Singapore, where each team of two men would transfer to an assault boat, towing an SB the rest of the way. Once within striking distance, one man would carry out a limpet attack in the SB while the other waited. When the SB returned, it would be sunk, along with the assault boat. The pair would then paddle a folboat back to the mothership. The fifteen assault boats, which were so weighty that they needed at least six men to lift them, were to be used 'with or without engines'. How a heavy assault boat, further encumbered by a 270 kilogram SB dragging along behind, was to be paddled by two men without engine assistance, was not disclosed.[16]

A fortnight after this fantastically ambitious and logistically outrageous plan had been decided upon, Hornbill as such was cancelled. It was no wonder. The Country Craft were hit by labour problems and would not be ready for delivery before the change of the monsoon. The extra American submarines, on which such high hopes had been pinned, had failed to materialise and, in any case, it was now thought doubtful that enough fuel could be carried by submarines to keep the Country Craft working at such a range. To add to the troubles, the stores from UK would not arrive in time to allow them to be taken to the Natunas before the strike dates.[17]

It was now decided to abandon all idea of using the Natunas and the Country Craft for the time being. Fortunately, the plan to use assault boats was also dropped and the operation spilt into two far more manageable sections. One, code-named Kookaburra, was to cover raids on the islands from Johore in the west to Sarawak in the east, the dates of which had not yet been set. The other operation was to concentrate solely on raiding Singapore Harbour, with the aim of sinking thirty enemy ships and substantially damaging thirty others.[18] Its commanding officer was to be Ivan Lyon, on whose chest was tattooed the head of the creature that would give its name to the operation — Rimau, the Malayan word for tiger.[19]

On July 6, the final planning conference for Rimau took place. Although far more streamlined than Hornbill, the plan was still far from simple. After setting up a rear base, Base A, they were to go in the submarine to a known junk route, where they would pirate a junk. While *Porpoise* returned to Australia with the shanghaied junk crew, the Rimau men would sail the junk, SBs on board, to a rendezvous point close to Singapore from where the attack would be launched. A small crew, left behind at the rendezvous to erect the folboats for a fast getaway, would dispose of any unnecessary stores and destroy all evidence that might incriminate them. As soon as the raiders returned, the SBs and junk would be sunk and the folboat teams would paddle back to Base A, where, two weeks later, *Porpoise* would return for them.[20]

The matter of who was to command the junk in the latter stages of the operation was taken out of Lyon's hands by the unexpected addition of a twenty-six-year-old Royal Marine, Major R.M. 'Otto' Ingleton, to the Rimau team. A former architect, Ingleton had taken up an appointment with an assault force known as Detachment 385 when he was seconded to SOE and given the job as SEAC observer for Hornbill. Too late, someone at the planning conference realised that Ingleton, described as a very big man, was not an ideal choice for the operation. Tipping the scales at 108 kilograms, he was far too large and heavy for an SB, which would sink under his weight. As he had already been appointed and was on his way, accompanying seventeen Free Frenchmen who had been recruited for the intended raid on Saigon, Lyon was given no option but to assign him to control the folboat withdrawal and take care of the waiting junk.[21]

This plan was still immensely complex. Although worried by its complicated structure, which, he confided to one of his colleagues, was 'too big', Lyon realised that if he were to return to Singapore before the change of the monsoon, it had to be now or never. With a nod of his head he put Rimau under way.[22]

The plans now galloped along at breakneck speed. The very day after the planning conference, eleven SRD men, who had been training at Fraser Island Commando School under the watchful eye of chief instructor Donald Davidson, were put on a train and sent to Perth. Six days later they, and twenty others, were marching along the short jetty at Careening Bay Camp, about twenty kilometres from Fremantle. The camp, which had been virgin bush six weeks before, had been hurriedly constructed and was still in a rather primitive state, much to the discomfort of its commandant, an elderly, retired naval officer named Commander Cox.[23]

Five of those automatically included in the Rimau team were Jaywick veterans Davidson, Page, Falls, Huston and Marsh, whose loyalty and devotion to Lyon had made it unthinkable that they should be omitted. Davidson and Page, now promoted to the ranks of Lieutenant-Commander and Captain respectively, had summed it up simply: 'We cannot let Ivan go on his own'. Huston was not the least surprised that Lyon had dreamed up another operation and that he had been asked to take part in it. On April 27, when Davidson had written to Andrew, congratulating him on his Distinguished Service Medal, he had signed off with a cryptic, 'Hoping you are having a good leave. I have not lost you yet'.[24] These six seasoned raiders, along with Major Ingleton, who had just arrived from Colombo, headed the list of twenty-two. Although nine of the remaining fourteen would be SB operators, each Rimau member, including the technical experts, had to be fit enough to paddle back to Base A, a distance of more than one hundred kilometres, in twelve days.[25]

Although there was quite a substantial pool of prospective SB operators, some did not make it past first base. All those with false teeth were immediately eliminated as the breathing equipment, incorporated into an underwater suit that looked like a science-fiction costume reject, had to be held firmly in the mouth. As final selection could not take place until the SBs arrived, the remainder had a rather long wait to see if they would prove suitable. In the meantime, with the help of four dummy SBs, hurriedly knocked up as a stop-gap measure, Davidson put them through a tough programme which eliminated quite a few more. On July 21, scarcely a week after the bulk of the trainees had arrived, eight had fallen by the wayside. Three moved out the next day, followed by two more on August 2. When the rest were subjected to an actual sea trial in one of three SBs (extricated with difficulty from a Melbourne-bound ship a few days later), some found the claustrophobic feeling unbearable and asked to be withdrawn.[26]

The SB training was exceptionally difficult. For a start, the time frame was far too tight to allow Rimau to follow the English training programme, where SB operators were required to undergo a rigorous period of familiarisation before they even sat in an SB. In addition, Careening Bay did not have proper training facilities and there was a shortage of adequately trained instructors. Although Lieutenant Holmes, more a technical officer than a qualified instructor, and Lieutenant Davis, whose knowledge of the SBs proved to be less than that of his students, did their best, the workings of the submersible boat remained an absolute mystery. It was not until SB test pilot, twenty-year-old Scottish Sub-Lieutenant Riggs, arrived from England with Bobby Ross on August 7 that things improved. Riggs at least knew how to trim the craft, a function that had so far eluded the best of them. However, when his students discovered that experts, no matter how enthusiastic or skilled, do not always make the best teachers, most of them were forced to go back to learning the hard way — by trial and error.[27] One trainee, Private Douglas Warne, from the New South Wales city of Newcastle, managed his SB with phenomenal skill. Trapped underwater in a sinking SB, he simply drove the craft out backwards to resurface with relative ease.[28]

This time, unlike Jaywick, all the potential raiders knew what was expected of them in advance. After explaining what had been achieved on that raid, Lyon used a large sand and cement map, showing the target area in a three dimensional form, to elaborate on how it would be done.[29] Because this information had been given out in advance, security at the camp was tight. A special officer was appointed to enforce rigid security measures, trainee operatives were isolated from the technical and camp staff, and fraternisation was deeply frowned upon lest someone become too nosy. Unfortunately, it was not quite so easy to maintain secrecy away from the camp. The sight of oddly attired English officers and men with strange regimental badges at large in Perth led to awkward questions that required adroit fielding. Although a fairly tight control was kept on the trainees, it did not stop some of the bachelors from doing an illegal disappearing act at night, particularly when the charms of the ladies at the nearby searchlight battery became known.[30]

On August 10, when *Porpoise* arrived from Ceylon, Commander Marsham was astounded to find that the plans called for him to depart within two days for a twenty-five-day reconnaissance voyage, return to Fremantle, load the J containers and stores, and then sail on the mission within another four days. Fortunately, this 'fantastic programme', was shelved by the non-arrival of the J containers. Although they had started out speedily enough, at Colombo they had been transferred to incredibly slow merchant vessels whose captains had insisted upon delivering them to Melbourne — the official destination on the manifest. Until the containers made the long trip back to the west it was impossible to plan stowage, modify the submarine's casing or carry out a dress rehearsal. By August 18, as neither the practice container nor the operational variety was in sight, it was decided to make a dummy wooden container so that some work could proceed.[31]

Time marched on. When the elusive containers, after many promises, finally put in an appearance on August 31, they were in an appalling state. The axles and the wheels, which were supposed to run easily along the mine rails, had rusted up solid and were far too small to take the load. Such was the friction created by each container's two and a half tonnes of weight on the tiny nine centimetre wheels that it took the combined strength of eight men, using a double block and tackle, to get them to move at all. With departure day set at September 14 at the latest, it was obvious that unless something drastic was done, Rimau would be cancelled.[32]

Marsham came to the rescue. He told an astounded Lyon, who had been told five months before that such a thing was impossible, that the obvious solution would be to slide the SBs through the forward hatch and store them in the empty torpedo compartments — the normal procedure when folboats and canoes had to be transported. As Marsham was certain that in the event of an emergency dive during unloading the hatch could be shut within one minute of the alarm being sounded, they adopted his suggestion with alacrity.[33]

The expensive J containers did not go to waste. Fortunately, Lyon had been loaned from the AIF the services of a talented and inventive Australian engineer, Warrant Officer Alf Warren, who had, Marsham observed, 'the finest mechanical flair, for which his countrymen are noted, and, when confronted with a problem he quickly provides a solution so simple that it's a wonder no one thought of it before'. Within a short space of time Warren had turned the useless J containers into a handy storage facility for the rest of the supplies by welding eight of them to the mine casing.[34]

While the drama of the J containers had been taking place, Lyon and Davidson had been scrutinising the final plans for Rimau. The documentation, handed to them on August 26, was split into five sections and covered many pages. They were lucky it was not longer. It was only the fact that the departure date had been so delayed and Rimau now had top priority that saved them at the last minute from a diversion to Java to drop off an SRD agent organising another special operation.[35]

The operational section had been worked out in minute detail. Base A was to be a small, densely wooded island named Merapas. Little more than one and a half kilometres in length and less than a kilometre in width, it was situated off the east coast of Bintan Island, about one hundred and ten kilometres from Singapore. The most easterly island in the Riouw group, Merapas appeared to have three things going for it — good cover, a probable lack of habitation and the fact that it was within island-hopping range of Singapore Harbour. The greatest stretch of water between it and the target area did not exceed twenty-four kilometres. Should Merapas prove to be unsuitable, they were to find an alternative base on one of the other islands to the south-west.

Once the three and a half tonnes of stores had been secreted on the island, the submarine was to proceed to a shipping channel that ran between Borneo and the Riouw Archipelago. In the vicinity of Pedjantan Island they were to seize a junk, tow or sail it to a secluded cove at Pedjantan and, over the next two nights, unload eleven tonnes of equipment and stores, including the SBs.

At this point the submarine's task for the outward journey would be finished. With the shanghaied junk's crew on board as compulsory passengers, *Porpoise* would return to Australia. After refuelling and revictualling, the submarine would return to Merapas to pick up the party, fifty-eight days after Rimau's initial departure from Australia. If the submarine did not return on that date, the party was to wait on Merapas for thirty days. If there was still no sign of a rescue submarine, they were to make whatever arrangements they could for an escape.

Once the submarine had left Pedjantan for Australia the junk was to make its way to Singapore, via the Temiang and Sugi Straits, a distance of 400 kilometres, in six days. At Kapala Djernith, off the coast of Batam Island, it was to anchor in a bay while two folboat teams, under the control of an officer, performed a reconnaissance of Pulau Labon, where it was planned that the junk would wait while the raid took place. While one of the teams returned to report on the suitability of Labon, the officer and his partner were to proceed to Subar, the old Jaywick observation post, to note shipping movements in readiness for the raid which would take place that night. As soon as it was dark, they would paddle to Pulau Labon with their information and join the others on the junk. The SBs would then disperse in various directions to attack six main objectives, stretching from Samboe Island to the mainland. Once the limpets had been put in place on the sixty ships, each SB would return to its pre-arranged rendezvous.

This meant that all but five men would make their way back to the junk. The four raiding the Eastern Anchorage would return to Subar, while the man attacking Samboe Wharves would head for nearby Dongas. From here, he and his canoe partner would begin the long, solitary journey back to the base around the top of Batam Island. When the Subar quartet had retrieved their carefully concealed folboats, they and the junk group would split up and return to Merapas by whichever route was thought best. A fortnight later they should all be safely back, with nothing else to do but await rescue by the submarine.[36]

The logistics involved in organising the stores to support this ambitious programme were immense. Every single thing had to be measured, weighed and packed. Everything from food to drinking water, clothing to toothpaste, weapons to condoms (for covering rifle barrels and for keeping small items such as watches dry) had to be listed, counted, checked and rechecked. There were Bren guns and silent Stens, an anti-tank weapon to repel attacks on the junk, plastic explosive and limpets, pistols, thousands of rounds of ammunition, yards of flannelette for cleaning the assorted arms, Boston Mark II radio stations and walkie-talkies, folboats and folding engineer's boats, stoves, kerosene, compasses, maps, knives, binoculars, ordinary rations, iron rations and comfort rations, hammocks, fishing lines, parachute cord for tying up prisoners, medical kits, skin stain, sunglasses, mosquito nets, and dozens of sundry items that might be useful, including a substantial amount of money in varying currencies and denominations. The maintenance stores for the SBs, which included a vast array of spare parts, had also been carefully worked out, right down to the last drop of oil.[37]

One of Lyon's last tasks was to organise the signal plan. Rejecting the usual cipher keys and tables on the grounds that they were too risky, he and Rimau's cipher clerk, Staff Sergeant Mary Ellis, decided on a far more simple scheme — a one-off code, impossible to break. After selecting two copies of a book, they chose a page at random and, starting at the top lefthand corner of that page, struck out every third word. The letters of each remaining word were given a number in running numerical order. When the message was ready to be encoded, the numbers that had been allotted to the letters on that page were substituted for the letters in the message. There was no break to signify the end of a word and no punctuation. The transmitted signal was therefore simply a string of jumbled numbers, which could be deciphered with relative ease, provided you had a copy of the book, knew the page number and the strike-out pattern. It was so simple that it could be used by anyone with a knowledge of Morse code and radio frequencies.[38]

It was now time to select the team. Although the Jaywick men, having passed all the required tests, were at the top of the list, there were other people whom Lyon could not leave out. Lieutenant Bobby Ross's many skills, including his working knowledge of Malay, made it impossible for him to be omitted. The same went for Gregor Riggs, the curly headed, cherubic-faced SB whiz, who decided it was time to swap his dummy raids for a real one, and the cool-headed Doug Warne, a powerfully built, unarmed combat expert whom a friend once described as being 'built like a brick shithouse and just as hard to punch a hole through'.[39]

Next came the only other officer operative — broad-shouldered and snowy-headed Lieutenant Albert Leslie Sargent, who hailed from the Victorian country town of Wangaratta. A seasoned soldier, 'Blondie' Sargent had seen fierce fighting in the Middle East and on the Kokoda Track in New Guinea. Described by his mates as a livewire, with an engaging smile that lit up a rather ruggedly handsome face, Lieutenant Sargent was the brains behind the Sargent Adaptor — a device for producing air bursts at any required height with the use of a three inch (eighty mm) mortar. A tough, as well as talented, man, Sargent had the distinction of being one of the last soldiers to be commissioned in the field.[40]

The next on the list, Victorian-born Jeffrey Willersdorf, had certainly packed a great deal into the two years in which he had been a soldier. Of average height and strong build, the fair-haired warrant officer was a trained parachutist who had already been on one SRD operation outside Australia.[41] Also selected were two Australian Army corporals, former jackeroo Archie Campbell, from Dalby in Queensland, and a Dublin-born former actor, Roland Fletcher. Campbell, son of a highly decorated First World War soldier, had enlisted shortly after war had been declared. Now, like Willersdorf, a trained parachutist, he had fought in Africa, where he had been wounded, and New Guinea, where he had been recruited by SRD. Completely won over by the force of Lyon's personality, Campbell had described him as 'the most wonderful man he had ever met . . . not only did he appear to *know* everything but he could do everything associated with the job for which they were trained — perfectly'. Before leaving on the mission Campbell had also confided that, although he could reveal nothing about what he was doing, he could say with complete confidence that Lyon was 'a leader for whom every one of them would be willing to die'.[42]

Campbell's fellow corporal, Ron Fletcher, had entered the world of Special Operations in a slightly less orthodox fashion. Trained as an actor in England, the adventurous Irishman had joined the merchant marine to see the world. On arrival in Australia he had jumped ship and had returned to his former profession before joining the AIF in late December 1941. The following August he had volunteered for, and was transferred to, the Northern Australia Observer Unit, commonly known as the 'Nackeroos'.

A tougher bunch of men would have been hard to find. The five hundred-strong Nackeroos had been hand picked to patrol the northern coastline of the continent on horseback, with orders to watch for signs of Japanese activity and remain behind to infiltrate enemy lines if an invasion took place. Forced, by erratic supply lines, to live off the land and survive in locations described by Fletcher's CO as 'the arsehole of the world', the troops had become very self reliant in time, tending to resemble bushmen rather than regular soldiers. By late 1943, when it was evident that the Japanese were no longer a threat to the area, the Nackeroos were disbanded. It was unfortunate that such a group of practical and hardened individuals were not kept as a specialised commando unit. When Fletcher was assigned to Rimau in June 1944, such was his versatility and ingenuity that Ivan Lyon would have been only too pleased to recruit the Nackeroos en masse.[43]

The last two on the solely operational side of the expedition were a pair of Lance Corporals by the name of Hardy and Pace. In September 1942 Jack Hardy had joined the army only to find that his job was the same as that in civvy street — driving lorries. Evidently wishing to undertake more adrenalin-producing activities and desperate to get into the war before it finished, Hardy had trained as a parachutist and joined SRD. Like his colleague Hugo Pace, he was a natural for the job.[44]

Pace was a man with an exotic background. Of French-Egyptian parentage, he came from Port Said. A yen for adventure had lured him first to the French Foreign Legion and then, on the urging of his father, who had met many Australian diggers during the First World War, to a clerical job on a station in Queensland, where he joined the AIF in March 1941. Within six months he had embarked upon a ship bound for the land of his birth, before being transferred to New Guinea, where he was wounded in action. After being evacuated, he returned to New Guinea, was detached for special duty and finally enrolled into the ranks of SRD on the same day as Campbell. Of above average height and rather spare build, the olive-skinned, dark-eyed Pace was noted for his smart appearance, his yarns about his life with the Legionnaires and his exceptional fitness. Always good for a sixteen kilometre run or a 1600 metre swim before breakfast, it was obvious that a bullet which had passed through his hip during his stint with the Foreign Legion had not affected him in the slightest.[45]

Of the seven specialist members of the team, one of whom was also an SB operator, by far the most important was Gilbert Islander Bruno Reymond, navigator and ship's captain. Although Lieutenant Richard Cox (one of those who had escaped with Lyon on *Sederhana Djohanes*) had arrived with Riggs and Ross on August 7 to take up the post, he had proved to be unsuitable, leaving Lyon with no alternative but urgently to seek a replacement. Reymond's late arrival at Careening Bay Camp had been a real shock to his system. With only five days to go before Rimau's departure, he had been put through a two-month folboat and training course in four days. Every morning at 8 o'clock, the thirty-year-old naval lieutenant had been dragged off by Lieutenant Walter Carey, brother of Sam Carey of Townsville raid notoriety, to be returned eighteen weary hours later at 2 am. Nevertheless, Carey's tactics had worked and by the end of the period, which Reymond, who was used to his creature comforts, endured with good humour and great stoicism, he was pronounced fit. With an extensive maritime background, dark, part-islander looks that would need no enhancement to effect a disguise, and intimate knowledge of the seas to the north of Australia, Reymond must have been an answer to Lyon's prayers.[46]

So too must have been Port Pirie's talented son, Warrant Officer Alf Warren, whose resourcefulness, so admired by Commander Marsham, had made him indispensible to the operation. He was joined by another technical wizard, twenty-one-year-old Sergeant Colin Cameron, who, prior to joining the army, had been employed at an electricity power station in Victoria. Standing well over 180 centimetres tall and weighing about seventy-six kilograms, the sportsloving Cameron had been so taken with army life that he intended to pursue a military career after the war.[47]

Fellow Victorian and SB operator/stores expert Sergeant David Peter Gooley, a former bootmaker from the town of Rushmore, had been earmarked for Rimau in May, when it had still been Hornbill. Before joining SRD, Gooley, like Doug Warne, had been at Queensland's Canungra Jungle Training Camp, where he was an infantry instructor. Finding the job rather too tame for his liking, he had tried for almost two years to be transferred to something more positive in a war that was threatening to pass him by. His chance came when he was recruited by SRD in June 1944. The following month, Gooley had been ordered to travel from Fraser Island to the west along with Fletcher and Warne. Gooley was a 'good bloke' but, being a serious-minded fellow, was found by some to be a little hard to get along with. Aged twenty-six and deeply religious, he took a dim view of the vivid recounting of female conquests and luridly bawdy jokes. When the tales of his team mates became too much he would turn his fiancée's photograph face down on the blankets, remarking, 'I don't think you should hear this, dear'.[48]

The two remaining specialists were both signallers from Western Australia. Eighteen months after war had broken out, Corporal Colin Craft had thrown in his schoolteaching job and enlisted, only to find that his exciting career in the army consisted of mowing down grass instead of the enemy. Fed up with constantly reducing the height of lushly green lawns, Craft had jumped at the chance of joining a 'different and dangerous outfit'. Within six months of transferring to SRD's Z Special Unit in November 1943, he had added parachuting to his list of accomplishments. A mean fiddler, he was a popular figure around the camp, playing well-known tunes on his rather battered violin, from which he was inseparable.[49]

Clair Mackie Stewart was senior to Craft in years, if not in rank — he and Davidson were the old men of the group. By rights, thirty-five-year-old Stewart should not even have been in the armed services. His age, married status and his reserved occupation as ganger with the WA Railways were enough to ensure that he was kept out of the war had Stewart not marched off the railway track and into the Royal Australian Air Force recruiting office. When rejected by the boys in blue because of less than perfect eyesight, he tried the army, which was able to accommodate him, reading glasses and all. Once in the AIF, Stewart trained as a signaller, a field in which he excelled. Such was his proficiency that SRD ignored his bespectacled status, recruiting him on 19 November 1943, the same day as that other tough character, Douglas Warne. After training as a parachutist with Craft, Campbell and Pace, he was sent to Careening Bay, where he arrived for training on July 31. Hardened by years of outdoor manual labour and with neck muscles that threatened to burst his collar buttons, Stewart was in superb physical condition. His signalling skills, his steadiness, his toughness and his maturity made him an excellent addition to the Rimau team.[50]

The chosen twenty-two were to be accompanied to Merapas by two more officers — Major Chapman, the SOE engineer from Baker Street, and Walter Carey, the instructor who had pummelled Bruno Reymond into shape in record time. In their role as 'Conducting Officers', they were to report on phase one, familiarise themselves with Base A for the pickup, photograph the seized junk, take charge of any papers found on it and act as escorts for the captured crew.[51]

Walter Carey had been raised on a small, poverty-ridden farm outside Sydney. At the age of twenty-three, a love of adventure and a cavalier attitude to life had led him first to New Guinea and then, when war erupted, to China in a vain attempt to organise guerilla groups as a member of Mission 204. Recruited by SRD for special operations, he was already the veteran of one mission before he arrived at Careening Bay to join Rimau. Known as 'Massa' because of his colourful reminiscences of life in New Guinea, Carey was a popular figure. Quite tall, with a strong but wiry build, the brown-eyed Lieutenant was filled with the blarney that sets the Irish apart. His capacity to tell the most outrageous tales with a deadly serious expression and such conviction that he was believed by everyone was legendary. So, too, was his dry humour, which gave him perhaps his most admirable trait — the ability to see the funny side of everything, even in adversity.[52] It was a talent which Lyon now had reason to covet, for, just as it seemed that everything was at last falling into place, a bombshell of monumental proportions hit. Someone had talked.

It was the age-old problem — loose talk by a person who should have known better. A Royal Naval Intelligence Officer attached to SRD, one Commander Geoffrey Branson, had managed to spill the beans not once, but twice. Privy to the fact that Rimau was about to leave, he had waltzed up to Commander Marsham, who was standing on the dock alongside *Porpoise*, and said to the astounded submarine captain, 'I hear you are off to Singapore'. Marsham, who was in an already tense state and war-weary from too many patrols, went immediately to his commanding officer, Captain Shadwell of the Eighth Submarine Flotilla. When it was discovered that there had been a further breach of security, Shadwell announced that Rimau would have to be cancelled.[53]

This second breach was perhaps potentially more serious. In answer to a question about Ivan Lyon, put to him by an American lady whom he had met at Perth's Peppermint Grove Hotel, Branson had told her everything, including the fact that Rimau's target was Singapore. When the woman, who worked for Admiral Christie, informed her boss, the panic was on. Both Shadwell and Marsham wanted to forget the entire operation, but Lyon argued that since Branson's position at Naval Intelligence required him to know about Rimau his comment to Marsham was not nearly as serious as it appeared. He was also convinced that the information given to the American had gone no further than Admiral Christie. Lyon's persuasive debate won the day and in any case he held the trump card — access to a 'hot line' to London. On September 6, with 'considerable misgivings', Shadwell, acting on behalf of Mountbatten and the Commander-in-Chief of the Eastern Fleet, gave his approval for the operation. Had he known that a third breach, which would eventually see Branson transferred, would come to light shortly after Rimau had left, he would have had no hesitation in rescinding his reluctant consent.[54]

The news of the security breaches had not diverted Lyon from his countdown timetable. Such was his confidence, he had confirmed on September 5, while the security question was still unresolved, that a trial run would proceed as planned. That night the stores were taken off the submarine in folding engineer's boats, ferried to the shore and hidden in the scrub — an exercise which took two and a half hours, the actual unloading from the sub accounting for a mere twenty minutes. The next two nights were spent rehearsing the offloading of the SBs and junk stores, and in carrying out a simulated limpet-attack on HMAS *Adelaide*.[55]

With all phases of the dress rehearsal an outstanding success, Lyon announced that they were ready to leave. This was the signal for last-minute letter writing and for Corporal Stewart, the only one who lived nearby, to slip away and see his wife and bid a farewell to his peacefully sleeping children. In faraway Queensland, the family of Andrew Huston received the message that he was going on a lengthy training exercise but expected everything to be organised for his twenty-first birthday celebrations, which fell on Christmas Day.[56]

On September 9, Lyon and Chapman carefully discussed with Marsham and Shadwell the 'Fremantle Submarine Operational Order No. 1' — a document of vital importance which set out the timetable and the procedures that the submarine was to follow, including the pickup drill. Marsham, perhaps believing that such a disclosure might persuade Lyon to change his mind, announced that, in view of the security breach, the submarine might not be able to pick them up. Lyon simply replied, 'In that case, we shall find some other method of getting back'. Such was his air of quiet confidence that Shadwell, who was watching this exchange, never doubted for a moment that he would do it.[57]

That night, after all the operational stores had been loaded, there was a party. And what a party it was! In a large marquee, overflowing with good food and good cheer, were all the Rimau team, the crews of *Porpoise* and visiting submarine *Sea Wolf,* the staff of the nearby Garden Island Naval Base and, not unnaturally, the girls from the searchlight battery. After the evening had progressed to the lively stage, a young naval lieutenant produced his white handkerchief, onto which, with the aid of an indelible pencil moistened by frequent dips in the puddles of beer that were now appearing on the festive tables, Lyon's tigers wrote their names for posterity. The following morning, with instructions from Rimau's Romeos to their shore-based mates to 'look after the girls on the hill', the men, now recovered from the frivolity of the previous night, boarded the submarine and stowed their gear.[58]

At 12.20 in the afternoon of September 11,[59] the great grey submarine slipped silently and without fanfare from her mooring to head up Cockburn Sound. Within her massive iron hull were twenty-two men hellbent on serving King and Country. Idealists all, they were unaware that Operation Rimau was simply the means to a political end. It was as well that they could not read the thoughts of Commander Marsham, already beset by doubts and plagued by grave misgivings, as he steered his submarine towards the open sea.

The entire operation reminded him of a similar raid, long ago, when a swashbuckling Sir Francis Drake, under the auspices of Admiral Hawkins, had cheekily sneaked into Cadiz harbour and, to the eternal embarrassment of the then mighty and hitherto invincible Spanish navy, set fire to the Spanish Fleet. Drake's subsequent humiliating defeat of the Armada, his constant raids upon the enemy's shores, his bravery, seamanship and coolheadedness ensured that he had earned a unique place in British history.

But the submarine commander was a seasoned warrior, an old campaigner grown cautious with the acquisition of age and experience, who knew that in this war such coups required more than raw courage and great daring. They needed an element of luck, a plan that could not go wrong and a foolproof backup system. Recalling the dramas, the hitches, the almost insurmountable problems that had frequently threatened to bring Operation Rimau to its knees, Marsham recorded that:

the whole business smacks of the days of Drake and Hawkins. An ambitious, dare-devil scheme proposed by a band of very gallant gentlemen; support and backing from high places and senior officers afloat [but hopelessly marred by] muddle and inefficiency [and by] self seeking and obstruction from those locally responsible for the supply and transport of stores and equipment.[60]

They were words that were to haunt him for the rest of his life.

Chapter 9
A Spot of Pirating

After such an inauspicious start, the six-day passage up the West Australian coast to the Java Sea was entirely uneventful. Apart from a junk, which came into sight as the submarine crossed the northern narrows, they saw nothing of interest as the vessel passed through the Lombok Strait. There was no sign of the large patrol boat that had so terrified Jaywick the year before, and indeed no evidence of any enemy activity whatever until they neared the Kangean Islands — the small island group that marked the point at which all those going in the direction of Singapore turned to the west. Even then, it was only a few aircraft flying overhead from the direction of Soerabaya, a town lying to the south-west on the long, narrow island of Java.[1]

If Lyon thought about this rather ramshackle, grubby little settlement at all, it would merely have been in passing, his attention drawn to its existence only by the close proximity of the aeroplanes. He had no way of knowing that, not one hundred and sixty kilometres away, rotting in the sandy soil of a carelessly filled, unmarked mass grave, lay the mortal remains of William Roy Reynolds.

When Bill Reynolds had been captured at Laoet the previous November, he had been taken 160 kilometres north to Balikpapan, where he was incarcerated in the Sentosa Barracks, a small building that was doing duty as a gaol. On 10 February 1944, he added to the already substantial scratchings on a door jamb the information that he was being taken to Soerabaya, where, for the next six months, he was allowed no contact with other prisoners because of his ability to speak Malay. Indeed, such was his fluency in the language that some of the Japanese guards believed that he was part Malay.

On August 8 the Japanese commander decided to dispose of a number of prisoners, including Reynolds. At 8 o'clock that morning, without any trial whatever, Reynolds was hustled from his cell and placed in a truck with several Indonesian inmates. Half an hour later they, and a second truck carrying a detachment of guards, arrived at the execution ground, which was about two hundred metres from the Eastern Entrance Fort of the Harbour and known to the Japanese as the Higashiguchi Battery.

Upon arrival the prisoners, who were handcuffed and blindfolded, squatted down in front of a hut to await a small bus carrying three more European prisoners, an interpreter and three guards. As an execution usually aroused a great deal of interest there was, besides those who had been ordered to attend, quite a substantial gallery. Among the fifty or so in attendance was Lieutenant Yoshimoto, who had given the order to execute the prisoners; his assistant commanding officer Ensign Okada, who had accompanied Reynolds from prison to the fort; the legal officer representing the court which had sentenced the Indonesians; interpreter Senuma; Warrant Officer Ikeda; five armed soldiers; officers from the Naval Base and a mish-mash of officers, NCOs and troops who were passing through Soerabaya and who had come to view the proceedings. To one side, ready and waiting, was a pit about two metres wide and two metres deep.

After Senuma had announced the death sentence to the victims in Malay, all but one of those who understood the language were in a state of near collapse. Numbed by the shock, the first group of Indonesians squatted meekly while volunteers from the army rank and file, led by Warrant Officer Ikeda, cut off their heads.

It was neither a clean nor a swift execution. The swordsman assigned to the third or fourth prisoner botched the job, only partially decapitating his victim. Annoyed by this inept display, Lieutenant Yoshimoto ordered Yamashita, a clerk attached to the Naval Unit, to deliver the coup de grâce with a spear that was resting against the wall of the hut.

The remaining seven prisoners were spared this form of execution, but for entirely different reasons. The last three Indonesians, scared witless by the prolonged nature of the decapitations and the hideous attempts to spear their comrade, were in such a state that they were now incapable of either standing or squatting. Unable to carry out the beheadings without reducing the entire proceedings to an even more bizarre spectacle, the Japanese were forced to shoot them.

This left the three Europeans and Reynolds, whose subsequent act of defiance would be long remembered by the Japanese. Dressed in shirt and pants, his beard long from his lengthy imprisonment, the tall Australian stood rigidly at attention, his bearing making it abundantly clear that he, uncowed and unbroken after months of confinement, was not going to accommodate the enemy. Watched by an interested gallery, which had already witnessed the bungled executions, the shooting of the Indonesians and the resulting loss of face by the executioners, Lieutenant Yoshimoto assessed the situation.

Clearly, here was a prisoner who would not concede an inch — a man so completely fearless and iron willed that he would never bend before his captors, who, when standing fully upright, scarcely reached his chest. Unable to do anything else, Yoshimoto called a detachment of six guards to one side and gave them fresh orders. A few minutes later they raised their rifles and took aim. The steadfast figure of William Roy Reynolds, defiant and unyielding to the end, crumpled only when the volley of shots forced the life from his body.[2]

However, as it would be forty-five years before information about Reynolds's gallant stand would be discovered, his young friend Lyon was unaware of his fate as *Porpoise* glided on towards the Carrimata Straits.[3] Once through the straits quite a number of junks were sighted, but not, Davidson and Lyon noted, as many as the previous year. When *Porpoise*, now travelling on the surface, approached one in the same manner as an enemy submarine by crossing its bows, the junk's crew gave a useful demonstration of the local boat drill. Up went the Port Registration of Singapore Flag (a white pennant with grey lines, a red star and oriental characters), and the more familiar Japanese ensign, confirming that the flags they had brought with them, sewn by the dextrous Mrs Manderson, were correct and that their intelligence on the behaviour of Japanese submarines had been spot on. Davidson took a long hard look at the junk, its rigging, its cargo and its crew before making suitable notes and sketches in his diary for the benefit of Allied intelligence.[4]

After spending a couple of anxious days dogged by an oil leak that threatened to betray their presence, *Porpoise* finally reached the island of Merapas on the afternoon of September 23, right on schedule. While the submarine circled just below the surface, Lyon and Davidson carried out a periscope reconnaissance which revealed that, apart from two small huts, a couple of local boats and a man wandering along the western shore, the island appeared to be deserted. With the reconnaissance completed, *Porpoise* headed out to sea. It was decided that as soon as it was dark, two men would be dropped off for a more detailed investigation.[5]

At 6.45 pm, to Commander Marsham's great disappointment, he spied an 8000 tonne tanker, just ripe for his torpedoes. As the proximity of Merapas precluded any attack he informed Lyon, tongue in cheek, that before the mission had even begun, Rimau's score was now eight thousand tonnes in the red.[6]

Within an hour they were back at Merapas and were ready to surface off the northern coastline. Since no one had taken into consideration that the Australian-made recce folboat, unlike its English counterpart, could not fit through the hatch erected, its launching took rather longer than Marsham would have wished. After passing out the package, the hatch was slammed tight, leaving Davidson and his partner Stewart, selected because of his signalling abilities, alone on the hull to erect the boat. Twenty minutes later, the submarine dived and the pair paddled off, knowing that they had twenty-four hours to carry out their task before the submarine returned.[7]

An hour and a half later, hampered by the strong rip tides, they had still not reached the shore. With some difficulty they eventually edged the boat towards the northern coast, which, although rocky with a considerable swell, was a good deal better than the windy western side with breakers pounding both its beaches. After slipping and sliding across the glassy black boulders they slung their hammocks between a couple of dead trees that had toppled against each other in a type of wigwam arrangement. To their suprise they found that, tired as they were, sleep eluded them, the transition from the close quarters of the submarine to the 'scented peace of the island' being far too abrupt. Davidson was so struck by the aromatic difference between the two that he felt compelled to write, 'The scent of the flowering trees and lily palms was more delicate than any scent that ever came out of Paris. A sigh of welcome'. When daylight came he was forced to turn to more practical matters. Finding that the area in the vicinity of the Hammock Tree, as Davidson named their resting place, was uninhabited, they began their detailed exploration, moving in a clockwise direction from their starting point, midway along the northern side.[8]

The three-sided island, eight kilometres from the neighbouring island of Mapor, was roughly in the shape of the head and neck of a greyhound — the rugged northern side representing the flat nose and forehead of the animal, the eastern edge the back of its neck, and the long curving westerly side the underjaw and throat. The northern shore, which rose steeply from the rocks at the base of the Hammock Tree, was dubbed Invasion Coast. The rocky bump that could be the greyhound's ear was christened Oyster Point, while the land crabs that scuttled behind the easterly beaches gave their name to the bay. There were three beaches along this side — one of sand, one of coral and the remaining a mixture of the two. On the southern most point of this shoreline the rocks returned, forming a point that was named in honour of Corporal Stewart. Behind Stewart Point was a banana plantation and nearby, on the first of the westerly beaches, an uninhabited dwelling. This western coast, the longest side of the island, was also the gentlest and easiest to approach. For this reason, the inhabitants had planted quite a large coconut grove and built two huts, in front of which were moored the small fishing koleks that Davidson and Lyon had seen through the submarine's periscope. As the mooring stakes appeared to be a permanent fixture inside a small sheltered reef, Davidson named it Kolek Bay. Beyond the dwellings was a large flat depression, filled with tussock grass and very thick undergrowth completely blanketed by creepers. It seemed to be an old swamp, so choked with vegetation that it was no longer marshy, but still providing fresh water fed by a now underground stream. As it was quite free of mosquitoes and was an ideal place in which to hide, Davidson named it Cache Swamp.

Just past Cache Swamp was another small coral beach, behind which grew wild sago — an excellent place to secrete folboats. Further around from the coral beach the rocks returned, forming the third point on the island, now named Punai Point. Once around Punai Point, the circumnavigation of the island was almost complete. Between Punai Point and the Hammock Tree they saw, sitting near a large overhanging tree, a kingfisher, which immediately prompted the name 'Kingfisher's Rest'.

In contrast to the flat, more open western section behind Kolek Bay, the interior of the island was of much higher ground, with the most elevated point, on the northern side, being about ninety metres above sea level. From this point, the ridge shelved gently towards Punai Point in a westerly direction, while a long arm ran the full length of the easterly side. Except for a cleared area that was an old coconut grove, the inland was covered in dense vegetation ranging from forest to jungle to thickly growing palms of various kinds. On the long ridge behind Land Crab Bay was an overgrown clearing that provided excellent cover, while further towards the banana plantation near Stewart Point the forest thinned to scattered tall timber. Between this more sparsely forested area and the beaches along the Bay was a veritable Garden of Eden. Although useless for permanent cover as it was liable to be visited, it was a gourmet's delight, filled with untended coconut, jackfruit, betel nut, banana and papaya trees and inhabited only by flying foxes.

At the summit of the hill, between the Hammock Tree and the coconut plantation, they saw a stumpy-tailed Malayan wild cat, which gave rise to the rather unimaginative Wild Cat Hill. Not far from here, overlooking Cache Swamp and Kolek Bay, was the disused coconut grove, which Davidson believed would make an excellent night camp.[9]

By the time nightfall came, the pair had completed their exhaustive assessment of the island. Shortly after 7.30 they picked up the silhouette of *Porpoise* as she surfaced off the Invasion Coast and twenty minutes later, smelling strongly of the jungle, were reporting their discoveries to Lyon. On learning that the locals were in residence, he amended the plan. To preclude the possibility of the Malays stumbling upon the stores in the three weeks until Rimau returned, Conducting Officer Walter Carey, armed with a silent Sten and a pistol, volunteered to remain behind and watch over them.[10]

This being settled, Sargent, Gooley, Campbell, Craft, Fletcher and Warne swung into action to erect the folding engineer's boats, which were to ferry the stores to the shore. For easy transportation, these boats, which were so heavy that they needed ten men to lift and six to paddle them, had been folded flat and secured to the hull of the submarine. Leaving everyone else inside the vessel, the six men stood on the heavy wooden base and erected the boat around themselves. The submarine then submerged, allowing the boat to drift off. Once afloat, the boat crew rowed back to the submarine (which had meantime resurfaced), tied up the boat and repeated the procedure with the second boat. The rest of the team then emerged from *Porpoise* to begin the task of unloading the stores from the J containers.[11]

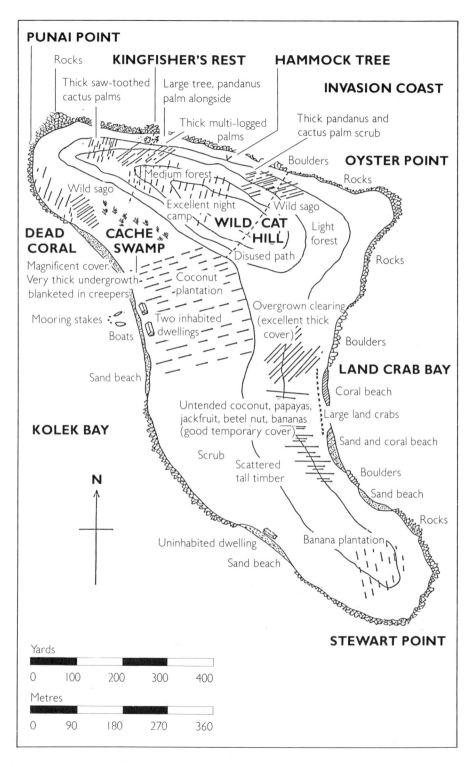

Map V. Merapas Island, from the original sketch by Donald Davidson.

Although they moved without fuss and worked efficiently, the men did not move fast enough in the opinion of, and to the great annoyance of, a very nervous Commander Marsham. Used to having his submariners move at the double when the submarine was on the surface, the Rimau men's 'leisurely manner of emerging from the conning tower' and 'sloping away to their appointed places' drove Marsham into an 'absolute frenzy'. This anger, induced by a feeling of vulnerability which the non-submariners apparently failed to comprehend, was heightened when he learned that the second boat had a hole in it, caused by friction during transit. Disturbed that the stores would take twice as long to move, he was greatly relieved when the hole was successfully plugged with cotton waste. The unexpected bonus of the J container doors being extremely easy to open calmed him down somewhat, since he had expected that the deep-sea pressure would have clamped them down tightly, making a further delay. However, as the cool Fremantle air inside them had expanded in the tropical heat, they popped open without any difficulty at all.[12]

A scant thirty-eight minutes after the unloading had begun, *Porpoise* had towed the boats to within four hundred metres of Kingfisher's Rest. Assisted by the tide, sixteen men in the less heavily laden boat then paddled towards the shore, towing the second boat, which held the bulk of the stores and the other three men. As Davidson had estimated that two hours would be needed to unload and hide the supplies, Marsham decided to wait close by on the surface instead of putting to sea to recharge the submarine's batteries. In case *Porpoise* suddenly had to retreat, leaving the working party behind on the island, Lyon, Ingleton, Reymond and Falls stayed on board, along with Chapman. If necessary they could go and find the junk and then return to collect the others when the coast was clear.[13]

This decision was unfortunate for two reasons. Firstly, the labour force for unloading the stores was now cut by about twenty per cent. Secondly, since Carey was to remain on Merapas, the conducting officer to do the pickup after the raid would have to be Chapman, who was still on the submarine. Not having landed, he was, and would remain, completely unfamiliar with the layout of the island.

The rendezvous arrangements for the returning raiders, as well as the rescue pickup, had been discussed before Carey left *Porpoise*. Starting on the night of October 15, the first date that the raiders could be expected to return, he was to go each evening to the Hammock Tree, sling his hammock and wait there until dawn. As the trees were dead, the distinctive shape of their trunks showed up starkly in the darkness, while a dark hammock, slung against an equally dark background, was invisible.

The returning raiders were to approach Merapas with caution. Although Kolek Bay was the easiest access, it was rejected as its proximity to Cache Swamp could put their hiding place at risk. The recommended route was by way of Land Crab Bay, whose beaches provided a safe landing place in all but an easterly wind. While the rest hid in the undergrowth, one of each party was to make a reconnaissance of the Hammock Tree. If Carey were there, all would be well. If not, they would know immediately that the base had been compromised.[14]

Exactly the same procedure was to be followed for the pickup. On the night of November 7, the first pickup date, and, if necessary, for the next thirty nights, until the submarine returned, a watch would be kept at the tree for the rescue party — Corporal Ron Croton, who had trained with the Rimau team and knew them well, and Chapman. It was likely that long before Croton and Chapman reached the tree from Land Crab Bay, the lookout would see them, since Davidson and Stewart spotted *Porpoise* as soon as it had resurfaced. If no one was waiting between the hours of dusk and dawn, Chapman would know that something had happened to all of them, including Carey.[15]

The first problem arising from the decision to split the party was now being felt. Not only was the working party under strength, but the movement of the stores across the slippery black boulders in the dark was proving to be extraordinarily difficult. After the containers and bags had been hauled laboriously out of the boats and across the nine metres of rocks to Kingfisher's Rest, they were secreted inside a stilt-legged palm thicket before being humped over the hill to the undergrowth of Cache Swamp. The minutes ticked by. Two hours came and went, then three, and still they were nowhere near finished.[16]

Out on the water, with the submarine's batteries running periously low, Marsham was becoming very toey. Unable to see any sign of the working party, he was beginning to wonder whether they might have all been washed away by the tide.[17] At one minute past midnight he had had enough. In desperation, since it had not been considered necessary to make any signal arrangements, he flashed a red torch in the hope of attracting their attention. Davidson, to whom the submarine had been in plain view for the entire time, took the signal to mean 'hurry up' and, much to Marsham's relief, all, apart from Carey, returned to *Porpoise* within thirty minutes. On the way, the recce folboat and one of the engineer's boats, which were impossible to restow, were sunk in deep water. On reaching the submarine the remaining boat was also sunk.[18]

Davidson was not happy to return. With the work only half completed, Carey faced a long hard job over the next three days, moving the stores from the palm thicket and into permanent cover on the other side of the island. Yet the task was not formidable enough to demand that they all return the next night. Although uneasy, Davidson's only consolation was that, for the time being, the stores were reasonably well hidden and that Carey would be fastidious in obliterating all tracks that might betray their presence. For this reason, a small rake had been included in the Base A stores list.[19]

While Carey was left to his lonely vigil, *Porpoise* headed out to sea to recharge her batteries and plot a course for Pedjantan Island, 270 kilometres away. At 3 o'clock that afternoon, twenty-six kilometres off the coast, they dived and approached at high speed so that a periscope reconnaissance of the sheltered northern side could be completed before dark.[20]

As he took his turn at the periscope, Davidson was ecstatic. Beyond the sandy beaches with their safe anchorages, the thick, jungle-covered land rose steeply, providing cover for hundreds of men. Better still, the island appeared to be completely uninhabited. The only sign of life was a group of carefree monkeys gambolling upon the beach. Completely satisfied that Pedjantan was ideal for phase two of the operation, Rimau set off to do a spot of pirating.[21]

Like taxis in wet weather and buses at peak hour, there was now not a junk to be seen. For the next two days, September 26 and 27, they cruised the shipping routes to the south and east of Pedjantan without sighting a single vessel. In desperation they decided on the second day to prevail upon the gods to help them. A small joss, intricately carved from a stick of carbon by Chapman, was brought forth. The torso was similar to a black magic ju-ju idol, while the lower half was fashioned into the shape of a spiral, designed to give it momentum when in the water. A Battle of Britain scarf, Lyon's charm, was wound around its neck and a monocle, Davidson's recognised totem, was placed to its eye while it was gyrated through 360 degrees. With great ceremony, each officer placed a finger on its head and chanted, 'Find me a junk. Get me a junk. Wichety Wichety. Bring me a junk'. They then cast it into the deep with a final twist to help it on its important and magical journey.

The idol took quite some time to carry out its job. Perhaps the combination of frightfully English scarf and eye piece, African voodoo-type carving and the chanting of an Australian Aboriginal word for a common grub (a little touch that can safely be attributed to Davidson), thoroughly confused it, although Davidson's contention was that it was either a case of extreme laziness or an inability to comprehend English. Whatever the reason, it was not until 9.20 the following morning, when prowling the Borneo coast near the Pontianak River, that they finally sighted two sails, some distance apart. *Porpoise* dived and tracked the one to the east. Conditions were not good for observation as there was considerable haze and the sea, which was the colour of tea, was fouled by driftwood and scum. Eventually, persistent squinting through the periscope revealed that it was a handsome Bughis prahu, but, being about one hundred tonnes, it was too large for Rimau's requirements. When they altered course to follow the second, it had disappeared.[22]

About an hour later, eleven kilometres from the Pontianak Roads, they resurfaced and located their quarry, only to see it steer towards the shore. Intending to sail towards Pulau Laut, Marsham turned south, but before they had travelled very far they spied a two-masted junk at anchor. As *Porpoise* dived and closed upon the hapless target, the vessel chose that very moment to raise its anchor and get under way, leading Marsham to believe that the periscope had been spotted. At 2 o'clock, having given chase for well over an hour, the submarine surfaced alongside the junk off an island named Padang Tikar. Meeting no resistance from the rather startled crew, who actually threw mooring lines to *Porpoise*, Lyon, Davidson, Ingleton, Warren, Cameron, Ross and Page went on board, while an ever anxious Marsham, his submarine again vulnerable upon the surface in sight of the enemy coastline, counted off the seconds.[23] Thirteen minutes later the successfully pirated vessel was sailing for Pedjantan.[24]

Marsham, who had probably envisioned that the ship would be in the style of a Chinese junk, thought it an appalling choice. Lyon and Davidson, who had seen many such vessels before the war and also, like all the Jaywick men, had encountered similar craft the previous year, were of a completely different opinion. Unlike the rather cumbersome profile of the Chinese-designed junks, the tonkans or prahus of Indonesia were extremely streamlined. Made without formal plans, they were built along the same lines that the country's skilled craftsmen had followed for centuries. With their raked timber hulls either oiled or painted white, the untrained eye could be excused for assuming that they were of European origin. This prahu, with a white stripe above its brown oiled hull, white-painted deckhouse, two masts and concertina-type sails was quite unremarkable and a perfect example of many of the small locally built vessels that plied the waters of Malaya and Indonesia.[25]

The ship that Lyon and Davidson had chosen was a forty tonne vessel from Ketapang, whose name — *Mustika* — was probably a corruption by the English tongue of Masa Tiga, a small island near Pontianak. Crewed by eight Malays under the control of owner/skipper Mohamed Juni Bin Haji Abdullah, *Mustika* now traded between her home port of Ketapang, where all the crew lived, and Pontianak. The Malays, who were not particularly worried that they had been shanghaied, told Bobby Ross that life had become difficult under Japanese rule. They were generally ill treated and were forced to bow to the conquerers in the streets, the penalty for failing to do so being a smart whack on the head. Large numbers of their people had been thrown into prison, many of the chiefs and rajas killed, and the sultanates completely disrupted. Trade, too, had suffered. Before the war, *Mustika* had regularly carried timber to Java and returned with a load of sugar to Pontianak. With lack of food forcing the people to grow rice on every bit of available land, rubber and sugar production had all but ceased and trading prahus had been reduced to carrying cargoes of wood. The vessel had just offloaded a consignment of roofing timbers at Pontianak and was returning empty to Ketapang when *Porpoise* intercepted her.[26]

The reason for the initial co-operation, when *Porpoise* suddenly appeared, was simple. Like the junk crew of a few days previously, *Mustika* had assumed that the submarine was Japanese. It was not until the Malays sighted the berets and white skins of the boarding party that they realised their error. They were not perturbed by this, or by the fact that they were to go to Australia. Indeed, had they not been concerned that their families would be worried when *Mustika* failed to return, they would have been perfectly content.[27]

The Rimau men found that the eighteen metre prahu sailed extremely well, reaching Pedjantan well ahead of the submarine. While *Mustika* anchored in a cove, *Porpoise* carried out a complete periscope reconnaissance before disappearing out to sea under cover of darkness to recharge her batteries.[28]

When Marsham returned shortly after midnight to unload six SBs and half the stores he learned that the purchase for the derrick, the responsibility of Major Ingleton, had been mislaid. Having taken the trouble to arrive with four SBs already on the casing in order to keep the timing tight, he was extremely angry. When the derrick problem was overcome by some innovative improvisation, he was further infuriated to discover that there would be more delays — the SBs could not be loaded through the prahu's hatch using the equipment they had brought with them. Pointing out in no uncertain terms that the Rimau men could have spent the waiting hours enlarging the hatch, thereby solving the problem, the submarine commander completely lost his temper. Fortunately for his blood pressure and all those who were on the receiving end of his rather violent outburst, someone came up with an alternative solution. After some more improvisation, seven SBs, one more than planned, were successfully stowed below *Mustika*'s decks. Meanwhile, Marsham managed to simmer down, later apologising for his hot-headed remarks and conceding that one hour and thirty-six minutes was not such a bad unloading time after all. With that, he took his submarine out to sea until after 7 o'clock that evening.[29]

While *Porpoise* was away, those on the prahu had enjoyed a carefree day. After a revitalising sleep on the open deck, luxuriating in the cool, fresh air of the tropical night — a welcome change after the hot stuffiness of the submarine — they organised the stowage of the equipment, before sending Lyon, Chapman, Page, Stewart and four of the Malays ashore to explore. On a small coral spit that extended out beyond the sandy beach, they found the remnants of a long-abandoned rail line. Apparently built around the turn of the century, it had been used to transport copra from a large, old and now very overgrown coconut plantation that stretched from the beach towards the mountainous, jungle-covered interior. While Lyon and Page followed the track inland, Chapman organised the Malays to cut coconuts, leaving himself and Stewart free to explore the beaches on either side of a small prominence, dubbed

Crab Rock. In contrast to the sea, with its brilliantly coloured fish that had leapt from the water and the stingrays that had glided away as the boat had neared the shore, the beach itself, apart from some bales of rubber and a large quantity of old timber, held nothing of interest.

Chapman and Stewart, their beach recce completed, turned inland, finding that the rail track, after passing through the plantation, wound in easy stages up a hill. Meeting up with Page and Lyon, the consensus was that Pedjantan Island, with its tinkling mountain stream, its abundant shellfish and luscious tropical fruit, was about as close to paradise as they were ever likely to come. After gathering up the large quantity of coconuts that the obliging Malays had collected, they returned to *Mustika* to allow the remainder of the party ashore for some recreation and to collect more coconuts. With memories of Marsham's peppery outburst still fresh, the rest of them made a concentrated effort to avoid any similar displays of temper when he returned that night by overhauling the derrick and enlarging the hatch.[30]

It was a prudent move. When the submarine drew up alongside, four of the SBs again lined up on the casing in readiness, the transfer was completed with a minimum of fuss and the unpleasantness of the previous night was not repeated. The rest of the J stores were loaded into the last remaining boat, which Marsham, anxious to avoid hanging around for any longer than necessary, had floated off in advance. By 10 o'clock, less than two hours after *Porpoise* had arrived, everything was stowed on *Mustika*, including 125 loaves of bread, baked by the submarine's chef as a parting gift. In return, Rimau presented the sub's crew with a large number of coconuts.[31]

While the stores were being transferred, Lyon, Ross and Davidson, all of whom spoke Malay, had interrogated the Malay crew thoroughly, obtaining a great deal of information about shipping routes and sailing regulations in the Singapore area. As this was a coastal trip, *Mustika* carried none of her signal flags, which were held by the Japanese authorities in Pontianak. The captain told the officers that if a Japanese patrol vessel approached it was imperative to follow three rules — make sure that there were no more than three men on deck, display no flags or signals and keep on sailing. After assuring Lyon that, with the steady monsoonal breeze that was blowing, sailing time to Singapore would be three days and three nights, he provided sarongs and singlets from the crew's belongings to clothe the Rimau men who were to appear on deck.[32]

Already one day ahead of schedule, since the unloading at Merapas had not been spread over two nights as planned, Lyon now had theoretically ten days to reach Singapore, where the attack was scheduled for the night of October 10. Even without the favourable breeze, they had plenty of time. Sailing at the planned rate of 1.8 knots an hour, it would take only six days to cover the 380 kilometres, leaving them with three or four days still up their sleeve. Always erring on the side of caution, Lyon stuck with the previously calculated figure, telling Chapman that he would spend the extra time at Pedjantan before leaving for the target area.[33]

It was now 10 o'clock on the evening of September 30 and time for the submarine to take her leave. Assuring Lyon that he would return to pick them up in forty days' time, Marsham gave the order to cast off. As the sub pulled away, leaving *Mustika* riding at anchor before a backdrop of stunning beauty, peace and tranquillity, the men on watch turned to give the traditional naval farewell. With three rousing cheers for 'this extremely gallant body of officers and men', the submariners headed for the Carimata Straits and home.[34]

Apart from a handful of Chinese and Malays, and the conquering Japanese, no one ever saw the men of Rimau again.

Chapter 10
Disaster

Porpoise had not long gone when Ivan Lyon began to revise two aspects of the operation that were less than satisfactory — Carey was alone on Merapas and there was no emergency escape plan. Evidently concluding that four days spent resting in the idyllic surroundings of Pedjantan could be more profitably spent in dealing with both problems, Lyon decided to return to Merapas. Although 270 kilometres away, Merapas was in the general direction of Singapore. The dog-legged detour would add a mere eighty kilometres to the total length of the trip.

To leave Carey behind, without any means of transport, had been simply a hurriedly conceived, stop-gap measure to prevent the coconut workers from accidently stumbling upon the stores. Although Davidson considered it unlikely that the islanders would leave the cleared area and venture into the jungle, guarding the supplies was a round-the-clock job. As this was clearly an impossible task for one person, Lyon decided to put another three men ashore.[1]

Whom would he choose? Those who were transferred would have to be reliable, level headed and not employed upon a task vital to the success of the mission. Ingleton, whom circumstances had thrown upon Lyon, was the most expendable. Always a problem because of his size[2], his role as junk master had only been created to keep SEAC happy. However, any suggestion that he join Carey was evidently unpopular with the Royal Marine, for he remained with the junk.

By a process of elimination,[3] Lyon settled on Hugo Pace, the tough, battle-experienced ex-Legionnaire, and the two men who had backups — resourceful engineer Alf Warren and signaller Colin Craft. In actual fact, except that he would have had a lot of explaining to do, Lyon could have left both signallers on Merapas. The reason was quite simple. As he had not brought the code book with him, the radios were useless. It had apparently been a deliberate act. With all the delays and troubles that had threatened to cancel Rimau before it began, Mary Ellis, Rimau's cipher officer, believed that Lyon had taken the decision that, come what may, they were not going to be recalled. Without the one-off code book, it was impossible to decode any message sent from Australia. Likewise, it was also impossible to transmit.[4]

Mustika arrived from Pedjantan without incident on October 4[5] to disembark Warren, Craft and Pace and to organise an alternate escape route, including a supply dump and an accessible bolt-hole, near a junk route. The question of supplies for the dump was easily solved by syphoning off some of the stores from the extensive Merapas stockpile, and of the hideout by choosing the one island that met the necessary criteria. It was near a junk route, was more or less on the way to the target area so they could drop off supplies, could be island hopped by folboat from Singapore and Merapas, was uninhabited, had a water supply and was well known to at least six of them. That island was Pompong.

Pompong was ideally positioned a little over one hundred kilometres to the south-west. Perched on the northerly end of the Lingga Archipelago, it was well sited for easy access from either Merapas or Singapore by any one of a number of routes. As five of the Jaywick team had already paddled from Singapore to Pompong and the sixth, Freddie Marsh, knew the island intimately, it was an excellent emergency rendezvous as well as a likely place to pirate a junk should the need arise.

They left Merapas Island on or about October 5, leaving two folboats behind as transportation for Carey, Warren, Craft and Pace and taking on a quantity of stores for Pompong. Instead of going by the most direct route, straight down the Telang Strait, they made a detour, sailing through the group of islands that hugged the south-easterly coast of Bintan Island. The prahu looked innocuous enough and, as it displayed no flags, was unlikely to attract any unnecessary attention. Nevertheless, stowed in a handy place were Mrs Manderson's excellent copies of the Japanese national flag and the Osame Gunsai Kambu. The latter was somewhat like the Rising Sun in design, but had additional lines and six Japanese characters which signified 'Shonan Military Administration Headquarters', Shonan being the Japanese name for Singapore. Should a plane look as if it might attack, the deck crew was instructed to display them prominently.[6]

The men were now in an area frequented by fishermen and by villagers moving constantly from island to island as they attended to their daily business. However, from a distance, the crew of *Mustika* was no longer made up of white soldiers. Since leaving Pedjantan they had given up wearing berets and had painted the exposed parts of their bodies with makeup. The officers had also removed their badges of rank, which were simply strips of cloth slipped over their shirt epaulettes. Lyon, Page, Davidson and five of the others had gone completely native, trading their jungle greens for sarongs and singlets and adding an extra touch of authenticity to their rig by placing wide-brimmed, oriental-style straw hats upon their heads.[7]

Sticking to the routine he had employed on *Sederhana Djohanes*, and following the advice of *Mustika*'s captain, Lyon allowed only three of those in island dress on deck at any one time. One of those kept below and not subjected to the donning of local garb was Otto Ingleton, whose size made it impossible for him to be anything other than an outrageously conspicuous giant in this land of small, fine-boned people. Although the disguises would not stand up to close scrutiny, when viewed from afar the blue eyes and brown-streaked fair hair were not distinguishable enough to arouse suspicion.[8]

Although confined below decks, the men were not idle. As the benefits of careful intelligence gathering on Jaywick had proved to be just as useful as sabotage,[9] observation was split into three categories — notes, sketches and photographs. Page was responsible for the photography, Ingleton for the sketching and Davidson, always a copious notetaker, for the written reports.[10] Lyon, his hands full with the running of the prahu, kept his information where he usually filed it — in his head.[11] As they neared the Bintan coastline they were kept busy. In his drawing book Ingleton sketched the bauxite mines, easily identifiable by the great red scars that marred an otherwise green landscape,[12] and Page took several photographs, including one of Davidson in his sarong and straw hat and another of Lyon, his pipe looking rather incongruous with the singlet and sarong ensemble.[13]

As they passed the end of the Riouw Straits, they had a fine view of the Japanese fleet, prompting more sketching, photographing and note taking. Ingleton, probably with the aid of the high-powered telescope, had no trouble in filling in the finer details of the ships, meticulously recording the guns, turrets and peculiarities of each vessel. Further south, nearing Pompong, they all noted that bauxite mining was apparently being carried out on Lingga Island. Nothing escaped their attention. The deposition and strength of Japanese defences, the descriptions of military installations, even the appearance and apparent attitude of the villagers were all carefully snapped, drawn and noted.[14]

Davidson and Ingleton were not the only ones committing what they saw to paper. Back on Merapas, Carey was relieving the boredom by recording everything that moved. Although he had no need to disguise himself, he occasionally shed his jungle greens as he found the sarong infinitely cooler than trousers. In his daily wanderings around the island he recorded the wind strength and direction, the movement of shipping and the description and flight paths of aircraft that passed overhead. The others also contributed items of interest for Carey's diary, which he hoped would be of value to the intelligence department as well as providing him with a unique souvenir of the mission.[15]

Then something unexpected occurred. The appearance of a visitor at the camp shot to pieces the theory that the locals would not bother to leave the plantation or wander into the thick jungle. In making this prediction, Davidson had forgotten that small children, especially boys, are universally curious creatures. Ten-year-old Karta was no exception.

It was not long before he had located Rimau's hideout and befriended them.

In the clearing behind Cache Swamp, Karta had been most intrigued by a palm tree that was lifted from its anonymity by the strange hieroglyphics that had been gouged into its soft trunk. Undoubtedly the work of Walter Carey, whose leg pulling was legendary, the unintelligible symbols were to cause much head scratching in the years to come. Inexplicably and indelibly carved upon the tree, more than two metres above the ground, the marks were believed by some to be a datum survey mark, while others were completely stumped. Despite hours spent puzzling over the possible meaning, the riddle remained unsolved for forty-five years.

Fed up with scribbling in his little note book, it appears that Carey had decided to indulge in graffiti with a difference — graffiti that would leave any island visitors, particularly those who might be Japanese, completely mystified. With the aid of his basic phrase book, the lanky Australian had reached above his head and neatly carved two bold Japanese characters high upon the trunk of a convenient coconut palm.

What the short-statured Japanese troops made of this lofty message when they eventually arrived at the previously unoccupied Merapas Island is anybody's guess. The symbols simply and inexplicably read 'Japanese Tree'. Karta, being unable to read either Japanese or English, and interested only in recognising the handiwork of his new-found friends, coined the phrase that was to last for decades — 'The British Coconut Tree'.[16]

While Carey was leaving this offbeat and very Australian joke for posterity, *Mustika* was making its way up one of the numerous straits that led to Kapala Djernith. The prahu had attracted not the slightest bit of attention, save for a Japanese navy plane that banked for a closer look. The sight of the flags, waved vigorously from the bow by Bob Page, evidently satisfied the pilot's curiousity, for he wiggled his wings and flew away. Fortunately, although SRD Intelligence had warned them that surveillance and patrols had been stepped up after the Jaywick raid, they had not so far encountered any trouble that might call for the contingency plan.[17]

Although marginally better than the fantastic scheme dreamed up by Davidson for Jaywick, the Contingency Plan Mark II, devised by SRD's Planning Department, was still very dicey. This time they were to foresake dinghies, breathing tubes and suicidal limpets, and rely instead upon pure subterfuge. Should a Japanese patrol wish to come on board, the decoy party was to lure them below, where they would be overpowered, silently garrotted and stripped of their uniforms. Some of the Rimau men, dressed in enemy clothing and with forage caps pulled down well over their faces, would then hustle the Rimau 'natives' to the patrol boat, as if carrying out a straightforward arrest. With the help of additional weapons concealed beneath the sarongs of the 'natives', they were to dispatch the remaining Japanese and move off smartly, away from *Mustika*. It was envisaged that any interested onlookers observing this pantomime would believe that a few local fishermen had been arrested and taken away for questioning. Once out of sight, the patrol boat would be sunk in deep water, taking the bodies of the Japanese with it.[18]

This plan had many weaknesses, not the least of which was the assumption that the deck crew could manage to carry out successfully a prolonged and convincing masquerade as Malays. At a pinch, Lyon, Reymond and Huston might stand up to more than a cursory examination, but even they could not hope to sustain the deception for long. As with Jaywick's contingency plan, the most sensible idea would have been to pray that they would never be placed in a position that would call for it to be put to the test.

Lyon's timetable, even allowing for the diversions to Merapas and Pompong, was still spot on. On the night of October 9 *Mustika* anchored in a quiet cove off Kapala Djernith, at the southern end of Phillip Channel, while the two recce parties, under Lieutenant Ross, paddled off to Pulau Labon, about eleven kilometres away. Leaving the other team to return to Lyon to report on the island's suitability as an SB transfer base, Ross and Huston paddled another eleven kilometres to Subar. For the second time in thirteen months, Jaywick veteran Andrew Huston was about to endure another uncomfortably hot day on this small, barren island observing the shipping in Singapore Harbour through a telescope. Although Ross had not set foot on Subar, he had a good pre-war knowledge of Singapore and had the added advantage of being able to speak Malay, should they accidently run into any trouble.[19]

While the recce pair lay sweltering beneath the miniscule amount of shade offered by the coarse bracken, *Mustika* left Kapala Djernith and moved in a north-easterly direction towards the maze of small islands lying off the Batam coast. With Japanese naval craft anchored at the southern entrance to the Riouw Straits, there was constant movement between that anchorage and Singapore, making the waters near Phillip Channel a rather risky spot to pass an entire day. By mid afternoon, they were threading their way north, past the multitude of mangrove-ringed islands that dotted the waters, to Kasu — a small, jungle-clad island that was home to a village of simple fishermen.[20]

Clustered along the edge of a bay and standing rather lopsidedly on poles above the water, the village was well sheltered from the wind by large banyan trees growing on the hill behind, and by a small cape that jutted into the water at the southern end of the cove. From the centre of the densely packed dwellings ran a bamboo jetty, sufficiently long to straddle the extensive mud-flats that were exposed at low tide. Opening out onto the jetty and for quite a distance along both sides, until the increasing height above the mud put a stop to development, the fishermen's houses perched precariously. In one of these houses lived the headman.

Another, requisitioned as a Water Police Post, was manned by village collaborators known as the Hei Ho, under the control of the Kempei Tai.[21]

None too popular with the locals, the Hei Ho threw their weight around, enforcing their authority by the wearing of uniforms identical to those worn by the Japanese army. The effect of the uniform, complete with regulation boots and cap with red star, was diminished somewhat by the fact that the villagers knew that the weapons carried by these quasi-policemen were fake. Nevertheless, being realistic in every detail, the wooden copies of Japanese army rifles served their purpose, enabling the Hei Ho to intimidate easily all those not in the know.[22]

From their small post halfway down the jetty, the police had a fine view of the waterway and of any vessel that might sail close enough to enable them to flex their muscles and demonstrate their authority. As Japanese naval craft were out of bounds and exempt from Hei Ho interference, the collaborators' jurisdiction extended only to local boats and fishing vessels.[23] This observation post was also well positioned for a strike upon passing craft, not only because of its convenient location but because of the island's topography. Facing the small channel that separated Kasu from the large island of Batam, this sleepy, quiet backwater was so well hidden from the south by the cape that strangers approaching from that direction were upon the settlement before they realised it.

At about four o'clock in the afternoon, *Mustika* rounded the point.[24] Sidek Bin Safar, one of the Hei Ho, who went by the lordly title of Police Inspector, immediately noticed the prahu when it came into view. As the tide was still low, the incoming current was sluggish and the wooden boat, its sails hanging limply in the windless air, was going nowhere fast. There was not the hint of a breeze, although the heavy, leaden-coloured clouds signified that a storm might soon break, relieving the oppressive heat of the late afternoon.[25] Sidek lifted his gaze. Idly watching the unidentified prahu drift by, he was jolted from his lethargy. The people on deck were not indigenous Malays but 'orang putehs' — white men.

There could be no doubt about it. The prahu, or tonkan, as the Indonesians called all wooden boats, was a mere twenty metres away. It was now so close that he could see that there were Europeans on board, badly disguised as northern Indians.[26]

Alerting underlings Yunus, Yahya and Atan, Sidek quickly fetched the only man in the village who could speak English. He was Ati, a Singaporian Chinese who had wisely moved back to the island when the Japanese occupied Singapore. Shoving their military caps upon their heads and carrying their imitation rifles, the four Malays, accompanied by Ati, scrambled over the side of the rickety jetty and down to the water where their police boat was moored. Measuring about seven and a half metres in length, the motor-driven launch was made of rough, oiled timber planks. In the stern was a small, box-like deckhouse, open at the front and with large, glassless apertures on either side.

Watched by every person in the village, the police boat chugged towards *Mustika*. As the onlookers prudently chose to remain within the confines of their houses, those whose homes lined the pier had the best view. Watching from the doorway and window of two of these houses, eighteen-year-old Arafin Bin Akup and Mahat Kunil, a thirty-three-year-old fisherman, had ringside seats.

In the very front of the launch stood Ati. The four Hei Ho were immediately behind, their well-developed sense of self preservation making sure that the Chinese was between them and potential danger. To the men on board *Mustika* they presented an instantly recognisable profile. The sight of four fully armed members of the Imperial Japanese Army, ranged in typically arrogant stance in the bows of a motor launch could mean only one thing — a Japanese patrol.[27]

As soon as the launch had left the pier the alarm had been raised on *Mustika* by the call of 'Patroller. Patroller'. Those below had instantly taken up their stations, Bren guns and Stens trained upon the launch through holes in the hull. For the present they could do nothing more than follow the advice of *Mustika*'s captain to the letter — no more than three men on deck and no signals.[28]

Lyon, with the others, waited in silence. There had been no indication from the police boat as to its intention and no one had hailed *Mustika*. As it was now raining, there was a possibility, albeit slender, that the boat might return to shore. If it did not, they would be in grave danger, perhaps forced into a position where they would have to use the contingency plan. If the Japanese kept coming and decided to board, would the plan work, or would Rimau's mission, due to begin in only three hours' time, be over before it had begun?

As the launch closed the gap to a distance of less than twenty metres, someone on the police boat shouted something unintelligible. This was the signal for a tall man, standing on the deck of *Mustika*, to order his companion to bend down and level a Bren gun across the edge of the decking, presumably in an effort to cover the enemy vessel.[29] The atmosphere below decks was electric, with sweat streaming from every pore and muscles aching from the strain. As the patrol boat drew nearer, an 'English engineer', unable to control his nerves, panicked and fired.[30]

In that split second, Operation Rimau was finished.

What made Ati realise that something was wrong before a shot was fired is not known. Perhaps the abnormal stillness as the launch neared the tonkan touched some sixth sense, telling him that it was time to take cover. For whatever reason, in one deft move he threw himself sideways and into the water before the first shots thudded into the launch. Exposed upon the bow, their human shield now inconveniently overboard, the Hei Ho made a prime target. Abruptly, they turned the boat, but it was too late. Before they could follow Ati into the water, Rimau's guns had cut down two of them.

Realising that Ati was a Chinese civilian, the marksmen on *Mustika* concentrated their fire upon the uniformed figures now in the water. Within seconds it was all over. The bullet-riddled body of the third man lay floating beside the boat, while the fourth had disappeared. Sidek Bin Safar was not, however, dead. With a remarkable talent for survival, he had not struck out for the shore but had clung to the rear of the boat, shielded by the deckhouse from the bullets that cracked across the water and buried themselves in the timbers. There he remained, hanging on for dear life long after the launch, its motor still running, became snared by the poles that supported the village houses.[31]

Inside their homes, quite safe from the fusillade of shots that had been directed at the Hei Ho and not at them, the villagers continued to observe the proceedings with interest. Although the rain was now coming down in torrents, they could still see what was happening on board the prahu as *Mustika* had made almost no headway in the last few minutes.[32]

On board the boat, Ivan Lyon, his plan now in tatters, told his men that the raid was aborted and that he had no option but to blow up *Mustika* and its secret equipment before someone alerted the Japanese. Calculating that there would be no more than three hours before the enemy arrived in great numbers from Singapore, he ordered twelve of the men to assemble the folboats and make for Merapas by whatever route they could manage.[33] Before the six folboats[34] pulled away from the side, Davidson, still on *Mustika*, grabbed the two flags (which might prove useful if the submarine did not turn up and they needed to pirate a ship), and threw them down into one of the boats.[35]

As the folboats moved off, the villagers took fright. The short battle they had just witnessed had been very exciting and, as the Hei Ho were not the most popular people in town, not at all distressing. However, the sight of six little rubber boats, manned by personnel who were obviously well armed, leaving the tonkan and making in their direction, was quite another matter. Believing that they might perhaps be next on the white men's hit list, the village people headed for the jungle-covered hill. They would get wet, but it was infinitely preferable to being stitched up by a row of machine-gun bullets.[36]

Peering from their new hiding places, Arafin and Mahat could still make out the shape of the tonkan through the rain and premature gloom brought about by the storm. As the wind had now begun to blow, the boat had moved further downstream. Although these two onlookers were unable to discern what was actually happening on board *Mustika*, Sidek Bin Safar was close enough to see everything. Hanging on to the back of the launch, still too terrified to move, he had a prime position.

Mustika, having at last started to make some headway, suddenly stopped and anchored in mid stream. Sidek watched intently as five men launched a large boat from the deck. After loading it with three unassembled folboats, a rubber raft, large quantities of ordinance material, ammunition, food and medical supplies, they paddled off in the direction of Singapore. Almost immediately there was a loud bang. The tonkan, holed beneath the waterline, slid slowly from sight beneath the waves. There was another, far more muffled explosion and then absolute silence.[36]

While the startled villagers crept back from the jungle to collect the dead and Sidek recovered his equilibrium, Ivan Lyon, Donald Davidson, Archie Campbell, Doug Warne and Clair Stewart paddled their folding engineer's boat as hard as they could for Subar, where Ross and Huston, quite unaware that disaster had overtaken the expedition, were waiting.[37]

Heading in the opposite direction, their energies now concentrated on reaching Merapas alive, were twelve bitterly disappointed men. They knew there was no going back. The explosions that they had all heard could mean only one thing — *Mustika* had been scuttled and the SBs were now sitting in the mud, a useless mass of twisted and fragmented metal. To have been beaten by sheer bad luck when on the very brink of success was almost too much to bear. Had the rain come a few minutes earlier they would have passed by Kasu undetected and been well on their way to victory. It was unbelievable — almost as unbelievable as hearing Ivan Lyon announce that he had decided to cancel the raid.[38]

Had they but known that the limpet mines, far from being fourteen metres under water, were at that very minute lying at Lyon's feet upon the wooden floor of the folding boat, their spirits would have soared. He may have been forced to destroy the Sleeping Beauties, but he had by no means entirely abandoned his plan. That very night Ivan Lyon would lead six men on a raid on Singapore Harbour, using folboats. It is inconceivable that he would have done anything less. To abort the mission totally because a few Japanese patrolmen on an isolated Indonesian island had met an unfortunate end would have been completely unacceptable to a man such as Lyon.[39]

All that was required to salvage the situation was a quick change of plan. Having efficiently disposed of the SBs, Lyon was free to pursue his objective by whatever means he thought fit. The fact that the Japanese, who would soon be aware of Rimau's presence, might make escape extremely difficult did not enter into his calculations. Every Rimau man knew that the mission was more important than the life of any individual.[40] Ivan had worked for months, had spent every minute of every day plotting, scheming and planning. He was not about to give up now.

Once Lyon and his group had collected Ross and Huston from Subar, the seven men assembled the folboats. With the recce kayak, they had four all told. The folding boat, having served its purpose, was exchanged for the rubber raft, which, apart from being capable of carrying their equipment, was far lighter to tow.[41] Doug Warne, a very strong canoeist, was to go it alone, leaving the other three boats paired by men who were either officers or Jaywick veterans. It was obviously a good combination. At about three o'clock the following morning they penetrated the outer defences of Singapore Harbour. All except Warne, who, for all his strength was beaten by the rip tide, then placed their limpets on shipping anchored in the Roads and waters near Samboe Island.[42] Early the next morning, for the second time in a little over a year, the Japanese were enraged and the local villagers astounded to hear the sound of explosions booming across the water. About twelve hours later, when night fell, there were several more.[43]

While the seven saboteurs spent a triumphant day admiring their handiwork, probably from the safety of Dongas Island,[44] the Indonesians in kampongs within earshot of the target areas were abuzz with speculation. Who had been responsible for the loud bangs? What had been blown up? Their questions were never answered and in the absence of any telltale signs such as great palls of smoke, they were not able to learn anything that might satisfy their curiousity.[45]

The next day, when Sidek Bin Safar arrived at Blankan Padang Island, near Samboe, to report the deaths of the three Hei Ho policemen, he was told by the villagers about the mysterious explosions.[46] His news that some white men had killed three island police and then sunk their tonkan aroused some interest, but not enough at this stage to bother informing Singapore headquarters.[47] However, calculating that the tonkan or the supplies it contained might be salvageable, a number of local police returned to Kasu with Sidek. Among them were people skilled in using diving equipment — probably workers from the ship-building yards on Samboe Island.[48] For the next day or so they provided the villagers with a new form of entertainment. After donning weird helmets, which Arafin and Mahat noticed were attached by tubes to some kind of machine, they disappeared under water for about half an hour at a time. The tonkan was located but, to the disappointment of both the searchers and the observers of this fascinating sideshow, the divers came up empty handed.[49]

Sidek, having survived the shooting, was naturally the centre of attention and, being the chief witness, was asked to make a full statement. Although nothing had been found on the tonkan, the Blankan Padang police, who, like those at Kasu, were under the control of the Water Kempei Tai, finally contacted Singapore on Friday October 13 to report that there had been 'a defensive stand' by about twenty people, including Caucasians, at Kasu earlier in the week. A copy of the message, which apparently carried no indication of priority, was put aside for the attention of Army Headquarters until after the weekend.[50]

When a report was received the following day that an American B-24 plane had been seen circling Bintan Island for over two hours on the day of the Kasu attack and had apparently made contact with someone on the ground, the Kempei Tai officers stirred themselves to action. Assuming that the incidents were linked and were the work of one of the enemy's pesky 'stay behind' parties, they telegraphed a message to Major Fugita, head of Bintan Island Garrison, and to all naval units, to begin an immediate search and maintain a strict watch in the Riouw Archipelago and the Durian Straits. The Kempei Tai then dispatched a search party of its own, hoping to make contact with the troublesome guerillas.[51] In the meantime, they turned their attention to what they believed to be another, quite unrelated matter.

In spite of the Number One Work, which had continued its brutal investigations for exactly twelve months, the sabotage had not been stopped. The purge had evidently not taught any of the civilians a lesson, for on October 11, a mere four days after prime suspect John Long had been returned to the civilian camp after almost one year in detention,[52] there had been another raid upon harbour shipping. As if the shock of the dawn raid had not been enough, in the early evening there had been more explosions, loud enough to be heard in Singapore and by all of the Indonesians in the villages around Samboe. Coming at a time when Japan was feeling the effect of United States submarine activity and was desperately short of ships, the attacks were an outrageous affront.[53] As at least three ships had been sunk,[54] the loss of face was immense.

Determined to put a stop to the activities of the saboteurs once and for all, the secret police, in a frenzy of bloody reprisals, set about extracting from the civilian population a hideous price as payment for this latest humiliation. Before many days had passed, the heads of innocent Chinese and Malays, thrust upon sharpened pikes, formed a ghastly pallisade along the streets of Singapore City.[55]

Chapter 11
For God, King and Country

The Singapore Kempei Tai may have been busy, but their colleagues in the offshore islands most certainly were not. Indeed, apart from the undersea diving at Kasu, there was no evidence at all to suggest that anything out of the ordinary had taken place. Singapore, a mere sixteen kilometres across the water, was blissfully unaware that a tonkan full of white men had wiped out three-quarters of the island's Military Police Force. It was little wonder. Neither war nor Japanese occupation had made the slightest difference to the inter-island communications system, which was hopelessly inefficient.

As the police post at Kasu was equipped with neither radio nor telephone, Sidek Bin Safar had been forced to go by boat to make his report to the Hei Hos at Blankan Padang Island. Since they had not bothered to pass on his information for two days, the frantic search that Lyon had envisioned would take place had not eventuated. The only unusual activity had been by Kempei Tai in Singapore, zealously trying to prove that the latest sabotage was another inside job.

By this stage, the raiders could have been expected to call it a day. However, Ivan Lyon had other ideas. With the rubber raft still full of useful ironmongery,[1] they paddled not to Merapas but to Pangkil — a small, elongated island in the Riouw Straits.

There was no way that anyone travelling along either of the Jaywick and Rimau escape routes and turning east at Pandjang Island could miss Pangkil, which straddled the entrance to the Tiung Straits and sat slap bang in the centre of the Riouw Straits. Not that it attracted much in the way of visitors. Barely rising from the sea, which fell back to reveal extensive rocky reefs at each low tide, and covered in occasional jungle patches and savannah-type grassland from which nondescript trees and occasional cultivated groves of coconuts emerged, Pangkil was not particularly inspiring. Neither was it of any strategic or economic importance. It was inhabited by fishermen and coconut workers, who lived in two villages which straggled out over the water at either end in the usual higgledy-piggledy fashion.[2] The Japanese had passed Pangkil by and Rimau would have too had it not been such a convenient place to hide during the daylight hours of October 14.[3]

The Riouw Archipelago was no place for men on the run. With a large naval fleet anchored at the southern end, near Mantang Island, the temporary anchorages in the deep water off Bintan Island, the entire area was bristling with Japanese.[4] Lyon knew full well, from previous intelligence and personal observation while on board *Mustika,* that the enemy frequented the waters of the strait in large numbers. The safe way to Merapas was across the top of Batam and Bintan Islands, or down the old Jaywick route and through the Dempo Straits. The Riouw route was so perilous that, unless there was an overwhelming reason to be there, only a madman would choose it. Lyon had an overwhelming reason. There is no possible motive for dragging a rubber boat, loaded with equipment, for more than one hundred kilometres, unless he intended to blow up the ships in the Riouw anchorages.

Pangkil was well suited for a preliminary reconnaissance. It was within easy paddling distance of Tapai or Fishermen's Island, a small island rising steeply from the sea a few miles to the south that gave a bird's-eye view of Japanese shipping at Mantang Island. As the people from the two villages might be able to supply some very useful information, the seven men broke cover at about four o'clock on the afternoon of October 14, unaware that a search ordered by the Singapore Kempei Tai was about to set off from Bintan Island. Taking sweets, cigarettes and chocolates, they split into two groups. While the other three headed north, Davidson, Campbell, Huston and Warne set off for Tandjung Kramat, the main settlement on the south-western tip of the island, where they met village headman Raja Rool. Standing nearby, quietly absorbing the scene, was Raja Rool's second son, Raja Muhammad.[5]

He learned from the tallest of the four, who spoke a little Malay, that the visitors, dressed in jungle greens and each carrying a Sten gun, pistol and numerous hand grenades, were 'Australian officers' who had come by submarine and had been on Pangkil since midnight. The eighteen-year-old Muhammad, casting an interested gaze over their two folboats, the black, inflatable rubber boat and their strange 'necklaces' (identity discs), assumed that the submarine must have surfaced in the deepwater channel between Pangkil and Karas Islands. By the time the discussions concluded, his father had a swag of goods and the Rimau men had learned something new — there were other Japanese ships anchored in the straits, apart from those at the Mantang Island base.[6]

Five kilometres away, at the other end of the island, Lyon, Ross and Stewart also met a headman — Penegat Island's Raja Mun. He was friendly enough, accepting cigarettes and learning that the soldiers, armed with two Bren guns and three pistols, had come to Pangkil in small, two-man canoes.[7]

The white visitors obviously must have felt secure, for they spent all the next day on Pangkil. The island appeared safe enough to them but, in light of their new information, it was useless as a surveillance post since it was impossible to see the ships riding at anchor to the north-east, between Dompak and Penegat Islands. Neatly excising that area from view was a flat, oval island, barely more than a blister, named Soreh.[8]

Soreh, or Afternoon Island, is tiny, so tiny that it can be circum-navigated on foot in less than one hour. Pretty enough to be considered an island paradise by peacetime adventurers, it was of no military significance. Roughly one kilometre in diameter, its green, palm-filled nucleus is ringed by wide, pure white, sandy beaches, that slope gently to the sea. The occasional Ru tree, with its multi-branched crown and convoluted buttress-roots, is a perfect foil for the pale green and grey backdrop provided by the stately coconut palms. Apart from a denser patch of vegetation towards the centre, there is no undergrowth, making it possible to see from one side of the island to the other.

As a hideout, it was a disaster. Worse still, there was a limited water supply, making it even less attractive than Pangkil. Soreh, however, had one feature that Pangkil could not match — position. Despite the fact that its height above sea level would not have exceeded six metres, the view of the shipping anchorage near Dompak Island was perfect.

On the evening of October 15, Lyon, Ross and Stewart left Pangkil and paddled off to Soreh. Less than ten hours later, Raja Rool made urgent contact with the others. They had been betrayed and must leave Pangkil immediately, before the Japanese arrived.

At 4 am, Raja Muhammad watched from the village as the remaining four split into two parties and paddled away. While Davidson and Campbell went to Soreh to warn Lyon, the others, with the rubber raft in tow, made for Tapai.[9]

The enemy informant was collaborator Raja Mun, the visiting Penegat headman who had engaged Lyon, Ross and Stewart in conversation. He had wasted little time in going by boat to Tandjung Pinang to report the presence of the white men to District Police Officer Mahamit, who gave him twenty dollars for his trouble. This not insubstantial reward was soon swelled to seventy dollars when Mun, accompanied by Mahamit, repeated his story to Yap Chin Yah at Tandjung Pinang Kempei Tai Headquarters. Not the most popular Chinese in town, Yap had been brought from his home at Dabo, on Singkep Island, to investigate local Indonesians who had worked for the Dutch.[10]

With all available troops already out and searching for white soldiers on Singapore's orders, the local Kempei Tai immediately telegraphed Raja Mun's intelligence to Singapore. By 8.40 on the morning of October 15 signals were being flashed to naval forces in the area to maintain a strict watch on the Durian Straits and the Riouw Archipelago.[11]

The following morning, an Indonesian coconut cutter by the name of Abdul Latif was quietly stoking up a fire inside his small hut on the island of Soreh, where he lived with his wife and small child. Part of Latif's job, as caretaker for Soreh's owner, Tenghu Haji Ahmad Tabib, entailed extracting the oil from the plentiful coconuts that grew all over the island. With no village and nothing of interest on the island save the nearby tomb of some long-forgotten king, Latif was accustomed to carrying out his work in peace and tranquillity.[12] Despite the war, that pattern had remained undisturbed until 8 o'clock on the morning of Monday 16 October 1944.[13]

Latif was hacking open coconuts about fifty metres from his house when he first saw them. The four white men, dressed in green and khaki shirts and trousers, were bareheaded and each carried a Sten gun and a pistol. Latif noticed also that two were taller than the others, two were older, and that around each man's shoulder was a rope cord, of the type usually attached to a pistol. They also had an 'army sign' or badge (more than likely their Rising Sun beret badges) attached to the front of their shirts.

The sudden appearance of these warriors and the size of their armoury did not alarm the young Indonesian, for he had seen some of the party on Pangkil in the past day or two. In passable Malay, they asked Latif if he would climb one of the trees and cut them some green coconuts. Happy to oblige his unexpected visitors, Latif did so. After they had drunk of Ivan Lyon's favourite tropical beverage and scooped out some of the juicy young meat, the strangers disappeared among the coconut palms, the only evidence of their passing the empty coconut shells that lay at Latif's feet.[14]

While Lyon, Ross, Davidson, Campbell and Stewart were lying up out of sight on Soreh, five kilometres away the island of Pangkil was the scene of frenetic activity. Although Mun's information had been received in Tandjung Pinang early on October 15, the local branch of the Kempei Tai had taken some time to become organised. With all available men already out searching Bintan Island on orders from Singapore, a full twenty-four hours had elapsed before Major Fugita managed to gather together a force large enough to take on the enemy band believed to be on Pangkil Island.[15]

As the Japanese considered that safety lay in numbers, their search patrols tended to be unnecessarily large. The usual tactic was to use a mob of thirty or forty men, supplemented by Hei Hos and a few local natives, who were impressed for the job if necessary. This passion for group travel made for very slow going. It also took a great deal of organisation and was a logistical nightmare. Consequently, the pursued had a fair chance of eluding the pursuers, who had a penchant for sticking to paths and an absolute horror of entering the jungle other than by recognised trails. In the absence of any track, they stuck to the coast and moved around the perimeter.[16]

Late that morning, unaware that the quarry had skedaddled to Soreh and Tapai during the night, Major Fugita and his entourage arrived at Pangkil. It was a daunting and impressive sight. In addition to a large number of men, he had brought along light machine-guns and two landing barges, which could not be beached as the tide was out, leaving the reef exposed. Nevertheless, one of the officers managed to come ashore and collared Raja Rool.

The demand that he reveal the whereabouts of the white soldiers met with stonewalling resistance from the unco-operative headman, who stated quite categorically, and quite truthfully, that there were no white men on the island. The Japanese, thwarted by Raja Rool's dogged persistence from gaining the information they required, tried a new tack. They would not take the headman away for questioning — they would take his son, Raja Muhammad, instead. Unmoved by the thought of his offspring in the clutches of the dreaded Kempei Tai, Raja Rool stuck to his story, leaving the Japanese officer with no option but to carry out the threat.[17]

The officer's decision to have Muhammad row him out to the landing barges in a small sampan turned out to be ill advised, for the Indonesian knew every inch of the waterway. Within minutes the boat collided with a rock and the commander, having been flung into deep water, was forced to swim to the shore while an unrepentant Muhammad stayed in the partially submerged boat. How long he might have stayed there is debatable, for another landing barge, loaded with excited Singapore Kempei Tai and Hei Hos, arrived with the sensational news that some of their party had been killed in a fierce battle with white men at Soreh Island.[18]

While the farcical scene at Pangkil had been taking place, Latif and his wife had been inside their house at Soreh, busily rendering coconut oil. Early in the afternoon, on hearing a strange noise coming from the beach, Mr Latif poked his head outside to investigate. To his alarm, he saw a Japanese landing barge, filled with Kempei Tai and Hei Hos, about fifty metres away, nosed onto the sand near the King's Tomb. It was the search party from Singapore, directed to Soreh by the ever-helpful local spy, Raja Mun. He had informed them that if the five white men believed to be on the island were still there, Latif would know about it.[19]

Latif knew that the arrival of the Kempei Tai meant trouble. Forcing his wife back into the safety of the building he ordered her to stay well hidden. About twenty-five Kempeis were now making their way inland towards Latif's house. As they passed through the trees, they saw the remains of the coconut shells upon the ground — irrefutable proof in Kempei terms that strangers had been on the island. When they met the coconut cutter, clad only in his shorts and singlet and still carrying his coconut knife, they asked the inevitable question — were there any white men on Soreh Island? Through the Kempei Tai's interpreter, a local Hei Ho named Raja Ibrahim, Latif denied all knowledge of any white men.[20]

The Kempei Tai were unconvinced. Determined to obtain some satisfactory information they tried more persuasive methods, offering Latif money in return for information, as advised by the devious Raja Mun. For the second time that day the Japanese learned that large numbers of the native people, unlike the traitorous Mun, were incorruptible. Latif, like Raja Rool, stuck to his guns. After an hour of unproductive questioning, the Kempei Tai, by now very angry indeed, decided to remove this unexpectedly stubborn individual to headquarters for further interrogation.[21]

The Kempei force now split in half and fanned out. The larger group which had gone to Latif's house began to search the island, while the other fifteen, including interpreter Raja Ibrahim, went back with their prisoner to wait on the barge.

Almost immediately, the stillness of the tropical afternoon exploded with the sound of concentrated gunfire. The search party had walked into an ambush.

Unable to see what was happening, those on the barge wisely kept a very low profile, aware that the staccato chatter of Bren guns indicated that the white men meant business. For two hours the battle continued unabated until, at about five o'clock, the Japanese were forced to retreat. When the remnants of the search party reached the safety of the barge, bringing their dead with them, Latif was very satisfied to see that five or six Kempei were either dead or injured.

Without further ado, the barge circled the island then headed for Pangkil to seek reinforcements, arriving shortly after six o'clock. On the way, the Japanese managed to extract from Latif the information that his elder brother Jalil was living on Pangkil. While Major Fugita, who had now assumed total command, organised his troops, Jalil was located and taken to the barges to join Latif and the unfortunate Muhammad, whose little episode with the overturned boat had not been forgotten. These three were probably less than enchanted to discover that they would be forced to endure the company of the man who was directly responsible for their present predicament — collaborator Raja Mun.[22]

On Soreh, everything was quiet. As soon as the Japanese had left, Mrs Latif had crept from her house, where she had huddled, terrified but safe, while the battle had raged outside. Making her way through the palms, she found the white men. Three were unhurt but the other two were wounded, one shot through the shoulder and the other through the chest. As she bent to help them, the others spoke to her in Malay, urging her to 'run away and hide, before the Japanese came back'. Aware of the danger, she returned to the house, the only place that offered any kind of refuge.[23]

Lyon realised that the situation was now very serious. Three things were obvious — the Japanese would be back, probably in less than two hours; Davidson and Campbell were injured, and there was still an hour or so to go before nightfall.[24]

If all five had been unhurt, it might have been possible to make a dash for it, but there was not enough time to move wounded men. The alternative was to stay and fight. Lyon, Ross and Stewart could fend off an attack and perhaps even escape, but Davidson and Campbell had almost no hope of survival unless they could leave before the Japanese returned. What Lyon needed most was time — enough time for Davidson and Campbell to reach Tapai, ten kilometres due south, where, waiting on the thick, jungle-covered island, were Huston, Warne and a stack of food, ammunition and medical supplies. In any case, with the Japanese on the offensive, Huston and Warne should be warned to wait no longer. As soon as it was dark, Davidson and Campbell, their pain and shock now substantially diminished by shots of morphine, set out on their perilous journey.[25]

Meanwhile, Major Fugita, who had left one lot of troops on Pangkil to carry out a thorough search, was on his way to Soreh with two barges containing a force that numbered close to one hundred men.[26] One hundred Japanese against three lone Allied soldiers. The odds were, as Lyon might have said, a bit steep.

In an effort to shorten these odds, Lyon studied the position closely. Being completely bereft of any proper cover, Soreh was a defensive nightmare that would require the use of clever tactics and subterfuge if the enemy were to be kept at bay. The silent Sten guns, highly effective over short range and almost impossible to detect, were the key to the plan. Placing Stewart and a swag of hand grenades in a wide, stone-lined ditch, thirty metres away on their rear right flank, Lyon and Ross climbed one of the few scalable trees on the island. It was a Ru tree, growing about fifty metres back from the north-east beach. The King's Tomb was roughly one hundred and thirty metres away to the east while Latif's house was at the same distance but in a more southerly direction, ensuring that Mrs Latif would not be caught in any crossfire. As the Ru tree's most distinguishable feature was its numerous, upward-spreading branches, they had an excellent and well-concealed position. Each man took with him his silent Sten and a large supply of ammunition. Once in position, the trio waited.[27]

They did not have long to wait. Some time after seven o'clock Major Fugita's men moved cautiously off the landing barges, which had come ashore on the northern beach. For the first half-hour, as the Japanese crept inland, there was silence. Then, without warning, the night erupted into total chaos as soldiers dropped in their tracks, victims of unseen but lethal weapons. What the Stens didn't pick off, the hand grenades made up for, as the powerfully built Stewart lobbed his hand propelled bombs. Superbly positioned in the ditch, Stewart was hidden by the grass and, unlike the pair in the tree, had a very stable platform from which to throw.

The Japanese, taken by surprise and pinned down without adequate cover, faced an impossible task. With the flashes from the exploding hand grenades illuminating the scene, Ross and Lyon had no trouble sighting and picking off the enemy. The dazzlingly brief bursts of light were of no use to the Japanese, however, as they had no idea from which direction the shots and grenades were originating. For the next four hours, bewildered by the lack of sound and unaware that Ross and Lyon were high above them, the Japanese forces made no headway and suffered heavy losses.[28]

It was not until almost midnight that someone finally spotted the muzzle flashes from the Stens. Impressed by the cunning of Lyon and Ross, one of the Japanese interpreters on the barge told Raja Muhammad, 'The white men are very smart. They hang like bats from the tree and shoot the people from there'.[29]

Lyon and Ross must have realised that, by climbing the tree, they had chosen a position from which there was no possible retreat. From the moment they had heaved themselves into its spindly branches they had known that, unless a miracle occurred, death was inevitable. On this isolated Indonesian island, Ivan faced the realisation that he would never again see his beloved Gabrielle and that soon he and Ross would give their lives for the British Empire ideals of God, King and Country. For over four hours, they fended off the Japanese attack, killing or wounding over sixty men and pinning down forty more,[30] in the hope that the others might yet escape. As midnight approached, on this sixteenth day of October 1944, their time was up.

A well-aimed Japanese hand grenade soared through the air. In that split second it was all over. The Ru tree, illuminated in a violent eruption of light, revealed the figures of Ross and Lyon, held like flies in a grotesque spider's web. As the projectile sprayed its murderous mixture of shrapnel and flying debris into the balmy tropical night, there was a deafening explosion, then two dull thuds. And then, absolute and utter silence.

When the smoke cleared, the Ru tree was empty. Crumpled upon the grass beneath lay the limp and lifeless forms of Lieutenant-Colonel Ivan Lyon and Lieutenant Bobby Ross.[31]

When Latif, whose barge had been sent to Karas Island to pick up twenty reinforcements, arrived back at Soreh, the action was all over. The remaining Japanese, too petrified to move forward in case another dozen such warriors were concealed behind or in the trees, had backed off to regain the safety of the landing barges. Somewhere, hidden among the foliage was Corporal Stewart. He was safe enough, for the Japanese had no intention of checking out the bodies or instigating another search until daylight.

At about one am, a barge, carrying Latif, Raja Muhammad, Jalil and some of the dead and wounded, left for the Kempei Tai post at Karas, about thirteen kilometres away, where Muhammad and Jalil were threatened and beaten by Kempei, trying to extract information that would lead them to Mrs Latif. It was probably the fact that Jalil was beaten so violently that he lost consciousness which saved his life. His inert body was thrown into a room with Muhammad who, being in far better condition, managed to steal a boat and get them both to Pangkil.

As he was of use to them, Latif temporarily escaped the attentions of the Kempei Tai. At about ten o'clock he and Raja Mun were taken back to Soreh and escorted to the foot of the Ru tree to confirm the identities of the white men, who had been stripped of everything except their clothing. Leaving the corpses to rot where they lay, the triumphant Kempei Tai carved the name of their unit on the trunk of a nearby palm tree before taking Latif and two folboats they had found back to Tandjung Pinang.

Their search of Soreh Island, if indeed there was any search at all, was at best superficial. Not only did they fail to find Mrs Latif and the baby hiding in the house, they also failed to find Stewart, who, with his folboat now in Japanese hands, was stranded. Major Fugita can hardly have been pleased with the results of the engagement. Two folboats, some equipment and two dead white soldiers did not stack up well against the loss of forty-four men and more than twenty others wounded by shrapnel. Although all but seven were local Hei Hos of little consequence to the Japanese, one of those killed had been Kempei Tai leader Lieutenant Muraroka. To add insult to injury, the other three white soldiers known to have been on Soreh had managed to escape. As the situation was far from satisfactory, Fugita did not relax his search for the missing men.[32] By the following morning he had found two of them. They were both dead.

By some incredible feat of endurance and determination, Davidson and Campbell had made Tapai. However, Huston and Warne were no longer there. With no sign of the others and alerted by the sounds of grenade explosions and Japanese gunfire clearly audible at Tapai, they had fled, leaving behind the rubber raft filled with ordinance material that would never now be used.[33] This decision to leave the equipment cannot have been taken lightly. To slash the rubber and sink the boat would have been simple, had they known for certain that the others would not follow. In weighing up the options, they must have decided that the risk of the Japanese finding the raft was preferable to depriving their comrades of essentials that might mean the difference between life and death.

After reaching Tapai, Davidson and Campbell had summoned sufficient energy to pull themselves up and over the rocks to a spot about six metres above the water line. Behind them, the vine and jungle-clad hill rose steeply, for Tapai is the most elevated of all the islands in the area. They sat side by side, resting their backs against a large, sloping rock, which gave ample support for their weary bodies. Their wounds, which had stopped bleeding, had formed dark, rust-coloured patches, almost indiscernable against the dark green of their saturated clothing. They had their pistols, but no ammunition and only one hand grenade. In the darkness, they had apparently been unable to locate the rubber raft, or perhaps they were simply too exhausted to look for it.[34]

In daylight it was possible to see all the way to Soreh Island. By dawn on the morning of October 17 there was every indication that all was not well. There had been no shooting since midnight and no sign of Lyon, Ross or Stewart. Donald Davidson and Archie Campbell settled themselves against the rock and waited.

At 7 am on October 18 two boats, carrying a Kempei Tai search party, Latif, Raja Mun and Raja Rool, approached the island. Alerted by Mun that white men had been seen paddling off in the direction of the island, the occupants were not surprised to see the figures of two men on a rocky ledge, well above the waterline. Ever mindful of their personal safety and unwilling to be on the receiving end of any more of the white men's tricks, the Kempei Tai pushed Raja Rool out of the boat and ordered him to move towards the figures, still sitting motionless against the rocks. Gingerly, the elderly man made his way across the slippery rock platform towards the two men, who had given no indication that they were aware of his presence.

It was some time before he realised that they were not merely unconscious, but dead. Although their clothing and their pistols were saturated from the rain and their skin grimy, they looked lifelike enough. And they had not been dead long, for the voracious ants and other insects had not yet invaded the bodies. But why were they dead at all? There had been no fighting here. Raja Rool could not understand it.

Neither could Latif, when he was brought from the second boat with Raja Mun to make an identification. They were the same men who had been on Soreh all right, Latif said — one tall, and one short, the same combination as those who lay dead beneath the Ru tree. When Mun's turn came to inspect the bodies, his inscrutable face did not betray his surprise that he had never seen either of these white men before. Not at all anxious to complicate his life any more than necessary, he told the Japanese that they were two of the men who had spoken to him at Pangkil.

Puzzled, Latif now took a closer look at the corpses, trying to determine the cause of death. Although wounded in the chest and shoulder, the blood was dried and it did not seem that these old wounds could have been fatal. Perhaps they had killed themselves, but with what and how? As the pistols that Raja Rool had seen had since been souvenired, he saw nothing except the lone hand grenade. In any case there were no fresh wounds to indicate that they may have shot either themselves or each other. Like Raja Rool, Latif was completely bewildered.[35]

If either of them had smelt the tell-tale odour of bitter almonds they had no inkling of its significance. It was not until the more worldly Japanese appeared on the scene that the picture fell into place. Here, upon the rocks of Tapai, lay the bodies of two extraordinarily brave men.[36]

'ANYTHING IS PREFERABLE TO FALLING INTO ENEMY HANDS', had warned Allied Intelligence. This instruction, printed in bold block capitals on intelligence summaries distributed to special operations personnel, had been heeded by both Davidson and Campbell. Wounded, without proper arms or ammunition and with no hope of offering anything other than token resistance, they had faced the inevitable with great courage and fortitude. Quite deliberately and with full knowledge that their act was irrevocable, they had crushed the glass of their cyanide capsules between their teeth. In placing the lives of twenty-one men above their own, Lieutenant-Commander Donald Davidson and Corporal Archie Campbell had performed the most selfless act that can be asked of any human being.[37]

After collecting the folboat, the rubber raft with all its supplies, and such sundry items as wristwatches, clothing, rations, binoculars, weapons, money and sunglasses, the search party returned to Major Fugita with the news that two men, including a Lieutenant-Commander, were now dead on Tapai Island. Unfortunately, they also had to report that there was no sign of the fifth man. Somehow, he must have escaped. There was some small consolation, for they had retrieved from the officer's body a rather waterlogged, but still legible notebook which, when translated, might reveal some useful information.[38]

Doubtless the Kempei Tai were pleased with this windfall. It might even help appease the top brass at Seventh Army Headquarters, who had been most put out to learn that information concerning the Kasu Island incident had taken three days to filter through to them. Arriving in the middle of the noon meal, the news had quite spoilt everyone's lunch.[39]

Although they could now account for four of the white men seen leaving the tonkan, the Japanese, believing that the rest were hiding out somewhere on Batam Island, continued their search.[40] In the meantime, to ensure that the locals would be less anxious to help the enemy in future, they decided to make an example of Mr and Mrs Latif.

When Mrs Latif arrived at Penegat Island (having been rescued from Soreh by a passing villager named Tambi Sukar), her husband, with whom she had hoped to be reunited, was not there. He was in Kempei Tai Headquarters at Tandjung Pinang hanging by his wrists from the torture room ceiling.

His tormentor was Yap Chin Yah, the Chinese import from Dabo, whose torture methods were such that Latif begged to be put out of his misery. His request for immediate death was denied, but he was informed he would be hanged in due course. Still alive after five days, he was taken to Pulau Buau, an island near the naval base at the top of the Riouw Straits, where he was imprisoned. After surviving six months on a starvation diet and still dressed in the same shorts and singlet, he was transferred to the Singapore Water Kempei Tai Headquarters at Tandjung Pagar.[41]

Mrs Latif was not free for long. In hindsight Penegat Island, being in Raja Mun's patch, was a very poor choice. Unable to break Latif, the Kempei had arrested his wife. It says much for her fortitude and constitution that she survived a hefty dose of the same treatment that had recently been doled out to her husband.[42]

While Abdul Latif languished in gaol, the search for the men of Rimau continued throughout the Thousand Islands without any success whatever. As the days merged into weeks with no reports of any sightings, the patrols became half hearted.[43] It was as if the white men had disappeared from the face of the earth. It was an opinion that was shared by Major Walter Chapman, for when he arrived at Merapas Island on November 21, thirteen days late, Rimau was nowhere to be seen.

Chapter 12
Right Place, Wrong Time

When *Porpoise* finally returned to Fremantle on October 11 after an uneventful journey from Pedjantan Island, both she and her commander were in need of attention — the submarine for a number of mechanical faults and Marsham for emotional stress. Burnt out by this latest sortie and unable to contemplate another mission in the claustrophobic confines of a submarine, he asked to be relieved of his command.[1]

The possibility then arose that *Porpoise*, even with a new commander at the helm, might not be repaired in time to make the rendezvous, forcing Shadwell to cast around for an alternate vessel. Although it had been mooted that one of Admiral Christie's submarines might be available, the military chiefs preferred not to invite the United States Navy to muscle in on what had been, up until now, an entirely British/Australian affair.[2]

They chose instead HMS *Tantalus*, a T-class submarine which, although scheduled to go on patrol, could perform a dual role and make the pickup from Merapas. Its commanding officer, Hugh 'Rufus' Mackenzie, an able man with an impressive record of 'kills' to his credit, was none too pleased to learn that *Tantalus* was to take over the role of Rimau's taxi. Like Captain Shadwell, Lieutenant-Commander Mackenzie believed that 'the most important task of a submarine is to sink enemy shipping'. Previous experience had convinced him that special operations, when he was 'forever landing people in little canoes and picking them up again' were, to put it bluntly, 'a pain in the neck'.[3]

On October 16, at about the same time as Lyon was making his acquaintance with Abdul Latif on Soreh Island, *Tantalus* slipped out of Fremantle harbour on her combined exercise, carrying Rimau's rescue team, Chapman and Croton, and a full load of seventeen lethal torpedoes. A far cry from *Porpoise*, with its cumbersome profile and lumbering ways, *Tantalus* was a streamlined hunter, captained by a man who was determined to live up to his reputation. With over three weeks before the submarine was due to break off patrol and proceed to Merapas, Mackenzie had high hopes of sinking quite a few enemy ships.[4]

Unfortunately, fate was not at all kind. After seeing nothing for twelve days, they spied a ship near Merapas only to have it scuttle into the safety of the Singapore Straits. Completely frustrated, Mackenzie resumed his search, the reports of the mauling that the Japanese Fleet was receiving near the Philippines serving only to make him envious as well as annoyed. This annoyance swelled five days later when, having finally stalked a convoy of four small merchantmen and sunk one of them, the submarine was ordered to call off the chase as her services were required elsewhere. Disparagingly referred to as 'life guard duty' by Mackenzie, the job involved standing by in case any American airmen were shot down during a bombing raid over Singapore. To Mackenzie's disgust, apart from a distant destroyer, they saw nothing; not even a US plane, let alone a downed pilot. When finally released from the purgatory of rescue duty on November 8, Mackenzie resumed his patrol.[5]

Although only sixty kilometres away at the time, he had made no attempt to land Chapman and Croton at Merapas on the night of November 7, nor did he attempt to do so on the following two days, when *Tantalus* was still within one hundred kilometres of the island. Without consulting his superior officers or sending any wireless messages seeking a change to 'Operation Order No. 44', Mackenzie decided to delay the pickup. The reason, according to his log, was because there were 'fifteen torpedoes still remaining' and 'further targets had to be found'. Later he tried further to rationalise his decision by stating that, as he had an extra fourteen days' fuel and stores in hand and believed that his main objective was 'offensive action against the enemy', it would have been 'improper' to abandon his patrol in order to pick up the party. In spite of his protestations, his decision was utterly indefensible.[6]

Everyone, from Captain Shadwell to Major Chapman, knew that Rimau's pickup date was November 7/8. Although Rimau had been instructed to wait for thirty days, this did not absolve the submarine commander of the responsibility of making every effort to keep the original rendezvous. The date agreed upon by Lyon, Chapman, Shadwell and Marsham had been quite explicit and Mackenzie's written orders plainly stated that 'subject to patrol requirements HMS *Tantalus* will leave her patrol at dark on 7th November and proceed to the vicinity of Merapas Island'.[7]

The patrol requirements at this stage were zero. They had found no masses of shipping whose destruction was vital to the war effort. Indeed, the patrol was evidently considered to be of such low priority that Mackenzie had been diverted to 'life guard duty' by senior officers who obviously placed more importance on the rescue of downed airmen than the possible destruction of enemy ships. Moreover, there was no practical reason why *Tantalus* could not have returned to Australia with fifteen unused torpedoes. Although conditions on a T-class submarine were rather cramped, Rimau's accommodation did not depend on using space occupied by the six reserve torpedoes. Even if it had, some of the torpedoes, although expensive, could have been dumped, for what was the loss of a few warheads — warheads that were often wasted when they misfired or the captain missed the target — against the lives of twenty-three men?[8]

In the end, human frailty triumphed over objective, cool-headed analysis. To return with only one trifling target to his credit, particularly when the Americans had been knocking off enemy shipping at a rate that was almost embarrassing, was evidently too much to ask of a man like Mackenzie.[9] With his own pride as well as that of the British Navy, if not the Empire, at stake, Mackenzie was looking for an opportunity to strut his stuff.

For three days he found nothing. Then, on November 11, *Tantalus* homed in on a target — a tiny wooden coastal trader crewed by eleven Malays and one Chinese, guarded by a lone Japanese soldier. Stuttering along the surface of the ocean to the north-east of Merapas, the *Pahang Maru*, loaded with seventy-five drums of fuel oil and nine drums of lubricating oil, was on a voyage from Malaya to Bangkok. It was obvious, from its stop-start progress, that it was experiencing serious engine trouble.

The submarine soon caught up with the ailing ship, which was travelling at a speed of only three knots. As the other vessel was unarmed, *Tantalus* surfaced. With his movie camera under his arm, Major Chapman accompanied the gun crew onto the submarine's turret to record the scene for posterity.

Without firing a single warning shot, *Tantalus*'s four inch (110 mm) gun opened up at a range of 540 metres. The first round started a fire amidships, while the next four killed both the captain and the assistant engineer and set the engine room ablaze. When the firing stopped, the remaining members of the *Pahang Maru*'s crew were observed hanging over the ship's railings, looking anxiously at the holes in the hull. As they showed no inclination to flee, a few more rounds were poured into the target, from a range of only 180 metres. The vessel, now well ablaze and breaking up, started to sink.

As the water reached deck level, nine of the crew abandoned ship and were immediately picked up. When the chief engineer indicated that the Japanese guard was making for the shore, the submarine aborted the rescue of the last Malay, still standing on the burning deck, and chased after the soldier instead. After he had been subdued by a blow to the head with a lead weight, following an unsuccessful attempt to drown himself, he was taken on board. Convinced that his last moment had come he was led below, where, contrary to his expectations, he was well looked after. His spirits however had taken such a pounding that he took no interest in life and spent the voyage back to Australia huddled in a miserable heap in a corner.

Fortunately, the remaining Malay crewman was an able swimmer. While the drama with the Japanese had been taking place he had taken to the water, where he was still paddling around, awaiting rescue. When he and his fellow crew members had recovered from the shock of being attacked, they were handed over to the accommodating captain of a Chinese junk, who relieved Mackenzie of his unwanted passengers in return for a tin of biscuits.[10]

On November 11 Mackenzie reassessed his position but, instead of sailing immediately for Merapas, he decided that he wanted to delay the pickup even further — another week to be exact. Clearly, as this would be pushing 'patrol requirements' to the limit, he would need formal permission. He 'consulted' Major Chapman, who, for some inexplicable reason, evidently 'concurred' with his argument that 'as their pickup could be any time between 7th November and 7th December . . . the most useful thing the submarine could do would be to continue on her patrol until the remaining torpedoes had been used up'. At 24 minutes to 11 on the evening of November 11, four days after the agreed rescue date, 'Rufus' Mackenzie transmitted a signal to Captain Shadwell requesting an additional week's deferment.[11]

The precise contents of the message are not known, but, whatever was said, it must have been persuasive. Against all logical explanation, Captain Shadwell, who had once been so worried that Rimau's safety had been compromised with the security leak that he advocated cancellation of the operation, gave Mackenzie the permission he sought.[12]

For the next nine days the submarine patrolled the waters between Singapore and the Natunas without success, sighting only three targets during the entire period, none of which was attacked. On November 19, on instructions received from headquarters, Tantalus carried out another round of lifeguard duty off the Malayan coast — a mission that was as uneventful as the previous one. On November 21, three days after the deferred but officially sanctioned pickup date, and fully two weeks after she was expected, Tantalus, her fifteen precious torpedoes still intact, eventually arrived at Merapas.

At seven that evening, after studying the northern coastline through the periscope, Chapman was satisfied that he had identified the Hammock Tree. On the southern shore he had spotted four people, whom he believed were Malays, walking along the beach near the huts and also spied one kolek tied to the mooring stake. The uninhabited house looked to be still uninhabited and the only sign of human occupation, apart from the four beach wanderers, was a fire burning in the banana plantation behind Stewart Point. It all seemed perfectly ordinary. He had seen no sign of any of the Rimau party, but that was only to be expected.[13]

At about one am the submarine, with the folboat and stores lashed firmly to the casing, stopped at a point 450 metres north-west of Oyster Point.[14] The pickup orders, drafted in Fremantle by someone who paid scant attention to the topography of the island or to Davidson's detailed notes, had actually directed that the drop-off be made on the lee side, which was about as far away from the Hammock Tree as it was possible to get. Mackenzie decided, however, that conditions were favourable enough to attempt a landing on the northern coast, which cut the distance to be travelled on foot by about half. Had they come directly inshore at this point, they would still have been about three hundred metres from the Hammock Tree. Unfortunately, it was three hundred metres to the west.

Since this was the wrong direction for the approach to the rendezvous, it is evident that no one, least of all Chapman, bothered to consult Davidson's instructions. Davidson had been quite specific. When approaching the island, they were to come ashore at Land Crab Bay. While one man waited, concealed in the dense cover behind the beach, the other was to continue on foot in a westerly direction until he reached the Hammock Tree.[15]

Launching the folboat from the submarine's fore hydroplanes, Chapman and Croton paddled towards a small stretch of sand, aided by a calm sea and cloudless sky. As they neared the shore, close to Punai Point, Chapman was alarmed by what he thought was the sound of waves smacking against the rocks and decided to land further around the point on the lee side. It was not far — about three or four hundred metres — but with each stroke of the paddle they moved further away from the rendezvous point, which had to be reached well before daybreak. After a bit of bother from a breaking sea, they touched bottom about five metres off Dead Coral Beach. It was now close to two am. After hiding the folboat in the thick undergrowth behind the beach, both men turned towards Punai Point. It is obvious that, in selecting this route, Chapman did not realise that, having landed on the far side of the island, the shortest and easiest route to the rendezvous was inland, across Cache Swamp and Wild Cat Hill. Chapman's choice was hopeless. Between Dead Coral and the Hammock Tree lay over five hundred metres of slippery black rocks.[16]

Had Chapman gone ashore to help with the unloading of the stores, he may have had some idea of just how difficult it would be to negotiate these boulders in the dark. Varying in size from twenty centimetres to ninety centimetres in diameter and as treacherous as polished glass, they were for the fit and very sure footed. Chapman was neither. Of the past seventy-one days he had spent only four on dry land. Coupled with the need for silence, Chapman's wobbly state made their speed excruciatingly slow. After two and a half hours of slipping and sliding, during which they covered a distance of only about three hundred metres, they finally neared the small patch of sand where they had originally intended to land. As they rounded Punai Point, Chapman produced a torch in an effort to light the way and make his task a little easier.[17]

Horrified that anyone could be so stupid, Corporal Croton cocked his silent Sten gun and informed his superior officer that he would shoot him if he did not extinguish the light. Almost exhausted, and convinced that, in spite of not having found the track, they had reached Kingfisher's

Rest, Chapman called a halt. About an hour later, with light flooding the horizon, he was ready to set off again.[18]

As he looked out to sea, the Major suddenly froze. Standing off the coastline were three large naval vessels. His panic subsided when a closer look revealed that they were simply some small, rocky, offshore islands, but there was a further delay while Chapman fretted about whether they might be seen by someone on the islands — a notion that was dismissed by Croton, who could not see what all the fuss was about. By the time they reached the Hammock Tree, about three hundred metres further on, it was almost full light. When Chapman looked for the hammock slung between the trunks of the trees, he found, to his consternation, that the space was completely empty.[19] It was little wonder. They had arrived far too late.

It is patently obvious that Chapman cannot have read Davidson's instructions. Not only had they come from the wrong direction, they had missed the rendezvous by at least one, if not two, hours. The arrangements were perfectly clear. If the rendezvous was not kept, the party would leave the tree at first light to seek cover during the daylight hours.[20]

Chapman searched the area but found nothing except a few small pieces of silver paper beneath a bush. He did not expect to find tracks, for the men had been trained to obliterate all signs of occupation. Deciding to carry out a search of the island, they avoided the path that ran up the hill from the tree, striking off a little to the east through a light jungle of palm trees and creepers. Although the hill at this point was reasonably steep, they scaled it without mishap until Chapman's boot disloged a small boulder, giving him his second fright of the day. He held his breath while it rolled down the hill with what seemed to him to be an incredibly loud noise. His nerves must have been on edge, for Croton, who was nearby, took absolutely no notice.[21]

On reaching the summit of the hill, they turned east to explore the remainder of the ridge. It was not very interesting — an overgrown banana plantation filled with rotting fruit and a wild sago patch. It was not until after they had passed the sago patch that they saw the Japanese. He was all alone except for a small, skinny native pi-dog, following about fifty metres behind. Croton and Chapman flattened themselves behind the nearest coconut trees as the man crossed their field of vision at right angles and disappeared over the rise. The dog, who was undisturbed by their presence, trotted after him.[22]

The corporal had no doubt that the man was Japanese. He had seen plenty of enemy soldiers when attached to Mission 204 in China and had, like Chapman, just spent ten days in close proximity with the Japanese prisoner on board *Tantalus*. Unlike the local inhabitants, who dressed in sarongs or shorts and singlet, the stranger was clad in a proper shirt and long trousers. Too tall for a local, his skin was pale and his oriental features quite unlike those of a Malay. Always one for direct action, Croton wanted to take him prisoner, but Chapman wouldn't have a bar of it. He insisted that it was impossible. They had neither rope for securing his hands and feet nor proper gag and, besides, as it was so early in the morning it would be too long to wait until the submarine returned.[23]

Obviously shaken by the close encounter, Chapman had Croton cover him with his Sten gun while he proceeded down the hill, parallel to the path which led to the native huts and along which the man and the dog had just disappeared. As soon as they reached the edge of Cache Swamp, they turned west and skirted the northern side, keeping well away from the obviously dangerous hut area.[24]

When they reached the western end of the swamp, near Dead Coral, the pair split up. Despite Croton's assurances that he had hidden the folboat properly, Chapman was unconvinced. He sat beneath a tree while his underling, under protest, went off to check. When he returned, having informed Chapman in no uncertain terms that the folboat was properly concealed and that his errand had been a 'bloody waste of time', the pair discovered two paths leading up the hill from a couple of waterholes, which Croton, a good bushman as well as a practical soldier, estimated had been dug about six to eight weeks previously. After noting a sweat rag and bandage hanging from a tree and four makeshift bailers lying on the ground, they followed the first path, which led almost immediately to a deserted clearing. Although there was ample evidence of recent occupation, it was evident that whoever had been there had left in a tearing great hurry.[25]

The area was dominated by a rudely constructed shelter, not unlike the framework of a bush lean-to. About seven and a half metres in length and three metres wide, it had been made by simply suspending a pole from a cleft in a tree to an overhanging branch and partially covering the framework with interwoven palm leaves. Nearby, half filled with stagnant water, was a large iron wok, probably the legacy of some long-gone plantation workers, under which were the remains of a fire. Several other much smaller fires, on which rested four or five Commando Cookers containing partially cooked meals, were also scattered around. Although now quite putrid, the contents were recognisable as being part of the Rimau rations and on closer inspection it was apparent that the fires had been hurriedly stamped out. Beneath some cut, quite dried-out brush, the sharp-eyed Croton spied a rubbish heap containing fifty empty food tins, while another heap about five metres away contained another thirty. Clearly, quite a number of the party had been here. The question was, where were they now?

A further search revealed other bits and pieces — an empty beer bottle, an oil can from the SB maintenance kit, the small rake given to Carey to eliminate footprints, empty cigarette packets, some lengths of rope, a cotton name tag with oriental characters written on it, a bunch of green bananas, some mostly rotten pawpaws, yam roots, a very ripe coconut, and, quite inexplicably, a set of completely unintelligible symbols, carved into the trunk of a coconut palm, well over two metres from the ground. Chapman could make neither head nor tail of it.[26]

Bewildered, the pair extended their search, looking for further evidence. Running from the top of the hill towards the Invasion Coast were three paths, which showed signs that they had been recently cut. The first, leading towards Kingfisher's Rest, revealed no evidence of usage and was not explored further. The second, which led down to the Hammock Tree, was partially investigated, yielding some more fragments of silver paper and a broken drinking bowl. The third path, which led nowhere in particular, yielded nothing.[27]

They then walked back along the ridge towards the east. Without actually venturing down to Stewart Point to check out the area thoroughly, Chapman came to the conclusion that the missing party was not hiding in the vicinity.[28] Finding nothing other than the overgrown banana plantation which they had seen before, they returned to Cache Swamp.

Here they found more evidence of Rimau's occupation. Scattered amongst the undergrowth were six small wood and palm-leaf shelters, much better constructed than the large lean-to. Big enough to accommodate two men, each contained tins of half-cooked food resting on the ashes of fires that were long since dead. There were also two other structures, quite devoid of any equipment or gear, that looked as if they may have been used to conceal folboats. Near the waterholes was a string that might have served as a clothes line but apart from that they found nothing — no weapons, no clothing, no note and definitely no sign whatever of the three tonnes of stores and equipment.

With Chapman satisfied that the party was nowhere on the island, he and Croton sat down in the clearing and waited. It was a very long wait. As the submarine was not due back until after dark, Chapman had plenty of time to think.[29]

What had happened? Where were they? How long had they been gone? With very few clues on which to base his assumptions and clouded by evidence that did not seem to add up, Chapman came to the conclusion that Rimau had returned to the island, perhaps in the junk, and that they had been surprised and captured without a fight.[30]

He briefly considered taking one of the locals off for interrogation, but dismissed the idea as being impracticable as well as dangerous. Dangerous it most certainly would have been, for the Merapas natives had been supplanted by a Japanese patrol. Resigning himself to the fact that Rimau had disappeared, Chapman fervently hoped that whatever had happened had taken place before November 7 — the day the submarine should have returned to rescue them.[31]

Chapman remained in the clearing, pondering the situation, until dusk approached. At about six o'clock, he and Croton moved down to Dead

Coral, retrieved the folboat and the stores and settled down on the rocky foreshore to await the arrival of the submarine. At 10 to 10, after four rather anxious hours, Chapman was relieved to see the comforting sight of *Tantalus* rounding Punai Point in the moonlight.[32]

Commander Mackenzie had had a rather trying day. As they had been obliged to spend the entire day underwater after being spotted by an enemy plane at 6 am, he was somewhat relieved on surfacing to find that all appeared to be well on Merapas. As he rounded Punai Point he was reassured to see the figures of Chapman and Croton moving about on the beach.[33]

By 20 past 10 Chapman had reached the submarine, reported to Mackenzie and informed him that the rescue was a lost cause. He told the submarine commander that, although there were signs that the party had been there, it had obviously left at least fourteen days before. Chapman was so adamant on this point that Mackenzie believed there was no point in waiting until the next night, as the orders specified, or in making any further attempt to establish contact. Indeed, he decided that to hang about any longer might only serve to jeopardise the safety of the submarine.[34]

With 'practically a full outfit of torpedoes remaining' it was not long before Mackenzie's attention was diverted away from Rimau and back to his patrol. Deciding against going straight home, he detoured to Java, hoping to find some rich pickings among the convoys travelling south. In spite of his high expectations, they did not find any targets until the morning of November 27, when a small merchantman with two escorts were spotted. Four torpedoes were fired but it was, to use his own words, a 'rotten attack'. The first two exploded prematurely and the second pair missed the ship altogether. As the enemy was now alerted to *Tantalus*'s presence, the submarine made herself scarce and headed for Lombok. Nine days later they were back in Western Australia, tying up in Fremantle harbour.[35]

As a rescue mission, the Sixth War Patrol of HMS *Tantalus* had been an abject failure. As a patrol it had not been much better. The expenditure of six torpedoes (four of which were wasted), fifteen rounds of ammunition and almost two hundred and sixty thousand litres of fuel did not look good when compared with the tally of one small freighter, one nondescript native vessel, two Malays killed by accident and one dejected prisoner of war. The best that could be said of this very expensive, fifty-two day patrol, which had covered over eighteen thousand, four hundred kilometres, was that it was the longest patrol by any British submarine. In the absence of anything else about which to crow, it was a claim that assumed a disproportionate importance.[36]

On their return, both Chapman and Croton were taken to SRD Headquarters. Croton was only briefly interrogated, but Chapman, being the officer, was not let off so lightly. By December 12 he had produced a lengthy written account of the entire operation, including details of the incidents that occurred while on the submarine. So painstaking was the Major in this part of the report that he included some interesting details that had been omitted, or differed, from those that appeared in the report written by the submarine commander.[37]

Perhaps it was the effort of recalling everything that had happened in this part of the sortie that made Chapman suffer a memory lapse when it came to the section in which he had played the major role. He made no reference to the fact that he had apparently been consulted about the change in the pickup date and that he had agreed. Although he remembered the little pi-dog with absolute clarity, he did not mention the Japanese at all, nor the fact that Croton had wanted to take the enemy soldier prisoner. He also had no recollection of the embarrassing fact that the corporal had threatened to shoot him. He did not, however, forget to submit to his superiors an Adverse Confidential Report on soldier Ron Croton.[38]

It can only be assumed, from the way in which he presented the reasons for the failure of the mission, that Major Walter Chapman was now a man consumed by doubt and guilt. Included in this report to SRD was a copy of Mackenzie's 'Patrol Report Appendix I', which gave his account of the pickup sortie. Two pages long, the retyped version was an exact copy until the final words of the tenth paragraph, in which Mackenzie had originally written, 'It is to be hoped that the delay in carrying out the operation was not the cause for the loss of this gallant party, but it must be considered as a possibility'. This had been altered to 'it is unfortunately very possible' (that the loss of the party was attributable to the delay), thereby shifting the blame to Mackenzie.[39]

In what appears to be an attempt to mitigate the sickening thought that he might be held responsible in some way for this late arrival, Chapman then presented evidence piece by piece to prove that, even if the submarine had turned up on the right date, Rimau would not have been there. The mangoes, the coconuts, the cut brush and the decaying food were all deemed by him to be at least two weeks old. He even decided that the unripened bananas had been cut fourteen days previously, obviously unaware that in the tropics green bananas ripen at a much faster rate than they do in England. To the average reader, there seemed to be no doubt about it. The Rimau men could not have possibly been on Merapas during the past two weeks, and, judging by the Major's allegedly thorough search of the island, were not anywhere in the vicinity.[40]

The astute intelligence officer who combed through Chapman's report and studied his lengthy analysis was by no means convinced. He was so suspicious that many stones may have been left unturned, that he began a campaign to mount a rescue operation named 'Rimexit'. It seemed to him that there was a fair chance that Rimau might still be on Merapas.[41] He was not wrong.

Although the party had quit the camp sixteen days before Chapman arrived, it had not gone far. For thirty anxious days, the remaining survivors of Operation Rimau had watched and waited for the submarine to come.[42]

On 5 May 1964, not long after this fact became known to him and shortly after being interviewed by an historian about his part in the operation, Walter Chapman, aged forty-nine, was found dead in his car on the road outside the Amersham Hospital in Buckinghamshire, England. In his pocket was a small, black, bakelite capsule, of a type not seen since the Second World War. It was quite empty. Even to a layman, the cause of death was obvious, for, permeating the corpse, was the unmistakeable smell of bitter almonds.[43] Twenty years on, Rimau had claimed its final victim.

Major-General H. Gordon Bennett, Commander of the
AIF Malaya 1941-1942. (AWM 8520).

The horror of the bombing. Grief-stricken Chinese women with the body of a small child
amid the ruins of Singapore city, February 1942. (AWM 11529/22).

The surrender party advances towards the Japanese at Bukit Timah, 15 February 1942.
Major Cyril Wild, carrying the white flag, is on the left, General Percival on the right.

Colonel Alan F. Warren, Royal Marines.

Lieutenant-Colonel Ivan Lyon of the Gordon Highlanders, c.1936.

Gabrielle Lyon, c.1939.

Ivan Lyon at the helm of *Sederhana Djohanes*, off the coast of Ceylon, 12 April 1942. Seated in front of him, the trilby-hatted Geoffrey Rowley-Conwy scans the horizon. They are, Rowley-Conwy has written on the back of the picture, 'trying to decide what the wind will do, and whether to go north or south'.

Lyon climbs along the bowsprit of *Sederhana Djohanes* as the *Anglo-Canadian* alters course to pick them up, 14 April 1942.

The dying moments of *Sederhana Djohanes* after her 2670 kilometre voyage from Sumatra, 14 April 1942.

Captain William Roy 'Bill' Reynolds, Master Mariner, whose
ship *Kofuku Maru* (later *Krait*) enabled Lyon to carry out
the raid on Singapore Harbour.

Lieutenant-Commander
Donald Davidson RNVR.

Refuge Bay, Camp 'X', October 1942. (Left to right). Sub-Lieutenant B. Overell (explosives expert), Ivan Lyon (now minus his moustache), Sergeant Clarrie Willoughby (gunnery instructor), Captain 'Gort' Chester, Donald Davidson, Jock Campbell.

A fully erected folboat with rations and equipment for two men.

A folboat in action. Major Tom Hall in rear cockpit.

The final Jaywick team, with Jock Campbell of SRD. (Back row) Moss Berryman, Boof Marsh, Joe Jones and Happy Huston. (Centre) Crilly the Cook, Cobber Cain, Paddy McDowell, Horrie Young, Poppa Falls, Taffy Morris. (Front) Ted Carse, Donald Davidson, Ivan Lyon, Jock Campbell, Bob Page.

The fully loaded *M V Krait,* formerly *Kofuku Maru* and *Suey Sin Fah,* under the expert guidance of Bill Reynolds, makes her way up the Brisbane River in January 1943 before leaving for Singapore.

On board *Krait,* September 1943. (Back row, left to right) Wally Falls, Cobber Cain, Ivan Lyon (with tattooed tiger on chest), Ted Carse, Paddy McDowell. (Front row, left to right) Andrew Huston, Moss Berryman, Horrie Young.

Lyon observing the shipping in the Singapore Roads from the western tip of Dongas Island, 23 or 24 September 1943.

(Left to right) Falls, Davidson, Huston, Lyon, Jones and Page drink a toast to Jaywick on 11 November 1943 at Meigunyah in Brisbane. Of eighty-one missions mounted by SRD during World War II, Jaywick would prove to be the only completely successful operation.

'Sleeping Beauty' expert, Sub-Lieutenant Gregor Riggs.

Launching a 273 kilogram SB at Careening Bay Camp, Western Australia, August 1944. Folboat on right.

Lieutenant Bruno Reymond, shown here during his secondment to the American Navy in 1943, lights a cigarette for a recently liberated Gilbert Islander.

Lieutenant Williams's handkerchief, on which all the Rimau men wrote their names the night before departure.

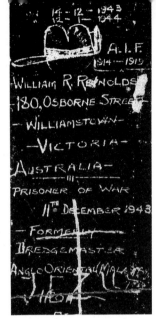

Lieutenant Walter Carey, the Conducting Officer who remained at Merapas to guard the stores.

The scratchings on the door jamb of Bill Reynolds's cell in Balikpapan. As Reynolds was never a member of the AIF, it is thought that he used the readily recognisable slouch hat and initials to identify himself as an Australian.

The hijacked Indonesian prahu, *Mustika*.

Eyewitnesses Mahat Kunil (left) and Arafin Bin Akup (right), aged thirty-three and eighteen in 1944, at Kasu Island, June 1989.

The village at Pangkil Island where Lyon, Stewart and Ross met traitor Raja Mun.

Lieutenant Bobby Ross and (below) Lieutenant-Colonel Ivan Lyon, killed at Soreh Island, 16 October 1944.

Corporal A.G.P. (Archie) Campbell, who died with
Lieutenant-Commander Donald Davidson at Tapai Island,
18 October 1944.

Abdul Latif, in 1989, beside the rock at Tapai Island where he found the bodies of Campbell
and Davidson.

Sergeant Colin Cameron.

A fish trap similar to that upon which Sargent was marooned.

Two great mates, Able Seamen Andrew 'Happy' Huston, drowned near Boeaja Island on 15 December 1944, and Freddie 'Boof' Marsh, died in Singapore 11 January 1945.

In September 1981 Karta (far left) and other Merapas Islanders uncover the stone sangar where Cameron made his last stand on 5 November 1944.

Corporal Colin Craft (left), drowned at Satai Cape, and Lance Corporal Hugo Pace, who died at Dili.

Lieutenant Albert 'Blondie' Sargent, captured at Maja Island 24 December 1944, beheaded at Bukit Timah 7 July 1945.

Private Douglas Warne, died at Soerabaya as a result of a tetanus experiment, April 1945.

Lieutenants John Sachs and (below) Clifford Perske, beheaded at Soerabaya 30 March 1945.

Despite Japanese claims that the Rimau men had been executed with full Samurai ceremony, they were beheaded in exactly the same way as this man, Sergeant L.G. Siffleet of 'M' Special Unit, the intelligence branch of AIB. Aitape, New Guinea, 24 October 1943. (AWM 101099).

Corporal Clair Stewart and (below) Captain Robert Page, beheaded at Bukit Timah with Fletcher, Carey, Gooley, Falls, Hardy, Ingleton, Sargent and Warren, 7 July 1945.

Standing alongside the Rimau graves at Bukit Timah, Major Cyril Wild (right) attempts to establish the identity of the victims by questioning Outram Road Commandant Colonel Mikizawa.

Warrant Officer Jeffrey Willersdorf who died of wounds, maltreatment and neglect at Dili, Timor, February 1945.

The grave of Lieutenant-Colonel Ivan Lyon at Kranji.

Kranji War Cemetery, Singapore. The graves of those beheaded at Bukit Timah are in the front row.

Presentation of the Commando Cross of Valour at the War Memorial, Hyde Park, Sydney on 8 July 1978. (Left to right) Colonel George Cardy, representing Lieutenant-Colonel Ivan Lyon; Debbie Brown, representing Lieutenant Albert 'Blondie' Sargent, and Mr Horrie Young, telegraphist on the Jaywick raid.

When the government refused to consider posthumous awards for Rimau, 1 Commando Association commissioned this specially designed Commando Cross of Valour.

Chapter 13
Pursued

Finding it impossible to keep together, the twelve whom Lyon had ordered to flee from Kasu had split up and returned to Merapas safely, where they were reunited with the party guarding the stores. A few days later, when they were joined by Warne and Huston, the number of Rimau men hiding on the island rose to eighteen. As this pair could not say with any degree of certainty what had happened to Lyon and the others, the possibility of their being alive was accepted as being remote, particularly in the absence of any planes suggesting that a search was in progress. Indeed, things were so quiet that on Merapas, a mere fifty kilometres from Major Fugita's headquarters at Tandjung Pinang, there had been no sign of any Japanese activity at all.[1]

Time rolled on. With only a few days to go until November 7, and nothing to indicate that the enemy was on their trail, there was every reason for the remaining eighteen to feel confident that they would get back to Australia in one piece. They would have done so, had a Japanese plane not developed engine trouble.

On November 3 a Singapore-bound aircraft, whose pilot noticed a sudden drop in oil pressure, made an emergency landing at Kidjang, twenty-five kilometres to the west of Merapas. Although the two Japanese passengers on board, one of whom was Mr Tanabi, manager of the Bintan Bauxite Mine, were not injured in the unexpected touchdown, they were very interested in the cause of the diversion, which proved to be a punctured oil line. Alarmed by the possibility that the damage may have been caused by a bullet, Singapore Headquarters ordered an investigation of the islands to the west of Kidjang, to eliminate the possibility that enemy agents may have fired on the plane as it passed overhead.

Kidjang's Captain Sungarno and Second Lieutenant Orzawa were instructed to take a search party to the island of Mapor, about eight kilometres to the north-west of Merapas. In line with the usual procedure, Orzawa impressed into service a young Indonesian with local knowledge — twenty-four-year-old Abdul Rachman Achap, an employee of Mr Frey, the Dutch Harbourmaster.[2]

The two boats, containing more than a dozen men, arrived at Mapor on the morning of November 4 to interrogate headman Abdul Wahab, who stated quite categorically that he had received no reports that Europeans were in the area. Achap had no doubt that Wahab was speaking the truth, for had the headman had any idea that European men were on Merapas the Japanese would have known about it weeks earlier. Recruited by the promise of a sack of rice per month plus two or three hundred rupiah for items of information, Wahab was a well-known informant.

For some reason, the Japanese were not satisfied. Taking Wahab with them, the search parties headed for Merapas where, on the south-west tip, they spotted one of the Malay fishermen, who was immediately apprehended and questioned. Although he must have known from young Karta that strangers were on the island, the Merapas islander stubbornly refused to reveal any information. When a severe beating did not encourage him to change his tune, Captain Sungarno, apparently content, left half of his force on the boat with Lieutenant Orzawa and sauntered inland from the beach.[3]

Coming right on meal time, the sound of the boats' engines had rudely interrupted the preparation of the Rimau team's lunch. Those who had been supervising the cooking grabbed their guns and took cover on the hill, while the remaining eight, who were occupied elsewhere, sought refuge in the jungle. Up on the hill, well hidden by the dense growth that lay between them and the beach, the lunch party watched as the boats neared the island. By the casual manner in which the craft approached, Captain Page was convinced that the landing was routine and that enemy suspicions had not been aroused.

His assumption was based on sound military logic. The bay near the huts was a woeful choice for troops on the offensive. Had they intended to storm the island, they should have landed on the Invasion Coast, which was far more difficult to defend. This lackadaisical, very incautious attitude indicated to Page that the visit was a low-key affair and it might well be that the Japanese, never too keen on entering thick jungle, would make a perfunctory search and leave. Provided the search party did not move away from the coconut grove, Bob Page believed there was a good chance that Rimau would remain undetected.

Tension was high as they watched Sungarno move away from the sand and into the grove — so high that, before the patrol had covered one hundred metres, one of the Rimau men accidentally discharged his gun. That in itself may not have been such a disaster had not the fusillade of shots from the silent Sten found its mark.[4] Captain Sungarno fell to the ground, stone dead. In a split second, another soldier, mortally wounded in the head, also pitched forward.[5]

For the first few seconds, the Japanese were stunned. With no noise other than a sound reminiscent of raindrops falling upon palm leaves they, like the troops at Soreh, were caught off guard. However, the sight of their dead commander· and their badly wounded comrade soon convinced them that the matter was serious. To a man, they hit the ground.

Second Lieutenant Orzawa, who had been watching from the boat, took over. Quickly recovering his wits, but with no idea of the size or deployment of the enemy, he ordered his troops to spray the hillside with machine-gun and rifle fire. The fire was returned but, as the hidden aggressors made no attempt to mount a counter-attack and as firing became sporadic at about four o'clock, Orzawa deduced that their numbers were not great.

With the daylight about to fade, he decided that it would be prudent to wait until morning before mounting a concentrated attack on the hill. While one of the boats was sent to Kidjang to report Sungarno's death and to request heavy reinforcements, he turned his attention to the dead and wounded. Unwilling to expose his men to enemy fire, he dispatched the fisherman and his wife to bring out Sungarno's corpse and rescue the injured soldier. From the safety of the shore, Abdul Wahab watched as the pair struggled to carry the captain's body to the boat, beaten all the way by enraged Japanese, who then detained them for further punishment.

Between eight and nine o'clock, several boats arrived with about one hundred reinforcements, which Orzawa, after forcing all native craft ashore, organised into sea and land patrols. While one group circled Merapas by boat at regular intervals, another mounted watch on the shoreline. Those not engaged in either of these activities spent the night in the locals' huts, confident that the white men had no chance of escape.[6] Unfortunately for Lieutenant Orzawa, he had underestimated the resourcefulness of the Rimau men.

When the alarm had been raised, the party had been split in two — nine hiding on the hillside with Bob Page, and the eight working away from the main camp area. The smaller group had been further fragmented and now comprised only six men — Blondie Sargent, Bruno Reymond, Doug Warne, Jeffrey Willersdorf, Colin Craft and Hugo Pace. It was unfortunate that in the flurry to take cover they had lost contact with two of their group. Somewhere, hiding in the jungle, were Sergeant Colin Cameron and Sub-Lieutenant Gregor Riggs.[7]

Up on the hillside, Page pondered what should be done. Provided they could hide somewhere until November 7, only three days hence, he knew that they had every chance of being rescued by the submarine. He decided that Mapor, which was within easy paddling distance of Merapas, might be just the place.

The Japanese foot patrol of the island cannot have extended any further than the hut area, for, as soon as it was dark, Page and his men recovered their folboats and packed them with stores from the camp in the clearing. Then, having ascertained that the water patrol circled the island once every two hours, they pushed off. Some made the journey in the water, probably towed behind the folboats — a procedure made possible by the use of improvised water wings. Page had previously discovered that a pair of trousers, stuffed with fibrous coconut husks, provided excellent flotational support. As they silently ferried the laden folboats across the eight kilometres of ocean to Mapor, they had no idea that Cameron and Riggs, who had not managed to catch up with either party, remained cut off and stranded.[8]

The following morning, Lieutenant Orzawa split his expeditionary force into two groups to storm the hill — one from the north and the other from the south. Achap, who had spent the night in one of the huts, watched from the beach near Stewart Point as the soldiers moved off. For some time he heard nothing. Then, from the vicinity of the hill, there came the sound of gunfire. On the fragmented skyline he caught a glimpse of a European soldier, racing frantically between the trees. Across the top of Wild Cat Hill he ran, down the spur towards Stewart Point, with the Japanese in hot pursuit. When he reached the end of the spur, he ran out of land. As there was nowhere else to go, he turned and faced his pursuers.

Three shots rang out, striking him in the chest. As the man rolled down the hill, to lie spreadeagled against a rock at its base, Achap ran forward. Cradling the badly wounded man in his arms, the Indonesian looked into eyes that betrayed no fear. The soldier returned his gaze. Then, quite calmly, and without uttering a single word, Sub-Lieutenant Gregor Riggs crossed himself and died.[9]

On the other side of the hill, near two small stone forts from which he and Riggs had made their final stand, lay the body of Sergeant Colin Cameron.[10] Left in the dark the previous evening, armed only with pistols and unable to flee the island, the duo had faced the fact that they were in a perilous position. With only a few hours in which to prepare a defensive position, they had hurriedly built two stone fortifications, about three metres apart, on either side of the Kingfisher's Rest path. In constructing these forts, or sangars as they were sometimes known, Cameron and Riggs had piled black stones, gathered from the foreshore, into two cylindrical shapes. With time running out, the constructions were rudely designed, without firing steps, nor slits through which a gun could be aimed. Since the walls tapered inwards, rather like an inverted ice-cream cone, there was barely enough room for one person.

While Achap had been watching the progress of the Japanese who had moved off the beach near Kolek Bay, the other group, which had made its way around to the Invasion Coast, had ultimately come to Kingfisher's Rest. With a limited field of fire and nothing but short-range pistols with which to defend themselves, the two Rimau men had not really stood a chance. When Riggs saw Cameron pitch backwards over his sangar, propelled by the force of the bullets that ripped into his head and chest, he decided it was time to quit his position. Although he would have lost some time in heaving himself over the rocky wall, he must have had a reasonable start on the Japanese, who were well below him on the slippery rocks.[11]

When Achap saw him weaving between the trees, he had run the best part of three hundred metres, most of it uphill. He may have outdistanced his pursuers, had not the other group arrived in time to take up the chase, the sound of their gunfire alerting Achap to the fugitive's plight. For the next few minutes he had stood transfixed, watching the erratic progress as Gregor Riggs ran for his life.

When Abdul Achap looked closely at the dead body that he held in his arms, he noticed a silver bracelet which he hoped that he might be able to keep, for it was a beautiful piece of work, emblazoned with some kind of emblem, beneath which was engraved the name of its owner. In spite of his high hopes, he was unsuccessful in his attempt to procure this piece of jewellery, for when the Japanese arrived, that was the end of the matter.[12]

It was probably the dramatic manner of his death, and the fact that his body was too close to the huts in which they intended to stay, that made the Japanese decide to bury Riggs. When he saw that the grave was to be simply a pile of rocks heaped randomly upon the body, Achap indicated that the soldier, obviously a Christian, should be buried in proper western style beneath the ground. Having spoken up, he was given the job of gravedigger. Choosing a spot away from the rocks, he lay the body of Riggs to rest in the soft earth in the shade of a large tree, not far from the beach at Stewart Point.[13] He must have done a good job as the Japanese later claimed credit for the burial, describing the grave, which had been marked and inscribed with Japanese characters, as 'very fine'.[14] For Cameron, who was out of sight on the other side of the island, there was no such refinement. He lay where he fell, the small stone sangar the only lasting reminder of his passing.[15]

By this stage the searchers as well as the onlookers believed that the rest of the European men had fled. Unable to explain their disappearance at the time, nor indeed in the years to come, the islanders came to the conclusion that all had been rescued by submarine.

Feeling a little more confident, the Japanese decided to investigate the hill more thoroughly, sending Achap on ahead to act as their shield. When he reached the clearing he found nothing but a couple of walkie-talkie radios, some bundles wrapped in sacking, two rifles, a pistol and more food than he had seen for quite some time. Concealing a walkie-talkie beneath his clothing, he tucked with relish into the lunchtime rations that had been abandoned by the Rimau party. Further up the hill he found the radio transmitter — smashed. Impressed by the fact that it had 'Australia' written on it and that it had short-wave frequency, Achap hoped that when the Japanese heard that the wireless was wrecked, they would not bother with it. Unfortunately the Japanese wanted the radio,

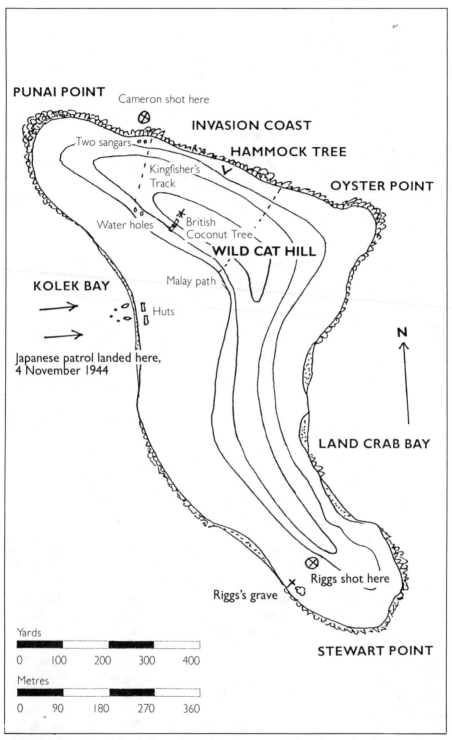

PUNAI POINT

Cameron shot here

INVASION COAST

Two sangars

HAMMOCK TREE

Kingfisher's
Track

OYSTER POINT

Water holes

British
Coconut Tree

WILD CAT HILL

Malay path

KOLEK BAY

Huts

N

Japanese patrol landed here,
4 November 1944

LAND CRAB BAY

Riggs shot here

Riggs's grave

Yards

| 0 | 100 | 200 | 300 | 400 |

Metres

| 0 | 90 | 180 | 270 | 360 |

STEWART POINT

Map VI. Merapas Island, from Davidson's original sketch, with additions by Tom Hall.

broken or not, so Achap had to content himself with the walkie-talkie, still concealed beneath his shirt.[16]

Back at the beach, Abdul Wahab watched with great interest as the booty, including three folboats and a camouflage hood, was loaded into the boats.[17] Considering the enormous amount of stores that had been on the island, Rimau had left very little behind. The only items that Page's group had been unable to retrieve were those in their personal kit. Of negligible monetary value, these small articles were, nevertheless, to lead them all to destruction.

By the time the Japanese had finished ransacking the men's belongings they had recovered Carey's notebook, Ingleton's sketch book, Page's camera, complete with film, Mrs Manderson's flags, and, from one of the huts near the beach, a document written in English. It is likely, from the terrible punishment inflicted upon the hut's occupants, that it was a testimonial written by the Rimau men in the hope that the Merapas islanders might be rewarded after the war.[18]

Leaving a small force, consisting mainly of Hei Ho, to remain on the island for the next four months, the Japanese left for Kidjang, taking Achap, Wahab and the Merapas islanders with them. On the boat, and much to his annoyance, Achap was relieved of the walkie-talkie by a keen-eyed Japanese soldier who had seen him pocketing it in the clearing. He returned home with nothing to show for his outing other than a few sizeable bruises and a belly full of good Australian tucker.

Although Wahab was able to return unscathed to Mapor post haste, the Malays, who had with such fortitude refused to betray Rimau, were not so lucky. For three weeks they were mercilessly beaten, the fisherman so badly that, twelve months after his ordeal, he was unable to speak above a whisper. To add to their misery, when they finally returned to Merapas they found that the Japanese had burnt down their house.[19]

When the documents, camera and flags arrived in Singapore, along with the news that there had been a battle on Merapas, the Kempei Tai turned up the heat. The contents of the notebooks and Ingleton's sketches, along with the visual evidence provided by the processed film, convinced the Kempei Tai that there was more to this enemy party than met the eye. While Hiroyuki Furuta, a civilian interpreter attached to the Army's Intelligence Branch, translated the documentation, puzzling over such cryptic entries as 'SB treatment over', Kakoshima Nasaki, chief of the 29th Naval Kempei Tai, ordered more Kempei troops into the area.[20]

Meantime, the Singapore Kempei Tai's special force was still trying to determine who had masterminded the sinking of the ships the previous month. As summary execution of a number of Chinese and Malays and the public display of their remains had not produced satisfactory results, the Kempei once again turned their attention to John Long, the Jaywick number one suspect who had miraculously survived twelve months in custody. To the Japanese, the situation appears to have been quite straightforward. As this second attack had taken place four days after Long had been released from gaol, he must be responsible. On November 25, John Long was rearrested. Two days later the Japanese cut off his head.[21]

Meanwhile, the real culprits were still free — Page and his men on Mapor, and Sargent's group on the high seas. The latter had had a charmed life, for, although they had been spotted at various islands, no one had informed the Japanese. Sargent and his five comrades, finding themselves isolated from Page at Merapas, had gone to ground. During the night, while Reymond collected his charts and his sextant from his kit, the rest had apparently succeeded in scavenging whatever stores and food stocks that were nearby. With no way of reaching the folboats and with the Japanese now in strength, they had hidden themselves in the jungle and settled down to wait.[22]

The following morning, alerted by the sound of shooting, they had watched, helpless, as the Japanese flushed Riggs into the open. Undetected by an enemy who seemed more intent on grabbing loot than conducting a proper search, they had waited patiently for an opportunity to implement Lyon's contingency plan — make for Pompong, hijack a junk and sail for home.[23]

Although this might have appeared somewhat ambitious, it was by no means unrealistic, for fate could not have handed them a better team — Sargent, Willersdorf and Pace, all experienced soldiers; the cool-headed Warne; Craft, an intelligent thinker with youth and enthusiasm on his side, and Reymond, sea captain and expert navigator. As the Japanese had confiscated their folboats, they simply waited until dark, stole two fishing koleks lying conveniently on the beach and headed for Beruan Island, their first port of call.[24]

While Sargent's group was fleeing towards Pompong, the other ten Rimau men awaited rescue on Mapor. When November 7 came and went with no sign of the submarine, they were not disheartened. As Japanese boats were still scuttling about the area Bob Page believed that the submarine commander had simply deferred the pickup until things quietened down.[25]

It is not feasible that the Rimau men simply sat on Mapor, watching for the submarine in the hope that someone could dash across eight kilometres of ocean to Merapas to make contact. The only way of ensuring that the rendezvous was not missed was to have two men paddle to Merapas each night, keep vigil by the tree and return to Mapor before dawn. As the key to survival lay at the Hammock Tree, there can be no doubt that on November 21, when *Tantalus* finally arrived, the Rimau men were waiting. That the two parties failed to meet was due to a number of unnecessary mistakes.

Firstly, Rimau had been expecting *Porpoise*, not *Tantalus*;[26] second, they had expected her to approach Merapas on or soon after November

7, and, third, from the direction of Stewart Point, thereby allowing the pickup party coming from Land Crab Bay to reach the Hammock Tree before first light. Last, and most important, if contact was not made, the orders quite clearly stated that the rescue party was to return on successive nights. Not one of these things occurred.

Tantalus arrived in place of *Porpoise*. This would not have made much difference had the substitute submarine surfaced in the correct position. Even with its streamlined hull well trimmed down to facilitate the launching of Chapman's folboat,[27] there is no way that Rimau could have missed seeing *Tantalus*, provided she had lain off Land Crab Bay. Had Major Chapman, late as he was, approached the tree from the east, the lookout would surely have spotted him scrambling over the rocks. In the unlikely event of the Rimau men failing to see either of these things, they would have had a second chance to make contact on the night of November 22, had the submarine not picked up Chapman and Croton, out of sight, on the southern side of the island. Needless though these mistakes were, the error that tipped the balance was Chapman's insistence that Rimau had gone. Had Chapman and Croton attempted a second rendezvous as ordered, they would have found the men of Rimau waiting in the darkness.

Furthermore, had Chapman, who had an exceptional sense of smell, rested at Kingfisher's Rest and later carried out his search of the island as thoroughly as he maintained, he could not have failed to find Cameron's unburied and rapidly decomposing body, nor missed the freshly turned mound of earth that marked the burial place of Riggs. Although the discovery of the remains may not have altered Chapman's decision to quit Merapas, it would have removed part of the mystery and gone some way towards establishing the fate of the Rimau men.[28]

When thirty days had passed without a sign of the submarine, Page decided to move to Pompong Island. During the next week his men worked their way south, following much the same route as that taken by *Mustika* as they skirted the southern entrance to the Riouw Straits. Although they made contact with a Chinese man at Buton as they threaded their way down the Buton Strait, they were not betrayed. Blondie Sargent's group, which had stopped off at Beruan, Borus and Lina Islands, a little to the east, had also been fortunate that not a single word of its progress had reached the ears of the Japanese.[29]

However, on November 27, Sargent's party was spotted at Temiang, a short distance from Pompong. Although the Japanese had lost contact with the party at Sebangka as it fled down the western coast of Lingga Island towards Tandjung Dato, the Kempei Tai, as well as native collaborators, were now very much on the alert.

When Page's group reached Pompong Island, it split into two — Page, Falls, Gooley and Fletcher in one group and Ingleton, Carey, Warren, Huston, Marsh and Hardy in the other. The two groups then headed further south, with the intention of making for Java. Through the Tjempa Straits they paddled, right into the heart of the Lingga Archipelago — and right into the arms of the Japanese.[30]

On December 15, a search party, consisting of Japanese naval personnel, a village headman named Engku Haji Said Nuh, and two Hei Ho, one of whom was called Soekarti, arrived at the island of Selajar with orders to look for white men, At about eleven am, having forced information from the locals, Engku's party came upon Page, Falls, Fletcher and Gooley near the village of Penuba. On seeing the four men, who were eating a meal, the Japanese opened fire. Wally Falls, taken completely by surprise as he bent cooking over the fire, was wounded in the right hip and captured. The other three, who were unhurt, split up and fled on foot.

Also on that day, but further north, between the islands of Pompong and Boeaja and dangerously close to the sea-plane base at Tjempa, Ingleton's party ran into a group of Kempei Tai and native Hei Hos. As they attempted to escape, the folboat manned by Huston and Marsh was holed and sunk by enemy gunfire. Although Freddie Marsh managed to extricate himself from the sinking craft to seek refuge with Carey and Warren on Tjempa Island,[31] his mate, the determined young man who had learned to swim simply to go on Jaywick, was not so lucky. Caught in the ferocious rip tide which swirled between the islands, he disappeared from sight. Shortly before noon on December 16, just nine days before his twenty-first birthday, on the southern headland of Boeaja Island — a place where many a sailor had finally come to rest — the Kempei Tai found the drowned body of Andrew Huston.[32]

Two days later at 5.24 pm, the Kempei caught up with Ingleton and Hardy, who was wounded in the shoulder, on nearby Gentung Island. All in all, December 18 was a very satisfactory day for the Japanese. Thirty-six minutes after Hardy and Ingleton were captured at Gentung, Bob Page was found hiding in a native hut on Selajar Island.[33] He had run out of steam. For three days he had been on the run, and now, bone weary and hungry, he could run no more. When the Japanese soldiers entered the hut, he lay flat, pretending to be asleep. Cautious as ever, the enemy troops approached on tiptoe, taking what seemed to be an eternity before they finally pounced. Page could have dispatched one or two of them with his pistol, but he was too exhausted to bother. In any case, he had accepted the fact that capture was inevitable.[34]

The next day, Fletcher and Gooley, the last remaining members of Page's party, were also captured on Selajar. They were taken by boat to Dabo Police Station, a low white Dutch colonial building of indeterminate age, situated on Singkep Island, where they joined Falls and Page, already behind bars. Shortly afterwards, when Ingleton and Hardy arrived from Gentung, the number of Rimau in custody rose to six. Each officially charged with being 'an enemy of the State', they were the object of much

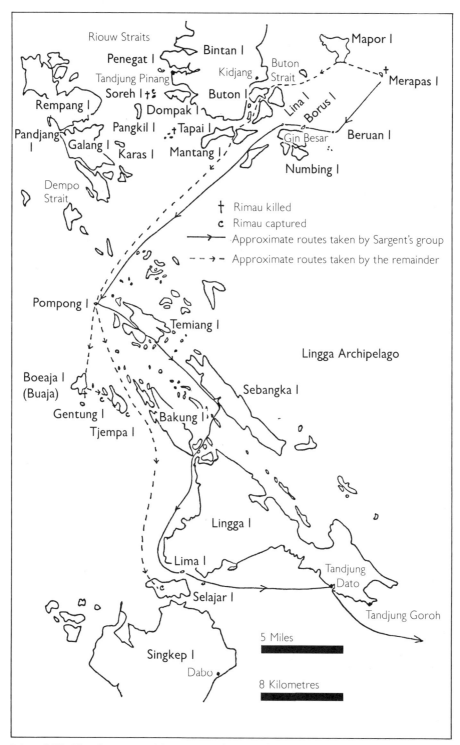

Riouw Straits

Mapor I

Penegat I

Bintan I

Buton
Strait

Kidjang

Tandjung Pinang

Merapas I

Soreh I

Buton I

Lina I

Rempang I

Dompak I

Borus I

Beruan I

Pandjang
I

Pangkil I

Tapai I

Gin Besar

Galang I

Karas I

Mantang I

Numbing I

Dempo
Strait

† Rimau killed

c Rimau captured

→ Approximate routes taken by Sargent's group

- - → Approximate routes taken by the remainder

Pompong I

Temiang I

Lingga Archipelago

Boeaja I
(Buaja)

Sebangka I

Gentung I

Bakung I

Tjempa I

Lingga I

Lima I

Tandjung
Dato

Selajar I

Tandjung Goroh

5 Miles

Singkep I

Dabo

8 Kilometres

Map VII. The Riouw and Lingga Archipelagoes, with routes taken by the men of Rimau and places where they were either killed or captured.

curiosity among the locals until December 23, when they left in two local fishing boats for Tandjung Pinang, where the Japanese Navy took over.[35]

They arrived in Singapore in two groups, one on Christmas Eve and the other two days later. The group that arrived on Boxing Day, having been detained for some time at Tandjung Pinang, made a splendid entrance. Australian POWs waiting on the wharf at Keppel Pier for shipment to Japan watched the arrival of the three heavily guarded prisoners with more than a passing interest. It was obvious, from the preponderance of armed sailors and the use of a naval vessel, that the three European men were more than ordinary prisoners.[36]

The following day, December 27, three days after discovering the remains of the Pompong Island supply dump, the Japanese bagged the last three fugitives, hiding on Tjempa Island. Although there had been no reports since early December on the whereabouts of Sargent's band, the Japanese authorities in Singkep waited for ten days, presumably in case they re-appeared, before sending Warren, Carey and Marsh, wounded by a bayonet in the upper chest, to join the other six in Singapore. Under heavy guard, they made the journey by boat, spending the night in the cells of Kidjang Police Station, where, once more the centre of attention, they were viewed by the local village people. Marsh was now so desperately ill that a rumour ran around town that he had died.[37]

By the time they arrived at Tandjung Pagar, the waterside headquarters of the infamous Kempei Tai, Marsh was indeed near death, suffering from a raging fever and so weak that he had to be carried in on a stretcher. For two fever-racked days he lingered, his cries clearly audible to his friends locked in a nearby room. Finally, on January 11, the moaning stopped. Freddie Marsh, the sailor for whom life had been a carefree, fun-filled stage, was dead. It is not known for certain what caused his death but, whether from wounds or disease, it was an unpleasant and painful end. The Japanese, not unexpectedly, declared that he had died of malaria.[38]

It is amazing how many people succumbed to this illness while guests of the Kempei Tai. In citing malaria, the Kempei had hit upon a most convenient method of explaining away deaths that should not have occurred. No matter what the actual cause of death, the official records were invariably the same. In accordance with normal practice, they also claimed that Marsh had been visited by a doctor and that, regrettably, nothing could be done for him. This was undoubtedly true. A doctor usually turned up at a Kempei Tai establishment when it appeared likely that a prisoner might inconveniently expire while still in custody.[39] The system worked very well. The medico looked, the patient died, and the official records were kept in order.

When the first three Rimau men had arrived in Singapore on Christmas Eve, two days before any of the others, the commandant of the Water Kempei Tai, Lieutenant Norio Hinomoto, had summoned several men to attend a conference. One of those who hurried through the Singapore streets, bright with Christmas decorations, was Hiroyuki Furuta, the Japanese civilian interpreter who had been translating Rimau's notebooks. At Water Kempei Tai Headquarters, housed in the Tandjung Pagar premises that formerly served as the Chinese YMCA, he was joined by Captain Nogushi, also from Garrison Headquarters, Warrant Officer Imanaka and two other interpreters.

Lieutenant Hinomoto told the meeting that he was seeking advice on how to handle the prisoners — members of a party which seemed to be a cut above ordinary soldiers. As two of them had fought to the death and another two had taken poison, the Kempei officer was of the opinion that violent methods of interrogation would achieve nothing. His opinion that the usual methods would elicit little information was undoubtedly also swayed by the fact that Corporal Stewart, captured on Soreh with the help of Raja Mun on October 18, had kept his mouth firmly shut for two and a half months, in spite of constant torture.[40]

Furuta, who was well travelled and had spent five years in England and Europe before the war, agreed with Hinomoto that the usual methods involving violence or systematic starvation would be non-productive. Realising that, as they had not been caught during combat, the soldiers' main concern would be about their status, he shrewdly suggested that the prisoners could be put at ease by a combination of gentle treatment and reassurance that the interrogators were not trying to gather evidence to convict them as spies.

The three prisoners, one of whom was Page, were then paraded before Hinomoto. They were exhausted. The strain of three months' constant running showed plainly on each drawn, bearded face, from which eyes glittered with nervous tension. Their tattered clothes were filthy and their unwashed bodies caked with sweat and grime. It was obvious that what they needed most was a good hot bath. To their astonishment, Hinomoto announced that they were to receive both a bath and a shave. Before this had time to sink in, he made another, equally amazing statement. Professing that out of respect for their Christian religion he would delay any questioning until after Christmas, he wished them a restful and Merry Christmas.

It is far more likely that Hinomoto's act of compassion was motivated by the fact that the next three prisoners had not turned up from Singkep. Nevertheless, considering the reputation of the Kempei Tai, Hinomoto's cordial Christmas Eve reception must have been almost beyond belief. When the bath and the shave materialised, along with clean clothing, it is surprising that the cynics amongst them did not wonder what the Japanese were up to. What Rimau failed to realise was that it was part of a cleverly orchestrated plan to gain their confidence and catch them off guard. Unfortunately, it worked.[41]

Undeniably, the Kempei Tai had a head start. Immediately after Christmas, armed with information obtained from Davidson's notebook, the skilled interrogators divided the prisoners into three groups and set to work, interrogating each man individually.[42] Keeping in mind that the security of the Sleeping Beauties must be maintained at all costs, the Rimau men studiously avoided all mention of them, sticking more or less to the cover stories prepared by SRD.

The institution of cover stories created a conflict. On the one hand, the members of special operations were exhorted to avoid capture at all costs, committing suicide if necessary. Should this prove to be impossible, it was stressed that, as the enemy was adept at extracting intelligence, the only information given should be name, rank and serial number. On the other hand, each man had also been presented with a cover story, to be learned by heart, in the perhaps unreasonable expectation that he would be in a state lucid enough to stick to it. Some stories, as in the case of Rimau, were complicated in the extreme. The men had three separate versions, each containing elements of the truth, with the choice dependant upon the place of capture. Unfortunately, as no one in SRD's planning department had thought past the pickup date, there was no specific cover story for the men of Rimau to recite when they were eventually captured. With three different stories and ten men, plus a probable fourth version dreamed up at the last minute, the possible combination of fact and fiction was almost endless. The final result, when added to the entries in the notebooks, must have been most illuminating. At the end of each day, Hinomoto, Noguchi and Imanaka compared notes, pooling the snippets of information and planning their next move.[43]

Not surprisingly, the Japanese soon discovered that some aspects of the prisoners' stories did not gel. Why, asked Lieutenant Colonel Kuwarbara, to whom Furuta reported, did they blow up the tonkan, their best means of escape, when all they had to do to preserve the secret of the limpets was to drop them overboard? Furuta's answer that the tonkan was an obvious target for pursuers did not allay the colonel's suspicions. He believed that the captured soldiers were hiding something, a notion that Furuta, who had built up a good rapport with the men, dismissed as being impossible. The following day he changed his mind.

The prisoners had all volunteered the information, which was actually correct, that the attack involved the use of folboats. When Furuta and the others noted discrepancies in the folboat pairings for this part of the operation, they did not take much notice. Hinomoto, however, was more astute. He figured it must mean something, but what?

Within twenty-four hours, they had their answer. On receiving a note from Imanaka which said, 'These people seem to be using some kind of special boat. Please verify', Furuta remembered the puzzling 'SB' references in the note book. Taking a punt, he asked Bob Page, 'What did you do with the SBs?' Believing that the Japanese knew all about them, Page inadvertently spilled the beans.[44]

It is not known for certain whether this benign process of intelligence gathering was speeded up in the early part by the judicious application of selective torture. A well-known tactic, it was used to good effect on those confined to the Kempei Tai's Outram Road Gaol, where the prisoners referred to it as the 'cigarettes and lolly racket'. If friendly overtures did not work, the Kempei tried more physical types of persuasion before reverting once more to kinder, even indulgent treatment. They used two sets of interrogators — one for the beatings and the other to act out the role of fairy godmother — and the psychological effect on prisoners of not knowing what kind of day was in store was most effective, probably achieving better results than consistent treatment of either kind.[45]

Despite Japanese assertions that the Kempei at Tandjung Pagar were at all times paragons of virtue in their handling of Rimau, it does not seem possible that Major Ingleton, for one, would have revealed some of his information voluntarily. Within days he had given details of SOE and SRD plans for the future and outlined methods by which they expected to infiltrate enemy territory. Irrespective of how this information was extracted, it was of little consequence. The Japanese were already exceedingly familiar with SRD organisation, personnel, training, aims and plans. As SRD counter-intelligence was well aware, this information had been gleaned from the reports of espionage agents and the interrogations of previously captured Allied personnel such as SRD's Sergeant Siffleet. In 1943 this unfortunate M Special agent, captured in New Guinea and subsequently beheaded, had, like Ingleton, 'volunteered' details of SRD organisation and his mission.[46]

Although it is impossible to assess how much intelligence was gathered from the Rimau prisoners, how much was deduced from the entries in the notebooks, given away with the cover stories or extracted by more forceful measures, one thing is abundantly clear. By January 9 the Kempei Tai knew almost everything: the date that Rimau had left Australia, their mode of transportation, the date of arrival at Merapas, the number in the group, the operational plan, the SRD training system, and the fact that the Allies had a new, secret weapon — the underwater submersible boat.[47] And when the results of Blondie Sargent's interrogations arrived from Soerabaya, they knew even more.

MALAYA

Kota Bharu
Trengganu
Medan
Kuantan
Mersing
Singapore
Riouw Archipelago
Lingga
Padang

Natuna Is
(Bunguran Is)

SARAWAK

THE PHILIPPINES

**CELEBES
(Sulawesi)**

0°

Moluccas

Pontianak
Pedjantan I
Maja I
Pelapis I
Bangka I
Palembang
Billiton I

**BORNEO
(Kalimantan)**

Balikpapan
Bandjarmasin

Makassar Straits

Laoet I
Katapongan I
Makassar

Tandjung
Puting

SUMATRA

Java Sea

Batavia (Jakarta)

Masalambo I Doangdoangan I
Kajuadi I
Romang I

140 mile
225 km
Nila I

Soerabaya
Kangean Is

Flores Sea

JAVA

Bali

Dili

Lombok Strait

Soemba I
(Sumba I)

TIMOR

To Australia 500 miles, 800 km

Miles

0 100 200 300 400 500

Kilometres

0 100   800

———— Route taken by Willersdorf
and Pace to Romang I

Map VIII. South-East Asia, with route taken by Willersdorf and Pace to
Romang Island.

Chapter 14
Dark Days at Soerabaya

By the time the Japanese had flushed out the Rimau fugitives from the Lingga Archipelago, Blondie Sargent, Reymond, Craft, Willersdorf, Warne and Pace were far away. On December 1, a week before the others had even left Mapor, they were at Tandjung Dato, on Lingga's southern tip, where Goking Riaz, a native of nearby Tandjung Goroh, repaired one of the koleks. So that they might have a better chance of finding a junk to replace their small wooden boats, which, being basically coastal craft equipped with a tiny triangular sail, were not the ideal choice as ocean-going vessels, they set sail for the southern coast of Sumatra. For the best part of three weeks they moved south until, having hatched a cunning plan, they managed to pirate a prahu manned by several Chinese.[1]

The captured boat then sailed due east, towards tiny Pelapis Island, a pickup point organised by Dutch intelligence for the rescue of fliers downed in Indonesian waters. Pelapis was evidently a rendezvous which did not appeal to the Chinese, who were not at all pleased to have been hijacked by a band of European men. As they neared the island, on or about December 21, the second night after their capture, the Chinese decided to rid themselves of their uninvited passengers by staging a revolt during the evening meal. Reymond, hit over the head with a club, fell over the side and disappeared, along with Craft. Sargent, who had by this stage been relieved of his weapons, escaped by jumping over the side.

After swimming about for some time he was rescued by a fishing boat, only to be pitched once more into the sea when the craft suddenly capsized. Clinging to a large log, he drifted with the current for the next ten hours, until washed against a fishtrap in the waters off Maja Island. Completely exhausted, suffering from immersion and minus his trousers, he dragged himself onto a platform formed by the stakes, where he clung for twenty-four hours until rescued by native fishermen. But, alas, luck was not on his side. Having saved him from certain death on the fishtrap, the fishermen then informed the Japanese.[2]

Two of his friends had also reached the shores of Maja. At Satai Cape, the benevolent tide that had brought Sargent to the shore also delivered up the drowned bodies of Bruno Reymond and Colin Craft.[3]

The local collaborators and Japanese garrison wasted little time in handing over their prize to the Kempei Tai, who took delivery of the prisoner in Pontianak, Borneo (Kalimantan), on Christmas Day. The following evening at about nine o'clock, Sargent was in the local police station, filling in a form with details of his personal history, when he was seen by Captain Chizuki Ozaki, an anti-sabotage naval officer attached to the intelligence section of the 2nd South Seas Expeditionary Fleet Headquarters at Soerabaya. Although in Pontianak for Christmas festivities, Ozaki decided to question the prisoner, who, having lost all his hair from the effects of his ordeal, looked decidedly 'aged'.[4]

Debilitated by his experiences, Sargent was in no condition to resist the persuasive talents of an interrogator as skilled as Ozaki, or to invent a plausible story and stick to it. Within one and a half hours Ozaki had extracted a great deal of information about Operation Rimau, including the details of Sargent's escape from Merapas, the number of ships that had been blown up and the technical specifications of the SBs. Believing this information to be of great importance, Ozaki immediately returned to his quarters, where he made out a report for his superiors by candlelight. Two days later Sargent was in custody in Soerabaya.

About a fortnight afterwards, the Japanese in Soerabaya learned that information similar to that of Sargent had been obtained from other Rimau prisoners. As a result, Fleet Headquarter's Staff Officer Tachino ordered Ozaki to re-interrogate Sargent, with particular reference to the expedition's equipment. This time it was not so easy. Ozaki was quite put out to find that Sargent, who had recovered much of his strength, was not at all pleased to see him. After one and a half frustrating hours, Ozaki had accomplished nothing, for Sargent, in his haughtiest manner, refused to elaborate. Neither did further questioning, in the several interrogations that followed, elicit anything new.

Shortly afterwards, Tachino received orders to dispatch Sargent to Tokyo's Ofuna Internment Camp by the first available air transport, orders which, owing to a shortage of aircraft, were soon amended to transportation by the first available means. As this meant a boat of some kind and an armed escort, Sargent was left cooling his heels in the naval stockade.[6]

In mid-February he was still there. When a car arrived one day to transport him to Commander Tatsuzaki's office in the court martial buildings for another round of interrogation, Sargent was startled to find that he was not its only passenger. Seated in the car, somewhat weatherworn but still very much alive, was Private Doug Warne.[7]

When Sargent had last seen his friend he had been diving over the side of the prahu to escape the Chinese. Somehow, Warne, Willersdorf and Pace had managed to regain control of the boat, apparently ditching the Chinese in the process. From Pelapis they had navigated the small vessel around the southern coast of Borneo, past Tandjung Puting to

Katapongan Island, where disaster had struck. Here, miles from medical help and surrounded by a hostile enemy, Warne had become very ill. With his delirium bordering on madness, the other two had faced the unpalatable fact that they could take him no further. Possibly believing that he had a better chance of survival either in the hands of villagers or in the custody of the Japanese, his friends had been forced to leave him behind at Katapongan, a speck in the ocean off the south-easterly tip of Borneo.

Doug Warne must have been blessed with a cast iron constitution. Instead of fading away, racked by illness, he recovered and when sufficiently well, quit Katapongan in a small kolek which the others evidently had the foresight to leave with him. With no charts, and no navigational equipment except perhaps his compass, he had spent several weeks in the Macassar Straits, floating from island to island, until betrayed by the locals to Japanese stationed at Bandjermasin. From Borneo he had been flown to Soerabaya.

Warne was in reasonable shape considering his ordeal, although he told his interrogators that he was troubled by a pain in his abdomen, just below his ribs on the left-hand side — probably an enlarged spleen, the legacy of a recent attack of malaria. The interrogation, conducted by Tachino and Ozaki, lasted an hour, and apparently achieved little in the way of information. The pair were re-examined several times by Ozaki, again with little result.

It was now time for Sargent to move on. Escorted by Warrant Officer Shirakawa and Lieutenant Nakamura, who were being transferred back to Japan, he was taken by train to Batavia (now Jakarta), whence he was to travel by ship to Tokyo, via Singapore. The trio had just reached Batavia when Nakamura was recalled to Soerabaya to answer questions about the loss of some documents for which he had been responsible. Whatever the documents were, they must have been important. Instead of reporting as ordered, the lieutenant committed suicide very publicly by shooting himself with a pistol in a Soerabayan restaurant.

The remaining escort took Sargent to Singapore, passing on the instructions that he was to be sent to Japan. Unfortunately, the Seventh Area Army had other ideas. With nine Rimau members under lock and key, it was not about to relinquish the tenth who had so fortuitously fallen into its hands. Without further ado Sargent found himself removed from the ship and incarcerated in Singapore's Outram Road Gaol.[8]

After Sargent had departed, Warne was taken by car to the court martial buildings, where he was paraded, in a generally dishevelled state, before the members of the court. His appearance lasted only a few minutes, and he was asked no questions. Although Warne had no idea of what was happening, it appears that this brief appearance was the Soerabayan equivalent of a military trial. This puzzling episode over, he was placed in the custody of an officer named Naotaki Noguchi.[9]

Sargent and Warne were not the only Australian prisoners to face interrogation in Soerabaya in early 1945. On about March 15 two more SRD operatives, a pair of army lieutenants by the name of Clifford Perske and John Sachs, also had the misfortune to fall into enemy hands. Members of a combined British/American operation known as 'Optician-Politician', they had left Fremantle on March 11 in US Submarine *Bream* to see what havoc they could wreak among Japanese installations and shipping. Although of vastly different backgrounds, Clifford Perske, a farmer from Queensland, and John Sachs, an oil representative of German/Australian descent, were bound by the same single-minded ambition — 'to kill the enemies of the King'.

In this, and other respects, John Sachs was an Australian version of Ivan Lyon. Aged thirty-one and the eldest son of a successful German immigrant who had embraced the concept of the British Empire with fervour, Sachs had been raised in an atmosphere of unbridled love of King and Country.

Young John Sachs, like Ivan Lyon, had delighted in all things military, joining the militia as an artilleryman and volunteering for service as soon as war was declared. A crack shot who had won many trophies for sharpshooting, he was renowned for his ability to split a business card held edgewise at twenty-five paces and shoot chalk from between the fingers of his accomplice by the light of a candle while standing on his head.

His skill with firearms had been put to good use in April 1941 during the last desperate hours of fighting in the debacle known as the Greek Campaign, when he had single-handedly wiped out a machine-gun nest, captured and rendered a large gun useless, rounded up a score of prisoners and accounted for the deaths of an untold number of the enemy. Shot three times and knowing, with huge enemy reinforcements due, that surrender was inevitable, Sachs had then allowed himself the luxury of lying down in the back of a truck and passing out.

When he came to, he was a prisoner of war. But it was not for long. As soon as his wounds were healed he escaped, was recaptured, escaped again and then, disguised as a Cypriot peasant, spent five months fighting in the mountains with the Greek resistance. Fed up with living a hand-to-mouth existence, he stole a boat and eventually made his way back to Cairo, via neutral Turkey.

As the last anyone had seen of John Sachs had been in Greece — a bloodsoaked and apparently lifeless body on the back of a truck — the general opinion was that he had been killed in action after a feat of exceptional bravery. Consequently, the wheels were already in motion to recommend him for a posthumous Victoria Cross. (In the end, the paperwork evidently lost in a mass of red tape, Sachs did not receive any recognition whatever for his heroic stand.) When he reappeared in Cairo, the news that Sachs, like Lazarus, had risen from the dead, caused a sensation.

As soon as he had regained his health he returned to Greece by submarine, extracted a number of key Allied personnel (earning the Military Medal in the process) and then transferred to the infantry in New Guinea, where he once again covered himself in glory by concocting a huge gelignite bomb to eject some well-dug-in Japanese who were holding up the Australian advance on the Komiatum Ridge.

Such single-minded determination and innovative techniques, on top of his earlier conspicuous efforts — all of which had been prominently reported in the press — did not go unnoticed by those organising special operations. In May 1944, after a short spell at Canungra, Lieutenant Sachs, jungle-warfare instructor, became Lieutenant Sachs, SRD.[10]

In late 1944, under the auspices of SRD but the direct control of America's Admiral Christie, Sachs was attached to Operation Politician, where his tasks were to assist in the rescue of downed airmen, ferry personnel for emergency evacuation, carry out reconnaissance duties, and blow up ships or installations whenever the opportunity arose.[11]

On 11 March 1945, one month after completing a rather dull patrol with US Submarine *Bream* to Ita Ubi Island he and Clifford Perske, who was on his first operation, were assigned to join the same submarine on a patrol to the South China Sea. During the afternoon of March 14, while proceeding to the patrol area, the submarine attacked a Japanese convoy sailing from Bandjermasin to Soerabaya. After sinking one vessel, *Bream* tracked the convoy to the eastern tip of Great Masalambo Island, where the ships had sheltered for the night.[12]

At fifteen minutes to midnight, Sachs and Perske were ready to set off in a folboat to blow up the remainder of the ships with a few well-placed limpet mines. Conditions were ideal — dark and rainy, with little wind. They had gone only a little over half the distance when, for reasons that could not be ascertained, the submarine's crew noticed that the folboat was about two thousand metres to the east of the intended destination. Unable to make radio contact with the pair, the submarine waited until the appointed time and then surfaced at the prescribed rendezvous.

Sachs and Perske were nowhere to be seen. Unbeknown to anyone on *Bream*, an unsuccessful attack by a British submarine on the same convoy at 5 o'clock that afternoon had placed the Japanese on full alert. Before the Australians had time to leave their lethal calling cards, they had been captured by a naval patrol.

Although harassed by destroyers, *Bream*'s commanding officer did not call off the search. Fully aware of the terrible risk he was taking, he continued to comb the sea to the north and east of the island without finding any sign of the missing pair. At four minutes to three on the morning of March 17, a radio signal was picked up on the allotted frequency. Although the Americans thought the voice sounded like that of Lieutenant Perske, the authenticator codeword was not given and the commander, fearing that it was a trap set by the Japanese, followed orders and did not proceed.

It is almost certain that the submarine officer had summed up the situation correctly. One of the first questions asked of Perske and Sachs would have been the wireless frequency for contacting the submarine. By giving this information but withholding the authenticator, they had gambled that *Bream*'s commander would realise that they had been captured and that the submarine's situation was perilous, as indeed it was. Badly damaged by the heavy depth charging, it was with great difficulty that *Bream* made her way back to Australia safely.

After their capture Sachs and Perske were transferred to Soerabaya's Guben prison. Here Tachino, the naval officer who had questioned Warne and Sargent, sought permission to interrogate them. It is doubtful that torture, which was often employed by Captain Shinohara's Special Base Unit, was used by Tachino. Indeed, Shinohara's techniques were a contentious issue, since the Japanese Fleet orders expressly forbade the use of torture during interrogations.

Whatever his methods, Tachino did not fare well. After two hours of questioning, Sachs, the operational leader, had revealed only that they had left Fremantle by submarine and that their intention had been to blow up ships at Masalambo with magnetic mines. As all attempts to induce Sachs to reveal the codes and frequencies for communication with Australia had failed, Tachino only bothered to ask Perske his name, rank and serial number. He then informed the Special Base Unit's Shinohara, who was conducting his own investigation, that he wished to question both prisoners at a later date.[13]

Shinohara was evidently a law unto himself. His methods of interrogation of both Sachs and Perske were such that he almost came to blows with an extremely angry Tachino, who had pointed out in no uncertain terms that such treatment was expressly forbidden. To this Shinohara replied, 'While they are under my care I can treat them as I wish. I can eat them if I wish, either boiled or roasted'.[14]

In the latter half of March the Japanese came to the conclusion that prisoners from whom all useful information had been extracted — Warne, Perske and Sachs, as well as four Americans and nineteen Indonesians — were to die at a date to be fixed.[15]

When he heard this, Dr Nakamura, a naval captain attached to 2 South Seas Fleet, became very interested. Since anti-tetanus serum was impossible to procure, the doctor had been searching for an alternate substance with which to inoculate his troops. When bacteriologist Commander Natase Ide evolved a new and revolutionary substance described as a 'denatured anatoxin', Dr Nakamura believed it might be a suitable substitute. As it was derived from tetanus bacteria, the dosage was critical: too much, and the patient would die. As he had little time to carry out a series of controlled experiments, increasing the dosage and observing the results, he needed expendable 'volunteers'.

Urged by Nakamura, Commander Tatsuzaki was persuaded to release all prisoners to the hospital medical staff. As soon as permission had been granted, all prisoners, Caucasian and Indonesian, were lined up for their inoculations. Two days later a second injection was given. As interpreter Junya Saito could not remember the Malay word for 'tetanus', he was instructed to tell the prisoners that they were being vaccinated against typhoid and that they might suffer a very high fever as a result.[16]

That was an understatement, to say the least. Within days, Doug Warne and all but two of the Indonesians became ill. Warne was admitted to the Naval Hospital at Darumo, about an hour's drive from Soerabaya, suffering from a complaint to one of his legs — evidently the first stage of a muscle paralysis similar to that experienced by tetanus victims. As the illness progressed and the paralysis began to affect his ability to swallow, he was taken off normal rations and fed soup and rice gruel.[17]

Also gravely ill in hospital as a result of the injections were two American merchant seamen, shipwrecked in the Indian Ocean when their oil tanker, Fort Lee, had been sunk by a German U-boat on November 2. Obviously, the doctor had miscalculated just how much Warne and the marine castaways, who had experienced extreme physical hardship, could stand, for they all fell ill. Nakamura, who had not expected this to happen, went to extraordinary lengths to keep them alive, informing the guards that 'as these prisoners of war are very important they must not be permitted to die'. It was all to no avail. About a fortnight after admission, Warne's guard, Petty Officer Noguchi, reported that his charge was in such a state that he could no longer move.

Tetanus is a disease for which there is no cure. Those who survive probably owe their lives to a strong constitution and constant nursing care, designed to help lessen the excruciating pain and violent seizures that wrack the victim's body. Towards the end, Warne, now pale, thin and desperately ill, was placed upon a soft bearskin rug, probably in an attempt to ease his suffering. But the constitution that had kept Warne from death's door at Katapongan could not hope to combat the effects of Dr Nakamura's preventative medical technique. He lapsed into unconsciousness, finally dying about fifteen days after admission to hospital. On the orders of Ozaki, his body was removed for burial in an unmarked place, along with those of the castaways, thereby effectively eliminating any trace of him.

The Japanese, who claimed that Warne was in good health before he became inexplicably ill, declared that he had died from the combined effects of 'stomach trouble', exposure and malnutrition. Not surprisingly, the castaways and the seventeen Indonesians were also deemed to have died from 'other' causes.[18]

Perske and Sachs, along with the two Indonesians and two American airmen, had not become ill. Whether routine inoculations before they left home, their fitness, the administration of a lesser amount of toxin (or none at all), saved the Europeans is not known. What is known is that the experiment provided Nakamura and Ide with an excellent guide to the correct dosage, for they went on to inoculate their troops successfully.[19]

While the seven survivors may have conquered the toxic effects of Dr Nakamura's hideous experiments, they had no hope of sidestepping their death sentence. When it became obvious that several of the prisoners had suffered no ill effects from the injections, Captain Shinohara took it upon himself to give orders for their immediate execution. Fourteen days after their arrival in Soerabaya, at about eleven-thirty in the morning, an order was issued to remove Perske and Sachs, along with the remaining Indonesians and the two airmen, from their cells.[20]

The two Americans, Flight Officer Mason Schow and Sergeant Donald Palmer, the sole surviving members of a B-24 which had disappeared on a bombing run over Borneo on 24 October 1944, had never had any chance of avoiding the death penalty. For some time, in defiance of orders to transport all fliers to Tokyo, the Japanese in Soerabaya had been executing all airmen who had the misfortune to fall into their hands. Now, blindfolded and handcuffed, they were placed on a truck with the others for the thirty-minute journey to the Eastern Fort execution ground.[21]

Many of the base personnel had no idea that an execution was about to take place until they saw about twenty armed men ranged around a truck outside the guardhouse. Alerted by the unusually large guard, Kazuyuki Mike observed the Australians, Americans and Indonesians being loaded into the truck. Mike, who had given the fliers chocolate and who had attended two of the interrogations of Sachs and Perske, was in no doubt as to the prisoners' identity — blindfolded or not. Dashing John Sachs, lean, dark haired, dark complexioned and with a high-bridged nose (the legacy of a German bullet which had slightly rearranged his features in Greece) stood almost one hundred and eighty-three centimetres tall. Perske, who was about seven or eight centimetres shorter, was equally as good looking but lighter in hair and skin colour than his friend. The Americans were easily recognisable, for the elder one sported a massive red-blond beard while his freshfaced, much younger companion was by far the shortest of the four. When Mike realised that all were bound for the killing ground, he made enquiries about the sudden decision to execute them, but was unable to obtain any satisfactory answers.

Down at the fort, a large crowd was gathering around a pit, dug by the members of the Special Attack Group (Sword Unit), who had been also ordered to demonstrate their skill in swordsmanship. On disembarking from the truck, which pulled up about ten metres away, the condemned men were taken to a small hut, where they waited for an hour as the grave-digging detail had not dug the pit deep enough. It was some time after one pm (Tokyo time) before the interpreter was ordered to tell the Indonesians that their deaths were imminent. Nothing whatever was said to the Europeans.

After an officer named Ikeda had executed the first Indonesian, John Sachs was led away. He can have been in no doubt about what was in store. By throwing back his head as he walked and aided by the bump on his nose, he was able to see from beneath his blindfold. Kneeling before the pit, he was decapitated by Lieutenant Okada.[22]

Thousands of kilometres away, in the Sachs family home in the Sydney suburb of Double Bay, at precisely 2.30 on the afternoon of Good Friday, 30 March 1945, Lieutenant John Sachs's framed Army Commission inexplicably crashed to the floor.[23] While Fritz Sachs, who had no idea that his son was even missing, stared at the shattered glass with a feeling of great foreboding, the officer in charge of the execution glared at Sachs's lifeless body in absolute fury.

It was typical of Sachs that even in death he was able to cause a ruction. In executing him, Lieutenant Okada had not performed his task well, nicking his sword and thereby incurring the wrath of Lieutenant Yoshimoto, who, after a great deal of yelling, ordered Petty Officer Tamura to produce some more youthful volunteers. When no one offered, he issued the order that 'men of the lowest rank shall cut', which caused Seamen Norimura, Nakauchi, Nakayama and Hashimoto to inherit the job.

Nakayama's victim, the youngest American airman (who had been kept segregated from the others), and Hashimoto's, the last of the Indonesians, had been roped to prevent their bodies from pitching into the hole. The reason for this was not obvious until several medical officers appeared on the scene to perform an on-the-spot dissection. After an anatomical lesson for the benefit of the onlookers, the hearts, livers and gall bladders were removed before the bodies were finally buried with the others.

The reason for this sickening procedure had been to satisfy the whim of one man — Captain Shinohara, a chronic asthmatic. Believing that the gall bladder of a bear had medicinal properties, he deduced, by some tortured form of reasoning, that the ingestion of a human gall bladder would cure his constant wheezing.[24]

While Shinohara's contemporaries may have been awed by his behaviour, they were untroubled by the fact that prisoners of war were executed. There were specific orders issued by the Fleet Commander which allowed for the disposal of POWs, all of whom were regarded as being of little consequence. Although they were supposed to be tried, this was never done, especially since all prisoners captured other than in combat were deemed to be spies.[25] Indeed, for the past three months the Japanese had been given an even freer reign to dispatch prisoners, 'spies' in particular. On February 10, Singapore's Seventh Area Army, having decided that anyone connected with Rimau was an enemy of the state, had relayed a very explicit order to all units:

> We want to punish the sabotage units which infiltrated from Australia and were captured in the Singapore area recently. Although the matter will in each case be left up to the unit concerned, we wish the investigations to be such that no one is left to do harm afterward.[26]

Had this order not been issued, it is quite possible that Warne, Sachs and Perske may have been dispatched to Tokyo and may well have survived the war. When the Japanese in Soerabaya had informed their superiors that Sargent had been captured, orders for his immediate transfer to Japan had been issued — orders which would have been carried out had not the Kempei Tai in Singapore taken matters into its own hands and removed him from the ship. But with the arrival of the Seventh Area Army message, the situation for Warne, Sachs and Perske had altered dramatically. The Japanese at Soerabaya, whose record of wholesale execution of prisoners was already well established, had looked upon this order as a licence to murder with impunity.

Warne, having confessed that he had been a member of the party that had blown up three ships in Singapore Harbour, had never stood a chance. Neither had Sachs and Perske who, apart from being 'spies', had unwittingly admitted to a mission that was indistinguishable from Rimau. As far as the Japanese were concerned, Sachs and Perske were as much Rimau men as the twenty-two who set off from Australia on 11 September 1944 with Ivan Lyon.

A few days after Lieutenants John Sachs and Clifford Perske met their bloody fate on the Eastern Fort execution ground, Tokyo, having learned that prisoners were being executed without trial, rescinded Singapore's order.[27]

Chapter 15
A Death Fit For Heroes?

Towards the end of February, after eight weeks detention in the Tandjung Pagar Headquarters of the Naval Kempei Tai, the Rimau prisoners, whose deaths were so desired by the Seventh Area Army, were still alive. The fact that they were also in good shape was due not to any change of heart on the part of the Kempei but to three quite disparate reasons — Hinomoto's decision that torture would achieve little, the illuminating entries in the notebooks, and last, but by no means least, information from the prisoners that Ivan Lyon was related to the family of Queen Elizabeth, consort of England's King George VI and formerly a Bowes-Lyon. Although the relationship was distant, this fact was so widely accepted that Ivan was often referred to as Ivan Bowes-Lyon. The Japanese, who could not have imagined any of Emperor Hirohito's relatives ever going to war, were exceedingly impressed by this news and, without a doubt, decided to tread very carefully indeed.[1]

Despite the fact that it was strictly forbidden for personnel to keep diaries or records when in enemy territory, the information in Davidson's waterstained but still legible notebook, seems to have been extraordinarily detailed. The Japanese even knew the name of the operation, which they preferred to call the 'Tora Kosuku Tai' or 'Tiger Operation Party', rather than Rimau. As a result, the interrogators, aided by the unassuming civilian interpreters and Hinomoto's clever tactics, had gleaned most of their intelligence without having to resort to more violent methods.[2]

By the first week of February, the Seventh Area Army had added to this intelligence other, quite startling, information that had arrived from Java and Timor, where Willersdorf and Pace had finally been captured.[3] When they learned that Ivan Lyon's men, and not internal saboteurs, were responsible for both Singapore raids, the Japanese hierarchy knew that they were sitting on a timebomb. Something would have to be done about Rimau — fast.

Had the Rimau men been ordinary POWs the situation would have been bad enough for the Japanese. Desperate to keep thousands of prisoners, and indeed their own rank and file, from knowing that the war was not going well for Japan, Japanese authorities had the option of either executing prisoners, particularly airmen, or placing them in solitary confinement in Outram Road Gaol, where, apart from being isolated, they might conveniently die from disease, malnutrition or ill treatment, thereby saving their captors a great deal of bother.[4]

But Rimau presented a special problem. Whereas pilots, under regulations laid down by General Tojo, could be disposed of without any trouble,[5] the summary execution of nine Allied soldiers was fraught with danger. On the other hand, imprisonment, even in Outram Road, from which many never returned, was also risky. The problem of Rimau was the immensely complex problem of face.

From the moment the Japanese learned that the raids upon shipping in Singapore Harbour were not inside jobs, the surviving members of Rimau were doomed. Should it ever be made public that a few men had come thousands of kilometres to thumb their noses at the enemy, not once, but twice, the Japanese would be a laughing stock. Worse, should it ever be revealed that the Kempei Tai, under the auspices of the Imperial Japanese Army, had tortured and murdered untold numbers of Asian and European civilians (executing the last one as recently as November),in the mistaken belief that internal saboteurs had been at work the shame would be unendurable. Even more humiliating was the fact that, at this very minute, there were a number of Malays accused and tried for blowing up ships in the harbour, upon whom sentence of death had been passed. For the Japanese to admit that the entire judicial system, from the investigators, to the prosecutors, to the judges, had been wrong and that Japanese justice was flawed was absolutely unthinkable.[6] In order to save the collective Japanese face, all of the Rimau men would have to die.

Once this had been decided, the Seventh Area Army transmitted the fatal signal, ordering all unit commanders to deal with the matter in such a way that 'no one is left to do harm afterwards'. While this order was promptly carried out in Soerabaya, a little more discretion was needed in Singapore. In order to avoid any repercussions, it was decided to pursue the line that the men of Rimau had committed a war crime, the penalty for which was death.[7]

As the Rimau prisoners at Tandjung Pagar had been lulled into a sense of security by the low-profile methods of the interrogations, it is little wonder that none of them had noticed a change as the questioning progressed. Indeed, it was not until severe re-interrogations began weeks later at Outram Road Gaol that Page and Ingleton realised that there had been a distinct shift of emphasis. Although they noticed the change they did not voice their suspicions to the others. Neither did the interpreter, Hiroyuki Furuta, who had realised for some time that the interrogations had ceased to be benign.

Furuta's association with Rimau had begun long before they had ever met, for he had been present at lunch at the Army's Raffles College headquarters on October 16, when word had arrived that Mustika had been scuttled and that the three Malay Hei Ho had been killed. When

Davidson's notebook, followed by Carey's diary, Ingleton's sketchbook and Mrs Manderson's flags, had been sent to Singapore, it was Furuta who had been given the job of examining them. But it was not until Christmas Eve, when the first of the prisoners had arrived, that he had actually come face to face with the personnel mentioned in the documents.[8]

Since then, being in attendance at many of their interrogations, he had built a rapport of sorts with the men, especially Page, Carey, Ingleton and Stewart. In common with all those who had ever met Bob Page, Furuta had fallen under the spell of his warm personality and ready smile. To the somewhat plain Japanese interpreter, the handsome features of the tall Australian rivalled those of the most dashing movie star.[9]

Always anxious to improve his English, Furuta took every opportunity to engage the Rimau prisoners in conversation. Stewart told him about his wife and children, Page about his medical studies at Sydney University and Fletcher about his acting experience. True to form, Carey had pulled his leg unmercifully, telling Furuta that it would be easy to find him in Australia as he was related to every Carey in the Sydney telephone book and, since he had been in the army so long that he must have been promoted to Captain by now, that he should be addressed in that manner. The idea of acceding to a Japanese request to draw plans of an SB also smacks of Wal Carey's jokey larrikinism — it is perhaps indicative of the nature of these so-called 'plans' that, despite their best efforts, Japanese engineers were unable to produce a prototype of the craft before the war ended.

It is also odds-on that it was Carey who had proffered the information that only small Australians had been picked to go on the Rimau raid. What Furuta made of Wally Falls, who was a well-built ninety kilograms (or, for that matter, any of the others, most of whom towered over him), is not disclosed. It is also evident that a remark made by Ingleton that he 'had never eaten so much rice in his life' and 'didn't know rice could be so tasty', was also lost on Furuta, who believed that conventional English tastebuds had adapted to oriental food with amazing rapidity. By the time Sargent arrived from Java and told Furuta that his hair had fallen out as a result of a high fever, Furuta didn't know whether to believe him or not.[10]

As his relationship with the Rimau men progressed, Furuta was torn between his allegiance to Japan and his growing friendship with men who were, in fact, the enemy. Haunted by the knowledge that the interrogations were leading them inexorably towards death, but not brave enough to warn them, he harboured unrealistic dreams that somehow he might be able to spirit them off to Changi Camp, where they could be hidden — an action far beyond the capacity of such a mild-mannered civilian.[11] Tormented, Furuta trod a shaky path as he attempted to serve his country and his Emperor while coming to terms with his conscience. But it was not until Bob Page made an unexpected confession that Furuta's divided loyalties really were put to the test.

It must be remembered that, apart from the most senior army officials, who had themselves just discovered this amazing fact, no Japanese had any idea that Jaywick and Rimau were anything other than the work of local saboteurs. Rumours, even at this high level, flew thick and fast, among them the ludicrous theory that the Kasu Hei Ho was part of the sabotage team, shot by mistake. Although he knew a great deal, Furuta had not learned anything about either raid from the prisoners since no one had breathed a word about Jaywick and none of those from the Rimau raid (apart from Stewart, who had said nothing during his two and a half months confinement), had been interrogated in Singapore. Since any disclosure of the facts would have weakened the spying case they were trying to construct, the Japanese Army, which always suppressed unfavourable news, ensured that there was a complete security clampdown. For this reason, Furuta knew nothing about the raids, neither did he have any idea of the real reason why the Army was anxious to rid itself of Rimau.[12]

One day, he mentioned quite casually to Page that a large number of Malays were to be executed for blowing up ships in the harbour 'last year'. Assuming that Furuta was referring to Jaywick, Page consulted the others, who, after a heated exchange, decided that he should come clean. The following day, fully aware of the fact that an admission to the sabotage of 1943 might do him and his companions immeasurable harm, he told Furuta that the Malays were innocent, explaining precisely why. When Furuta, who had not been long in Singapore, checked on the details for Jaywick, he found that Page was telling the truth.

Furuta was now in a real bind. Unaware that his superiors already knew the facts, he fought a great battle with his conscience, knowing that if he passed on this information, Captain Page would be in an even more perilous position and if he did not, he might well find himself in serious trouble. He eventually confided in Colonel Nagayaki Koshida, his Divisional Chief, who, being a very senior officer, was privy to all the facts. An astute man, he told Furuta that he was to forget the whole incident, reminding him that as the trial had been held, the Malays had confessed, the papers had been signed and the execution had been arranged, the loss of face among the investigators and the judiciary would be too great to contemplate.[13]

Convincing himself that he had done everything in his power to save the lives of the condemned men, Furuta took Koshida's advice, after telling Page to keep mum and to leave everything up to him. Although the unfortunate Malays, regarded as expendable, were duly executed, Furuta was consoled by the thought that at least he had done something to prevent Page from getting himself into even more hot water, for, by this stage, he knew that all the prisoners were in dire trouble. He also knew there was precious little he could do about it.

Being a mere civilian interpreter, a job ranked by the Japanese Army as being below that of a carrier pigeon, Furuta was in no position to voice any opposition when he realised that it was the Army's intention to pin a capital charge on Rimau. In fact, by interfering, he would have run the risk of being replaced by someone who was less kindly disposed towards the prisoners whom he sought to protect. Realising that stalling for time might help, he dreamed up two schemes — the compilation of a military dictionary and the creation of propaganda messages designed for Japanese radio broadcasts to Australia. Telling Bob Page that it didn't matter if the details for the broadcasts were accurate or not, just as long as they produced something between them, the pair came up with a number of scenarios that evidently satisfied Furuta's superiors.[14]

But these delaying tactics were not enough. In about mid-February, after the Kempei had finished its preliminary investigation and the Army had decided that Rimau would have to be eliminated, the nine prisoners were moved from the Tandjung Pagar building to Outram Road Gaol.[15]

Outram Road was the place where miscreants from the Japanese military and Allied prison camps were confined by the Kempei Tai for punishment. It was Kempei policy to confine prisoners here only when it had extracted every bit of information it required. Constructed in the style of many nineteen-century British prisons, of impregnable stone and containing a large number of cells, the gaol was tailor-made for the needs of the Kempei, who had moved in as soon as the British had moved out — the transition from His Majesty's Prison to Kempei Tai Gaol being greatly facilitated when it was discovered that the departing British had thoughtfully left the keys to all the cells hanging neatly on the wall. Since 1942, the number of prisoners, Japanese as well as Allied, who had gone through the gates of Outram Road alive and come out dead was considerable.

During the first two years of the war the conditions at Outram Road — daily beatings, every possible variety of torture, a starvation diet and an almost total lack of sanitation, breeding vermin and disease — were so terrible that, by comparison, Changi POW Camp was considered to be a paradise. Indeed, some prisoners, teetering on the thin line dividing life from death, owed their survival solely to the fact that the Kempei, who were not anxious for too many prisoners to die in their custody, had sent them off to Changi hospital when death had appeared to be imminent. If they died, the blame could then be apportioned to incompetent Allied medical staff. Even when the tide of the war started to turn against the Japanese and conditions at the gaol marginally improved, Outram Road remained a place of great misery and suffering.

It was here that the Kempei Tai sent the men of Rimau. Since the Japanese wished to keep them strictly isolated from the rest of the prisoners, they were placed two to a cell according to rank, in a special portion of the lower storey normally reserved for 'spies'. Even under ideal conditions, the cells, like those in all prisons dating back to the Victorian era, could never have been called homely. Under Japanese occupation they were even less so. Four thick walls rose from a concrete floor on which rested the bed and the 'binkei' bucket, which was either emptied by the prisoner or, in the case of those who were not permitted to leave the cells, by a special latrine party. A small dollop of rice with occasional traces of vegetable matter topped by an evil-smelling paste made of decomposing crabs and prawns was served three times a day from a wooden cart that was trundled down the corridor. The massive steel and wooden door, through which the food was pushed by way of a small hatch, also had a spy hole. Peering through it, the guards kept a close eye on their charges, aided by the meagre light that filtered through a small barred window by day, and the glow of a naked globe that burned throughout the hours of darkness.[16]

There is no doubt whatever that, although the gaol conditions had slightly improved, the methods of the gaolers had not. (Indeed, Furuta, who made much song and dance about the good treatment at Tandjung Pagar, was suspiciously tight lipped about the conditions in Outram Road — as well he might be.[17]) Furthermore, many of those placed in solitary confinement endured appalling conditions.[18] Segregated from the rest of the inmates, the Rimau men's lives in Outram Road would have been even less tolerable than usual had the small gestures of kindness, already extended to them at Tandjung Pagar by Furuta, not continued. In the guise of working on the military dictionary, he visited Rimau regularly in Outram Road, keeping them supplied with occasional cigarettes and a considerable amount of his own reading matter.[19]

Perhaps these attempts to bring a touch of humanity into a world that was otherwise bereft of any trace of civilised behaviour helped Furuta to cope, for he was in an invidious position. On one hand, confronted daily with the awfulness of Outram Road and other Kempei Tai establishments, he could not help but see the results of brutal treatment. On the other, he was one of the few who knew that steps were being taken to charge the Rimau men with espionage — a secret that he must share with no one, least of all the prisoners.[20]

On 1 March 1945, shortly after Rimau had been transferred to Outram Road, a report, based on the Tandjung Pagar interrogations, was referred to the Judicial Department for confirmation that it was legitimate to classify the Rimau prisoners as spies. Consequently, the investigation passed from the Kempei to the Judicial Department's Major-General Otsuka, who ordered prosecutor Major Kamiya to pursue the matter.

By the end of March, having studied the report very closely, Kamiya informed Otsuka that there appeared to be several violations of law under which the prisoners could be tried. When General Itagaki, the new

Commander-in-Chief of the Seventh Area Army, ordered Kamiya to organise a trial and ensure that a sentence of death was handed down, Kamiya began in earnest to lay the foundations of a case that confirmed Furuta's gravest fears. He knew that by the time the Major had finished, every Rimau member would face the executioner.[21]

Kamiya was progressing quite well when the order was issued from Tokyo, a few days after the deaths of Sachs and Perske, that executions without proper trial were to cease. Mindful that certain Japanese might have to account for their actions, Tokyo had evidently decided that it was time to exercise restraint. Although Kamiya and Otsuka had concluded that there was sufficient evidence to proceed with a trial under Japanese law, they were now a little apprehensive about its validity under international law. On April 20, Kamiya travelled to Japanese Headquarters in Saigon for consultation with his superiors.[22]

Although Saigon's Major-General Hidaka agreed with Kamiya's opinion, he wanted more evidence, particularly in relation to Rimau's clothing, since a charge of espionage could not be levelled under either Japanese or international law if those collecting the information were uniformed military personnel. After a further period of 'severe' interrogation that lasted a month, Otsuka came up with the answers he required and re-submitted the evidence to Saigon. This time Kamiya received the sanction he sought. He was given instructions that the offences were to be tried under Japanese martial law and that the subsequent death sentence must be handed down by a judge.[23]

This meant, in effect, that the accused had almost no hope of acquittal. Under Japanese law, the very fact that the prosecutor had made out a case and taken it to court meant that the verdict was invariably 'guilty'. Since the decision was worked out in advance, it required very powerful evidence to overturn it. Quite unknown in English law, which presumes innocence unless proven otherwise, this procedure followed the European system and was used in Japanese criminal and military courts. As the judges usually rubber stamped the prosecutor's opinion, it had the distinct advantage for the prosecutor of achieving the outcome he desired.[24]

Obtaining a verdict that would satisfy the prosecution was ensured when Major Mitsuo Jifuku, Kamiya's colleague, was appointed one of the judges and handed all the papers pertaining to the case. At the end of May he began a close examination of the documentation. It is significant that by this time the war in Europe was over and Germans were being rounded up in large numbers to face war crimes trials — a sobering thought indeed for Major Jifuku. After a week's careful deliberation, he decided that, although the paperwork was excellent, he would seek further evidence from additional witnesses to back up the statements made by the accused.[25]

The fact that the trial was delayed for some weeks in an effort to obtain these additional statements underlines the extraordinary lengths to which the Japanese were prepared to go. In the past, executions had taken place without any formality whatever. Indeed, it was a rare occurrence for the accused to face even the most rudimentary of trials.[26]

The Japanese case rested on the charges of perfidy and espionage. The perfidy related to the allegation that Rimau had not worn proper uniforms and that *Mustika* had breached international law by displaying a Japanese national flag when it attacked the police boat at Kasu. The charge of espionage concerned the information in the notebooks, the sketches and the photographs, some of which had been collected while in disguise. Although the prisoners had admitted to removing their berets and badges, to carrying Japanese flags which they had waved once, and to taking notes on military installations and the like, Jifuku wanted additional statements from eyewitnesses at Kasu and Merapas to prove that international law as well as Japanese law had been breached, and to forestall any accusations that the prisoners had been condemned on confessions obtained under duress.

On June 5, he ordered the Kempei Tai to obtain the necessary statements within seven days. Finally, on June 20, he received an affadavit by Sidek Bin Safar, who had been visited at Kasu by the Kempei Tai. He had been most co-operative. In his statement was an account of the attack on the police boat, a description of *Mustika* and of the clothing worn by Rimau. Most conveniently, he had also come up with a brand new 'fact' — the Japanese national flag had been 'marked' on the stern of the tonkan.

Having been ordered by Otsuka to expedite the date of the trial, Major Jifuku decided that he could not wait any longer for further evidence from Merapas. As, in the opinion of both the local and chief judiciary departments, the case was already clearly evidenced and must not be further delayed, on June 28 he gave the go-ahead for the trial to proceed.[27]

Kamiya now busied himself with the job of finding two more judges who would be prepared to hand down the correct verdict. As the senior judge had to outrank the accused, he needed someone with the rank of colonel at the very least. Unfortunately, since the presiding judge had to be selected from a combat unit, Kamiya was forced to look outside his own, very co-operative department.

He ran into trouble almost immediately. Furuta's superior, Colonel Yoshida, who knew that the trial was a set-up and that he would be expected to endorse the demand for capital punishment, refused to have anything to do with it. Fully conversant with all the facts, he told Furuta that he would not be used as 'a tool of the Judiciary Department just to read out the death sentence prepared by that department'. Declaring that, if he had a free hand, he would find the Rimau men 'not guilty' and send them all to a POW camp, he also confided to Furuta that he considered them to be heroes, not war criminals. His view that they should be accorded POW status was one which was shared by several other lesser-ranking officers who, from the fragmented information available to them, did not believe that the Rimau prisoners were guilty of war crimes. Unfortunately, Yoshida did not have the courage of his convictions. Knowing that, in the light of orders issued at a high level, it would be impossible to go against the wishes of the prosecution, he took the line of least resistance and dissociated himself from the affair.

If Colonel Yoshida refused to participate in a trial that he knew to be nothing more than a device to sanction judicial murder, Colonel Masayoshi Towatari of Garrison Headquarters had no such qualms. Considered by Furuta to be a 'swaggerer and a general nuisance', he accepted the position as President of the Court on July 1. When staff officer Major Myosha Hisada was appointed as the second assistant judge the same day, the tribunal was complete. As soon as the arrangements had been confirmed, Jifuku met his fellow judges and explained what was required of them. Two days later, at around noon on 3 July 1945, the ten Rimau prisoners were removed from their cells at Outram Road and taken to what was formerly a professor's residence in the grounds of Raffles College for trial.

The Military Court was packed. As Presiding Judge, Colonel Towatari was positioned in the centre of the dais, with Jifuku on his right and Hisada on his left. Seated on the same level as the judges was prosecutor Kamiya, while off to one side sat the official court recorder, Warrant Officer Rikichi Asuka. In front of Kamiya, but below the dais, was interpreter Hiroyuki Furuta, who, in deference to the occasion, had eschewed his civilian garb for that of an army lieutenant. In the gallery was Major-General Otsuka, flanked by scores of military personnel who, resplendent in full dress uniform with campaign ribbons emblazoned upon their chests, had come to watch the interesting and unusual spectacle of Allied prisoners being put through the motions of a full military trial. Lined up ominously in a rack beside the door, were dozens of ceremonial swords belonging to the officers present.

Had there been a western observer present he would have been struck forcibly by the fact that one person, whose presence is considered vital in an English court of law, was conspicuous by his absence. In accordance with Japanese court procedure, there was no defence counsel.

At 1 o'clock, dressed in Japanese military clothing and with their normally bare feet encased in Japanese army boots, the prisoners were escorted into the courtroom. They were lined up before the judges, ranged from right to left, more or less according to rank. Ingleton, being the senior officer, was first, followed by Page, Carey, Sargent, Warren, Stewart, Fletcher, Gooley, Hardy and finally, the lone sailor among them, Wally Falls. Since they were dressed in clothing that was not their own, they wore no badges of rank and displayed no insignia. However, their hair was close cropped and their faces clean shaven. After each man had given his name, rank, age, birthplace and military unit, Major Kamiya read out the carefully prepared charges.[28]

The charge of perfidy had several strands. It stated that the Rimau men, dressed in green shirts and trousers, had removed their berets and badges of rank; all had applied stain to their skin and some, including Page, had worn sarongs. While wearing these clothes, on a tonkan flying a Japanese flag belonging to the original Malay crew, they had entered Singapore waters and had killed four members of the Malayan police. They had then fled to Merapas, where they had engaged in a battle with the Japanese. As a result of the fighting on Soreh, Tapai and Merapas, eight Japanese had been killed. Because of these activities, the accused were charged with 'engaging in hostile activities without wearing uniforms to qualify them for fighting and also using the vessel which lacked qualification for fighting'. The charge of espionage centred on the allegations that Davidson, Ingleton and Page had collected information while in disguise, and that Carey had made observations at Merapas. (It is worth noting that the 'crimes' of the dead, such as the fighting at Soreh and the wearing of sarongs by Davidson and Lyon, had been intermingled with those of the living, thereby allowing all those on trial to be regarded as accomplices for acts in which they did not take part.)

When Kamiya had finished speaking, he handed to the judges a weighty volume which contained the evidence that he had gathered — the statements made by the prisoners during interrogation, Sidek's affidavit, a report made by the chief of the Singapore Garrison, and five pieces of evidence pertaining to the persons being charged. The latter were a Japanese national flag, Carey's notebook, Ingleton's sketch book, and Page's camera and photographs. For some reason, Davidson's notebook, although it contained a great deal of information, was not formally admitted as evidence.

As the judges had already seen this file and Major Jifuku was himself responsible for collecting some of the evidence in it, the review of the contents was superficial. After flicking through it, the judges were ready to move to Act Two.

In trials such as this it was usual for judges now to ask questions of the accused. This was not to assist them in deciding the guilt or innocence of the person, but to make sure that the prosecution had not fudged the evidence — a sensible precaution in the case of evidence obtained by the Kempei Tai. In Rimau's case, since the trial was a carefully orchestrated plot, the judges simply went through the motions.[29]

Ingleton was brought forward first. After being asked if he had any objection to the facts read out, he answered that he did not. It is little wonder. As his only chance to assess the validity of the charge was to try and follow it as Furuta made the translation, it must have been extremely difficult. He did not challenge the incorrect statements by the prosecutor that *Mustika* had been flying a Japanese flag belonging to the

Malays, or that four men had been killed at Kasu. Neither did he forcibly point out that jungle green clothing was the recognised Australian military uniform in the tropics.[30] While Furuta seems to have had some degree of fluency with the English language, it appears that translating military and legal jargon may not have been his strong point. In June 1944 he had interpreted at the trial of James Bradley and three others who had been charged with 'deserting' from their working party on the infamous Burma Railway. Saved from immediate execution by the intervention of Colonel Dillon (the same Colonel Dillon from Lyon's escape route) and a Japanese-speaking English major named Cyril Wild, Bradley had been brought to trial. He had no idea of what was going on and had actually thought, from Furuta's translation, that he was being charged with 'keeping within him cholera germs'.[31] Unless Furuta's command of English had improved out of sight in twelve months, it is not surprising that Ingleton failed to pick up errors or distortions.

The discrepency in the number of deaths at Kasu was of little consequence, but the accusation that they were flying *Mustika*'s Japanese flag from the stern was a complete and utter fabrication.

Although Mrs Manderson's flags had been kept in a handy place so that they could be produced and waved if necessary, *Mustika*, which was not masquerading, as *Krait* had done, as a Japanese vessel but as an Indonesian prahu, was displaying no flags at all. As the Malayan crew had not needed them for their trip, they had been, and still were, securely locked in the Japanese port office at Pontianak in Borneo.[32]

After confirming that Ingleton had no objection to the charges, the judges proceeded. He was asked one or two questions about his job and the composition of the Rimau party before his inquisitors finally got down to the nitty-gritty — the clothing worn by the prisoners while on *Mustika*.

They did not accept Ingleton's explanation that badges of rank had been removed as the party all knew each other well. In fact, the prosecution actually had Ingleton agree that rank identification was to enable outsiders to recognise them as military personnel. Since badges of rank in the Australian Army were not obtrusive, often being little more than simple white tape, it appears that 'badges of rank' as a term was being interchanged with 'emblems'. If this was the case, the judges had just asked Ingleton, a Royal Marine with scant experience in the Australian military system, a loaded question.

Members of the British Army, unlike those of the AIF, were always festooned with highly polished and often very ornate badges which identified at a glance the regiment to which the soldier belonged. The Australian Army was far more sombre, issuing only two small metal badges to its personnel — the 'rising sun' and the word 'Australia', both coated in non-reflective black paint which made them indistinguishable except at very short range. Therefore, while the British Army may have used badges to enable others to identify its personnel, the Australian Army most certainly did not. Had this notion been put to anyone but Major Ingleton, it would have met with an emphatic denial.

Once the topic of badges had been covered, the tribunal moved on to the question of the camouflage dye and the fact that berets had not been worn. Ingleton was forced to concede that, even though some of them had been dressed in shirt and trousers, the application of the skin dye and the lack of headgear did not make any of them readily recognisable as Australian soldiers. Unfortunately, he did not know enough about military law to realise that, as this was allowable under international law, it was a perfectly legitimate ruse.

He was then asked to confirm the identity of Davidson. A photograph was produced, showing him dressed in a sarong. Once this had been established, the judges moved back to *Mustika*'s flag.

Ingleton, who had no idea what was really going on, was unaware that Kamiya had up his sleeve a choice piece of 'evidence' — the revelation by Sidek, after his memory-jogging visit from the Kempei Tai, that a Japanese flag was 'painted' on *Mustika*'s stern. Failing to grasp the significance of the questioning, Ingleton conceded that, although he could not recall seeing one, it was possible that a flag may have been painted on the stern. In response to further questioning, he also stated that they had not displayed either Mrs Manderson's flag or a British flag at Kasu. Significantly, if the issue of whether *Mustika*'s original flag was actually flying was raised, it was not recorded in the court proceedings, even though this was part of the charge. A number of questions were then asked about the fight at Kasu, the identity of the sketchbook and the reasons why the sketches had been made. Satisfied with Ingleton's answers, the judges called Page.

He had nothing to add during his brief examination except to state that he had once seen Lyon wearing his badge of rank on the junk. Questioned by the judges, Page admitted that he had worn a sarong while taking his photographs and that he had fired at the police boat at Kasu. When asked 'Did you yourself kill any Japanese soldiers?', Page replied in clear and deliberate tones, 'I am an officer in the British Army and I know that my aim is good'. After identifying his camera and admitting to fighting at Kasu and Merapas, he was replaced on the stand by Carey.

Apart from stating that he had always been on the island with the stores and was never on *Mustika*, Carey did not challenge the charges. He admitted that he had worn a loin cloth on Merapas as it was cooler and had taken notes of enemy shipping and aircraft that came by the island. He also admitted that, although Warren and the other two had not kept notes, they had given him items of interest to add to his report. After confirming that he had engaged in fighting at Merapas and another island [near Boeaja], he too was dismissed.

The others, headed by Sargent and Warren, had little to add or subtract. Warren pointed out that he had been on Merapas, Sargent confirmed that Japanese flags brought from Australia had been waved at the enemy aircraft and the others admitted that they had kept their eyes peeled for useful information. Wally Falls challenged the question of badges of rank by stating, 'I am a navy man and therefore do not wear badges of rank'. The judges then smartly came up with the obvious question — if jungle green uniforms were recognised army dress, why was a navy man wearing one? If Falls gave the answer that the Australian Navy wore tropical kit that was almost identical with that of the Army, the answer, like the judge's question, was not formally recorded.

After the questioning was complete, each of the accused was asked to voice any objections about statements made by his fellow accused. There being none, the statements made by the prisoners to the Water Kempei Tai and Major Kamiya were read out. As there were again no objections, the prosecutor read out the affidavit of Sidek Bin Safar. Except for querying whether or not there was a flag painted on the stern, the prisoners confirmed that his statement was correct. Sidek's evidence was followed by the report of the Garrison chief and the identification of each of the exhibits. With no objections lodged and no one wishing to add anything or emphasise any point of evidence advantageous to him, it was time for the prosecutor to address the court.[33]

The contents of this fairly long dissertation came as no surprise to the judges or to Major-General Otsuka, who had already reviewed and sanctioned it. After running through the facts and evidence, Kamiya began to consolidate his case. The accused, he stated, had been proven guilty of displaying the Japanese flags they had brought from Australia and of wearing Malay dress. Although he admitted that it had not been proved conclusively that *Mustika* had a flag marked upon the stern, he evaded the question of whether Rimau had attacked the police boat while flying a Japanese flag by stating that there was no doubt whatever that no British flag had been hoisted before shooting took place. This, said Kamiya, was in direct contravention of the Hague Convention of 1907.

He was wrong. According to the Hague Convention, flying the flag of the enemy and even dressing in his uniform, is classified as a legitimate ruse and is therefore not forbidden. The Hague Rules do, however, prohibit its 'improper use'. Although this is not actually defined, to open fire while employing this ruse is recognised unanimously as being 'improper'. Despite Kamiya's assertions, there does not appear to be anything in the Hague Convention which insists that the aggressors' own national flag must be shown when attacking the enemy (clearly demonstrated by the fact that ambushes and surprise naval bombardments are legitimate and that submarines and aircraft attack without warning), although international judges such as Heaton and Oppenheim have ruled that if approaching under the enemy's flag, the attackers must reveal their true identity before hostilities begin. As *Mustika* was flying no Japanese flags and the members of Rimau were not masquerading as Japanese soldiers, this rule cannot have been breached. Kamiya was, therefore, on very shaky ground.

When assessing Rimau's dress he evaded the issue of whether or not jungle green was a recognised uniform and did not mention that Japanese badges of rank, being scarlet and gold collar tabs, were quite unlike the Australians' nondescript epaulette tapes. In what seems to be an acute case of colour blindness, he asserted that the quite definitely khaki green of the Japanese Army was so close to Rimau's distinctly jungle green that badges of rank should have been displayed. In so doing, he ignored the Hague Convention's ruling that removal of badges from uniforms is also a legitimate ruse.

This lapse of memory and allegation of similarity of colour enabled Kamiya to level the accusation that, although Malay clothing was worn by some of the party only for some of the time, all had participated in hostile activities while wearing a uniform that was a de facto disguise. Had he been able to prove that the Rimau party was dressed in Japanese uniforms, he would have had a case under international law. Since he could not, he simply disregarded the fact that engaging in battle while in disguise is punishable only if the enemy's uniform is worn or if military personnel masquerade as civilians without being ordered to do so by their commander or government. With disguise an integral part of Plan Rimau, the entire party should have been safe from retribution since, under the Hague Rules, those issuing the order, not those obeying, were answerable.[34]

Having 'proven' that everyone was illegally in disguise, the question of espionage was easier to tackle. It is interesting that, although the men were being tried under Japanese law, Kamiya, when it suited him, referred constantly to the Hague Convention of 1907, which, unlike the Geneva Convention, was recognised by the Japanese. It appears that Kamiya, in attempting to validate the charges under international law was already thinking ahead. After the war, it was the Hague, not the Geneva, Convention that was used as the yardstick when assessing whether or not a war crime had been committed.[35]

Kamiya now declared that, according to that Convention, 'a spy is defined to be a person who is mainly engaged in the collection of informations in the above manner' [while in disguise] and that 'such action is not illegal on his part but the country which capture [sic] such spy can punish him'. Although these words are basically correct, Kamiya's definition of what constituted an illegal disguise was not. According to Article 29, in the section pertaining to spies, of the same Convention which he was so fond of quoting, anyone clandestinely collecting information, including soldiers *not* in uniform, can be classified as a spy. One of the few exceptions is military personnel dressed *in* uniform.

Had the Australian uniforms, badges or not, been accepted as correct military dress, Kamiya could only have pinned his espionage charge on those who were disguised as Malays.

The only person still alive who was known, beyond all doubt, to have dressed in this manner was Bob Page. Indeed, it had been established by the Kempei that Ingleton for one, because of his size, had never abandoned his military clothing in favour of Malay dress.

Having convinced the court that the Rimau men were spies and that the punishment of spies was legal, Kamiya broached the subject of punishment for those who had participated in hostile activities while in disguise. Employing logical sleight of hand, he announced that, since he had found nothing in the Convention which prohibited it, punishment was therefore permissible.

In stating that punishment was not prohibited, he was quite right. What he did not say was that, as the Hague Rules do not recognise that, in circumstances similar to that of Rimau, these activities constitute a crime there is, naturally, no mention of any punishment for this non-existent breach of military law. By now, the accused were completely enmeshed in a tangle of lies, half-truths and judiciously selected fact and it was impossible for any of them to escape from the intricate web which Kamiya had so carefully and cleverly woven.

By deciding that the uniform was not a uniform but a disguise, he had made irrelevant the tricky aspect of who was wearing Malay dress. All were now spies, including all those who had not actually made recorded observations and all those not on *Mustika*. Carey was included in the list as he had worn local-style clothing while he was collecting his information on Merapas. Since Warren had not replaced his beret and badges of rank (removed on the voyage between Pedjantan and Merapas) before supplying verbal information to Carey, he too was a spy.

With everyone now a known spy, Kamiya solved the problem of identifying who had actually taken part in any hostile activity by declaring that, as all had had a common objective, all were equally guilty. He then stated that since the Hague Convention allowed spies to be punished, and did not prohibit the punishment of those engaged in hostile activities while disguised, Japanese law could be used in deciding the penalty.[36]

Having wrapped up his case so eloquently, Kamiya launched into a piece of inspired oration. He declared that the Rimau men, being supplied with poison which they had intended to use, were obviously heroes whose intentions had been thwarted. He then moved to the question of whether it was permissible to execute such men. A precedent, he reminded the court, had already been set. After citing the case of two great Japanese heroes, Oki and Yokogawa, who had been executed by a Russian court for exploding railway bridges in the Russian-Japanese war, he went on to declare:

Comparing the heroes of Rimau Operation to both heroes Oki and Yokogawa, the two parties are identical with each other in their action viewed from the standpoint of international laws and in the value of patriotism to their respective countries.

It has been proven to the Court beyond any doubt that the accused are guilty of the charges. When the guilt is so clear, it would be disgracing the fine spirit of those heroes if we tried or thought of saving their lives.

When they left their homeland, they put aside the matter of their lives. All they cared about was the success of [their] mission, lives were nothing in the face of heated patriotism.

When their action deserved death, I am sure that they would rather die than save their lives at the mercy of the captor, because dying gloriously is the way to immortalize their names on the history.

We were told that our two heroes who attacked the Port of Sydney in a tiny submarine were given a cordial funeral ceremony. The Australians are the people who have real sense of honour. They respected our heroes because they found true heroism in death.

Let us pay them the same respect, same admiration to the heroes, and send them to the glory of death to glorify the last of the heroes.

Let us not disgrace their spirit by supposing that they may want to be alive. Sending them to death is the only way to send them to an eternal glory. Let us do this.

With that, Kamiya formally demanded the death penalty.[37]

Before handing down judgement, the President of the Court asked the accused if they had anything to say. It must have been a stunned Ingleton who now rose to his feet. After thanking Kamiya for the remarks about his being a patriotic hero he stated that, although he realised that Rimau's modus operandi may have been an unfair method of warfare, he did not know until this present moment that they were such grave offences — thereby confirming that he had no idea he was on trial for his life. The others, probably too shocked to think, echoed the sentiments of their senior officer. Six hours after the trial had begun it was all over. After a short adjournment, the Presiding Judge handed down the verdict of the court.

Guilty. At a time and place to be fixed, they would all be executed.[38]

Chief Judge Towatari's conscience must have been bothering him. Before the prisoners left for Outram Road he spoke privately to them in an attempt to explain that, as a military man acting under orders, he had no alternative but to find them guilty. Page and Ingleton accepted his explanation, but it must have been cold comfort for them to know that the President of the Court actually knew they were innocent. Furuta, completely taken in by the elaborate courtroom drama that had just unfolded, believed that the judge's reluctance to condemn them to death stemmed not from the fact that they were innocent, but from the fact that they were heroes. It was a fallacy to which he clung for the rest of his life.[39]

Back at Outram Road the Japanese acceded to the men of Rimau's request to be together by transferring them to a large cell on the upper level. As they were still permitted no contact with the other prisoners, the front of the cell, which was composed entirely of bars, was draped with blankets.

Now that the ten had been condemned to death, their treatment changed dramatically. The food which, in common with the rations of the other inmates, had been even more miserable of late, assumed feast-like proportions. They were also given cigarettes, tins of condensed milk, blankets on which to sleep in relative comfort, and were allowed to mix freely with each other within their section of the prison. Furuta was also permitted to visit them. As he was the only Japanese whom they trusted, Page and Stewart gave him messages for their families, which he promised to deliver to the Allies when the war had ended. He also undertook to look for Bob Page's father, whom Page, not knowing that he was long dead, believed was still a prisoner of the Japanese. In return, Page and the others handed Furuta a testimonial in the hope that he would be exempted from any reprisals after their deaths. Some of the men also confided to Furuta their anger at not being told by SRD that their activities might land them on death row. Believing that after the trial they would be classified as regular prisoners and sent to a POW camp, they had been unaware that they were facing a capital charge until they heard the death sentence handed down.[40]

It would not be an overstatement to say that Furuta was devastated by the court's verdict. Horrified by the thought that all were to die, he felt compelled to do something. Not knowing that General Itagaki had specifically ordered the death sentence, he asked Otsuka to appeal to the General for clemency, even though he had been told by Kamiya months before that it was a lost cause. Otsuka's reaction was predictable. He told Furuta that, being a civilian, he did not understand the psychology of the warrior and that his persistent requests only made him look ridiculous. Rebuffed, but certain that Otsuka had refused to enter a plea because he was a weak-minded intellectual, Furuta made another, somewhat feeble attempt to solicit help from two other senior officers. Once again, he ran into the same brick wall.[41]

Five months after conceiving its February 10 plot to rid itself of the men of Rimau, the Seventh Area Army finally attained its objective. On July 6 an order for their execution was issued by General Itagaki, the very man on whom Furuta, in his ignorance, had pinned his last hope.[42]

The elaborate precautions taken to seal off the Rimau men from the rest of the world did not stop Australian Bert Rollason from managing to snatch a few words with them as he passed by on binkei duty. It was not much of a conversation — simply that they were now being better treated and were being given good food and cigarettes. The last time he spoke to them, some time on July 6, he learned that they were to be executed the following day. As with the date of the infamous Double Tenth massacre, there was an ominous ring about the seventh day of the seventh month.

The next morning the gaol's prisoners were alerted to the fact that something was up by the great kerfuffle which erupted as the guards sought to prevent anyone from seeing the condemned men being led outside. Dressed in khaki shirts and pants, the ten barefooted prisoners were securely fastened in single file to a central chain. Later, while being loaded into the two vehicles that were to take them to the execution ground at Bukit Timah, they were seen fleetingly by Rollason, whose guard had been less than vigilant.

If any of them were frightened or even nervous that they were about to take their last ride, they certainly did not show it. In common with many of their countrymen who had been placed in the same situation since 1942, they put on an outstanding performance for the benefit of the watching Japanese. Laughing and joking in a way that filled the onlookers with admiration and of which Bill Reynolds and Ivan Lyon would have heartily approved, they boarded the vehicles as if they had not a care in the world.[43]

By 10 o'clock they had arrived at Bukit Timah. Situated not far from Reformatory Road and lacking the lush green foliage of the tropical jungle, the execution ground was a desolate place. The sandy soil, little more than a hilly wasteland, was pitted with half-filled and open graves, which were scattered among the stunted, scrubby bushes and flourishing clumps of a carnivorous plant known as Dutchman's Pipe.

In common with most executions, there was a sizeable gallery. The army top brass was represented by Chief Judge Towatari, Major-General Otsuka, Major Kamiya, the Commander of Outram Road's military gaol, Major Shuzo Kobayashi, and his civilian gaol counterpart, Major Koshiro Mikizawa, who had expressed a wish to witness a decapitation. The actual executions, under the direction of Major Hisada, who, having been the judge was now the executioner, were to be performed by Sergeants Nibara, Tsukudu, Okamura and Shimoi and Corporal Hirata. There was nothing special about these five men, who were simply Kempei Tai personnel, known to the prisoners by such names as Woof Woof, Cookhouse and Boofhead. Standing by, ready to fill in the three pits that had been dug, were four Japanese convicts, one of whom was known as Kadino or Convict Warder No. 6.[44]

The only person missing was Hiroyuki Furuta. Unable to face up to the thought of the execution and the fact that he would have to translate the final order, he had asked another interpreter, Yoshimura, to take his place while he waited in his quarters in Nassim Road. But, at the eleventh hour, the suspense became overpowering. Jumping into a car, he drove to Bukit Timah, where, unable to come face to face with the men he had come to regard as friends rather than enemies, he watched from behind a bush.

Once the prisoners had been assembled, the gaol commandant formally announced that they were to be beheaded. Although the official record would state, as it invariably did, that the executions had been by firing squad, the Japanese used this method very rarely. Not only did decapitation save on ammunition, which was now in short supply, it also had the advantage of being whisper quiet. The echo of rifle shots could be heard far away. The sound of a sword swishing through the air was almost negligible.

Furuta, peering from his hiding place, saw that the prisoners, having been temporarily released from their bonds, were smoking cigarettes. Still demonstrating the same bravado they had exhibited when leaving Outram Road, they were joking and laughing, determined that the Japanese would not break them. When the rest period was over, they still displayed no emotion. Shaking hands, they simply wished each 'good luck'.

Ingleton then turned to face the throng as he made his final speech. After asking Kamiya and the gaol commandant to thank those who had been responsible for their recent good treatment, he broached the subject of Furuta. As his voice travelled clearly through the air Furuta heard him say:

'We have one regret. This is that we cannot see at this place Mr Furuta who has been so kind to us. We all wanted to thank him once more, but I suppose he has his duty. Please tell him we thanked him before we died.'

Almost blinded by tears, Furuta was incapable of movement. As an officer shouted 'Ki-o-tsuke' (attention), followed by 'Ichi-ni-tsuke' (take your position), Major Ingleton, hands tied behind his back, was escorted at bayonet point and forced to kneel at the edge of one of the pits. But when the swordsman raised his weapon in both his hands, its ice cold blade glinting in the brilliant sunlight, Furuta's nerve gave way. Covering his ears so that he could not hear the shriek of the executioner as he brought down his sword, he ran from the scene.[45]

It was as well for someone as civilised as Furuta that he did not witness the proceedings. After the four officers had been executed, the others were brought forward. Of the ten, only five were blindfolded. Far from being a ritualistic Samurai-style execution, full of pomp and ceremony and befitting the heroic status of the prisoners that Kamiya had so impressed upon the court, the proceedings were no different from any one of hundreds carried out by the Japanese during the war. The executioners were not highly born swordsmen but common soldiers whose expertise left a lot to be desired. The execution of two of the victims was so botched that decapitation was incomplete and, when it was over, the three pits containing the bodies piled one on top of each other —

four in one grave and three in the other two — were hurriedly filled in, like those of common criminals.

Before he had left for Bukit Timah that morning, Outram Road's Commandant Kobayashi (known as Major Felix owing to his habit of poking his head over walls to spy on the prisoners, in much the same way as the feline cartoon character) had ordered the gaol's 300 prisoners into the courtyard, where they had been informed that ten Allied prisoners were to be executed. Since the convict grave diggers had been forbidden to talk when they returned from the execution ground, further details were unknown. However, in the warders' room were two Korean prisoners named Noh Bok Kun and Kim Hyong Soon. Conscripted by the Japanese, they had been employed as POW guards until falling foul of the Kempei Tai. While ostensibly engaged in cleaning the room, they overheard the executioners laughing and joking about the grisly task they had just performed and taunting Nibara for being so unskilled that he had required two or three cuts to complete his tasks. Barely a month later, when the atomic bombs were dropped on Hiroshima and Nagasaki, ending the war with a suddenness that took everyone by surprise, Noh was interested to learn that a Japanese prisoner by the name of Noburu Yamane had been dispatched in great haste to stick six wooden crosses on the three mass graves at Bukit Timah.[46]

By the time the Japanese surrendered, all was in order. Although there had been no time to rid themselves of witnesses by executing all Allied prisoners as planned, the Kempei were well prepared. With the last resting places of the heroes reverently and Christianly marked, those responsible for their executions had only to ensure that the paperwork was impeccable. In this they succeeded beyond their wildest dreams. When the Allied investigating teams turned up in Singapore a few weeks later, they swallowed the Kempei Tai story hook, line and sinker. As the Kempei Tai later so rightly recorded, 'because of the Kempei's proper management, no one was accused as war criminals'.[47]

Chapter 16
Only Partial Retribution

In August 1945, the nations of the world, still recovering from the shock of the Nazi holocaust, once more recoiled with horror. It was hard to believe that the skeletal creatures who now dragged themselves from jungle huts, euphemistically described by the Japanese as POW Camps, could ever have been normal human beings.

Japan had not intended that anyone should ever learn of her acts of gross inhumanity, for the High Command had ordered the massacre of all prisoners, instructing unit commanders 'to annihilate them all, and not to leave any traces'. In the first week of August, mass graves had been dug at jungle camps and measures had been taken to ensure that all would be 'destroyed individually or in groups by mass bombing, poisonous smoke, poisons, drowning, decapitations or what' by the end of the month. Some prisoners had only six hours left to live when, at noon on August 15, the very day of the intended executions, Emperor Hirohito stunned everyone by announcing Japan's unconditional surrender.[1]

It was not until the Allied troops penetrated the jungles of the Far East that the enormity of the situation hit the Australian people. Day after day the figures rolled in, accompanied by graphic descriptions and hideous photographs of men, barely more than spectres, lying by the thousand on bamboo slats, awaiting rescue and rehabilitation. Even more sickening, to a society which treated its womenfolk with respect, was the revelation that many nurses and female civilian prisoners had endured conditions equal to that of the men. Australia, a small nation who had given Mother England the cream of her youth for the second consecutive generation, was so appalled that the need to punish those responsible was temporarily overshadowed by a greater need — to bring her men home.

There is no question that repatriation was the only sane course of action, but as each shipload of ex-prisoners sailed south, the prime witnesses to Japanese acts of atrocity all but vanished, dispersed into homes and hospitals across the length and breadth of Australia. Although there was a concentrated effort to obtain statements on the repatriation ships, the follow-up work was extremely difficult. By the time many of the deponents were tracked down by investigating teams requiring additional statements, many of the Japanese responsible for three and a half years of torment had disappeared.

Even those Japanese who did not flee had a fair chance of evading retribution. In an attempt to establish the whereabouts of 50 000 Allied prisoners, POW Recovery Teams had been forced to work round the clock for two and a half months, processing what amounted to almost seven hundred cases a day. As this work, often carried out by personnel whose talents lay elsewhere, was by necessity superficial, the actual fate of many prisoners was never determined and many war crimes remained undetected. Indeed, it was often only by the remotest chance that investigators had any idea that a war crime may have been committed.[2]

Major Cyril Wild, the Japanese-speaking British officer who had been given the unenviable task of carrying the white flag at Singapore's surrender, and who had later saved James Bradley from certain execution, had been seconded on his release from Changi to investigate the fate of missing pilots, most of whom had simply vanished on capture. A tip from a Malay driver named Samson, who remembered he had driven his Japanese master to an execution at Bukit Timah in July, pointed Wild in the direction of Outram Road Gaol and to Mikizawa, the commandant of the civil section, in particular. Mikizawa, no doubt in an attempt to mitigate the fact that 1200 Asians in his custody had died from starvation during the last fourteen months of the war, decided to co-operate. Leading Wild to a lonely stretch of wasteland at Bukit Timah, he poked around in the scrub until he found three newly made mounds with six wooden crosses, which he declared marked the graves of Chinese and perhaps 'one or two Europeans', whom he had seen executed. Wild, on viewing the distinctly Christian markers, was at once suspicious. Despite close questioning, Mikizawa protested that he knew nothing more and Wild, unable to obtain permission to exhume the bodies, was forced to let the matter rest.

About a week later a young deposed Malay chieftain turned up in Singapore from Lingga Archipelago, looking for an Englishman by the name of Salmond. Mr Salmond had good reason to remember Amir Silahili, for it had been the Amir who had organised the rescue of Mr Salmond and hundreds of others from the waters of Pompong Island and passed them on to Lyon's escape route. When the time had come for Salmond to flee to the Indragiri River, he had promised the Amir that 'when the day comes I shall return from Singapore with the British Navy to drive out the Japanese'. To which Silahili had replied, 'No, Tuan. I shall come to Singapore to meet you and we shall return together with the British Navy to liberate my people'.

After three years of Japanese occupation, the stalwart young chieftain, stripped of his titles and deposed by the victorious Japanese, had come to Singapore to call in his debts. Mr Salmond, being only too willing to oblige, took him to Wild, who listened with great interest to his story, and to two facts in particular. Silahili revealed that a garrison of heavily armed Japanese, twenty-seven of whom were Kempei Tai wanted for the Double Tenth massacre, were still terrorising the Lingga Archipelago. His second piece of information disclosed that in December of 1944 about ten British and Australians, members of a raiding party, had been taken to Singapore after being imprisoned on Singkep Island.

Tantalising as these stories were, the authorities, snowed under by the gigantic task of re-occupying Singapore and Malaya, were not in a position to act upon the information until October 1, when four motor launches, carrying naval personnel, Wild, Salmond, the Amir, two civilians investigating the Double Tenth incident and half a platoon of paratroops, set forth for Singkep to help the Amir liberate his people. On arrival, the party split into four groups to undertake its various tasks, which were completed to the satisfaction of everyone except the Japanese — the Amir had been restored to power, the Japanese had been arrested, a great deal of information about the capture of European men in the Lingga Archipelago had been collated and last, but by no means least, Wild had in his custody the Dabo Police Admission book and a scrap of paper bearing the names, Warren, Carey and Marsh.

The Police Book was a real puzzle, for it showed that six 'white men' had been admitted to gaol on December 18 and 19 and three more on December 28-29, for crimes described as 'enemy of the state'. Their identities, except for 'R.M. Ingleton, Major, Royal Marines, British', were not clear to Wild as their surnames had been omitted, although a column alongside the various entries indicated that almost all were Australian. With this scant information Wild returned to Singapore to begin a search for the nine men. To his consternation, he found that there was no evidence that they had ever been in a POW Camp and the Japanese were in a conspiracy to tell him nothing.[3]

It was about this time, mid-October, that another group of investigators returned to Singapore from the island of Bintan. They were Australians, members of a POW inquiry team, which had originally been asked to investigate reports that 6000 Allied prisoners were on Bintan Island. When the team's observers, peering from the doorway of a reconnaissance plane, reported that they had seen no sign of any Europeans, a ground party was sent in with additional instructions from SRD's Captain Ellis to make enquiries about Rimau, whose disappearance had been confirmed. On arrival in Kidjang on October 8, some of the team tackled Major Fugita and his cohorts while others questioned the local population. In establishing that their information had been incorrect and that no POWs, let alone 6000, had ever been incarcerated on the island, they inadvertently stumbled upon two other, very disturbing incidents.[4]

Shortly after Singapore had capitulated, about thirty-four Australians had surrendered to the Japanese at Tandjung Pinang. At first they had been put to work, but on the second day all had been taken to a tennis court, bayoneted, shot or beheaded, and the bodies, some of them still alive, thrown into an air raid shelter and a well. One officer who had escaped the initial massacre was subsequently decapitated on the beach.[5]

As the investigators were collecting this grisly evidence, three men had come forward — Abdul Wahab, the headman of Mapor; Alexander Ouvarow, an English-speaking Russian planter from the island of Numbing who had interpreted for the Japanese, and Mr Tobing, a Malay employee of the Dutch Administration at Tandjung Pinang. They alleged that a number of white men, after being involved in a battle with Japanese troops on Merapas Island, had been pursued down the archipelago and that three white men, captured on Singkep, had been lodged in the Tandjung Pinang Police Station overnight while en route to Singapore.[6]

While the civilians were pouring out their tale, Major Fugita, head of the Tandjung Pinang garrison, had decided to tell all he knew about the incidents at Kasu, Soreh, Tapai and Merapas. Yap Chin Yah, who had been responsible for Abdul Latif's torture, was rounded up, along with Chizu of the Kempei Tai, collaborators Raja Mun and Mahamit, and the headman of Pangkil, Raja Rool. By the time they had all made their statements, the investigating team knew of the various fights that had taken place, that some men had been killed and that prisoners had been taken to Singapore.

A search of Bintan, Mapor and Merapas yielded nothing except a set of dentures and Riggs's grave (thought to be that of a Japanese) on Merapas, and irrefutable evidence that Rimau had been on the island. For some reason, no attempt was made to visit the easily accessible islands of Soreh and Tapai, where the bodies of Lyon, Ross, Davidson and Campbell still lay — although by this time they were nothing more than bones. However, the additional information, from Abdul Wahab, that five men had been seen on the nearby, uninhabited island of Sentut in July 1945, raised hopes to such an extent that a search party was sent to investigate. They found nothing apart from indications that several small saplings had been sawn down, possibly to construct a raft, and also a length of rubber hose, apparently used to divert smoke from a fire, long since dead. This expedition to Sentut was nothing more than a wild goose chase. Forty years later it would be discovered that the five were escapees from the bauxite mine, betrayed to the Japanese by Abdul Wahab himself.[7]

When the results of the Australian investigation were brought back to Singapore and added to that of Wild, the investigation was stepped up. From the Koreans Noh and Kim, Wild learned that ten European men had been taken out of Outram Road Gaol in early July and had been executed. When it was discovered that the officers and the Kempei Tai responsible, with the exception of Commandant Koboyashi, who had fled, were already in custody for other crimes, it did not take long for the story to emerge.

Unable to deny what had happened, Major General Otsuka and Major Kamiya promptly produced their trump card — the trial documents. When Wild read through their contents he released Furuta, who was then thoroughly interrogated. By the time the Japanese interpreter had finished delivering his heavily embroidered mixture of fact and hearsay, Wild was convinced that the men of Rimau had committed crimes contrary to the Hague Convention of 1907 and that the Japanese, after giving them the best of care, had reluctantly executed them in a manner befitting heroes.

It is evident that if Furuta witnessed any violence during Rimau's incarceration, he erased it from his mind. As was pointed out in later war crimes trials, the Japanese appeared to be extremely adept at structuring their thinking in such a way that unpleasant thoughts could be either pushed into the background or disappear completely, as if the unpleasantness had never occurred. By the same token, small gestures of kindness could be blown out of all proportion, allowing one or two incidents to become the rule, rather than the exception. As a middle aged, well educated, fairly cultured and much travelled man, it is doubtful that without employing this device, Furuta would have been able to come to terms with violence of the type usually doled out to prisoners by the Kempei Tai, and with which he was familiar.[8]

While he was being interviewed, Furuta also handed over the two messages which he had promised to pass on for Page and Stewart. Bob Page's was for his father and stated, 'I trust my father will approve the way I took in giving up my studies and joining the Army', while the message from Corporal Stewart read, 'I hope my wife will excuse me for not saying a special goodbye when I saw her the night before I left for the operation. I did not want to worry her with my danger'.[9] Having committed these poignant statements to memory and recorded them verbatim, Furuta felt satisfied that he had at last fulfilled the dying wish of two men for whom he held a great respect.

He might just as well not have bothered. The Australian and British governments did not ever take the trouble to deliver them.[10]

When Wild and his Australian counterpart in Singapore, Colonel Pritchard, viewed the trial papers, they were exceedingly impressed, as well they might be. By Japanese standards, it was an exceptionally detailed document, for normal trial summaries, if they existed at all, were very perfunctory and did not contain the details or examples of cross examination which appeared in Rimau's paperwork. With Furuta backing up everything that appeared in the written record, and SRD headquarters withholding the information that the message ordering Rimau's execution had been intercepted and decoded in February 1945, it is little wonder that the investigators had no inkling that the entire trial and its documentation were a sham.[11]

Although the war was over, SRD, in common with many other clandestine agencies, was paranoid about keeping the fact that the Allies had broken the enemy codes a closely guarded secret. This cloak of secrecy was so effective that it was not until three decades after the war had finished that the public learned what a phenomenally useful weapon the intercepted material had been.

During the war the knowledge being gained from the decoded intercepts proved so valuable that drastic measures had been taken to safeguard secrecy. Fully aware that Coventry was to be bombed, Winston Churchill had been unable to do anything to warn either the city or its people. As Japan's diplomatic code had been broken long before she entered into hostilities with the Allies, it has been accepted that President Roosevelt knew for certain that the Pacific Bases would be attacked. In 1989 it was learned from the wartime diary of Australian cryptanalyst Eric Nave that Japan's naval code had been broken in November 1941 and that Churchill knew of the impending attack on Pearl Harbour. Although the question of whether this information was made available to Roosevelt remains unresolved, it is possible that the removal of the aircraft carriers out to sea from Pearl Harbour, just prior to the bombing raid, was not nearly as 'coincidental' as it might seem. From Nave's diary it appears that, by sacrificing the lives of 2400 sailors on the ships still in port, the secret of the intercepts was preserved and an outraged America was at last brought into the war without jeopardising Roosevelt's political status.[12]

Unaware that high-ranking SRD officers had known for a very long time that the Rimau prisoners' execution had been ordered, the investigators in Singapore tackled the question of whether or not a war crime had been committed. That ten men had been beheaded was irrefutable. According to the Japanese, the execution had been in grand style, in keeping with their status as heroes. Furuta confirmed that after the execution Otsuka, in an attempt to bolster the morale of his own men, had waxed lyrical about the bravery of his victims, with words such as 'flowers of chivalry' flowing easily from his lips.[13]

Wild, in particular, was mightily impressed by this account, for it was the embodiment of all he had ever learned about the Samurai way of death and the legendary code of the Knights of Bushido. Unfortunately, Wild's love of Japanese mythology was such that it had coloured his judgement, enabling him to accept the atrocities he had witnessed and the beatings he had endured during his imprisonment, in the belief that the behaviour of the Japanese was based on 'a living, honest thing, that belonged to the Samurai warrior — the Code of the Warrior'. Although various investigators were also fooled by other elaborate Japanese cover-ups, it was perhaps the mistaken belief that Wild had a great understanding of the Japanese mind that caused his colleagues to accept his opinion without question.[14] Consequently, after a half-hearted attempt to verify whether uniforms had been worn, Wild and Pritchard accepted the evidence that the men of Rimau had been executed legally as spies who had opened fire on the enemy while in disguise and while flying the enemy flag. No effort was made to find any of the many witnesses to the Kasu incident, nor to make independent investigations at the other islands. The investigators also chose to ignore the report by RAMC Captain Ross, who had exhumed the bodies of the executed Rimau men and the unfortunate John Long (also executed at Bukit Timah), that their deaths and the subsequent burial had definitely not been fit for heroes. Incredibly, in the face of this damning evidence, which completely supported the statements of Noh and Kim, the investigators believed the story of the Japanese rather than the testimony of the Koreans and the forensic evidence of Ross. It was this decision to accept that each remaining Rimau man had been accorded a hero's death, in keeping with the code of the Knights of Bushido, that was ultimately responsible for suppressing the truth and subverting the course of military history.[15]

When the various reports on Rimau and the Bintan massacre arrived, army personnel in Australia were not nearly as gullible. They cabled Singapore to enquire whether either or both were war crimes and, if so, what was going to be done about it. The answer, which included the trial documentation, was forwarded with several opinions stating that, in the case of Rimau, no crime had been committed and intimating that, because of lack of evidence, the Bintan massacre was virtually a lost cause. In this correspondence, sent on 29 January 1946, the personnel in Australia, who were being asked to give an opinion on the matter, were also reminded that no suspect was to be brought to trial unless a conviction was assured. The reason was allegedly twofold — firstly, there was already a backlog of cases requiring attention and, secondly, anything more than a few acquittals would have an adverse affect on public morale.[16]

This reply appears to be a very liberal interpretation of a policy laid down by Mountbatten. Immediately hostilities had ceased he had declared that:

> the Japanese should be tried on criminal charges only, that is to say brutality, etc. . . . that no one should be charged unless there was very strong prima facie evidence that he would be convicted on evidence which could be clearly seen to be irrefutable . . . nothing would diminish our prestige more than if we appeared to be instigating vindictive trials against individuals of a beaten enemy nation.[17]

Quite obviously, the premise on which the British judicial system had operated satisfactorily for centuries — that of the presumption of innocence until proven guilty — had been brushed aside by the fear that

Japanese public opinion might perceive the British Empire's pursual of war criminals as something which was not quite 'cricket'.

It seems that this all-important preservation of the public image was one of the reasons why Wild's colleagues in Singapore did not press the matter further. The explanations outlined in their reply did not, however, satisfy some members of the Australian War Crimes Section. On 16 February 1946 they raised the question of the validity of the executions of the Rimau men and of Douglas Hatfield, who had been beheaded in 1942 for trying to escape. Not until June 7 — almost four months later — did the Director of Prisoners of War and Internees find the time to reply. During this time, Legal Service's Brigadier Allaway had also examined the documentation and had reached the same conclusion as Wild's advisors.[18]

The much-delayed opinion from the DPW & I dealt with the matter in some depth. It advised that, although decapitation was abhorrent to the western mind, it was perfectly legal provided that the prisoner had been properly tried in accordance with Japanese law. Members of a court who tried a prisoner could only be classified as war criminals 'if they acted without jurisdiction . . . or if the trial was not conducted bona fide or was unfair'. If this had occurred, 'the members of the court, and the officer who confirms the proceedings are blameworthy and may be charged with an offence as war criminals'.[19] As there was no way now of establishing that the Japanese, having deliberately set the Rimau men up, had committed two of these offences, those agitating for further action were effectively silenced.

Nevertheless, it is astounding that the Singapore investigators did not suspect that skulduggery may have taken place. On December 27 they had discovered that nine New Zealand airmen had been executed out of hand and that the whole incident had been covered up. Captured during a strike against Sumatra in January 1945, they had been sent to Outram Road Gaol, much to the annoyance of several junior Japanese officers who had advocated their immediate execution. The resentment had smouldered and erupted into such a fury when it was learned that the atomic bombs had been dropped on Japan that the airmen had been taken to Changi Beach, beheaded, and their bodies sunk in deep water. When worried senior Kempei officers learned of these illegal executions, they decided that, as in the case of 'the former' beheading incident, it would be prudent to keep the matter dark. Accordingly, it was reported that 'a boat sailed from Singapore carrying these nine British airmen to Japan, and that the boat met aerial bombings off Camoulahan [Cam Ranh] and was lost together with the entire personnel on board'. This conspiracy was only exposed when the officers involved wrote a full confession before committing suicide.[20]

Ironically, although the handling of the Rimau investigations did not result in those responsible for their deaths being brought to trial, fate or the War Crimes Commission eventually caught up with almost all of them, for their many crimes against prisoners of war had extended well beyond the sham trial and execution of the men of Rimau. Corporal Hirata, one of the executioners, committed suicide. General Dihihara, who had issued the order of February 10, was hanged. So too were General Itagaki, who had authorised the trial and insisted upon the death sentence, Major General Otsuka, who had been responsible for the legal proceedings, and the two commandants of Outram Road Goal, Majors Kobayashi and Mikizawa. Major Kamiya, who had so brilliantly manipulated the 'evidence' to bring about the men of Rimau's death, was himself sentenced to life imprisonment. The remaining four executioners were given sentences ranging from five to ten years.[21]

One person delighted by the news that Otsuka was to die was Furuta, who had never forgiven Otsuka for his refusal to intercede on the Rimau men's behalf, and who had been further disgusted when Otsuka had turned informer in an attempt to save his skin. Interestingly, although he loathed Otsuka, Furuta believed that Outram Road Commandant Kobayashi was essentially a 'fair and kind man' and 'could not give prisoners as much comfort and treatment as the British authorities expected him to give'. This lack of understanding, said Furuta, had 'caused him death'. He also clung tenaciously to the delusion that Major Kamiya had been forced to take the Rimau prisoners to trial very much against his will. As for Furuta, he was absolved of any complicity and offered a job. In perhaps the unkindest irony of all, this quiet, inoffensive interpreter, who had once been forced to interpret at the trials of Allied prisoners, was now put to work translating for the British judiciary at the trials of the Japanese.[22]

By June 1946 SRD had been dissolved and all interest in Rimau had evaporated. Since, according to the available evidence, the mission had not been accomplished, there was no question of any recognition. As early as January 1945, a committee, consisting of General Blamey, General Northcott, Brigadier Lloyd and SRD's Colonel Chapman-Walker, had met for high level and secret discussions. From the contents of intercepted Japanese signals, they decided that the Rimau men had given away too much information and that someone on *Mustika* must have panicked and fired. Although all reference to Ingleton and the intelligence he had revealed was subsequently deleted from the intercept summary, the fact that other information was known to the enemy and that someone had fired prematurely resulted in a decision that no honours or awards could be bestowed upon any of the twenty-three men. It must have been a widely held opinion as the message telegraphed on 7 December 1945 from SOE in London to Jock Campbell, one of Ivan Lyon's closest friends and colleagues and now SRD's new Director, suggesting that the Rimau men should receive a Mention in Despatches, was ignored.[23]

Consequently, by 27 March 1947, when Corporal Hardy's mother wrote to Cyril Chambers, Minister for the Army, asking what recognition would be conferred upon her son and what punishment had been meted out to the Japanese responsible for his death, the army had decided upon its official version. She was informed that the party had given up their uniforms and spied upon the Japanese on their own initiative, that they had displayed Japanese flags and when finally captured were all still without either uniforms or any badges to suggest that they were members of any fighting force. The Minister stated that by being dressed in non-military attire, 'these intrepid Australians voluntarily deprived themselves of the right to be treated as prisoners according to the custom and usage of war' and had been 'tried before a legally constituted Japanese Military Court'.[24]

By asserting that the adoption of a disguise had been voluntary, when in fact it had been an integral part of the plan, by not conducting any investigation into the matter, and by regurgitating the 'facts' supplied by the Japanese, the Australian government neatly distanced itself from potentially embarrassing questions about Operation Rimau, for which it was answerable. In less than two years, the fabrications of the Japanese, aggravated by the poor assessments of senior army officers, and the distortions of truth, such as those found in the statements of Chambers, had turned Operation Rimau from a testament to courage and tenacity into an episode that was perceived to be both humiliating and shameful. Through ignorance and apathy, the authorities had cast a terrible and lasting slur on the memories of twenty-three men who had simply died for their country. Swept under the carpet, they and their operation were all but forgotten. Indeed, the words 'war crimes' in connection with Rimau would probably never have surfaced again had it not been for a message scrawled upon the wall of a cell in Soerabaya.

On the cessation of hostilities, investigation teams had been sent to Soerabaya only to discover that there was not a single prisoner, European or Asian, in custody. Neither was there any evidence of the mass graves at the Eastern Fort, since all remains had been hurriedly exhumed and cremated, leaving only small, isolated bones scattered below the sand. Such was the cover-up by the Japanese that preliminary questioning elicited no information about any Australians, and no hint whatever that all Allied prisoners had been executed without trial, some of them after the surrender. When three team members conducting investigations near Batavia were murdered in April 1946 by Japanese prisoners, who then committed suicide, the Japanese in Soerabaya could have been excused for thinking that they had succeeded in evading Allied retribution. But fate was about to overtake them, just as it had their comrades in Singapore.[25]

In late July 1946 a Dutchman, Private G.L. Bakker, was imprisoned in Soerabaya for thirty days for a misdemeanour. While reading the graffiti scribbled on the walls of his cell by former occupants, he came across a message written sixteen months before by Lieutenant Mason Schow, one of the airmen executed with Sachs and Perske.

> After the war — whoever reads this send a post card [sic] with this on it to Mr M.R. Schow, P.E.D. 1 Fluverenk, Jamestown, New York, U.S.A.
> Dear Dad, It is 25 February 1945 and I have been a prisoner here. Soerabaja [sic], for about three months. What will happen from now on I don't know. Love Bob.

At some later date he added:

> P.S. Donald Palmer, Clif Peask [sic], Aussie, Brisbane, Australia. John Sachs — Australia. Same cell. God bless whoever sends this message for me.[26]

As soon as he was released, Bakker responded to the airman's plea. When the postcard reached the United States, Mr Schow informed the authorities, who in turn contacted their counterparts in Australia. On 18 June 1947 a Dutch judge by the name of Van Beek began a preliminary investigation at Soerabaya. As all the cell walls had been whitewashed by the Dutch, effectively destroying any other clues, his enquiry raised more questions than it answered. Since a thorough investigation was clearly required, Australia appointed Captain Jack Sylvester in the latter half of 1947 to investigate the disappearance of Sachs and Perske, still officially listed as 'Missing — Believed Prisoner of War'. Although SRD knew that both men had been captured and, if intelligence sources could be believed, probably murdered, post-war investigations had so far shed no light on their fate.[27]

When Sylvester arrived in Japan there was a conspiracy of silence. Nobody, it seemed, had either seen or heard of any Allied prisoners ever being held at Soerabaya. Determined to get to the bottom of the story, Sylvester chipped patiently away until various Japanese, in an effort to disengage themselves from the investigator's clutches, began dropping names of people who might be able to help him. For two long years Sylvester interrogated and re-interrogated suspects, probing and worrying at every detail until the whole, terrible story emerged. He was aided in his search for the truth by the fact that almost all of the Japanese afflicted with total amnesia in 1947 had, by the end of 1949, made a miraculous recovery, recalling various events and dates with the utmost clarity. Under Sylvester's persistent questioning, one suspect, who had stated quite categorically that no prisoners had been held at Soerabaya, was able to remember that not only had prisoners been confined in the stockade, but that they had been executed. Moreover, in a flash of total recall, he suddenly remembered that he himself had been one of the executioners.[28]

Aided by confessions such as this, Sylvester inadvertently learned of many things besides the fate of Sachs and Perske. Some of the crimes were horrendous and clear cut, others were equally horrific but unsolvable because of their complexity and the misinformation that was mixed with factual evidence. Without realising it, Sylvester uncovered the fate of both Bill Reynolds and Doug Warne. Although Reynolds's death was more or less established later by investigators assessing the evidence, Doug Warne was identified as another SOE man of a similar name — an operative who had been working behind the lines with Freddie Spencer Chapman in Malaya and who ultimately survived the war. A New Zealander by birth, he was Lieutenant-Colonel Douglas Richardson, who had never been listed as missing and who had never been in Java. Amazingly, not one of the people examining Sylvester's file, all of whom had a list of SRD's missing men, realised that the name given by the Japanese as 'Douglas Richardson', was really Douglas Richard Warne.[29]

Although he was not familiar with the names of all of the Rimau personnel, Sylvester knew of the fate of some of them, since by this time the executions in Singapore were common knowledge. Consequently, when he learned that an order for their execution had been received in Soerabaya in February 1945, he realised that the death sentence had preceeded the trial by almost five months. In early 1949, shortly after this independent evidence came to light, the Australian War Crimes Section in Tokyo again raised the question of whether a war crime had been committed. With Major Wild dead, killed in an air crash in Hong Kong in September 1946, the inquiry was eventually passed on to the Army Legal Section, Singapore. The old file was located and once more the original opinion was transmitted to Tokyo, effectively putting paid to any further speculation by the investigators. In any case, with more startling revelations emerging from Sylvester's investigation — such as the previously undetected massacre of 250 Allied soldiers by the crew of a Japanese minesweeper — his staff were too fully occupied with taking down statements to press the matter further.[30]

Although the perpetrators of many of the crimes he had uncovered would never be brought to trial, Sylvester did succeed in amassing sufficient evidence to ensure that in 1951 those responsible for the deaths of Warne, Sachs and Perske were arraigned before a military court on the Admiralty Island of Los Negros. Although some of the accused were acquitted, the court decided that Rear Admiral Tanaka; executioners Yoshimoto, Okada and Ikeda; Doctor Nakamura and his accomplice Tatsuzaki; medical officers Yoshino and Konishi, and the evil Shinohara, must be punished.[31]

Fortunately for many of the accused, and unfortunately for people like Sylvester who had worked so hard and for so long to see that justice was done, Australia by this time was attempting to enter into an anti-communist alliance with Japan. For this reason, the British and Americans had been either acquitting or severely reducing the sentences being handed down to war criminals — a point which was raised by the defence lawyer at Los Negros when petitioning the court for clemency. Consequently, the executioners and the medical staff from Soerabaya (some of whom had been accused of injecting only the Indonesians with toxin, a crime to which they admitted) were given sentences ranging from one to seven years, while Tanaka's death sentence was commuted to fifteen years by Australia's General Sturdee, in whose hands alone lay the responsibility for either confirming or mitigating sentences.[32]

However, the many sins of Shinohara ensured that for him there was no such reprieve. On 11 June 1951 the Australian government found a permanent cure for the asthma which had so plagued him at Soerabaya. They hanged him.[33]

With the death of Shinohara, and the sentences handed out to the others, the deaths of Perske, Sachs, Warne and Bill Reynolds could be considered to have been avenged. Yet the very people who might have obtained some grim satisfaction in justice at least being seen to be done — the families of the men — were not only unaware that any trials had taken place, they were also never informed of the fate of their relatives.[34]

While the facts surrounding these deaths at Soerabaya were virtually lost in a mound of government apathy and red tape, further to the east, on the island of Timor, something even more shocking had taken place. The fate of Jefferey Willersdorf and Hugo Pace, the last of the Rimau men, had become inextricably enmeshed in a matter so sinister that, had it been made public, it would have created a scandal of monumental proportions and undermined the confidence of the entire nation. It was one of the darkest secrets of the war and its name was Operation Lagarto.

Chapter 17

The Timor Conspiracy

Australia's closest Indonesian neighbour, Portuguese-Dutch Timor, had been invaded by the Japanese early in 1942. Although the neutral Portuguese administration had been forced, by some rather strong-arm tactics, to accept Japanese occupation of its territory, many pro-Allied Timorese and Portuguese bands had continued to resist until reprisals against their countrymen diminished aid alarmingly and pushed them deep into the jungle. When their position became perilous, Australia dispatched Lieutenant Pires, a Portuguese Army pilot and SRD agent, to organise their evacuation and to set up an SRD operation which would undertake covert work.[1]

When the evacuees were successfully rescued on 3 August 1943, an Australian signaller, SRD's Sergeant Alfred Ellwood, joined the party. As Pires's English was not altogether fluent and as he was a rather volatile, highly-strung type, the level-headed Ellwood, aged twenty-one and already a veteran of operations in Timor, had instructions to keep an eye on him. Although there was already a signaller, one Patricio Luz, SRD was anxious to be kept properly informed of the activities of the party, known by the code name of Lagarto — Portuguese for 'lizard' or 'cunning fellow'.

Unfortunately, Pires was most resentful of Ellwood's presence, refusing to relinquish any of the signalling work and totally unreceptive to any advice. In addition to Pires's rather 'gung ho' attitude to the operation, Ellwood was horrified to find that Lagarto was hamstrung by an enormous entourage. Besides the actual party, which numbered eight, there were twelve servants, thirteen assorted bearers and Timorese chiefs (who had simply attached themselves to the group) and, to Ellwood's amazement, two women, one of whom was pregnant and continuously ill, accompanying Pires and his offsider Matos Da Silva.

Not surprisingly, the logistics of feeding, hiding and moving this retinue were overwhelming. The day after Ellwood arrived the party was forced to keep on the move by the inopportune arrival of some pro-Japanese locals and had been unable to retrieve its stores from the beach. With available rations soon exhausted and villagers loath to help for fear of reprisals, the group was reduced to a hand-to-mouth existence as it tried to keep one jump ahead of the Japanese. After two months, with Pires rejecting all suggestions to split the party into manageable groups and relying on intuition rather than military strategy, Ellwood informed SRD that, unless it acceded to requests to organise immediate evacuation, capture appeared to be inevitable. By the time SRD made up its mind to do so, it was too late. On September 29, aided by hostile Timorese and the confessions of tortured villagers, the Japanese closed in.

Only eight of those who survived the machine-gun fire regrouped. This small band, including Pires and Ellwood, made for the beach, where Ellwood, being without dry matches to burn his cipher, signal plan and papers, buried them in the sand. When an exhausted Pires announced that he could go no further, Ellwood, unlike wireless operator Luz and two of the others, did not abandon his superior officer. Realising that resistance was futile, they surrendered quietly.[2]

They were taken by truck to Dili, the capital of Portuguese Timor and Headquarters of the 48th Division Japanese Army, for interrogation by the Kempei Tai. When a 'softening up' period of no sleep and paralysingly tight bonds, followed by the usual beatings failed to loosen Ellwood's tongue, he was given salty food and water and kept awake. Maddened by thirst, his brain numbed by lack of sleep and his body bruised and battered, he begged the Japanese to execute him or allow him to shoot himself. When the Japanese found suicide capsules on Pires, it only made matters worse. Unable to withstand the interrogation, which included being strung up by his thumbs, Pires declared that Ellwood had intended to poison the Japanese. This false information elicited treatment so brutal that Ellwood once more begged for merciful release.[3]

Meantime, Pires, who had lost control completely, had given the Kempei a message enciphered in his emergency code which the Japanese wanted Ellwood to transmit to SRD. When he refused to do so, he was subjected to bouts of re-interrogation and returned to a filthy, fly-and-mosquito-infested cell beneath the verandah of the Kempei building, where his bonds cut into his rapidly swelling flesh, producing running sores, and his feet began to rot inside his boots. Finally, on October 5, after six days of almost non-stop interrogation, his resolve weakened by lack of sleep and mental and physical torture, Ellwood's resistance broke down. The experienced Japanese wireless operator, like his fellow officers, was able to speak English and could easily have transmitted the signal. However, the Kempei was determined to subject its victim to one more degradation. Holding Ellwood's hand on the transmitting key, the Kempei forced him to 'send' the message.

From A.B.C. [Pires] to H.B.M. [Mr Manderson, head of Timor Section]. Continue big pursue against us. In this moment our H.Q. stay in Waqui Mountain where we are hiding. Our operator Patricio Luz run away. We lost cypher book.[4]

Had SRD bothered to take basic security precautions, the authenticity of this message could have been immediately checked. By transmitting a pre-arranged 'authenticator word', which then had to appear in the answering signal, it was possible to establish whether or not an operator was in enemy control. For some reason, Ellwood had been provided with neither an authenticator word nor a cover story. With no fallback position, he had therefore had no option but to withstand his interrogation for as long as possible. He later learned that his resistance had been futile. Pires sang like a bird and the Japanese, who already possessed many ciphers, messages and documents captured from other areas, as well as Ellwood's recovered from the beach, had had the upper hand from the start.

As there was no answer to Pires's message, the Japanese ordered Ellwood to compose another on October 6. When he signalled that the party was now at Obaqui, it was with the expectation that SRD, which was, after all, an intelligence organisation, might actually exercise its collective brains. As they knew from previous messages that Lagarto's capture was imminent, it is incomprehensible that, on receiving the Obaqui message, SRD did not deduce at once that the party had been caught. Obaqui was not only thirty-two kilometres from Lagarto's last reported position, it was also thirty-two kilometres back in the heart of the area which SRD knew to be full of Japanese patrols and hostile local Timorese. There is no doubt that SRD consulted a map, for, in response to the rest of the signal, it replied that a food drop would be made.

As if failing to pick up this warning was not bad enough, SRD in Melbourne committed an unforgivable breach of security by mentioning the names of other operatives who were in Timor. 'ABC say Luz run away. Is this a fact or a precaution. Are you with ABC or separated. Who is operating,' they asked. The next day, when the Japanese had Ellwood reply, 'Confirm ABC lost cypher book during pursuit by Jap patrol. At same time Luz run away. I am with ABC and am operating wireless', they paved the way for their total control of Operation Lagarto.[5]

Ellwood knew that as long as he transmitted, Lagarto's lives might be spared. The problem was how to indicate to SRD that he was compromised. Fearful that allowing signals to be transmitted with glaring errors would cause an over-reaction from Melbourne and bring about the party's immediate liquidation, Ellwood vetted the Japanese messages, trying to make them as boring, banal and colourless as possible in the hope that such trite information would alert SRD to the fact that something was wrong. Expecting that someone would question his motives, he then stubbornly refused SRD's offer to extract him, although this had been a firm arrangement before he left Australia.[6]

Both his ploys failed miserably. On Christmas Eve, with a complete and utter disregard for security, SRD signalled that it intended to insert another party, code named Cobra. It topped this security breach a few days later by transmitting the details of MacArthur's strategy to regain control of the South-West Pacific by island hopping. In a fit of enthusiasm, it also decided, on receipt of a glowing recce 'report' from Lagarto on the suitability of Cobra's operational zone, to change the Cobra party's original role, of a three week reconnaissance, to a semi-permanent base.[7]

Ellwood was now in an invidious position. His messages had so far only resulted in his being forced to accompany the Japanese to collect regular supply drops. While it was galling to know that the enemy was the beneficiary of a large amount of equipment and food, it was unthinkable simply to allow his countrymen to be captured without trying to warn them.

The arrangements for Cobra's insertion at Edemomo were quite straightforward. On January 29, after the correct signals had been flashed from shore to ship, the party would be escorted to safety by three Lagarto native Timorese. Apart from replacing the Lagarto personnel with three pro-Japanese Timorese, the Kempei intended to stick to this plan.

Any hopes that Ellwood may have entertained of warning the Cobra party were dashed when the Japanese elected to keep him in a hut at Edemomo under lock and key instead of taking him to the beach with the signal party. Determined to signal Cobra before it left the ship, he managed to appropriate enough material to make a simple lamp. When zero hour neared he asked to be taken to the latrines, where he swung a violent punch at his guard. As the guard ducked, Ellwood broke a few teeth and felled him, but, unfortunately, did not render him unconscious. As the guard bellowed, Ellwood ran, pursued by Japanese and Timorese who came from all directions. With his progress slowed by the effects of beriberi, a debilitating vitamin deficiency disease, he was caught and struck over the head with a sword. Saved from immediate decapitation only by the number of people pressed around him, he was trussed securely, kicked and beaten senseless and left in the broiling sun without food or water for two days. His misery was absolute when, during a lucid period, he heard the voice of an Australian, signifying that Cobra had been captured. Roped behind a horse and forced to move at a trot until he collapsed, he was taken back to Dili, where he was subjected to further punishment and once more put to work transmitting bogus messages.[8]

The Cobra party, composed of Captain Cashman, radio operator Lieutenant Liversidge and three native Timorese, had met up with the three native Timorese 'guides' and moved inland without any trouble. After about an hour, when the leading Timorese guide pretended that he had lost his way and asked Cashman for a light, the Japanese sprang their trap. When Cashman, knocked unconscious by a blow to the head, regained his senses, he found that Liversidge and one of Cobra's Timorese had also been captured and that all were securely bound. After a preliminary bout of questioning, accompanied by the usual kicks and blows, all three were taken to Dili, where they were subjected to even worse treatment than that meted out to Ellwood.[9]

Part of Cashman's early interrogation was aimed at discovering the meaning of the phrase, '2926 Slender Silk Key' — Cobra's code and authenticator which, contrary to all regulations, Liversidge had recorded in his notebook. Although Cashman was able to satisfy the Japanese with a plausible explanation, he was not able to prevent them from sending SRD a message on February 8, indicating that all was well.

SRD was overjoyed to hear from Cobra, which was to have sent its first message on February 5. Indeed, such was the euphoria that for eighteen days no one bothered to check whether or not Cobra was actually safe. Even then, it was the Japanese, not prudence, that prompted the challenge, for on February 26 SRD learned from an intercept that Cashman was reported to be in enemy hands.[10]

Although the security check was simple, it was also almost completely useless. The arrangement for SRD to transmit the authenticator word — in Cobra's case, 'slender' — was an entirely random procedure, unlike the arrangement for SOE, which had a check built into every signal. In an attempt to gain confirmation one way or the other, SRD issued the challenge 'Slender girl sends greetings'. As the authenticator was not included in the reply, two days later SRD tried again, using a more devious 'Please acknowledge in last sentence from this particular girl. It will relieve her feelings and ours. We do not know her name but she is not, repeat not the fat repeat fat one'.[11]

The Japanese could not make head or tail of this incredible communication and sought clarification from Cashman, who again offered a plausible explanation. As, from their point of view, there was no sensible answer to this latest message, the Japanese did not bother to reply to it.

When four days passed with no news from Cobra, an alarmed SRD sought help from Lagarto. After informing Ellwood that an intercept indicated that all was not well and that the challenge had not been answered, Melbourne called for suggestions. Lagarto replied non-committally but offered to send Matos to 'investigate'. Before this suggestion was acknowledged, SRD again signalled Cobra, this time without any subtlety whatever. After a preamble containing war news from Rabaul, the message concluded with 'Jap chances escape encompassed troops very slender, repeat slender, repeat slender'.

The Kempei finally realised that there was a connection between the entry in Liversidge's notebook and the message just received. Under torture, Cashman revealed the secret. It did not matter that he had done so, however, for the very next day, March 3, SRD signalled Lagarto, ordering, 'Matsilva to go Edemomo at once. If he finds Cobra to be OK tell 452 [Cashman] to work slender repeat slender as authenticator in message confirming his safety'. These instructions to Ellwood concluded with the useful information that Lagarto now had an authenticator — 'compact'.[12]

With this great flood of information, the Japanese had no trouble sending an authenticated reply. But before this was received in Australia, SRD, which must have been verging on panic, dispatched yet another message to Cobra. The contents were designed, should Cobra indeed have been captured, to lure the enemy into the open. Out of the blue, Melbourne advised that £10 000 in gold was available for Cashman's use, provided a safe method of delivery could be arranged. As the Japanese could not work out what this message was about, Cashman was subjected to another round of violent interrogation.

Meanwhile, the Cobra signal with the correct authenticator was received in Melbourne. This reduced SRD to such a state of relief that it threw all caution to the wind. Its reply, announcing that an intercepted Japanese message had claimed Cashman's capture, was followed by another signal which divulged Lagarto's authenticator word. Yet another message disclosed that the offer of £10 000 in gold had been nothing but a ruse.

Luckily for the security of the entire Allied intelligence network, the Japanese refused to believe that Japanese messages had been intercepted and decoded, reasoning that if their code had been broken, no one would be stupid enough to disclose such a thing. Fortunately, their overestimation of the level of intelligence of those running SRD prevented the destruction of the Allies' ultimate secret weapon.

The Japanese must have been so busy being incredulous over SRD's 'intercept' information that they failed to notice that Lagarto, on March 16, had been challenged with 'Is Matsilva back. Send us compact signal to assure us finally re safety 452'. Ten days later Lagarto finally replied, 'Matsilva not yet returned. Will send required signal when he returns'. That this message failed to contain the authenticator word 'compact' went unnoticed by SRD, which simply resumed its usual stream of signals, sending information about personnel whom it intended to insert to relieve Lagarto.[13]

In spite of SRD's obtuseness, Ellwood did not abandon his campaign to warn Australia that he, and therefore Cobra, had been captured. His messages became ridiculous, giving inane 'information' about such things as village fiestas and offering weak excuses as to why none of his party could be extracted. Eventually the issue could no longer be sidestepped. When messages started to arrive at SRD insisting that a submarine would be the best method of extraction — a clever but vain attempt by the Japanese to lure a submarine into their patch — no one suspected that there might be an ulterior motive. Never once did SRD ask how the party had evaded capture or query the fact that the hideout, surrounded by pro-Japanese Timorese, remained unchanged for over twelve months. Neither did anyone think it odd that the drop zones were in country known to be populated, or that Ellwood never stirred from his base except to receive substantial amounts of stores. For almost two years not a single person ever questioned the value of his alleged intelligence or asked him precisely what he was doing. SRD did, however, with the assistance of the RAAF, keep up the regular supply drops, resulting in the enemy gaining vast amounts of valuable material, and continued to break security by needlessly giving information which led to the deaths of other operatives. It was the same story for Cobra. Before six months had passed, Cobra's wireless, with the help of SRD, would lure two unsuspecting men to their deaths.[14]

Although Cobra's Cashman, unlike Ellwood, was not actually transmitting, he was originating many of the signals and enciphering and deciphering all of them. With no way of alerting SRD to his predicament, now that the secret of the authenticator had been blown, he sent a stream of 'intelligence' just as stupid as that sent by Lagarto, only to have Brigadier Wills, the Director of AIB, compile this puerile information into official 'Information Reports'.

His other attempt to warn SRD, by giving the right location name but the wrong navigational references for drop zones or insertion points, thereby placing an easily identifiable geographical feature into, say, the middle of the ocean, was just as futile. The navigational information, which was evidently not checked for accuracy, was merely passed to the RAAF, which, believing that an error had occurred during transcription, simply corrected the reference to suit the geography. It is also evident that no attempt was made to check on either Cashman or Ellwood by comparing the 'fingerprints' of their transmission idiosyncrasies with a master copy, held on graphically interpreted tapes in Melbourne.[15]

Shortly after wireless links had been established with Cobra, SRD began planning the insertion of another party. Code named Adder, it consisted of two Australian soldiers — Captain J. Grimson (one of Sam Carey's Scorpion men) and signaller Sergeant E.H. Gregg — and three Portuguese Timorese. Although there had been no arrangements made through Cobra or Lagarto to 'welcome' the party, the Japanese knew, from signals sent by SRD, that the landing point at Cape Ile Hoi had been reconnoitred. Consequently, early on August 24, Adder was ambushed. In the ensuing struggle Gregg and one of the Timorese were killed. That same evening, about three hundred metres away, there was a second skirmish. The following day the body of Captain Grimson was found.

The Japanese knew that it was not the slight wound to his left eye that had caused his death. The bullet which had passed from his lower right jaw to the left side of his head clearly showed that rather than fall into enemy hands Grimson, like Rimau's Davidson and Campbell, had obeyed his orders absolutely. In a rare show of respect, the Japanese buried the Australians together, marking the place with a wooden pillar in traditional fashion.[16]

Meanwhile, SRD's suggestion of withdrawing both Ellwood and Cashman for consultation was apparently causing the enemy some concern, judging by what appear to be delaying tactics. It was perhaps this evasiveness, and the fact that intelligence sent by Cobra did not tie in with RAAF reconnaissance information, that prompted SRD on October 9 to seek reassurance that Cobra was not in enemy control.[17]

It is astonishing that this was not done much earlier. Since April 30 there had not been a single challenge issued. Security was so lax that, when SRD became concerned at the lack of communication from Adder, it gave Cobra, without any renewed security check, details of the insertion and asked Cobra to investigate — a request that Cobra countered with the excuse that there was too much enemy activity in the area. Shortly after this message had been received, SRD made the security check. On October 11, in answer to SRD's Signal 34, Cobra transmitted 'slender', allowing Melbourne to relax once more.[18]

The apparently comatose state of those at SRD, into which they had settled in September 1943, would have continued indefinitely had SRD not finally been jolted from its lethargy in March 1945 by the realisation that one, or possibly both, parties seemed to be in Japanese control. Consequently, orders were issued to put an immediate halt to plans to supply the parties with new codes and frequencies as suggested by a security conscious SOE major by the name of Seymour Bingham.

On reviewing the Timor operations, shortly after assuming control of SRD's Darwin-based Group D, which had taken over part control of Timor in December 1944, Bingham had become concerned that the signal plans, ciphers and wireless frequencies for both parties had been in use for far too long and were therefore a security risk. His caution had been born of experience, for the unfortunate major had already had his fingers burnt in the matter of security. Indeed, it was he who had been the scapegoat for the failure of an SOE operation in Holland which had resulted in the capture of sixty-four agents.[19] (See Appendix II.)

Innocent of any wrong-doing, Seymour Bingham had been banished from SOE Headquarters in London to the colony of Australia in much the same way as unwanted citizens had been expelled 150 years earlier. One can only imagine his feelings when, on 10 March 1945, he learned that security in Timor appeared to have been breached and that Cobra and/or Lagarto were suspected of being compromised.[20]

It had taken SRD weeks to reach this conclusion. On receiving in early February a report based on an intercept, which indicated that 'some chaps in hiding' had been captured in Timor, SRD accepted at face value the Department of Intelligence suggestion that they might be members of the Adder party. This was in spite of the fact that the same top secret report repeated previously intercepted Japanese information that, 'Lt

Pirusu [Pires], who is an agent, landed on the south coast of Timor on 3rd July [1943] from an Australian submarine'. Indeed, it was not until the evidence became overwhelming that SRD began to suspect that something might be amiss.

On January 19 and February 4 a memorandum listing items of intelligence required by AIB had been dropped to Lagarto and Cobra. Five weeks later, on March 10, Melbourne learned from a Japanese intercept that a copy of this document was in Japanese hands in Timor. Four days later, a wide-awake wireless operator, maintaining a listening watch in Australia, reported that he had eavesdropped on signal traffic between two parties, one of which used Cobra's call sign to send 'Q' signals — a secret SOE code which had been recently dropped to both Lagarto and Cobra. After some consultation, SRD dismissed his information as being impossible. Had someone employed some lateral thinking he may have deduced that the mystery signals were probably Cobra and Lagarto's Japanese wireless operators amusing themselves by sending the newly captured signal codes to each other.

Having missed the significance of the wireless transmissions and the earlier information, SRD was undisturbed by the implications of the March Japanese intercept, since eleven days passed before guarded questions were asked of either party. When further signals, enquiring whether the parties still had all copies of the memorandum, finally elicited an affirmative reply on April 2 from Cobra only, SRD decided that Lagarto alone was in enemy control. This deduction must have been especially sickening when SRD realised that four pages of closely typed secret plans, written in plain language, containing 'crack' codes, passwords, and the most exacting details for Lagarto's extraction, were now undoubtedly in Japanese hands, having been dropped by parachute in March.[21]

With SRD now harbouring doubts about Lagarto, it is amazing that no one considered the likelihood of Cobra's also being captured. Indeed, the satisfactory reply about the memo was evidently so reassuring that SRD did not take any notice of a report transmitted on May 6 which pointed out that every drop-zone reference point given by Cobra had been incorrect.

In June 1945, an enormous upheaval erupted in the upper echelons of SRD, causing Director Chapman-Walker and Major Bingham to be replaced. Although the reason for the shake-up is not clear, it is odds-on that Lagarto and Cobra had something to do with it. It may well be that the mishandling of Timor also provided AIB with the perfect excuse to replace Chapman-Walker (who, in common with former Director Major Mott, did not enjoy cordial relations with everyone, including AIB's Brigadier Wills) with Jock Campbell.[22]

Whatever the cause for Bingham's sudden departure, it was a case of déjà vu. For the second time in just over twelve months he had been innocently involved in a scandal of monstrous proportions. Irrespective of how he felt at the time, it was fortunate for Bingham that he was recalled. Within weeks circumstances would reveal that those controlling the Timor operations were guilty of bungling, gross stupidity and massive incompetence at a very high level.

While SRD was busily being reorganised, the plan to investigate Lagarto was grinding on with interminable slowness, for no other apparent reason than SRD's inability to come to terms with the fact that the party was in Japanese control. While doubts were being entertained, signal traffic went on as usual. Perhaps it was this failure to face reality that was responsible for an act of unbelievable idiocy which occurred on June 27. Four days before the check on Lagarto was to be made, yet another operational party was inserted into Timor.

Within hours of its arrival, the presence of the party, code-named Sunable, had been reported by pro-Japanese natives. For the next week it was dogged by Japanese patrols and ambushed three times before party leader Lieutenant Williams, during a fight on July 5, was fatally wounded. The other three, Sergeants White, Shand and Curran, evaded their pursuers for another week until lack of food and water forced them to surrender. During the various encounters, four Japanese were killed and several were wounded.[23]

It may well be that the unfortunate Sunable party diverted attention away from Sunlag. Led by Captain Stevenson, Sunlag parachuted into Timor on June 29, with the aim of investigating Lagarto. Having ascertained that Sunlag had arrived without mishap, SRD signalled Lagarto that a relief party was confirmed for the evening of July 1. Right on schedule, unaware that three pairs of eyes were watching their every move, Ellwood and his Japanese guards appeared at the drop zone. Unfortunately, because of wireless problems, Stevenson was not able to inform SRD until July 3 that its worst fears were confirmed, and another six weeks passed before Stevenson reported in person. Sunlag's seaborne rescue party, partly through what the SRD report later bluntly described as 'inexcusable' incompetence, had failed to pick up the operatives, forcing the team to spend five weeks dodging Japanese and existing on the scantiest of food after the eight-day ration supply had been exhausted.[24]

At least they retained their freedom. Suncob, the party which was sent to check on Cobra was not nearly as lucky. In another display of exceedingly poor judgement, SRD, without waiting to hear from Stevenson, had inserted them on July 2. Even before Captain Wynne and Corporal Lawrence parachuted into the area where Cobra was supposed to be hiding, things began to go wrong. The pair became separated by the wind, both parachutes hit trees and large numbers of excited locals witnessed their arrival. Helped by some of the Timorese, who were unexpectedly friendly, Wynne evaded capture until July 16, when he was surrounded by Japanese. As they opened fire he was felled, not by a bullet but by a rock, thrown by someone who exhibited marksmanship far superior to that of the riflemen.

His companion Lawrence had not fared as well. Captured on July 5, he had been taken to Lautem and Baucau where, during sixteen days of torture which sickened even the Japanese interpreter, he told his captors nothing. Such was his resolution that he attempted to bite off his tongue and dash out his brains upon the wall of his cell. But it was all for naught. When Captain Wynne was brought in for interrogation he offered little or no resistance.[25]

With the capture of Suncob, SRD had no idea that Cobra had also been compromised. Apparently incapable of weighing up the overwhelming possibility that this was so, SRD sent another 'slender' signal which was, naturally, correctly acknowledged. By this time, however, SRD's forward base at Morotai had become exceedingly suspicious, voicing the opinion that this latest 'evidence' that Cobra was still free was highly suspect. Against its better judgement, it allowed the next drop to take place and agreed, for the time being, that it would be better to keep from the highly placed 'SASO' (Senior Air Staff Officer), the fact that Lagarto, and possibly Cobra, were in enemy control.[26]

With Suncob and Sunable, as well as Lagarto and Cobra, in the bag, the Japanese tally of captured prisoners was quite impressive. Sadly, there was ample room for the new arrivals. From the Lagarto party, only Ellwood and Luz, who managed to evade capture completely, survived. Lieutenant Pires had died, insane, in February 1944 and the others, except for one who was killed in a cliff fall, had perished from maltreatment, illness and starvation, were crucified or buried alive. Of the Cobra party of five, only two survived — Cashman and Sancho Da Silva, brother of Matos. Lieutenant Liversidge died on 20 November 1944 from a combination of malaria, beriberi and starvation. The remaining two Timorese were murdered by the Japanese, as were the two surviving members of the Adder party.[27]

The entire SRD effort in Timor had achieved nothing but death and suffering. Every attempt to insert parties ended in unmitigated disaster, including the loss of all those on board a Liberator which was shot down in May 1945, while attempting to insert Sunbaker, another party which SRD, despite security fears, had decided to send to Timor. The tally of Allied dead, which can be attributed directly or indirectly to SRD's massive incompetence is thirty-one. The number of loyal Timorese, tortured to death or massacred for helping members of SRD parties, is incalculable.[28]

As if this gruesome roll-call was not enough, the manner in which the Japanese put an end to the Cobra/Lagarto charade really rubbed salt into the wound. On August 12, three days before the Japanese surrender, SRD was astounded and infuriated to receive two messages. From those controlling Cobra came:

For ABC [SRD Melbourne] from Nippon. Thanks for your information this long while. Herewith present a few words to you. Quote. Control enemy thousands of miles out by preparing tactics within. Unquote. Nippon Army.

And from Lagarto:

Nippon for LMS [the SRD section in Darwin which supplied transport for the drops and personnel]. Thanks for your assistance this long while. Hope to see you again. But until then wish you good health. Nippon Army.

After some debate an enraged SRD sent off two carefully worded replies. Lagarto's Japanese were warned in the strongest terms that the party must come to no harm, while the message to Cobra reflected SRD's disbelief that it was in enemy hands, stating, 'We are most surprised your information. Can you tell us whether our soldiers are safe and well?'[29]

As soon as was practicable, Captain Stevenson was dispatched to Timor to ascertain the whereabouts of all personnel. He arrived at Koepang, in Dutch Timor, on September 11, too late to catch up with those still alive. The Japanese, in an effort to prevent an early identification of those who had committed war crimes, had sent them to Bali on the pretext that Allied troops would pick them up there.[30]

Stevenson arrived in Portuguese Timor on September 22 to find that no investigation into war crimes would be permitted until a proper mission, complete with visas, was organised between the Australian and Portuguese governments. He was, therefore, forced to make 'unofficial enquiries' of the one lone witness who could help — a local Timorese by the name of Francisco Madiera. He and his father disclosed that three Australian prisoners had died in Dili Gaol — two from malnutrition and beatings and the other reportedly in an air raid — and that three airmen, who had parachuted from the crashing Liberator, had been shot on landing. As he was unable to investigate further, Stevenson had to content himself with inspecting the aircraft's wreckage.

When he returned to Koepang and questioned some of the Japanese who had been rounded up with the permission of the Dutch, he was very puzzled. According to his list of Timor agents, only three Australians — Gregg and Grimson from the Adder party, and Cobra's Liversidge — were missing. As he had reports of three dead men in Dili, the matter would have ended there had not the Japanese insisted that the two Australians from the Adder party had been killed on arrival in Timor, giving Stevenson five dead bodies but only three names. The statements of Ellwood and others simply added to the confusion. From the information of Sancho, Ellwood thought that the Dili Gaol victims appeared to be Gregg and Grimson, which was very puzzling as both he and Cashman had been told by Japanese officers in August 1944 and again when they left for Bali, that the two Adder men had been killed at the entry point.[31]

Stevenson began an investigation to establish the identity of the men who had died in the gaol. He was hamstrung from the start since information (obtained from Japanese intercepts in January 1945) that a warrant officer and a sergeant from the Rimau party had been captured and taken to Dili for interrogation was withheld. Stevenson's list from SRD did not contain this information or the names of the missing Rimau party despite the fact that Lieutenant-Colonel J.E.B. Finlay, Director of Plans, noted in a September intelligence summary that Rimau operatives had been captured in the Timor area. Although Stevenson's enquiries about Perske and Sachs, who were on his list, naturally brought no result, he did learn from Indonesians on Nila Island that two Australians had been captured at Romang. Deducing that they might be Rimau survivors, Stevenson requested photographs of the entire Rimau party to be forwarded from the Rimau planning department for the purpose of identification. This request was evidently ignored and, since the identity of the five bodies was never resolved, it appears that Stevenson did not pursue the matter.

It is evident that even the General Staff Officer, Intelligence, Advanced Headquarters AMF, one Lieutenant-Colonel Charles H. Finlay, was unaware of the Rimau information held by his namesake, J.E.B. Finlay. On November 13, some time after J.E.B. Finlay had received sufficient information to more or less establish the fate of Willersdorf and Pace, Charles Finlay was airing the opinion that the Japanese must have given out false information about the deaths of Adder's Gregg and Grimson in an attempt to frighten or impress their Lagarto and Cobra prisoners. In making this assumption, Charles Finlay was evidently unaware that Stevenson (now busily investigating Lagarto and Cobra) had passed to his superiors an urgent cable, received on November 10 from a Japanese Intelligence Officer, Captain Goto, containing a blow-by-blow description of Gregg and Grimson's death and details of their burial place.[32]

Although high-ranking officers withheld vital information it is surprising that the identity of those who died in the Dili Gaol was not discovered by less senior army officers reviewing the information that *was* available. Stevenson had made some useful deductions, Captain Goto had verified the fate of Gregg and Grimson, and Sancho Da Silva had given the name of one of the men who had died in the Dili Gaol as 'Peace'.[33] Had someone bothered to compare this name with the list of missing men, he could not have failed to realise that the name was a corruption of Pace.

The superficial nature of the Timor investigation combined with the inability of supposedly mentally alert army officers to put basic evidence together was one of two reasons why the fate of Willersdorf and Pace remained unknown to all but a select few for almost forty years. The other reason was the Lagarto cover up.

When the whole story began to emerge from Ellwood's and Chapman's candid statements and frank operational reports submitted to SRD on October 23 and 24, it was obvious that if the facts became public, heads would roll — not the heads of the rank and file, but those of various directors of military intelligence, highly placed SRD personnel and indeed, General Blamey himself.[34] The only alternative was to keep the truth about Timor under wraps.

When SRD had selected Stevenson to investigate the Lagarto affair, it had picked a good man. Although he had arrived too late to prevent Ellwood and Cashman making any statements without his advice, he had been able to see their reports, and several Japanese confessions which were now in the hands of Timforce — the team rounding up Japanese suspected of war crimes in Timor. These particular documents, as Stevenson pointed out in his final report on November 29, had been carefully perused by him and fortunately 'contained no reference which would cause derogatory comments in the Military Court'. He went on to observe that:

> it would not be surprising if during cross examination at the trials, the activities of Cashman and Ellwood under duress come out, but since it is completely irrelevant to war crimes, and my opinion is that Timforce [interested only in war crimes] would not be interested in the other aspect [the Cobra and Lagarto fiasco], it is doubtful if any enquiry will ensue.

These reassurances about the likelihood of the story leaking out were not required. Within a week of the penning of this report, General Blamey issued a directive to Z Special Unit that 'no member of this organisation will be used as witnesses' in war crimes trials.[35]

This caused immediate problems for those collecting evidence in Timor, since some of the SRD statements lacked vital information or were unsigned. Timforce, which could not understand why such an extraordinary directive had been given, was so incredulous that it asked for confirmation, pointing out that the matter was urgent as some statements were now questionable as evidence. Had the deponents been allowed to appear as witnesses for the prosecution, any irregularities in the statements could have been resolved with a few pertinent questions. Although the rules for war trials were far more relaxed than for an ordinary criminal trial (allowing diaries, unsigned documents, letters, etc to be accepted as evidence, even though the authors of such documents were unavailable for cross examination), Timforce was worried that the existing evidence might not stand up in court.[36]

The prosecution was also very pressed for time. It is interesting that, except where evidence was overwhelmingly clear, Australian war trials took years to get to court. A notable exception was the Timor trial. Considering that no SRD witnesses were allowed to appear, the evidence needed to be of the calibre of that collected by Captain Sylvester, who, in bringing Shinohara and his gang to justice, required two years to amass the evidence and another two to assess it.[37]

No such concession was allowed for Timor. As the Australian authorities knew full well that the Portuguese government, by insisting that various diplomatic procedures had to be adopted, had disrupted and delayed the war crimes investigation, the expedition of the trial was inexcusable. In February 1946 the prosecution was forced to go to court without the benefit of vital and corroborative evidence, much of which was not collected until June the same year.[38]

Without witnesses to cross examine, without evidence essential to the case, the trial was a sham. Even then, the prosecution may have succeeded had the President of the Court, Lieutenant-Colonel Brown, not inexplicably dismissed five vital pieces of evidence on the grounds that the statements were unsigned (allowable under conditions laid down by a charter set up for trials of Far East war criminals), and had the admissible evidence of Ellwood and others not been merely a watered-down version of the frank reports made to SRD. With the Japanese admitting to only minor tortures or to none at all, no witnesses to give evidence to the contrary, and a great chunk of the documentation disallowed, it is little wonder that the court acquitted all but three defendants.[39]

The trial, which was conducted in Darwin, attracted great interest, particularly from the Eighth Division, which had suffered so hideously at the hands of the Japanese. Not surprisingly, the information available to the public was censored. Although descriptions of some of the torture had been included in newspaper reports, the fact that evidence had been disallowed or that witnesses had not been permitted to testify was not revealed.

When the verdict was announced, the Australian public was astounded. So too were the Japanese in the dock. Looks of incredulity were clearly visible on nine otherwise inscrutable Oriental faces as the judge read out his findings. They were even more stunned when they learned that the sentences imposed on those who had been found guilty ranged from one to three months imprisonment. Saiki, who had received the longer sentence, was so disbelieving that he immediately sought reassurance from the interpreter that the length of time was three months, not three years.

The astonishment in Australia quickly turned to outrage. General Bennett was so infuriated that he publicly stated that 'it was difficult to conceive that such brutal crimes should result in such absurdly small sentences. Either the accused were innocent and should be acquitted, or they were guilty and must be very heavily sentenced'. To underline the leniency of the court, Bennett added that the punishment for being absent without leave in the Australian Army was one month's detention, while the President of the Ex-Servicemen's Legion observed that cruelty to a dog incurred a similar penalty.

These attacks and the vehement protests of others achieved nothing. Lieutenant-Colonel Brown merely stated that he was 'absolutely happy' about the outcome of the trials and that 'when the public knows the full facts as we do, they [sic] too will be quite happy at our verdicts'.[40]

The public was never given the chance. All public debate on the matter ceased immediately. The press, not usually noted for its reticence, was strangely quiet. It was as if the Darwin trials had never taken place.

With the trials over, all those implicated in the Timor affair were safe. Ellwood and Cashman, who might have expected at the very least a military enquiry to take place, had been given leave and demobbed, thereby eliminating any possibility that their frank and forthright reports would be made public.[41]

This quiet and quick disposal of the key figures in the Timor debacle is significant, particularly as others were brought with alacrity to answer questions about incidents which were far less serious. The case of Major Charles Cousens, accused of treason for taking part in a Japanese propaganda broadcast under duress, and the court martial of Captain John Murphy, accused of supplying information to the enemy, received enormous press coverage until the charges against Cousens were dropped and Murphy was honourably discharged when his was found to be a case of mistaken identity (the collaborator had been an elderly German with a similar name). So zealous was the government in its pursuit of persons believed to have committed misdemeanours while in uniform that Group Captain 'Killer' Callwell was stripped of his rank after a very public hearing in which he was found to have used an aeroplane belonging to the RAAF to supply liquor to the Americans. Yet the army made no move to investigate the conduct of Ellwood and Cashman, whose activities, in some quarters, might have been perceived to be highly treasonable. As the true facts were never placed on the public record, the part played by Ellwood in particular was taken out of context in later years. As a result, his conduct has been viewed with great suspicion, while the stupidity and negligence of highly placed personnel have remained undetected.[42]

Of all those involved in the Timor affair, the person with most to lose by exposure of the facts was General Blamey, who had already been involved in two high-level scandals when Victorian Chief of Police. The first involved the use of his Police Badge by a patron during a raid on an establishment where assignations with accommodating ladies were known to take place. The second was far more serious and resulted in a Royal Commission. In 1936, having served eleven turbulent years as Police Chief, Blamey attempted, for reasons best known to himself, to cover up the nature of the shooting of his CIB Superintendent in what appear to be irregular circumstances. When word leaked out that the shooting had not been self inflicted and accidental as claimed, an enquiry was held and Blamey was called to testify. As Judge Macindoe declared, 'I tried my best to steer him to the true story but he was immovable. I couldn't save him from himself', giving the reason for his perjury as, 'Being jealous of the reputation of the force which he commands, he thought that that reputation might be endangered if the whole truth was disclosed'. As there was no love lost between the staunchly conservative Blamey and the more socialist Victorian Premier, he was forced to resign, much to the delight of the press, whom Blamey had antagonised for years.[43]

In the ten years that had passed since this incident, Blamey had grown in stature, power and influence. As Commander-in-Chief of the AIF and autocratic by nature, he had created powerful alliances and made many enemies, none of whom would have grieved at his downfall. Given the long-standing enmity between Bennett and Blamey, it is interesting to speculate on what General Bennett and his supporters would have done had they had access to the file on the Timor operations. Surrounded by many who would have rejoiced to see him cut down to size, Blamey must have breathed a sigh of relief that he had not been brought to book over the actions of SRD, over which he had ultimate control. Although he had left the army in late 1945, the disclosure of the Timor affair, coupled with his well-documented and unsavoury past, would have resulted in his ruination. As Blamey's prominent and politically influential friends could not have avoided contamination by any scandal, the relief undoubtedly felt by the General must have been shared by many — particularly Liberal Party leader and former Prime Minister Robert Gordon Menzies, who had high hopes of ousting the Chifley Labor Government later that year.

Any scandal would also have put paid to Blamey's involvement in a right wing, fiercely anti-communist 'secret army', known as The Association, which was formed eighteen months after the war ended. Privately funded and decidedly anti-Labor, it was controlled by a core of high-ranking military and intelligence officers, headed by Blamey himself, all of whom were committed to the suppression of communism. In its own words, The Association was to 'organise the civil population to meet the unexpected, sudden emergency caused by a communist uprising'. It was intended that this uprising, which was spelt out in suitably lurid language, would be met by the determined resistance of The Association, whose members, many of them pillars of society, aspiring politicians and ex-servicemen, numbered into the tens of thousands. It appears that the secrecy of this private army was strictly maintained and that it was prepared, if necessary, to organise a right-wing coup should the Labor Party (which intended to nationalise the banks) retain power in the 1949 election.[44]

Perhaps Blamey's dexterity in handling what would have been an explosive situation was one reason, among many, why his good friend Menzies, who had been Victoria's Attorney General during Blamey's reign as Chief of Police, chose to bestow on him a high and great honour. On 16 September 1950, having attained his ambition to regain the Prime Ministership the previous year, Menzies had Blamey created Field Marshal — an elevation of rank which the Labor Party had fiercely resisted. In order to do this, Menzies created a precedent by restoring Blamey, who was on his death bed, to the Active List.[45]

The expeditious nature of the Darwin trials effectively put an end to any further interest in Timor. Any additional information, collected far too late for inclusion in the proceedings, was therefore of little consequence. As the file closed on the whole sorry mess, any chance of the fate of Willersdorf and Pace being discovered was lost. Like the other members of Rimau, whose mission was decreed an abject failure and whose story was lost in a maze of military bungling and ineptitude, they were destined to become forgotten heroes.

When Jeffrey Willersdorf and Hugo Pace had left Warne, delirious and raving at Katapongan Island in December, they had continued sailing in an easterly direction. Aided by a steady monsoonal breeze, their prahu carried them towards a Dutch pickup point at Nila Island. They had navigated their way with extreme accuracy, finding and noting the names of islands that were little more than dots on Reymond's navigational charts. From Katapongan they had called at Mesalima, Doangdoangan, Dewakang and Kajuadi Islands, before reaching Romang Island by January 17. Away to the north-east, only 230 kilometres distant and a little over two days' sailing, lay Nila, and safety. Equipped with their automatic weapons as well as their pistols and binoculars, they landed at Parao, on Romang, unaware that the village headman was a Japanese collaborator. They must have felt safe, for they made no attempt to leave. Two days later, on the morning of January 19, the Japanese swooped on their hiding place.

When Willersdorf and Pace arrived in Dili from Lautem, the closest Japanese base to Romang, they were in a pitiful condition. Both had been beaten. In addition to two large holes in his legs, caused by a bayonet, Willersdorf's hands and feet were a mess, the flesh between every finger and toe having been cut. Pace was suffering from general ill treatment and was tightly bound, apparently with telephone cable, which the Japanese were fond of passing through, rather than round, the wrists. The torture had been such that by January 23 the interrogators had managed to extract from these very tough and resolute Australians the purpose of their mission. Some time later, further questioning elicited the fact that they had been forced to leave Warne (whom the Japanese were told had 'gone mad') at Katapongan Island. They also gave up details of their route and revealed that their craft had been repaired by Goking at Tandjung Dato.

On February 10, when Singapore ordered that all Rimau men were to be 'dealt with', Jeffrey Willersdorf was no longer a problem. Having received no medical treatment, his flyblown wounds had mortified, resulting in his death a week after his arrival in Dili. Pace was allowed simply to waste away, his wounds infected and his body so emaciated by starvation and racked by disease that he too died in June. The pair were buried on a hill at Tiabesse, about two hundred metres south-east of the old Dili Power Station, which had served as the gaol.[46]

As their fate was unknown, their bodies, unlike that of Lyon, Ross, Davidson, Campbell and the Outram Road group, were never recovered. In February 1946 Abdul Latif accompanied the Dutch to Soreh and Tapai Islands, where the skeletal remains of those who had died were transferred to wooden coffins for burial in Singapore. The bodies of the Singapore victims, which had been exhumed in November 1945 with the help of Japanese labour, had been reburied in shallow graves until such time as a more fitting place was prepared.[47]

In late 1946, all were taken to Kranji War Cemetery, a grassy knoll that overlooks the spot where the Imperial Japanese Army stormed the shores of Singapore Island on the night of 8 February 1942. It is a peaceful place. Dominated by a simple bronze sword superimposed upon a towering white marble cross and surrounded by lush, well-laid-out gardens, Kranji is far removed from the hustle and bustle of Singapore City.

The row upon row of plain white headstones are a sobering sight, a reminder that war is a terrible thing, measured not in terms of territory lost or gained but in the sacrifice of ordinary, decent men. About midway up the hill are the graves of Ivan Lyon and Bobby Ross, while Archie Campbell and Donald Davidson probably lie close by, buried beneath headstones marked 'A Soldier of the Second World War'. A short distance away, united in death as they were in life, lie the ten who lost their lives on the killing ground at Bukit Timah. For the others, at Merapas, Boeaja, Borneo, Java and Timor, there are no marked graves. Like Bill Reynolds, John Sachs and Clifford Perske, their mortal remains lie in a place known only to God.[48] Let these words serve as an epitaph for them, and for all men who gave their lives, no matter where they lie:

> Greater love hath no man than this, that a man lay down his life for his friends.
>
> John 15:13

The forgotten heroes of Operation Rimau.

Lieutenant-Colonel Ivan Lyon, DSO, MBE (Gordon Highlanders), died at Soreh Island, Riouw Archipelago, 16 October 1944, aged twenty-nine.

Lieutenant-Commander Donald Davidson, DSO (RNVR), died at Tapai Island, Riouw Archipelago, 18 October 1944, aged thirty-five.

Major Reginald M. Ingleton (Royal Marines), died at Bukit Timah, Singapore, 7 July 1945, aged twenty-five.

Captain Robert C. Page, DSO (AIF), died at Bukit Timah, Singapore, 7 July 1945, aged twenty-four.

Lieutenant Walter G. Carey (AIF), died at Bukit Timah, Singapore, 7 July 1945, aged thirty-one.

Lieutenant Bruno P. Reymond (RANR), died off Satai Cape, Borneo, 21 December, 1944, aged thirty-one.

Lieutenant H. Robert Ross (British Army), died at Soreh Island, Riouw Archipelago, 16 October 1944, aged twenty-seven.

Lieutenant Albert L. Sargent (AIF), died at Bukit Timah, Singapore, 7 July 1945, aged twenty-five.

Sub-Lieutenant J. Gregor Riggs (RNVR), died at Merapas Island, Riouw Archipelago, 5 November 1944, aged twenty-one.

Warrant Officer Alfred Warren (AIF), died at Bukit Timah, Singapore, 7 July 1945, aged thirty-two.

Warrant Officer Jeffrey Willersdorf (AIF), died at Dili, Timor, February 1945, aged twenty-two.

Sergeant Colin B. Cameron (AIF), died at Merapas Island, Riouw Archipelago, 5 November 1944, aged twenty-one.

Sergeant David P. Gooley (AIF), died at Bukit Timah, Singapore, 7 July 1945, aged twenty-seven.

Corporal Archibald G. Campbell (AIF), died at Tapai Island, Riouw Archipelago, 18 October 1944, aged twenty-four.

Corporal Colin M. Craft (AIF), died off Satai Cape, Borneo, 21 December 1944, aged twenty-one.

Corporal Roland B. Fletcher (AIF), died at Bukit Timah, Singapore, 7 July 1945, aged twenty-nine.

Corporal Clair M. Stewart (AIF), died at Bukit Timah, Singapore, 7 July 1945, aged thirty-five.

Able Seaman Walter G. Falls, DSM (RANR), died at Bukit Timah, Singapore, 7 July 1945, aged twenty-five.

Able Seaman Andrew W.E. Huston, DSM (RANR), died off Boeaja Island, Lingga Archipelago, 16 December 1944, aged twenty.

Able Seaman Frederick W. Marsh (RANR), died at Tandjung Pagar, Singapore, 11 January 1945, aged twenty-one.

Lance Corporal John T. Hardy (AIF), died at Bukit Timah, Singapore, 7 July 1945, aged twenty-three.

Lance Corporal Hugo J. Pace (AIF), died at Dili, Timor, June 1945, aged twenty-five.

Private Douglas R. Warne (AIF), died at Soerabaya, Java, April 1945, aged twenty-four.

And also **Lieutenants Clifford Perske** and **John Sachs, MM (AIF),** who died at Soerabaya, Java as a direct result of the Rimau raid, 30 March 1945, aged twenty-seven and thirty-one.

Epilogue

Merapas Island, May 1989. Two figures, one white and one brown, oblivious to everything but the patch of ground beneath their feet, stand motionless in the shade of a tree at Stewart Point. After what seems an eternity, Abdul Achap nods. This is the place where he buried Gregor Riggs forty-five years before. The middle-aged Australian looks away, his emotions in utter turmoil, the waiting over at last. With the discovery of Riggs's grave, the last piece of evidence has slipped into place. Tom Hall's thirty-one-year search to discover the truth about Operation Rimau is over.

Achap waits patiently, aware, from the tension in the air, that his white friend is struggling to come to terms with something that the Indonesian knows he will never be able fully to understand. Hall, now composed, turns back. But his thoughts are far away, spinning through the kaleidoscope of events that have led him once more to Merapas Island.

Hall's efforts to prove that the Rimau raid was not a failure and that the subsequent executions were unjustified have taken him alternately through periods of joy and despair. So often his relief at finally making a breakthrough in his investigation has been shattered by the discovery that people purporting to have vital evidence were simply rehashing useless information, heard in some pub or other. He is first to agree, however, that these disappointments have been offset by periods of immense satisfaction. There were some real highlights, such as the successful restoration of *Krait* to Australia, in which he had played a major part, and the formation of a pressure group, One Commando Association, which led (with the help of ABC Radio) to his locating the families of the Jaywick and Rimau men. This had culminated, in July 1978, in the presentation to them of a specially designed Commando Cross of Valour in a moving ceremony at the Great War Memorial in Sydney's Hyde Park. Not so satisfying is the fact that a block of land in that same park, deeded to him by Lord Mayor Leo Port, is still without its memorial, the plans shelved because of interference by politicians and fringe organisations who wanted to bask in the limelight.

It is also disappointing that his attempt to have a film made on Rimau's exploits came to grief in 1983 when a government-backed film corporation wanted to distort the facts for dramatic effect. He concedes that the one positive thing to come out of this exercise was his trip to England. There, he uncovered a great deal of archival material, contacted Lyon's son and colleagues and was entrusted with a mountain of private papers which had given the story a new dimension. Perhaps most galling is the knowledge that the confidentiality of some of his early 'information', later found to be incorrect, was breached and passed on by opportunists, thereby adding to the confusion and distortion of facts that have surrounded Rimau. Much more pleasant to recollect is his private trip to Indonesia in 1981 when, worried that there was still much to find, he had located many eyewitnesses to the events of 1944, including Abdul and Mrs Latif, Abdul Achap and Sidek Bin Safar, whose memories were so vivid that they recalled every detail of the actions they had witnessed with absolute clarity.

But it was here at Merapas that he had experienced his greatest shock, greater even than the one he had just received in finding the grave of Gregor Riggs. In 1981, Karta, the young boy befriended by Walter Carey and now a grown man, had handed to Hall a cardboard box containing the skull of Riggs's mate Colin Cameron, which Karta had discovered near the sangar in 1976 and kept beneath his bed ever since, confident that one day someone would return to ask about the white soldiers. Hall's attempt to bring the remains (purchased from Karta for 98 000 rupiah) back to Australia for forensic analysis had been a hair-raising episode, involving his arrest by Indonesian marine police and a rather nail-biting time in Sydney Airport's customs' hall, which ended satisfactorily when a customs' official had waved him through.

Yet not all the shocks had been physical. There was the startling revelation by several Rimau family members that details of their inexplicable and disturbing ESP experiences of 1944 and 1945 dovetailed with Hall's factual evidence, of which they had no prior knowledge. On a purely personal note, the sudden realisation, on piecing together the Lagarto and Cobra fiasco, that his research difficulties stemmed from the day that he, in his naivity, had written to Robert Menzies about Timor, had been almost as great a surprise as discovering that Willersdorf and Pace, the two who were supposed to have paddled to Timor's Romang Island, had actually sailed all the way in a prahu and that Blondie Sargent, the alleged third member of the party, had not gone to Timor at all. It was ironic, really, to think that he had spent all these years investigating a story based on a false premise!

As Hall momentarily returns to the present, lifting his gaze to meet the dark enquiring eyes of Achap, he concludes that, apart from the satisfaction of arriving at the truth, it is the reactions of Rimau's families that has made it all worthwhile. Having heard nothing from the government, they are touchingly grateful for the slightest scrap of information. His sense of failure at the memory of finding that Gabrielle

Lyon had died before he could tell her about Ivan is mitigated somewhat as he recalls the admiration he felt when Clive Lyon told him of Gabrielle's remarkable survival in the prison camp, and of her courage when she discovered that Ivan was dead and that both her parents had been murdered pro-Japanese Vichy French.

In all, he muses, it has been a long and lonely road. Although he had never sought recognition for himself, he is now glad that he agreed to accept in 1988 the honour of being named one of the Australian Bicentennial's '200 Unsung Heroes'. Indeed, such was his reluctance to be singled out that it was only the feeling that he was accepting the medal on behalf of twenty-three men that had persuaded him to go to Government House at all. Yet he had to admit that, indirectly, it was this decision which had led him back to Merapas Island. This time, however, he was no longer alone in his battle to uncover the truth.

I had not seen Tom Hall for a number of years when I renewed my acquaintance with him on a suburban street in 1988, shortly after he had been informed of his Bicentennial Award and his inclusion in the commemorative book, in which, by coincidence, I was involved as a writer. By even stranger coincidence it was July 7 — the seventh day of the seventh month and the forty-third anniversary of the executions at Bukit Timah, a day that was indelibly etched on Tom's mind. When he told me he was afraid that Operation Rimau would remain a regurgitated mixture of fact and fiction unless it was properly documented, I offered to write a completely factual account using the evidence he had collected during his thirty years of meticulous research. My only proviso, with which he thoroughly concurred, was that, in the interests of truth, it must be drawn entirely from documented evidence, unsullied by hearsay or fantasy or wishful thinking.

So began a monumental project. Twelve months later, having assessed a mountain of Allied and Japanese documents, listened to hours of recorded interviews, travelled to Singapore and Indonesia to see where the action had taken place and recheck the eyewitness accounts (discovering Kasu eyewitnesses Mahat and Arafin and the story of Riggs's death in the process), and embarked upon a war of words with various members of the Defence Department (who were actively opposing the release of archival material), I finally understood what had been driving Tom Hall for thirty-one years. I am humbled that he has entrusted me with his life's work and that I should be the one privileged to write for him the story of Operation Rimau.

The Heroes of Rimau is more than the mere chronicling of one of the most amazing stories to emerge from World War II. It is a tribute to twenty-four men — twenty-three of whom paid the ultimate price in defence of their country. The other, a lone soldier — a young army officer of another generation — was determined that their sacrifice should not be in vain.

Appendix I
Citizen Soldier:
The Case of Major-General
H. Gordon Bennett

After the fall of Singapore, all Allied military personnel who had not managed to escape were taken into custody by the victorious Japanese. On 8 March 1943, while in captivity, General Percival wrote a letter to the Military Board in Australia explaining why it had been necessary to appoint Brigadier C.A. Callaghan as GOC, AIF, in place of Bennett, who had escaped to Australia. This letter was given to Callaghan. Immediately after the war, having been welcomed home by Bennett, Callaghan delivered the letter.

Its contents were to prove to be Bennett's ruination. Percival had accused Bennett, who believed that after the ceasefire at 8.30 on the night of 15 February 1942 he was a free agent, of 'voluntarily and without permission relinquishing command of the AIF', a charge that was paraphrased by Bennett's long-time enemy and head of the AIF, General Blamey, into one of 'desertion'. At Blamey's request, Percival confirmed the accusations in another letter written on 4 September 1945, conveniently forgetting that the Air and Naval Chiefs, Pulford and Spooner, as well as Brigadier Paris, had also escaped from Singapore. In this manner, Percival tightened the screws on the unfortunate Bennett, whose only crime seems to be that he survived while the other three perished. Pursued by Blamey and factions of the army who, jealous of his comparative youth and seniority, had long and unforgiving memories about Bennett's outspoken and well-deserved criticism, Bennett was put through both the military and public wringer. Percival, who had started the ruccus, remained silent about Wavell's orders to escape, asserting only that Bennett had left Singapore without asking him.[1]

Strangely, the two separate inquiries (the second of which was instituted to placate a public enraged by the army's treatment of Bennett), having found, on what appear to be purely technical grounds, that Bennett was 'not justified in handing over his command or in leaving Singapore',[2] did not recommend any censure. Neither was any further action suggested by the Military Board, which had already inflicted a far more subtle and exquisite punishment.

On his return to Sydney on 1 March 1942, Bennett's enemies on the Staff Corps had been ready, their knives out and sharpened, anxious to accuse Bennett of abandoning his men. Backed by his enthusiastic and loyal public, the Prime Minister and almost the entire Cabinet — all of whom believed it was the General's duty to escape — Bennett weathered the initial storm. However, he had trodden on far too many toes and bruised far too many precious egos during his long career to escape scot free.

The fighting general was given a non-combatant job in Western Australia, about as far removed from the war action as could possibly be devised. Bennett stuck it out until August 1944, and then resigned, thereby becoming the first general ever to resign his commission in wartime. The inquiries that followed after Percival's allegations in 1945 were simply the last nail in Bennett's military coffin.[3] In 1948, too late to save Bennett's reputation, an eminent military lawyer published his opinion of the legal aspects of the public inquiry, which shot the finding full of holes.[4] But it made no difference to the hardline views of the anti-Bennett brigade, led by General Blamey. The army hierarchy gave the fiery Bennett the cold shoulder for the rest of his life.

However, he never lost the admiration of the people or his troops, who still treated him with an affection akin to hero worship. It is interesting, considering the controversy surrounding Bennett that, having been a prime mover in his ultimate downfall, Percival never made any reference at all to the General's escape in his Despatches, or in his book published in 1949.[5] Perhaps he realised that so publicly to condemn, in print and for all time, a man who was only doing what had been expected of him, was carrying the hypocrisy just a little too far.

Appendix II
The Case of
Major Seymour Bingham

In the course of researching the incidents on Timor, we discovered that Seymour Bingham had been suspected of treachery in England, resulting in the collapse of an SOE operation in Holland and the loss of many lives. To eliminate the possibility, however remote, that he may have been an enemy agent operating in Australia as an SRD officer, we investigated his activities with SOE. It was not until the available and quite fragmented evidence was examined that the full story of Major Bingham's involvement in the Dutch SOE operation emerged.

The incident, code-named England Spiel or Operation Nordpol by the Germans, had begun in March 1942, when a Dutch SOE agent named Lauwers was caught in Holland with three encoded signals. Aided by these signals and information extracted from other captured agents, German Intelligence set up a bogus wireless link with London. After a suitable show of reluctance, Lauwers transmitted encoded messages for the Germans, confident that the omission of his security checks — including a deliberate mistake in every sixteenth letter — would alert SOE to his capture. His faith in the system was misplaced, for London began to make arrangements to send in another party, forcing Lauwers to devise an ingenious method whereby the letters CAUGH T appeared three times in his next message. It made no difference. The SOE agents were captured on arrival and, with another wireless soon in operation, England Spiel was under way.

In the months that followed, the capture of dozens of agents resulted in eleven separate wireless links, all in German control. Onto thirty fake dropping zones were also delivered 570 containers and 150 parcels containing 15 200 kilograms of explosive; 3000 Sten guns; 5000 small arms; 300 Bren guns; 2000 hand grenades; 75 radio transmitters; Aldis lamps, torches, signal apparatus, Eureka sets and S-phones; half a million rounds of ammunition; 40 bicycles; half a million Dutch Guilders (about stg£50 000); several thousand pounds in other currency; and a large quantity of bicycle tyres, clothing, tobacco, cigarettes, tinned food, coffee and chocolate.[1]

In all, sixty-four agents were caught. Of the fifty-nine who were unable to escape, forty-eight were exterminated in Mauthausen Concentration Camp in September 1944, three were shot in an escape attempt and the rest simply disappeared. At the end of the war only five agents were still alive.[2]

England Spiel ended when questions being asked by some personnel in SOE could no longer be ignored and when the Royal Air Force discovered, in the winter of 1943–44, that it had lost twelve aircraft and eighty-three men on special missions over Holland — five times the norm. Suspicions had surfaced in SOE in late 1943, when agents incarcerated in Haaren Prison managed to smuggle a message to the underground that nine of their number, including 'Doulin' and 'Arabe', had been captured. When this was passed to SOE via MI-6, it did not create a panic. The general opinion was that, coming from MI-6, one of SOE's rivals, the message was suspect and, in any case, the names of the agents were incorrectly spelled. In September, SOE chiefs also dismissed as being unlikely the information from agent Dessing (who had narrowly avoided walking into a Gestapo trap), that certain agents appeared to be in enemy hands. Major Bingham, now in charge of the Dutch Section and evidently a little worried by this stage, instituted an internal inquiry. When it was inconclusive, he asked for two agents to be recalled for consultation. They never arrived.[3]

Shortly afterwards, two agents who had actually managed to escape from Haaren Prison arrived in Switzerland after a three-month journey. Their detailed report, sent from Berne, was also treated with suspicion as German Intelligence, on finding that the birds had flown, signalled London that they had gone over to the Germans. This message was evidently so convincing that when the unfortunate pair arrived in England they were clapped into gaol.[4]

When RAF command announced that it would fly no more sorties until there was an investigation, all hell broke loose. The situation became so sticky that it was only the spirited defence of the Minister responsible for SOE, Lord Selbourne, and the personal intervention of Churchill, whose brain child SOE was, that saved the organisation from obliteration. In spite of evidence that the enemy had control of the agents, Churchill immediately ordered the flights to resume and operations to recommence.[5]

While this upheaval had been taking place, signal traffic to Holland had been maintained by sending messages containing information of little or no significance. Believing that the low-level intelligence was a clear indication that the British knew that their agents were in enemy control and that the game was up, the Germans decided to kill off England Spiel by sending a message to SOE on April Fool's Day, 1944.

To Messrs Blunt, Bingham and Successors Ltd. You are trying to make business in the Netherlands without our assistance. We think this rather unfair in view our long and successful co-operation as your sole agent. But never mind when you come to pay a visit to the continent you may be assured that you will be received with same care and result as all those you sent us before. So long.[6]

When this message was received, indicating that SOE had been duped, the British High Command looked about for a scapegoat. With Major Blunt, head of the Dutch Section when England Spiel began, safely ensconced in another, far more senior position, the axe fell on his successor, Major Bingham. With almost indecent haste, he was removed from his position and transported to Australia, which was about as remote a position as SOE could devise.[7]

After the war the Dutch demanded action in order to find out who was responsible for what was perceived to be a most incredible fiasco. An eleven-year enquiry followed. The Dutch, whose surviving agents had been told as much by the Germans, believed that there had been a traitor at work in SOE. Bingham was nominated as the prime suspect, even though he had not been in charge when England Spiel began. Although he was officially cleared of treachery, the Foreign Office announced that England Spiel was the result of gross incompetence and grave errors of judgement on the part of those heading the Dutch section.

Unfortunately for Bingham, there was no way of checking whether this was true or not for, quite unaccountably, every piece of paper relating to England Spiel had disappeared.[8]

The official verdict by the Foreign Office left many questions unanswered and, indeed, the real reason for England Spiel seems to run far deeper than the alleged incompetence of Majors Blunt and Bingham. With the benefit of first-hand statements by H.J. Giskes, the Chief of German Military Counter-Espionage for the region and the man who masterminded the German end; Pieter Dourlein, an agent who escaped and returned to England; H. Lauwers, whose capture started the entire affair; and the evidence of a brilliantly perceptive, civilian SOE code expert named Leo Marks, a far more complex picture emerges.

At about the same time that SOE received the first signals from Lauwers, indicating that he and his wireless were being controlled by the Germans, Russia was readying herself for a battle which would determine her very existence — a battle which would ultimately turn the tide of the war. Knowing that Russia's destiny lay in her ability to withstand the pressure being exerted by Hitler's armies, Joseph Stalin urged his allies, Churchill and Roosevelt, to divert Germany's attention from his beleaguered nation by starting a second front in Western Europe.[9]

Such a request, at this stage of the war, was impossible. Subterfuge, however, was not. Provided that Germany could be made to believe that invasion from the north-east was a distinct possibility, German troops, weapons and energies could be diverted away from the Russian front.

Should the German High Command 'learn' that a 'secret army' was being raised throughout Holland in preparation for an Allied invasion, it might just swallow the bait.[10]

It seems that it was for this reason that SOE's General Colin Gubbins formulated 'Plan Holland' — ostensibly plans of an operation designed to raise and equip a secret army of over a thousand men. Shortly afterwards, in June 1942, a Dutch agent with five containers of detailed and secret documents relating to the plan, was captured on arrival at one of the German-controlled drop zones. The Germans may have been suspicious of this prize which had fallen so fortuitously into their hands had SOE not begun to drop enough weapons, ammunition and equipment to outfit an army and to supply sabotage groups with sufficient material to blow up a dozen cities. As a timely follow up, less than six months after Germany had captured 'Plan Holland', a message was received on SOE's frequency which read:

> For the commander OD [Dutch Underground]. Allied landings along Dutch coast should be expected shortly. Landing parties will make contact with enemy. Civilian population and OD men must strictly refrain from interfering. Further instructions follow.

These messages were followed by others in a similar vein. Consequently, in anticipation that a second front would open up in Western Europe, Germany was forced to keep divisions in reserve instead of deploying them to counter the great Russian offensive on the Stalingrad front in November 1942. Within weeks, the Germans had capitulated at Stalingrad and the Russians were victorious at Kharkov, Rostov and Kursk, marking the beginning of Germany's slide towards ultimate defeat. Had not the German High Command been tricked into keeping back reinforcements in the west that might otherwise have been sent to the east, the war may well have taken a decidedly different turn.[11]

When quizzed by the Dutch Resistance chiefs, SOE denied that any messages in relation to an invasion along the Dutch coast had ever been sent.[12] The denials are hardly surprising. These bogus signals, the cold-blooded insertion of personnel, and the deliberate dropping of equipment and arms into German hands were evidently a closely guarded secret, unknown to all except those at the very top.

It was not until decades later that British code expert Leo Marks revealed that the absence of security checks, which had in fact been queried by him and others as early as June 1942, had been brushed aside with the quite erroneous statement that security checks were always being omitted, and the explanation that Dutch agents were of such a high calibre that they would never be compromised. Not to be put off, when Marks realised in early 1943 that the signals coming from Holland were far too 'pat' and contained technical coding errors, he used his coding expertise to set a highly unauthorised trap for the Germans. He then went directly to General Gubbins with irrefutable evidence that all the Dutch agents had been compromised. After congratulating Marks on his 'good work', Gubbins ordered him to say nothing to anyone in SOE and dismissed him with the reassurance that the matter would be taken care of.[13] That it was not points to the fact that Churchill, Roosevelt and other highly placed personnel could not allow this great charade, which had been so brilliantly devised, to be interrupted. Apart from tricking the German High Command, SOE had been able to cause great problems by sending messages on the radio links demanding the liquidation of key enemy personnel, ordering that installations such as the U-boat wireless control station be blown up, requesting that a known collaborator be sent to England to receive the Military Cross and making arrangements to extract key agents. The manpower required to circumvent such demands and to keep track of a fictitious underground movement invented to keep London happy took the entire resources of espionage chief Giskes and his department.[14]

It is little wonder therefore, with the D-Day invasion fast becoming a reality, that Churchill pulled out all stops in early 1944 to ensure that the England Spiel charade continued. Although it has never been admitted that SOE's continued deception was part of a master plan, after the war Churchill revealed that the conclusion by the Germans, that the Allies' main thrust would be at Pas de Calais, was brought about by 'the most complex scheme ever devised'. As he wrote in 1955, 'It would not be proper even now to describe all methods employed to mislead the enemy . . . The final result was admirable'.[15]

Yet, in spite of the overwhelming evidence that England Spiel was a brilliant piece of counter-intelligence, the Foreign Office verdict that it was a disaster brought about by massive incompetence still stands. Leo Marks, by his refusal to disclose all that he knows on the grounds that it would make life difficult for those in high places and cause 'great problems if the truth became known' only adds fuel to the fire. There are many Dutch who believe that one 'great problem' would be the revelation that Churchill and Roosevelt deliberately sacrificed Dutch lives in order to fool the German High Command. If they did, the ends could be said to justify the means. The fifty-nine agents who ultimately died, a number of resistance workers who were unavoidably arrested and the eighty-three RAF personnel whose planes were shot down while ferrying material to the drop zones, must have seemed a small price to pay for cementing the alliance with Stalin, changing the course of the war, paving the way for the Allied invasion of Normandy and tying up the German Intelligence network in Holland for almost two years.[16]

Yet Seymour Bingham knew nothing of this. Neither, it appears, did anyone in SOE below Gubbins. The direct intervention by Churchill and Selbourne, in having operations resumed in spite of evidence that agents had been captured and that others, reported as being 'dead', were in prison and alive, points to the fact that the truth was confined to a handful of highly placed people. This secrecy, coupled with the assertions of the Foreign Office and the disappearance of all documentation, has ensured that Bingham, a man innocent of any negligence and most certainly innocent of any duplicity, has remained the official scapegoat for the Allied High Command.

Notes

Abbreviations
AA ACT: Australian Archives, Canberra, ACT.
AA VIC: Australian Archives, Melbourne, Victoria.
AWM: Australian War Memorial, Canberra, ACT.
DODA ACT: Department of Defence Archives, ACT.
LFC: Lyon Family Correspondence.
LFP: Lyon Family Papers.
PRO: Public Record Office, London, UK.
THP: Tom Hall Papers.
USNA: United States National Archives, Washington DC.

References
The references for each paragraph or section are here collected together in one note. For individual references, see the first draft of *The Heroes of Rimau* which will be deposited with the Tom Hall Papers at the Australian War Memorial in Canberra.

Spelling
Because of the great variation in the spelling of Indonesian and Malaysian place names, that which appears on the original documents or, if inapplicable, on current British Naval Charts has been followed here.

Chapter I: A Fool's Paradise

1) The background for Singapore before the war is taken from eyewitness accounts such as those found in Ronald McKie, *This Was Singapore*, Sydney 1942, and from conversations between the author and Chinese citizens still living in Singapore.

2) Major-General S. Woodburn Kirby, *Singapore: The Chain of Disaster*, London 1971, pp. 15-18, 29,7.

3) Ibid, p. 49; David Day, *The Great Betrayal*, Sydney 1988, p. 119.

4) Extract from the *Straits Times*, quoted in Lionel Wigmore, *Australia in the War of 1939-45, The Japanese Thrust*, Canberra 1957, p. 74.

5) Timothy Hall, *The Fall of Singapore 1942*, Australia 1983, pp. 25-27.

6) The Japanese encountered no real opposition until five weeks after landing as Percival had not put his best troops in the front line. See note 64 below.

7) Kirby, *Singapore*, pp. 14, 30-31; Lieut.-General A.E. Percival, Despatches to The Secretary of State for War, April 25 1946, published in *The London Gazette*, Second Supplement, February 26 1948, Appendix A, Deductions from Japanese Appreciation of the Attack on Singapore 1937, p. 1339.

8) Percival's Despatches, p. 1250.

9) Kirby, *Singapore*, pp. 30, 32.

10) Ibid; Ivan Simson, *Singapore: Too Little, Too Late*, London 1970, p. 38. Compare Simson's statement with that in Sir John Smyth, *Percival and the Tragedy of Singapore*, London 1971, p. 81, which states that defences were not built as there was a ruthless cut in funding.

11) Kirby, *Singapore*, p. 30.

12) Air Chief Marshall Sir Robert Brooke-Popham, Despatches to the British Chiefs of Staff, May 28 1942, published in Supplement to *The London Gazette*, January 22 1948, p. 546; Air Vice-Marshall Sir Paul Maltby, Despatches to the Secretary of State for Air, July 26 1947, published in the Third Supplement to *The London Gazette*, February 26 1948, pp. 1359, 1408; Simpson p. 32; Lieut.-General A.E. Percival, *The War in Malaya*, London 1949, pp. 42-43.

13) Simson, pp. 37,72; War Diary of Sir Shenton Thomas, entries dated December 10, 31 1941, January 1, 9 1942, quoted in Brian Montgomery, *Shenton of Singapore*, London 1984, pp. 87,105,106,108; Duff Cooper to Winston Churchill, December 18 1941, an enclosure in Tennant to Churchill January 6 1942, POREM 3, 161/1 (PRO); Percival's Despatches, pp. 1264-65; Brooke-Popham's Despatches, pp. 357-58.

14) James Leasor, *Singapore*, London 1968, p. 220.

15) Percival's Despatches, p. 1309-10.

16) Kirby, *Singapore*, p. 35; Prime Minister to General Ismay, January 19 1942, quoted in Winston S. Churchill, *The Second World War, Vol. 7, The Onslaught of Japan*, London 1951, p. 43; Churchill to Roosevelt, quoted in Day, p. 255.

17) Smyth, p. 54.

18) Kirby, *Singapore*, pp. 35-36 and Day, p. 118.

19) Smyth, p. 55; Maltby's Despatches, p. 553.

20) Percival's Despatches, p. 1250; Maltby's Despatches, p. 1349. There is a discrepancy in the date of this report, given as July in Maltby, p. 1349 and as August 15 in Brooke-Popham, p. 550.

21) Ibid; Brooke-Popham's Despatches, p. 550; Smyth, p. 57.

22) Richard Gough, *The Escape from Singapore*, London 1987, pp. 13-14.

23) Percival's Despatches, p. 1251; Maltby's Despatches, p. 1349; Brooke-Popham's Despatches, p. 550-51.

24) Advisory War Council Minute 39, 25 November 1940, A 2682, Vol. 1. (AA ACT).

25) Day, pp. 118-19; Smyth, p. 55.

26) Statements by Menzies, quoted in Day, pp. 127, 131.

27) Lieut-Gen. H. Gordon Bennett, *Why Singapore Fell*, Sydney 1944, p. 4; Percival's Despatches, p. 1251.

28) Bennett, pp. 4-5; Brooke-Popham's Despatches, p. 570.

29) Bennett, pp. 5,6; Percival's Despatches, p. 1257; Brooke-Popham's Despatches, p. 570.

30) Hall, pp. 29-30.

31) Ibid, pp. 30-32; Major-General S. Woodburn Kirby, *History of the Second World War, The War Against Japan, Vol. 1*, London 1957, Appendix 12 'Notes on the Australian Imperial Forces', p. 516.

32) Simson, pp. 24,27,21,28-29.
33) Kirby, *Singapore*, p. 129; Duff Cooper to Winston Churchill December 18, 20 1941; Thomas's War Diary for February 9 1942, quoted in Montgomery, pp. 118,130. Note: Percival was never a schoolmaster. On leaving Rugby School he joined an iron ore company in London and then enlisted in the army in 1914.
34) Simson, p. 28.
35) Smyth, p. 50.
36) Simson, pp. 33, 41. For more details of the lack of equipment see Brooke-Popham's Despatches, p. 553.
37) Russell Braddon, *The Naked Island*, London 1952, pp. 40-43.
38) Kirby, *War Against Japan*, pp. 166-67. The statements in the pamphlet were to prove to be accurate, see Percival's Despatches, p. 1331.
39) Simson, pp. 42-43; Percival's Despatches, p. 1250; Interview by Tom Hall with Geoffrey Rowley-Conwy, January 1981, tape transcript p. 2 (THP); Bennett, pp. 12-18.
40) Simson, p. 42.
41) Hall, pp. 31-32.
42) Colonel Masanobu Tsuji, *Singapore, The Japanese Version*, Appendix 1, *Read This Alone — And The War Can Be Won*, Sydney 1960, pp. 295-350.
43) Simson, p. 36-37,33,111-13; Percival's Despatches, p. 1261.
44) Simson, pp. 106,37.
45) Day, pp. 189, 176,196.
46) Bennett, p. 56. Note: There is some doubt as to the origin of this cable which Bennett asserted arrived December 3 1941 — see A.B. Lodge, *The Fall of General Gordon Bennett*, Sydney 1986, p. 304 and note 23, p. 335.
47) Day, p. 202. These were the sentiments of Sir Horace Seymour of the Foreign Office.
48) Brooke-Popham's Despatches, pp. 570,571,565; Hall, p. 40.
49) Hall, p. 40; Brooke-Popham's Despatches, p. 553; Day, pp. 124-25.
50) Hall, pp. 63, 53.
51) Day, p. 207; *The Memoirs of Lord Ismay*, London 1960, p. 241.
52) Maltby's Despatches, p. 1363-64; Brooke-Popham's Despatches, p. 555; Douglas Gillison, *Australia in the War of 1939-1945, The Royal Australian Air Force*, Canberra 1962, pp. 200-04.
53) Brooke-Popham's Despatches, p. 555; Maltby's Despatches, p. 1364; Percival's Despatches, pp. 1252,1267-69; Kirby, *War Against Japan*, p. 78, 173-75, 181-82; Statement by Brigadier I.R. Graeme, April 1982, quoted in Montgomery, p. 91.
54) Gillison, p. 204.
55) Brooke-Popham's Despatches, p. 555; Hall, p. 59; Thomas's War Diary for December 8 1941, quoted in Montgomery, p. 83. There is a discrepancy in the time of the bombing. Brooke-Popham puts it at 3 am while Thomas's diary notes that it is after 4 am.
56) Rowley-Conwy Interview, p. 2.
57) Squadron Leader T.C. Carter, History of RDF Organisation in the Far East 1941-1942, (n.d.), Carter Papers TCC 2/1/ (IWM); Statement by Flight-Lieutenant Harry Grumber, April 1982, quoted in Montgomery, p. 80. This is in direct conflict with statements made in Brooke-Popham's Despatches, p. 555.
58) Hall, p. 59.
59) Ibid, p. 60-61; Brooke-Popham's Despatches, p. 556.
60) Bowden to Evatt, December 23 1941, A 5954, Box 571 (AA ACT).
61) Day, p. 211; Smyth, p. 106; Kirby, p. 86. The ships arrived in Singapore on December 2 1941.
62) Brooke-Popham's Despatches, pp. 557-58; Maltby's Despatches, pp. 1368-69; Percival's Despatches, p. 1272; Gillison, pp. 250-54.
63) Kirby, *War Against Japan*, pp. 274-81.
64) Hall, p. 94.
65) Hall, pp. 94-97, 99-102; Wigmore, pp. 217-20, 343-47; Percival's Despatches, p. 1298.
66) Mamoru Shinozaki, *Syonan — My Story*, Singapore 1975, p. 77. There does not appear to be any detailed record of this incident in any existing official history, other than a brief mention in Oswald L. Ziegler (ed), *Men May Smoke*, final edition of the 2/18 Bn. AIF Magazine, circa 1947, Sydey. As many of the details recorded by Shinozaki do not tally with the account of the well-documented ambush on the Nithsdale Estate, sixteen kilometres to the north of Jemaluang, by 2/18 Battalion, it is believed that this Jemaluang village incident is a separate

The Heroes of Rimau

skirmish involving D Company, the details of which have gone unrecorded by the Allies. The cross erected upon the graves of the Australians was not unique. Ziegler, p. 45, records that on July 4 1942 a group of Australians noticed a small white cross, inscribed with the words 'Australian Soldiers', in the Japanese camp at Parit Sulong. They were told that it was Japan's intention to erect it alongside the Muar Road.

67) Cablegram SP.299, Bennett to Sturdee, January 19 1942, Document 54, 553/2/3 (AWM); War Cabinet Minute, March 2 1942, notes on discussion with Major-General Gordon Bennett, A 2673 Vol II (AA ACT).
68) Tsuji, pp. 183-85.
69) Ibid.
70) Leasor, p. 213.
71) F. Spencer Chapman, The Jungle is Neutral, London 1949, p. 27-28.
72) Percival's Despatches, p. 1292 and Kirby, p. 179.

Chapter 2: The Fortress Falls

1) Hall, p. 107.
2) Wavell to Prime Minister, January 16 1942 and statement by Churchill, quoted in Churchill, pp. 41-42.
3) Prime Minister to General Ismay, January 19 1942, quoted in Churchill, p. 43.
4) Churchill, p. 52, Prime Minister to Wavell, January 20 1942, quoted in Churchill, p. 45-46; Prime Minister to Ismay, January 19 1942, quoted in Churchill, pp. 43-44.
5) Prime Minister to Ismay, January 21 and 20 1942, quoted in Churchill, pp. 49,46.
6) Mr Curtin to Prime Minister, January 23 1942, quoted in Churchill, p. 50; Cablegram 12, Curtin to Page (for Churchill), January 25 1942, M 100 (AA ACT). This cable cannot have been sent by Curtin, who was absent in Perth, Western Australia at the time. Dr. Evatt probably composed it, under the auspices of Deputy Prime Minister F.M. Forde, see Day, p. 248.
7) See note 4 above; Wavell to Prime Minister, February 3 1942, quoted in Churchill, p. 85; Air Vice-Marshall Sir Paul Maltby, Despatches to Secretary

of State for Air, July 26 1947, published in the Third Supplement to The London Gazette, February 26 1948, pp. 1381-82; Lieut.-General A.E. Percival, Despatches to the Secretary of State for War, April 25 1946, published in The London Gazette, Second Supplement, February 26 1948, p. 1305; Wigmore, p. 289; Maltby's Despatches, pp. 1377, 1379,1381,1382.
8) Maltby's Despatches, p. 1381.
9) Wigmore, pp. 258,296.
10) Ibid, p. 258, note 4.
11) Australian Defence Act 1903-53, Regulations and Orders for the Australian Military Forces, Sections 49, 117; Article by General Gordon Bennett, Daily Mail, November 15 1951, quoted in Smyth, p. 88.
12) Smyth, pp. 212-213; Wigmore, p. 290.
13) Smyth, p. 204; Hall, p. 103.
14) Walter Gibson, The Boat, London 1952, p. 41; Smyth, pp. 204-5.
15) Percival's Despatches, p. 1328; Churchill, p. 82.
16) Kirby, Singapore, pp. 220-21, 222. In this reference Percival admits that statements he had made to the contrary about this incident were incorrect.
17) Ibid, p. 222; Percival, p. 268.
18) Wavell to Prime Minister, January 16, 19 1942, quoted in Churchill, pp. 41,47; Percival's Despatches, p. 1308.
19) Hall, pp. 111,112,117.
20) Ibid, pp. 116,107; Montgomery, p. 199. It was also claimed in Air Chief Marshall Sir Robert Brooke-Popham, Despatches to the British Chiefs of Staff, May 28 1942, published in Supplement to The London Gazette, January 22 1948, p. 548, that the ground was too marshy. However, the post-war development of Singapore, including the construction of underground car parks and an underground rail system has proved this to be a misleading statement.
21) Hall, p. 122. It is estimated that 9000 Chinese died during the bombing. After the surrender, at least 6000 more were massacred by the Japanese in a purge to eliminate those who had fought against them. Another 147 were executed at Outram Road Gaol and 1470 died in prison from other causes. The total number of victims was

266

therefore around 17 000. See Shinozaki, p. 115.

22) Hall, pp. 110; 115,106; 113-14; 128.

23) Ibid, pp. 109,115.

24) Wigmore, pp. 299,304; Hall, pp. 159-60; Statement by Roy Whitecross of 8th Division Headquarters (who was a witness), to Lynette Silver, March 28 1990 (THP).

25) Wigmore, p. 304; Hall, p. 160.

26) Ian Skidmore, Escape from the Rising Sun, London 1973, pp. 2-10. Although written by Skidmore, this book is the personal account of the experiences of Major Rowley-Conwy, now Lord Langford.

27) Kirby, Singapore, p. 234.

28) Ibid, pp. 226-227; Simson, p. 107.

29) Kirby, Singapore, pp. 220-21.

30) Hall, p. 129.

31) Leasor, p. 225.

32) Louis Allen, The Policies and Strategy of the Second World War, Singapore 1941-1942, London 1977, pp. 251-52; Mamoru Shinozaki, My Wartime Experiences in Singapore, (Oral history Project No. 3), Institute of Southeast Asian Studies, Singapore 1973, p. 39; Ian Morrison, Malayan Postscript, London 1942, p. 174.

33) Gough, Escape, p. 47; Leasor, p. 230-31.

34) Gough, Escape, p. 47; Allen, p. 252; Footage of archival material in BBC television documentary, Arms and the Dragon (THP), shows the Dalforce men armed with Martini Henry rifles and a converted version of the same weapon, which have been identified in weapons manuals.

35) Tsuji, pp. 230,234-37; Kirby, Singapore, pp. 224-25; Hall, p. 162.

36) Hall, pp. 161-62.

37) Percival's Despatches, p. 1316; Thomas's War Diary, February 8 1942, quoted in Montgomery, p. 131.

38) Percival's Despatches, p. 1316-17.

39) Leasor, pp. 235-6.

40) Hall, p. 163.

41) Richard Gough, SOE Singapore 1941-42, London 1985, pp. 143-44.

42) Allen, p. 160; Whitecross's Statement.

43) Hall, pp. 121-23.

44) Hall, p. 176; Skidmore, p. 18.

45) Hall, pp. 124-25; Gough, Escape, pp. 21,203.

46) Smyth, p. 224,226.

47) Hall, p. 125. See also Churchill, pp. 83,90.

48) Wavell to Prime Minister, February 11 1942, quoted in Churchill, p. 88, Maltby's Despatches, p. 1383 and Wigmore, p. 342.

49) Prime Minister to Wavell, February 10 1942, quoted in Churchill, pp. 87-88.

50) Smyth, p. 228.

51) Frederick Howard, Kent Hughes, Melbourne 1972, p. 98.

52) Wigmore, p. 353.

53) Kirby, p. 241.

54) Bennett, p. 212; Wigmore, p. 96; Howard, p. 97. The figure of 2000 stragglers, identified as 'green' reinforcements from the General Base Depot, does not add up. On 25 January 1907 reinforcements had arrived. As 940 were immediately distributed to 2/18, 2/19 and 2/20 Battalions (see Wigmore, p. 296) there were 967 left. By the time more troops had been distributed to various groups over the next three weeks, the potential pool of troublemakers, when Singapore fell, was therefore very small indeed. This supports the statements made by General Bennett, see Bennett, p. 212. The erroneous statement that the AIF was undisciplined has been regurgitated in history books ever since, despite the fact that the statements were soon found to be untrue, e.g. see article by Ian Morrison, a London Times reporter who had seen the Australians in action in Malaya. His article, refuting the rumours, and originally published in the Times is reprinted in Salt, Vol. 7, No. 9, January 3 1944, p. 19.

55) Gough, Escape, p. 65.

56) Gibson, pp. 39-41.

57) Percival's Despatches, p. 1322; Gough, Escape, pp. 62-67, 80-82; Statement on the Evacuation by Shenton Thomas, quoted in Montgomery, pp. 169-70.

58) Geoffrey Brooke, Singapore's Dunkirk, London 1989, p. 88; Reports by A.N. Wootten on Escape from Singapore and Death of A.V. Bowden, October 17, 19 1945, A 1066 Item H45/580/6/4 (AA ACT).

59) Bennett, p. 186; Percival, p. 286; Wavell to Percival and Percival to

Wavell, February 13 1942, quoted in Churchill, p. 91.

60) Bennett, pp. 186-87.

61) Statement by William Edward Roberts, Commissioner of the Australian Red Cross, reporting on the eyewitness accounts of Colonel Craven, Padre Wearne and others, to Board of Enquiry, DWP and I, Item 86, Evidential Document 5056 (THP); Kirby, Singapore, p. 244; Wigmore, p. 374; Percival's Despatches, p. 1323.

62) Wavell to Percival, February 14 1942, quoted in Churchill, pp. 91-92; Allen, p. 180; Cablegram 81, Bowden to Evatt, January 26 1942, A 5954, Box 571 (AA ACT); Duff Cooper to Churchill, December 18,20 1941 enclosed in Tennant to Churchill January 6 1942, PREM 3, 161/1 (PRO).

63) Percival's Despatches, pp. 1324,1325.

64) Kirby, Singapore, p. 232.

65) Percival's Despatches, p. 1325.

66) Prime Minister to Wavell and Wavell to Prime Minister, February 14 1942, and Wavell to Percival, February 15 1942, quoted in Churchill, pp. 92,93.

67) Wavell to Percival, February 15 1942, quoted in Churchill, p. 94.

68) Wavell to Percival, February 13 1942, quoted in Churchill, p. 91.

69) Bennett, p. 197.

70) Percival's Despatches, p. 1325.

71) Interview by Tom Hall with Geoffrey Brooke, January 19 1981, tape transcription p. 4 (THP).

72) Wigmore, p. 378; Percival's Despatches, p. 1326; Wootten's Escape Report.

73) Statements and information from the Papers of William Roy Reynolds; Log of HMAS Goulburn, December 8 1941, SP 551 Bundle 238 (AA NSW); Memorandum, Krait AA 1981/155/1 Item 605/2D/1 (AA VIC); John Bostock, Australian Ships at War, Sydney 1975, pp. 178,186. Note: The claims by ex-crew members of HMAS Goulburn, that Kofuku Maru was captured by that ship and was the first enemy prize, are incorrect. The first prize ship was Fukuyu Maru, claimed and taken in tow by the senior ship of the 21st Minesweeping Flotilla, HMAS Maryborough, captained by Lt.-Commander G.L. Cant, RAN. Goulburn did not capture any enemy ships for the month of December 1941, although several of her crew were transferred as a prize crew to Shofuku Maru, captured by USS Esdall on Dec 11 — see Log, Bostock, p.86 and Papers on the capture and identity of Kofuku Maru (THP). It seems certain that the motor vessel rescuing Dutch nationals from Tandjung Pinang, mentioned in 2/19 Association, The Grim Glory, The History of the 2/19 Battalion AIF, Sydney 1975, p. 380, par. 4, is Kofuku Maru, captained by Bill Reynolds.

74) Interview by Tom Hall with Ron Morris, January 1981, tape transcript pp. 9-10 (THP).

Chapter 3: Escape from Singapore

The sources for the escape route section of this chapter rely heavily on the recorded, first-hand accounts of Ron Morris and Brian Passmore given during interviews with Tom Hall. As Brian Passmore had been ill and was suffering from a speech handicap, an edited version of his evidence has been placed in the Hall Papers. Where absolutely necessary, secondary sources have also been used. However, two of the texts, both by Richard Gough, which allegedly record some of the events portrayed in this chapter, often differ substantially in their factual content. Neither text gives any sources. For this reason, only eyewitness accounts or secondary sources that can be cross referenced have been used.

1) Lyon's description has been collated from information from Clive Lyon, Francis Moir-Byres, Bettina Reid, Ron Morris, army officers and men under his command and photographs (all THP). Lyon's eyes, which were most definitely a brown shade, have been described by those who did not know him well as being alternately very green or very blue. These statements have led to the conclusion that Lyon could not assume the disguise of a Malay. In fact, when deeply suntanned and dressed in a sarong, Lyon made a very convincing Malay.

2) Taped interview by Tom Hall with Clive Lyon, January 13 1981 (THP).

3) Ibid.
4) Reid's information, supported indirectly by Geoffrey Brooke in his draft of *Alarm Starboard*, p. 14 (THP).
5) Lyon interview: Taped interview with Geoffrey Brooke, January 1981, transciption side B, p. 2 (THP).
6) Moir-Byres information.
7) Ibid. For further information of the voyages of *Vinette*, see G.F. Moir-Byres, 'Malayan Sailing', October 7 1938 edition of *The Yachting World*, pp. 340-42 and Ivan Lyon, 'Malaya to Indo-China', November 11 1938 edition of the same publication, pp. 472-74, 504-06.
8) Ibid; G.F. Moir-Byres to Tom Hall, June 24 1981, pp. 1-2 (THP); For description of the Swimming Club see Jessie Elizabeth Simons, *In Japanese Hands*, Melbourne 1954, p. 3.
9) Moir-Byres information; Lyon's 'Malaya to Indo-China'.
10) Lyon interview.
11) Ibid.
12) Ibid; Lyon's letters to Gabrielle (LFP).
13) Lyon's letters.
14) Moir-Byres information.
15) Lyon's letters.
16) Moir-Byres information; Brooke, *Dunkirk*, p. 76; Gordon Grimsdale to General Lyon, February 2 1946 and Lt-Col. A. Warren to Brigadier Lyon, September 30 1946 (LFC).
17) Gough, *SOE*, pp. 131-33.
18) Gough, *Escape*, pp. 34-37; Gough, *SOE*, 147.
19) Brian Passmore to Geoffrey Rowley-Conwy, January 22 1974 (THP).
20) Gough, *Escape*, p. 35; Geoffrey Brooke, *Alarm Starboard*, Cambridge 1982, p. 162.
21) Gough, *SOE*, p. 28; Interview by Tom Hall with Ron Morris, MM, BEM, at Chester, England, 14 January 1981, tape transcription p. 1 (THP); BBC Documentary, *Arms and the Dragon*, on SOE operations; Leasor, p. 230.
22) *The Jungle is Neutral* is an autobiographical account of Chapman's exploits.
23) Morris interview, pp. 1-3; Gough, *Escape*, p. 37-38. Note: Although there was a food dump at Moro, on Sugibawah Island, where there were villagers to re-direct refugees, Lyon's HQ was at Durian, not Moro 'Island' as has been stated by several historians and writers.
24) Gough, *Escape*, p. 38,123.
25) Ibid, pp. 124-25.
26) Ibid, pp. 212,213,226; Brooke, *Alarm*, pp. 136,143,157.
27) Cyril Wild, 'Expedition to Singkep', *Blackwood's Magazine*, No. 1572, Vol. 260, October 1946, p. 218.
28) Citation for MBE awarded to William Roy Reynolds, Reynolds Family Papers and special file in THP; Gough, *Escape*, p. 132. Note: One of the 76 people rescued by Reynolds on his first trip to Pompong was Australian Dr Marjorie Lyon, whose epic story is recounted in Suzy Baldwin (ed), *Unsung Heroes and Heroines of Australia*, Melbourne 1988, pp. 247-48.
29) Skidmore, *Escape from the Rising Sun*, gives a first-hand account of the escape of Rowley-Conwy; Interview by Tom Hall with Geoffrey Rowley-Conwy, January 1981, tape transcription p. 3 (THP).
30) Gough, *Escape*, pp. 38-40; Gough, *SOE*, pp. 141-42; Brooke, *Dunkirk*, p. 76; Passmore to Rowley-Conwy, pp. 1-2. Note: Vanrennan is spelt in various sources as Vanrahen, Vanrehan and Vanrahan.
31) Gough, *SOE*, pp. 142-43; Brooke, *Dunkirk*, p. 76.
32) Gough, *SOE*, pp. 146-47; Passmore to Rowley-Conwy, p. 1; Summary of interview by Tom Hall with Brian Passmore, January 21 1981 (THP).
33) Passmore summary.
34) Gough, *SOE*, p. 147.
35) Passmore summary; Passmore to Rowley-Conwy, p. 1.
36) Gough, *SOE*, p. 169.
37) Passmore to Rowley-Conwy, p. 1; Passmore summary.
38) Gough, *SOE*, p. 161-65.
39) Gough, *Escape*, p. 160.
40) Morris interview, p. 3; Gough, *Escape*, p. 125.
41) Morris interview, pp. 4-5,9-10.
42) Rowley-Conwy interview, p. 5.
43) Morris interview, p. 10.
44) Brooke, *Dunkirk*, pp. 29,39,55-60; Gough, *Escape*, pp. 126-44.
45) Morris interview, p. 8. According to Gough, *Escape*, p. 154, the vehicle was an open tourer.

Chapter 4: The Incredible Voyage of the *Sederhana Djohanes*

This chapter has largely been constructed from an official account marked 'Secret'; from interviews conducted by Tom Hall in 1981 with Brian Passmore, Geoffrey Rowley-Conwy and Geoffrey Brooke; copies of correspondence between Rowley-Conwy and Passmore; and the original draft of Brooke's *Alarm Starboard*, (all THP); and from the eyewitness accounts of Rowley-Conwy and Brooke, which appear in Skidmore, pp. 93-197 and in Brooke, *Alarm Starboard* pp. 172-95, and *Dunkirk*, pp. 80-105.

1) Skidmore and Brooke, see introductory note; 2/19 Association, *The Grim Glory* Appendix 4 Escape Parties, p. 381; Gough, SOE, p. 176; Interview by Tom Hall with Ron Morris, January 14 1981, tape transcript pp. 9,11 (THP).

2) Skidmore and Brooke; Gough, SOE, p. 175.

3) Bennett, pp. 197-219; Kirby, *Singapore*, p. 246; Gough, SOE, p. 170; *The Grim Story*, pp. 379,382-3. Note: According to those who fought along the Kokoda Track, the term 'trail' was coined by an American journalist in Port Moresby and then popularised by the press — see Victor Austin (ed), *To Kokoda and Beyond. The Story of the 39th Battalion 1941-1943*, Melbourne 1988, p. 81.

4) Gibson, pp. 41,44.

5) Gough, SOE, p. 171; Skidmore and Brooke.

6) Gibson, p. 18; Gough, *Escape*, p. 152; Gough, SOE, pp. 176,177. It appears that the ship left on February 28 — see Colonel Warren's Diary, quoted in Gough, SOE, p. 171.

7) Gibson, pp. 7-8,34,40,70. Note: Brooke, *Dunkirk*, p. 220, explains the fate of Doris Lim, who was not executed by the Japanese as Gibson believed.

8) Ibid, pp. 41,14; Gough, *Escape*, pp. 163,172.

9) Gough, *Escape*, p. 148 and SOE, pp. 179-80.

10) Summary of interview by Tom Hall with Brian Passmore, January 21 1981 (THP); Brian Passmore to Geoffrey Rowley-Conwy, January 22 1974, p. 2 (THP).

11) Gough, SOE, pp. 174,179-80. Note: Colonel Dillon did not ever take over Warren's command. Warren remained behind to face ultimate capture, leaving Dillon free to escape from Sumatra in another prahu, *Setia Berganti*, purchased from the fishing village of Sasak, further up the coast. However, en route to Ceylon the vessel was captured by an enemy tanker. Warren survived three and a half years as a prisoner of war, see Gough, *Escape*, and Brooke, *Dunkirk*.

12) Skidmore and Brooke; Draft of Brooke, *Alarm Starboard*, pp. 9,10,14-15,38. (THP); Statement by A.R. North and accompanying note, quoted in Brooke, *Dunkirk*, pp. 109-110.

13) Brooke's draft, pp. 15-16.

14) Skidmore and Brooke.

15) Statement by Major W. Waller (THP).

16) Skidmore and Brooke; Passmore to Rowley-Conwy, p. 3.

17) Skidmore and Brooke.

18) Account, marked 'Secret'. *Sederhana Djohanes* Escape party, p. 3 (THP).

19) The accounts in Skidmore, Brooke and the evidence of Rowley-Conwy are a little confused on this point. The scenario presented in the current work seems to be the most likely.

20) Interview by Tom Hall with Geoffrey Rowley-Conwy, January 1981, tape transcription, p. 4 (THP).

21) Brooke's draft, p. 51; Skidmore and Brooke. Note: See note 11 above for details of Dillon's escape.

22) Skidmore and Brooke; Passmore to Rowley-Conwy, p. 3 and Rowley-Conwy to Passmore, Febraury 5 1974, p. 1 (THP), clears up the reason why the opinions were split.

23) Skidmore and Brooke.

24) Bettina Reid [the Department of Intelligence assistant/typist who worked on Operation Jaywick with Ivan Lyon], to Gabrielle Lyon, 13 December 1948 (LFC); Summary of information from Bettina Reid to Tom Hall, January 1989 (THP).

Chapter 5: Jaywick Begins

1) Reynolds's account of his experiences from Malaya to India; undated news-

clipping, 'How an Australian Tin Miner won the MBE; citation for Reynolds's MBE and Log of the *Suey Sin Fah*, March 12-14, 1942. All in papers of William Roy Reynolds.

2) *Suey* Log, March 13-17 1942.

3) Reynolds's Naval Commission, dated June 21 1918, Reynolds Papers.

4) *Suey* Log, March 17 1942.

5) Ibid, March 18-April 1 1942; Memorandum 'Krait' by DNI February 9 1943, p. 1, A 1981/155/1 Item 605/2D/1 (AA ACT).

6) Preliminary Papers for Jaywick, p. 4, A 3269, Item E 2 (AA ACT).

7) Statements by Margaret Reynolds to Tom Hall, May 1989 (THP).

8) Bernard Fergusson, *Wavell, Portrait of a Soldier*, London 1961, p. 75.

9) Ibid; Map showing zones of responsibility of SWPA and SEAC, A 3269/1 Item E 8 (AA ACT).

10) Lyon Family Papers.

11) Karl August Muggenthaler, *German Raiders of World War II*, London 1978, pp. 225-227; Jock Campbell to Brigadier Lyon, March 9 1942 (LFC).

12) Statement by Bettina Reid to Tom Hall (THP).

13) Interview by Tom Hall with Ron Morris, January 1981, tape transcript pp. 11-12 (THP).

14) Reynolds Papers.

15) Statement by Francis Moir-Byres to Tom Hall, recorded in a report dated November 1981 (THP).

16) Ivan Southall Notes, Formation of ISD pp. 1-5, AIB pp. 1-2, A 3269 Item Z1 (AA ACT); Statement by Samuel Warren Carey, July 1989, p. 2 (THP).

17) Southall, ISD pp. 1,4; Communications, SP 87/2574 [W10 SRD No 9], A 3269 (AA ACT); Article, 'Z Force Home For Sale', *Australian*, p. 7 October 28 1977; Carey's Statement, pp. 2,4,3,6.

18) D.M. Horner, *High Command*, Sydney 1982, p. 231; Carey's Statement, p.3; Summary of Field Operations, SRD, Australian War Memorial Private papers, 85/325 (AWM); A 3269 Item W9 (AA ACT). For examples of the use of secret numbers, see Rimau Papers A 3269 Item E 4 (AA ACT).

19) Jaywick's Preliminary Papers, pp. 1,2 and Statement of Expenditure; AIB

Activities, 1942-45, Press Release dated September 13 1945, p. 3 (THP); Governor Duggan's Secretary to Brigadier Lyon, March 8 1946, pp. 1-2 (LFC); Morris interview, p. 6.

20) Interview by Tom Hall with Alan Davidson, January 11 1981, tape transcript p. 9 (THP).

21) Ibid, pp. 2,9-12,14; Interview by Tom Hall with Donald Davidson's widow, Noel Wynyard, January 16 1981, tape transcript, pp. 1,10,13,14 (THP).

22) List of personnel who volunteered for training and Jaywick Log August 16-28 1942, p. 5, in A 3296 Item Jaywick Log E 2 (AA ACT).

23) Jaywick Preliminary Papers, pp. 1-3.

24) Ibid; photographs of the site (THP); Morris interview, p. 13.

25) Morris interview, p. 14.

26) Donald Davidson, X Training Camp including Notes and Observations on Training; Appendices I,II; Endurance Tests I,II,III; and Donald Davidson's Diary of Jaywick Log Training Camp September 6 1942-January 17 1943, all located in A 3269, Item Jaywick Log E 2 (AA ACT).

27) Statement by Ron Morris, recorded under A Short Story (THP).

28) Morris interview, pp. 6,26.

29) Memorandum 'Krait', pp. 1-2; Jaywick Report March 24 1943, pp.1-4, A3269 Item Jaywick E 2 (AA ACT).

30) Davidson's Diary; List of Personnel; Davidson's Notes.

31) Jaywick Preliminary Papers, p. 5; Staff Officer Naval Intelligence to Director Naval Intelligence February 2 1943, List of Personnel and Stores List Darwin, A 3269 (AA ACT). The latter confirms that eighteen men were to sail on *Krait*.

32) Davidson's Diary, January 13,15,16 1943.

33) Ibid, January 17 1943; Jaywick Preliminary Papers, p. 5. Monk is missing from the personnel list of February 2 1943 (see note 31 above). As there is no mention of him after he left camp for extensive dental treatment, it is assumed that he did not return. Kerr and Mackay were eliminated for reasons that can be established by reading Davidson's Diary.

34) Morris interview, pp. 5-6.

35 *Krait* Log January 18 1943, Appendix on *Krait* p. 1, A 3269 (AA ACT).

Chapter 6: Singapore Bound

1) Appendix on *Krait*, A3269 Jaywick E 2 (AA ACT) and information in statement by Bettina Reid (THP).

2) Jaywick Preliminary Plans p. 4, A 3269 (AA ACT); Admiralty Report of Operation Jaywick, XC/B 3197 ADM 1/16678 (PRO); Interior and exterior photographs of *Krait* (AWM, THP); Information of Donald Davidson, published in Noel Wynyard, *Winning Hazard*, London c. 1948; H.B. Manderson to Mrs F. Lyon, January 5 1948 (LFC); Memorandum 'Krait' by DNI February 9 1943 p. 1, A 1981/155/1 Item 605/2D/1 (AA ACT).

3) Ivan Lyon to Bettina Reid, January 31 1943, Reid Papers; Taped interview by Tom Hall with Ron Morris, January 14 1981, transcription p. 6, and Statements by Ron Morris, television documentary *This is Your Life* (THP); Appendix on *Krait*; Memorandum 'Krait', p. 4.

4) Muggenthaler, pp. 225-6,261; Gabrielle Lyon's Diary (LFP); Jock Campbell to Brigadier Francis Lyon, March 9 1943 (LFC); Appendix on *Krait* p. 3; Jaywick Report March 23 1943, A 3269 (AA ACT).

5) Memorandum 'Krait', p. 4; Motor Vessel *Krait* Defect List, Brisbane 6/2/42, A 1981/155/1 Item 605/2D/1 (AA ACT).

6) Wynyard, p. 44; Memorandum 'Jaywick Operation', Chief of Naval Staff to Flag Officer Commanding, Royal Indian navy, Calcutta, p. 1, A 1981/155/1 Item 605/2D/1 (AA ACT).

7) Papers of William Roy Reynolds.

8) Jaywick Report of April 8 1943, by B/B 187 [Jock Campbell], A 3269 (AA ACT); Memorandum 'Jaywick Operation', pp. 1-2.

9) Reynolds Papers.

10) Memo by R.E.M. Long, Motor Vessel *Krait*, A 3269 (AA ACT).

11) Correspondence between Mott, Blamey and others, Papers of Field Marshall Sir Thomas Blamey, 3 DRL 6643 Item 45/56.3 (AWM); Papers relating to Operation Scorpion, including letters by Carey, Blamey and Mott, AWM 3/6643 Item 2/58 (AWM); Statements by S. Warren Carey, July 1989 (THP).

12) Reynolds Papers; Lyon to Reid, mid 1943; Revised Jaywick Operation, July 3 1943, A 3269 (AA ACT).

13) Written and taped statements of Horrie Young to Tom Hall, August 14 1981 and Profile on Horrie Young (THP).

14) Profile on K.P. Cain and Morris Interview, tape 2 side 2, (not transcribed), both THP.

15) Papers of Edward Carse (THP).

16) Morris Interview, p. 28; Revised Jaywick Operation and List of Personnel; *Krait* Log, preliminary pages, Exhibition Document 154 (AWM).

17) Operation Python, SP 87/2574 [W 10 SRD 9], A 3269 (AA ACT); List of SRD Operations (THP); Lyon to Reid, July 20 1943.

18) Profile and Papers on Robert Page (THP); Morris Interview, pp. 17-18.

19) Revised Jaywick Operation; Profile on Andrew Crilley (THP); Crilley to Brigadier Lyon, February 12 1946 (LFC).

20) Davidson's *Krait* Log, reprinted in Wynyard, pp. 169-70.

21) Profile and Papers on Walter Falls (THP); Davidson's Jaywick Log Training Diary, A 3269 (AA ACT); Morris interview, pp 20-22.

22) Profile and Papers on Frederick Marsh (THP); Davidson's Jaywick Log; Morris interview, p. 25.

23) Profile and Papers on Andrew Huston (THP); Davidson's Jaywick Log; Morris interview, pp. 19-20.

24) Profile and Papers on Moystyn Berryman (THP); Davidson's Jaywick Log and Personnel Comments; Morris interview, p. 24.

25) Profile and Papers on Arthur Jones (THP); Davidson's Jaywick Log; Morris interview, p. 23.

26) Wynyard, pp. 46-7; Morris interview, pp. 18-19; Log of *Krait*, typescript p. 7.

27) Davidson's *Krait* Log, p. 175; Wynyard, p. 5; Diary of Horrie Young, p. 6 (THP); Morris's statement, *This is Your Life*.

28) Admiral Christie to Brigadier Francis

Lyon, April 11 1946; Thomas De Pledge to Brigadier Francis Lyon January 10 1946; Tom Argyle to Brigadier Francis Lyon February 17 1946. (All LFC).

29) Specifications of Stores to be freighted by air to Exmouth Gulf, and Report from Exmouth Gulf by Donald Davidson, September 1 1943, A 3269 Jaywick E 2 Copy 1 (AA ACT).

30) Signal from Admiral Royle to Radio Potshot, 301132 August 1943, A 3269 (AA ACT); Davidson's *Krait* Log, p. 175; Young's Diary, p. 1; *Krait* Log, p. 1; Morris interview, tape 2 side 2.

31) Davidson's *Krait* Log, p. 177; Young's Diary, p. 1; Jaywick Admiralty Report, Part II, p. 1; Wynyard, pp. 60-1.

32) Young's Diary, p. 1; Wynyard, pp. 52, 62-63; Morris's statement, *This is Your Life*; Statements by Horrie Young and Arthur Jones, television documentary *Snakes and Tigers* (THP); Statement by Reid.

33) Young's Diary, p. 2; Young's statement, *Snakes and Tigers*; photographs taken on *Sederhana Djohanes* and *Krait* (THP); Wynyard, pp. 63-64.

34) Young's Diary, p. 1; Wynyard, p. 62; H.B. Manderson to Brigadier Francis Lyon, January 5 1948 (LFC).

35) Taped statement by Horrie Young (not transcribed) and Statement in television documentary, *This is Your Life*, (THP); Wynyard, pp. 52-3.

36) Young's taped statement; Statements by Jones and Young, *Snakes and Tigers* and narrative, *This is Your Life*; Morris interview, tape 2 side 2; *Krait* Log, p. 34.

37) Berryman's statements, *Snakes and Tigers*, *This is Your Life*; Jaywick Admiralty Report, Part II, pp. .1-2; Operation Jaywick Report, July 21 1944, p. 1, A 3269 (AA ACT); *Krait* Log, pp. 6-7,19; Young's Diary, p. 1; Morris interview, tape 2 side 2. Note: Close scrutiny of *Krait's* Log and Navigational Log reveals the extent of the detour before Lombok Strait was found.

38) *Krait* Log, pp. 7-8.

39) Ibid, p. 13; Young's Diary, p. 2; Jones's statement, *This is Your Life*; Davidson's *Krait* Log, p. 180; Young's Diary, p. 2; *Krait* Log, pp. 13-15; Jaywick Admi-

ralty Report, Part II, p. 2; Collated Intelligence, p. 2, A 3269 (AA ACT).

40) Young's Diary, p. 3; *Krait* Log, pp. 16-17; Statement by K.P. Cain, television documentary *This is Your Life* (THP); Jaywick Admiralty Report, Part II, p. 2; Davidson's *Krait* Log, p. 180; Wynyard, p. 79; Record of Interview with K.P. Cain (THP).

41) Wynyard, pp. 80-81; Collated Intelligence, Appendix B; Jaywick Admiralty report, Part II, p. 2; *Krait* Log, pp. 16-18.

42) Davidson's *Krait* Log, p. 180; Revised Jaywick Operation; Jaywick Admiralty Report, Part II, p. 2; *Krait* Log, p. 16.

43) Cain's statement, *This is Your Life*; Jaywick Admiralty Report, Part II, p. 3; Davidson's *Krait* Log, p. 181; *Krait* Log, p. 17A; Wynyard, p. 87.

44) Jaywick Admiralty Report, Part I, p. 1 and Part II, pp. 3,6; Report, Confidential Operation X, p. 1, (copy in THP); Morris's statement, *Snakes and Tigers*.

Chapter 7: Mission Accomplished

1) Operation Jaywick Admiralty Report, Part II, p. 3, XC/B 3197 ADM 1/16678 (PRO); Report marked 'Confidential Operation X', p. 1 and Operation Jaywick Report, July 21 1944, p. 2, A 3269 Jaywick E2 (AA ACT); Information of Donald Davidson in Wynyard, pp. 90,96-97.

2) Jaywick Admiralty Report, Part I, p. 1 and Part II, p. 3; Operation Jaywick Report, October 25 1943, p. 1, A 3269 Jaywick E2 (AA ACT); Operation X, p. 1; July Jaywick Report, p. 2; Statement by Arthur Jones in television documentary, *Snakes and Tigers* (THP).

3) Operation X, p. 2; July Jaywick Report, p. 2; Wynyard, pp. 99-102.

4) Jaywick Admiralty Report, Part II, p. 4; Operation X, p. 2; July Jaywick Report, p. 2; Wynyard, pp. 102-110.

5) Ibid. Note: Wynyard states that the lights of Samboe Island were seen from Kapala Djernith. However, the raiders did not go via Kapala Djrenith as the plans were amended (see official reports and maps). It appears that Wynyard's statements were based on

notes from the original plan.

6) Revised Jaywick Operation and Lyon's hand drawn diagram, A 3269 Jaywick E 2 (AA ACT). Note: Hill 120, the original site chosen, is thirteen kilometres west of Dongas. The first mention of Dongas Island appears in Jaywick Admiralty Report, Part I, p. 1 and Part II, p. 2; July Jaywick Report, p. 2; Operation X, p. 2.

7) Jaywick Admiralty Report, Part II, p. 4; July Jaywick Report, p. 3; Wynyard, pp. 128-131; Collated Intelligence Reports, A 3269 Jaywick E2 P 2 (AA ACT); Observations of Lynette Silver and Tom Hall, June 1989 (THP).

8) Jones's statement, Snakes and Tigers; Jaywick Admiralty Report, Part I, p.1 and Part II, pp. 4-5; July Jaywick Report, p. 3; October Jaywick Report, p. 1; Wynyard, pp. 128-131.

9) Jaywick Admiralty Report, Part I, p. 1 and Part II, p. 5; July Jaywick Report, p. 3; October Jaywick Report, p. 1; Wynyard, pp. 128-131.

10) Statement by S. Warren Carey, July 1989, and Diary Of Horrie Young, p. 2 (THP); Jones's statement, Snakes and Tigers.

11) Jaywick Admiralty Report, Appendix A (Davidson's report); July Jaywick Report, p. 4; Collated Intelligence Report, Appendices A, B, C, D; Wynyard, pp. 135-42.

12) Jaywick Admiralty Report, Part II, p. 5; Operation X, p. 4 (Lyon's Report).

13) Jones's statements in Snakes and Tigers and in television documentary This is Your Life (THP); Jaywick Admiralty Report, Appendix B, (Report of Page and Jones); Report by Jones (THP).

14) Jaywick Admiralty Report, Part I, p. 1, Part II, p. 5 and Part IV, pp. 7,10-11; July Jaywick Report, p. 4; October Jaywick Report, p. 1; Operation X, p. 4; Jones's statements, Snakes and Tigers.

15) Young's Diary, p. 5; Wynyard, pp. 144-45.

16) Jaywick Admiralty Report, Part II, Appendix A and Part IV, pp. 11-12; July Jaywick Report, p. 5; Wynyard, pp. 145-55; Statement by K.P. Cain, This is Your Life.

17) Jaywick Admiralty Report, Part II, p. 6; Operation X, p. 5; Jones's statement, Snakes and Tigers. Note: Statements by

writers that Lyon's group was on the wrong beach (there is only one beach at Pompong) are erroneous.

18) Ibid.

19) Ibid; Jaywick Admiralty Report, Part IV, p. 12.

20) Wynyard, p. 127; Statements by K.P. Cain, M. Berryman and R. Grimwade, 1981-89 (THP).

21) Cain Statement, supported indirectly by Ron Morris in Interview with Tom Hall, January 14, 1981, p. 31 (THP).

22) Young's Diary, p. 5; Krait Log, transcription pp. 37-40, Exhibition Document 154 (AWM); Operation X, p. 5; July Jaywick Report, p. 5; Jaywick Admiralty Report, Part II, p. 6.

23) Statement by Ron Morris, television documentary This is Your Life. (This information is supported by a statement by E. Carse, Army newspaper, September 6 1967, p. 6, in Carse Papers. However, this version is a highly coloured account that contains grave factual errors and omissions and needs to be checked against other reports, logs and diaries.)

24) Krait Log, pp. 18-36; Young's Diary, pp. 3-5; Statement by Horris Young, television documentaries Snakes and Tigers and This is Your Life.

25) Krait Log, pp. 22,28,33-34; Carse's statement; Statement by R. Grimwade to Lynette Silver, 1989 (THP).

26) Young's Diary, p. 6.

27) Krait Log, p. 49; Original Krait Log, pp. 57-58 (consulted since the transcribed log had not been completed by AWM); Young's Diary, p. 6; July Jaywick Report, p. 5; Operation X, p. 5; Jaywick Admiralty Report, Part II, p. 7 and Part IV, pp. 1-2; Wynyard, pp. 163-65; Statements by Young, Berryman, Morris and Jones, Snakes and Tigers and This is Your Life; Hague Convention 1907, Spies, Article 29 and Law on Land, Article 23; Hague Rules 23, 24; Australian Manual of Military Law 1941, Chapter XIV, paragraph 144.

28) Krait Log, p. 49.

29) Original Krait Log, pp. 57-58; Lyon's Report to Reid (THP). That Carse considered himself to be in comand, see p. 60 of original log, which has his signature, followed by 'O.C. Krait'.

30) Carse's statement to the press; Morris interview, pp. 28-29. For examples of the esteem and affection in which Lyon was held see letters from Andrew Crilley, Paddy McDowell, Mrs Huston, Roma Page and the family of Rimau's A.G.P. Campbell (LFC).

31) Young's Diary, p. 6; Harry Manderson to Gabrielle Lyon, September 25 1947 (LFC).

32) Young's Diary, p. 7; Jaywick Admiralty Report, Part II, p. 7; Operation X, p. 5; Profile and Papers on Falls, statement by Norman Owen (THP).

33) Telegram, To India No. 214, November 2 1943, A 3269 Jaywick E 2 (AA ACT); Contents of intercepted signal, quoted in Lieutenant-Colonel A.G. Oldham to General T. Blamey, 7 February 1944, A 3269 Jaywick E2 P 4 (AA ACT).

34) Extract from Admiral Christie's diary quoted in Christie to Brigadier Lyon, April 11 1946 (LFC).

35) Signal 55 S/6 November 3 1943, Signal 29 AK 161 [Lyon] to Melbourne October 30 1943, Signal 58 from Melbourne to AK 126 [Page] October 31 1943, Signal 30 from AK 160 [Jock Campbell] to Melbourne November 1 1943, Signal 39 from Lugger Maintenance Section [a division of SRD] to Melbourne November 10 1943 — A 3269 Jaywick E2 (AA ACT); Morris interview, p. 37; Manderson to Lyon; Statement by R. Grimwade, Snakes and Tigers.

36) Letter from R. H. Hopper, Java, July 21 1946; Sworn statement of Chikari Ozaki, September 6 1948, MP 742/1 File 336-1-1939 Pt 1 (AA VIC); Information scratched on a doorjamb at Balikpapan, now in AWM; Statement by M. Reynolds, Papers of William Roy Reynolds.

37) Telegram, India 214.

38) Young's Diary, p. 3.

Chapter 8: Lyon's Tigers

1) Transcripts of the trial of Japanese war criminals, reprinted in Colin Sleeman and S.C. Silkin (ed), The Trial of Sumida Haruzo and Twenty Others. (The 'Double Tenth' Trial), London, 1951; Shinozaki Sionan, and his interview with Kim Yoon Lin, My Wartime Experiences in Singapore, Institute of Southeast Asian Studies, Singapore 1973. Note: According to Shinozaki, the death toll of Chinese by February 21 1942 was close to 17 000.

2) Memorandum on Operations by SOE in SEAC, September 20 1944, A 3269, Item N 1 Pt 1 (AA ACT).

3) Statement on political situation by Major-General Finlay (THP); A.J. Wilson to General Northcott, May 20 1944, pp. 1-2, A 3269/1 Item H 14 (AA ACT).

4) Jaywick and Preliminary Plans, A 3269 Item E 2 Copy 1 (AA ACT); Finlay on Politics.

5) Memorandum on Operations Hornbill Papers, A 3869, Item E 4. (Note: the memorandum dated 1.5.43 is obviously 1944 as the SBs were not invented until June 1943); Specifications for Country Craft (THP).

6) Lieutenant-Colonel Chapman-Walker, Signal No. 55 S/6, November 3 1942, A 3269 Jaywick E 2 Copy 1; Memorandum on SOE Operations; MacArthur to the Chiefs-of-Staff, Correspondence AIB, A 3269 Item N1 Pt 1 (AA ACT); Chapman-Walker, November 3 1943.

7) Memorandum on SOE Operations; Hornbill Operations May 30 1944, Hornbill Papers; Major Walter W. Chapman's Technical Report on Operation Rimau April 4 1945, A 3269, Item E 4 (AA ACT); Statements of Walter Chapman, quoted in Brian Connell, Return of the Tiger, London 1965.

8) A. Cecil Hampshire, The Secret Navies, London 1978, pp. 124-25, 149-52; Sir Robert H. Davis, Deep Diving and Submarine Operations, London n.d., pp. 316-19.

9) Statements by Chapman; Statements by Bettina Reid (THP).

10) Chapman's Technical Report, pp. 2-3; Commander Hubert Marsham to Captain 8th Submarine Flotilla September 29 1944, p. 21 and Captain Shadwell to Commander-in-Chief, Eastern Fleet, October 30 1944, p. 3 XC/B 3197 ADM 199/513 (PRO); Memo M 0583292/44, January 6 1944, p. 1, XC/B 3197 ADM 199/513 (PRO).

11) Shadwell to C-in-C, p. 3; Chapman's Technical Report, pp. 3-4.
12) Papers of the Ross family (THP); Diary of H.R. Oppenheim [one of Ross's fellow escapees], British Association of Malayasia Collection, Royal Commonwealth Society, London.
13) Memorandum on SOE Operations, p. 1; Lieutenant-Colonel Chapman-Walker Director SRD to Colonel Roberts Controller AIB, September 19 1944, p. 1, A 3269/1; Item H 13 (AA ACT); Papers related to Jaywick Decorations, XC/B 3197 ADM 1/16678 (PRO); Lord Selbourne to Brigadier Lyon, February 11 1946 (LFC).
14) Jaywick Decorations; Recommendations of Chapman-Walker to General Blamey and Sir Guy Royle, A 3269, Jaywick E 1 Copy 1 (AA ACT).
15) Mrs F. Lyon to Bettina Reid December 29 1945 (Reid Papers); Eric Gannon to Brigadier Lyon, December 7 1945, Mrs F. Lyon to Bettina Reid and Red Cross Message to Herve Gilis (LFC).
16) Hornbill Operations; Chapman's Technical Report, p. 1.
17) Document marked 'Secret', June 15 1944, Hornbill Operations; Memorandum on SOE Operations; Chapman's Technical Report, pp. 1-2; memo by NID (Q) dated December 24 1944, XC/B3197 ADM 199/153 (PRO); Chapman-Walker to Roberts, p. 2.
18) Memo on SOE Operations; Security, Hornbill Operations; Kookaburra Papers, A 3269/1 Item E 8; Plan Rimau, Folio 1, p. 1 A 3269 Item E 4. (AA ACT).
19) Minutes of Final Planning Conference, July 7 1944, A 3269 Item E 4 (AA ACT). Note: Ivan Lyon's secret number was AK 161, the number which appears in these documents, not AK 231 as listed on cards in AWM files. AK 161 is the number assigned to him for Jaywick (see signals) and Rimau (see operational plan and minutes).
20) Minutes of Final Conference.
21) Ibid; Ingleton's Military Papers (THP); Letter by Major-General Sir Humphrey Tollemache CO Small Operations Group, April 24 1977 (THP).
22) Reid statements.
23) Ivan Southall Notes, SRD Organisation, A 3269 Item Z1 (AA ACT); Telegram 99 July 7 1944, A 3269, Item E 4 (AA ACT); Statements by J.C. Williams (THP).
24) Army Record of Robert Page; Statement by Roma Page to Tom Hall 1977 (THP); Donald Davidson to Andrew Huston, April 27 1944 (THP).
25) Plan Rimau, Operational Plan, Folio 1 and Appendix 1.
26) Interview by Tom Hall with Harry Browne, August 7 1981 (THP); Davis, p. 317; Southall, Western Base, p. 1; Williams's statement; Plan Rimau, Folio 5, p. 2; Chapman's statements.
27) Southall, Training, p. 5; Hampshire, pp. 180-81; Browne interview; Williams's statement. That Ross and Riggs travelled together is confirmed by photograph showing Ross, Riggs and Lieutenant Richard Cox (ex *Sederhana Djohanes*) in San Francisco in July 1944 and Ross's letter to his parents July 1944, Ross Papers.
28) Browne interview.
29) Statement by N. Voigt (THP); Notes on conversation between Tom Hall and Mrs Bruno Reymond (THP).
30) Rimau Plans, Folio 5, p. 2; Williams's statement; Southall, Western Base, p. 2; Statement by Lloyd Victor Teakle (THP).
31) Commander Marsham, HM Submarine *Porpoise*, to Senior Officer (Submarines) Eastern Fleet, August 18 1944 and Marsham to Captain (S) Eighth Submarine Flotilla [Shadwell] September 29 1944 XC/B 3197 ADM 199/513 (PRO); Chapman's statements.
32) Marsham to Shadwell, September 29 1944; Chapman's Technical Report, pp. 3-5 and annexure, Comments on Individual Stores, p. 1.
33) Marsham to Shadwell September 29 1944.
34) Ibid; Chapman's stores comments, p. 1; Profile and papers on Alfred Warren (THP).
35) Plan Rimau; Colonel Roberts Controller AIB to Colonel Chapman-Walker Director SRD August 22 1944, A 3269/1 Item H 13 (AA ACT).
36) Plan Rimau, Preface and Folio 1.

37) Ibid, Q Plan and all Stores Lists.
38) Ibid, Folio 4; Report of Tom Hall's interview with Mary Lennox (nee Ellis), October 25 1981 (THP).
39) Browne interview.
40) Profile on Albert Leslie Sargent, Sargent Papers and General Personnel File (THP).
41) Profile on Jeffrey Willersdorf, Willersdorf Papers and General Personnel File (THP).
42) Profile on A.G.P. Campbell, Campbell Papers and General Personnel File (THP); A.E.G. Campbell to Brigadier F. Lyon and Mrs Lyon, July 24 1946 (LFC); Statement by Lady Campbell in television documentary, Snakes and Tigers (THP).
43) Profile on Roland Fletcher, Fletcher Papers and General Personnel File (THP); Richard and Helen Walker, Curtin's Cowboys, Australia's Secret Bush Commandos, Sydney 1986.
44) Profile on Jack T. Hardy and General Personnel File (THP).
45) Profile on Hugo Pace, Pace Papers, General Personnel File and information of Teakle (THP).
46) Report on Operation Rimau, Special Operations Australia — Organisation, A 3270, Vol. 1 (AA ACT). Papers of Bruno Reymond (THP); Williams's statement.
47) Profile on Colin Cameron, Cameron Papers and General Personnel File (THP).
48) Hornbill Operation, May 30 1944; Profile on David Gooley, Gooley Papers and General Personnel File (THP).
49) General Personnel File (THP); Article in Western Australian newspaper, Weekend Mail, June 25 1960, p. 10.
50) Profile on Clair Stewart, Stewart Papers and General Personnel File (THP).
51) Plan Rimau — Personnel Selected, Folio 5 and Conducting Officer's Report.
52) Profile on Walter Carey, Papers of Walter and Sam Carey (THP); The Grim Glory, pp. 109-10, and Appendix 9, pp. 824-26; Williams's statement; Browne interview.
53) Statements by Commander Marsham, report dated December 12 1981, p. 10

and Report of Interview by Tom Hall with Commander Hubert Marsham, January 1981, p. 1 (THP); Southall, Naval Directorate, p. 1; Weekend Mail June 25 1960, p. 10; Tom Argyle to Brigadier Lyon, February 17 1946 (LFC).
54) Marsham to C-in-C Eastern Fleet; Weekend Mail; Lennox interview report; Commando Memorial Trust Report, November 2 1981 and Report of interview with the family of Clair Stewart, October 1981, p. 4 (THP); SRD Papers on Breach of Security, A 3269 Item V 7 (AA ACT); Special Operations Activities Organisation, A 3770 Vol. 1 (AA ACT).
55) Chapman's Technical Report, pp. 8-11.
56) Hiroyuki Furuta, 'The Harimu Party Sleeps Here', originally published in a Japanese magazine, Bungei Shinju February 1957 (THP), original Foreign Office translation (O) pp. 10-11, second version corrected by Furuta (C), p. 16 (THP) Note: Some of the facts altered by Furuta for dramatic effect in his original version, which was written as an entry in a competition, were later corrected by him. The versions are not identical in content, with one version often containing facts not included in the other. Browne interview; Grimwade statements, Snakes and Tigers.
57) Plan Rimau, F.S.O. No. 1, September 9 1944; Statements by Marsham Report, p. 10; Interview by Tom Hall with Commander Hubert Marsham and Vice-Admiral Sir Hugh Mackenzie, January 23 1981, statement by Marsham, p. 1 (THP).
58) Chapman's Technical Report, p. 10; Mary Lennox to Tom Hall, June 28 1982 and Statements by Captain A.D. Stevenson to Tom Hall, 1978 (THP); Teakle's statement. Note: A Dutch banknote, later sent to Lyon's son, was also signed — see George Astley to Gabrielle Lyon, December 14 1944 (LFC).
59) Monthly Report of HM Submarine Porpoise, entry for September 11 1944, ADM 173/18592 (PRO).
60) Marsham to Shadwell, September 29 1944, p. 2.

Chapter 9: A Spot of Pirating

1) SRD Intelligence Branch, Rimau Project, Lieutenant-Commander Donald Davidson's Diary, September 11 - September 30 1944, p. 1, Sketch 1 Appendix B, A 3269 Item E 4 (AA ACT); HM Submarine *Porpoise*, Commander Marsham's Report of the 28th War Patrol, October 15 1944 and Captain Shadwell's Report October 30 1944, XC/B 3197 ADM 199/513 (PRO); Monthly Log of HM Submarine *Porpoise*, September 1944, ADM 173/18591 (PRO).

2) Sworn statements of Hirai March 17 1948, Takahashi May 20 1948, Moriyama May 24 1948, Uchida June 15 1948, Hamada September 3 1948, Ozaki September 13 1948, Yamashita December 28 1948, Bunyu May 31 and June 21 1949, Hirokawa June 28 1949, Yamashita July 12 1949; Report by Deputy Judge Advocate W.E. Van Beek, June 19 1947; Report on Interrogation of Uchida June 15 1948; 2 Australian War Crimes Section SEC SCAP, Missing personnel SWPA captured by Japanese and presumed dead, November 12 1948, p. 3 and Appendix A Item 16; Signal A 140, File 153/2, May 18 1949. MP 742/1 File No, 336/1/1939 Pt 1 (AA VIC).

3) In 1949, Australian investigators established that Reynolds had been executed in August 1944, information which was never passed on to his family. However, the entire story was not established until the many fragments of evidence were pieced together during the researching and writing of this book.

4) Marsham's Report, p. 8; Davidson's Diary, pp. 1-2 and Sketch 2, Appendix B; H.B. Manderson to Brigadier F. Lyon, January 5 1948 (LFC).

5) Shadwell's Report, p. 1; Marsham's Report, pp. 4,9 and Appendix 1, p. 4; Report of interview by Tom Hall with Commander Hubert Marsham, January 20 1981, pp. 1-2 (THP); *Porpoise* Log, September 23 1944; Technical Report by Major W.W. Chapman on First Sortie of Operation Rimau in HM Submarine *Porpoise*, December 19 1944, p. 1 A 3269 Item E 4 (AA ACT); Davidson's Diary, p. 2; Chapman's Report, p. 1.

6) Appendix 1, p. 4; Shadwell's Report, p. 2; Marsham's Report, pp. 4,8; Davidson's Diary, p. 5.

7) Appendix 1, p. 4; Chapman's Report, p. 1; Davidson's Diary, p. 3.

8) Appendix 1, p. 4; Davidson's Diary, p. 2.

9) Davidson's Diary, pp. 2, 4 and accompanying map of Merapas Island, with annotations; Photographs, slides and movie footage of Merapas Island, taken by Tom Hall, September 1981 and May 1989 (THP).

10) Davidson's Diary, p. 3; Appendix 1, p. 5; Chapman's Report, pp. 2,3.

11) Chapman's Report, p. 2; Appendix 1, pp. 3,5.

12) Chapman's Report, p. 3; Appendix 1, pp. 5,10; Captain Shadwell to Commander-in-Chief Eastern Fleet, October 30 1944, p. 4 XC/B 3197 ADM 199/513 (PRO).

13) Appendix 1, p. 5; Chapman's Report, p. 3; Davidson's Diary, p. 3; Note: Marsham states that ninety minutes were allowed, Davidson states a total of two hours. The latter is considered to be more correct.

14) Davidson's Diary, pp. 3-5. Although fourteen days at eight kilometres a day was the allowed time, it was expected that strong canoeists such as Davidson would cover the distance in much less time, probably as little as five days. Therefore the raiders were expected back between October 15 and October 24.

15) Interview by Tom Hall with Ron Croton, January 1982 (THP); Plan Rimau, Personnel List and Signal No. 99, Fraser Commando School, July 7 1944, and Report of Attempted Pick Up of Rimau Party by Major W.W. Chapman, December 12 1944, pp. 1-3, all in A 3269 Item E 4 (AA ACT); Davidson's Diary, p. 3. Note: While unloading the stores, the submarine was in constant view of the working party.

16) Davidson's Diary, p. 3; Chapman's Report, p. 3.

17) Appendix 1, pp. 5,10.

18) Ibid, p. 5; Davidson's Diary, p. 3;

Chapman's Report, p. 3-4; Appendix 1, p. 3.

19) Davidson's Diary, p. 3; Plan Rimau, Folio 2, Table A (Amended Stores Lists).

20) Appendix 1, pp. 5,6; SWPA Distances map, A 3269/1 Item E 8 (AA ACT); Chapman's Report, p. 4.

21) Appendix 1, p. 6; Davidson's Diary, pp. 5,6. Note: Davidson's entries for September 26 and 27 have the wrong dates. September 26 should read September 25, September 26 should be September 27 — see Marsham's entries recorded in Appendix 1, pp. 6,7 and Chapman's Report, p. 4.

22) Ibid.

23) Ibid; Report on Interrogation of Mustika Crew by G.C. Ripley, October 12 1944, A 3269 Item E 4 (AA ACT). Note: Pulau Laout has been spelled 'Laut' (modern spelling) to avoid confusion with the island of the same name on which Reynolds was captured, which lay much further to the south. For identification of this Pulau Laout (Laut), see Appendix 1, p. 7.

24) Appendix 1, p. 7.

25) Report of Hall's interview with Marsham, p. 1 and additional comments, p. 4; Taped interview by Tom Hall with Commander Hubert Marsham and Vice-Admiral Sir Hugh Mackenzie, January 23 1981, Statement by Marsham, transcription p. 1 (THP); Chapman's Report, p. 5; Appendix 1, p. 7; Log of Krait, p. 15, Exhibition Document 154 (AWM); Davidson's sketches, Chapman's photographs, and observations of Indonesian craft still being made in the traditional way today.

26) Davidson's Diary, p. 6; Appendix 1, p. 7; Krait Log, p. 10; Ripley's Interrogation; Report by Lieutenant Ross on Junk Mustika, Rimau Phase 2, September 28 1944, A 3269 Item E 4 (AA ACT).

27) Ross's Report; Appendix 1, p. 9.

28) Chapman's Report, p. 5; Appendix 1, pp. 7-10; Davidson's Diary, p. 6.

29) Ibid; Report of Marsham interview, p.4.

30) Davidson's Diary, p. 7; Chapman's Report, pp. 6-7; Appendix 1, p. 9.

31) Chapman's Report, pp. 7-8; Appendix 1, p. 9.

32) Statement of Mohamed Juni, Tuesday January 9 1945 at Richmond NSW, Rimau Report Copy II, A 3269, Item E 4 (AA ACT); Chapman's Report, p. 8.

33) Chapman's Report, p. 7; Plan Rimau, Folio 1.

34) Statement by Marsham, Additional notes to Marsham/Mackenzie Interview; Report of Marsham interview, p. 2; Appendix 1, p. 9. Note: Marsham denies that the cheering, as asserted by Chapman, was particularly loud, and states that only he and the men on watch were present to bid them farewell.

Chapter 10: Disaster

The events in this chapter have been reconstructed from eyewitness accounts of Indonesians and from the written reports of the Japanese. As Japanese versions are sometimes telescoped in time and confused by hearsay, they have been extensively cross checked with other available sources. When Japanese versions do not agree with other proven evidence or are obviously inaccurate (dates, time, numbers, etc), they have been disregarded. The process of elimination in order to deduce which Rimau member was present at any particular scene has been made possible by the knowledge of their roles, their place and time of death, their evidence at the Military Court Proceedings and the operational plan.

1) Interrogation of Interpreter Furuta, October 21 1945 Appendix A, ADM 1/18596-3231 (PRO); Translations of Proceedings of Military Court of 7th Area Army, p. 13-2, MP 742 File 336-1-755 (AA VIC); (For distances, see Maps of Bintan and Lingga Archipelago, (THP).

2) Furuta, Harimu (C). See also note 56, chapter 8 of the current work.

3) The three people who remained on Merapas with Carey were Warren, who was named and who confirmed this fact at the Military Court, and two others, see Furuta Interrogation Appendix A; Court Proceedings, p. 13-2; Full Account of Australian Special Operations Operational Party, Judicial

Department of 7th Area Army, p. 31-12, MP 742 File 334-1-755 (AA VIC). These men were not present at the court, were not on *Mustika* and were not with the seven men (six of whom were positively identified), who took part in the raid. The choice is narrowed to Willersdorf, Marsh, Huston, Craft and Pace. To leave Willersdorf, an operative and a warrant officer, on Merapas would have meant that the island group was top heavy with officers, while Marsh, the Jaywick reserve, and Huston, a Jaywick raider, had localised knowledge that Lyon could not afford to waste. Craft was available for Merapas, as it is known that fellow signaller Stewart was captured in the Riouw Straits after the raid. The only other person available to complete the trio was Hugo Pace, who was an excellent choice as he was not an officer and was an experienced soldier.

4) Report of interview by Tom Hall with Mary Lennox, (nee Ellis), who found Lyon's copy of the book among his papers after he had left on the operation, October 1981 (THP).

5) Japanese I Staff Message No. 211 January 9 1945, J 16625 C Serial No. 23577 (USNA).

6) Kempei Tai Documents, translation p. 8, which state that a large amount of equipment was found on Pompong Island (THP); Statement of Mohamed Juni Tuesday January 9 1945 at Richmond NSW, Rimau Report Copy II, A 3269 Item E 4 (AA ACT); Statement by Furuta 1957 Document I (THP); Furuta, *Harimu*, original (O), p. 6, corrected (C), p. 10; Interrogation of Interpreter Furuta October 21 1945 Appendix E, p. 1, ADM 1/18596-3231 (PRO); Judicial Department Account, p. 31-7; Kagayaki Staff 2 Signal 227, January 25 1945, Box 38 J 21138A,B,C, Serial No. SR 29841/2 and 3 (USNA). Note: The bauxite mines which Ingleton sketched are located on the SE end of Bintan Island and can be seen only from the inner channel — see aerial photographs taken by Tom hall 1981 (THP).

7) Military Court translation, p. 13-3; Judicial Department account, pp. 31-6,7,11,14.

8) Juni's statement; Furuta, *Harimu*, p. 6 (O), p. 9 (C); Judicial Department account, p. 31-6.

9) Harry Manderson to Gabrielle Lyon, September 25 1947 (LFC). For indication of the extent of the intelligence, which was used by the High Command to plan the retaking of Malaya, see Jaywick Operation, Collated Intelligence XC/B3197 ADM 1/16678 (PRO).

10) Judicial Department account, pp. 31-10,11,12; Military Court translation p. 13-3; Furuta, *Harimu*, p. 7 (C).

11) It appears that no notebooks were found on Lyon's body. His reports were always succinct and exceptionally brief (see Jaywick report and report on Endurance Test, Jaywick Papers). It was an aspect of his work particularly noted by SRD's Harry Manderson in his letter to Gabrielle Lyon 25 September 1947. By comparison, Davidson recorded everything, making notes that were so exhaustive that his wife was able to write a book about Jaywick using this material.

12) Military Court translation p. 13-3; Tom Hall's aerial photographs.

13) For description of Davidson see Judicial Department account, p. 31-7. For description of Lyon (whom Furuta, who had seen neither man, incorrectly identified as Davidson, who did not smoke), see Furuta's Interrogation Appendix E.

14) Military Court translation, p. 13-3; Furuta, *Harimu* p. 3 (O), p. 4 (C).

15) Judicial Department account, p. 31-13.

16) Statement by Karta to Lieutenant R.W. Lowry in 'A Report on Exercise Jaywick', p. 18, *Army Journal* 1971; Report by Major W.W. Chapman, Attempted Pick Up of Rimau Party by HMS *Tantulus*, p. 5, and analysis of Pick Up Sortie, A 3269 Item E 4 (AA ACT); Report by Tom Hall on his 1981 visit to Merapas (THP).

17 Furuta Interrogation Appendix E; Furuta, *Harimu* p. 7 (O), p. 10 (C); SRD Intelligence Report and D/Plans II, A 3269, Items E 4 and M I (AA ACT).

18) Statements by Major-General Finlay (CO Z Special Unit and GSOI SRD)

on contingency plan, May 1981 (THP).

19) Plan Rimau, hand-written unsigned addendum, A 3269, Item E 4 (AA ACT). The officer at Subar went on the raid. The three officers who took part in the raid were all killed — Lyon, Davidson and Ross. As Lyon and Davidson were on *Mustika* at Kasu (both named at court martial), they were not on Subar. Neither were any of the officers at the court martial, since all admitted to being at Kasu, and Reymond must have been on *Mustika* at all times, being the navigator. Ross was therefore the only possible candidate. An operative, he had the added advantage of being able to speak Malay and had been in Singapore before the war. His companion, by necessity, also went on the raid. As all other ranks at the court martial, said they were at Kasu, the 'other rank' on Subar must have been either Huston, Campbell, Cameron, Warne or Marsh. Cameron's job, charging up the SB batteries and ensuring that they were in working order, precludes the possibility of his being on Subar, and in any case it would have been pointless to send a non-operative as an observer. The best person to send of the remaining four would have been the one who knew Subar and Singapore Harbour. Therefore Huston would almost certainly have been the man to accompany Ross on this very important reconnaissance.

20) Furuta, *Harimu*, p. 7 (O), p. 10 (C). As Kasu is off the main shipping channels, the ships mentioned by Page must have been in the Phillip Channel.

21) Photographs and observations made at Kasu Island by the author and Tom Hall June 1989 and additional statements made by Sidek Bin Safar 1981 (THP).

22) Interview by the author and Tom Hall with eyewitnesses Arafin Bin Akup and Mahat Kunil, June 1989 (THP).

23) Furuta, *Harimu*, p. 7 (O), pp. 10-11 (C).

24) Arafin and Mahat interview; Interview by Tom Hall with Sidek Bin Safar 1981 (THP); Furuta's Interrogation Appendix A. Note: The Japanese throughout the occupied territories worked on Tokyo time. Therefore 5 pm was really

4 pm at Kasu, the time given by the local villagers.

25) Ibid; Military Court translation, p. 13-3. Note: Sidek Bin Safar is incorrectly named in this document as Bin Shiapell. No one of that name ever existed at Kasu and the only people involved in the Kasu incident are those named by eyewitnesses Sidek, Arafin and Mahat. On p. 31-3 of the Judicial Department account, this person is correctly identified as Ende (a corruption of Sidek) Bin Safar.

26) Arafi and Mahat interview; Sidek's additional statements; Report by Colonel L.F.G. Pritchard on Missing Personnel October 13 1945, ADM 1/ 18596- 3231 (PRO). Note: The term 'northern Indians' refers to Bengali Indians who made up part of the indigenous people of Malaya and Indonesia.

27) Arafi and Mahat interview; Sidek interview; Furuta's Interrogation Appendix A; Military Court translation p. 13-3; Furuta, *Harimu*, p. 7 (O), p. 11 (C).

28) Judicial Department account, p. 31-8; Arafi and Mahat interview.

29) Arafi and Mahat interview; Sidek interview and statement; Judicial Department account, p. 31-9. Whether the Hei Ho shouted in Malay or English is not clear from the statements of Sidek. As the Chinese man spoke English and the others Malay it may well be that words in either language may have been shouted. Major Ingleton stated that he heard them yell out 'something'. Whether it was unintelligible to him because he did not hear properly or because it was in Malay was not disclosed. Arafi and Mahat state that they heard nothing shouted at all, but with the rain starting, they may have been out of earshot.

30) Kempei Tai documents, translation p. 2. There is no identification of the person other than this. Speculation suggests that it may have been English architect Major Ingleton, who was untrained for SRD work. Although of an affable nature, he made a very poor impression on Commander Hubert Marsham who described him as a 'buffoon'. While Ingleton's statement

in the Judicial Accounts indicates that someone else fired first, it does not seem possible that any of the soldiers trained for the mission would have opened fire without being ordered to do so.

31) Arafi and Mahat interview; Sidek interview. Although the Military Court translation states that four Hei Ho were killed, there were three, a number confirmed by eyewitnesses Sidek, Arafi and Mahat and also Japanese signals Kagayaki Staff 2 Signal 227 and Oka Staff Number 2 Message 799, October 21 1944, Box 45, J 250251 A/B and D, Serial No. SR 35040-42 (USNA).

32) Arafi and Mahat interview.

33) Judicial Department account, p. 31-9; Furuta's Interrogation Appendix A; Military Court translation, p. 13-3.

34) Arafi and Mahat interview; Pritchard's report. Note: The statement that thirteen men were in six folboats is incorrect and is perhaps a typographical error. As there were four men at Merapas, two on Subar and four with Lyon — a total of eleven — twelve must have left Mustika in the first group, consisting of six folboats with two men in each. Later, in reconstructing the events in Oka Staff Message Number 2, the Japanese state that the escape from the junk was in nine folboats. This was correct from their viewpoint — the six seen by Arafi and Mahat and also mentioned by Pritchard and the three recovered in the Riouw Archipelago between October 17-18. Later, when the Japanese can account for eleven folboats, the number is raised.

35) Judicial Department account, p. 31-9. Although, according to the Judicial Department account, only the Japanese National Flag was produced in court, Furuta states on pp. 9-10 of the corrected Harimu that he examined two flags, one a national flag and one the Administration Flag, both made in Australia. Neither flag was flying at the time of the Kasu raid.

36) Arafi and Mahat interview; Sidek's interview and additional statement; Kagayaki Staff 2 Signal No. 227. Note: This signal relays the information that a large amount of material and supplies

were recovered, along with a 'rubber raft' and folboat on October 18 1944, the date that the Japanese found the bodies of Campbell and Davidson on Tapai, see Statement by Major Fugita CO Garrison Bintang [sic] Island MP 742 Defence, Army, Correspondence Files, Multiple Number Series, 1943-1951 (AA VIC).

37) Japanese signal, 48 Division [Timor] Staff Message No. 4024 February 3 1945, A 3269 (AA ACT), states that 'Lt Col Lyon and six men in September 44 penetrated to the vicinity of Singapore and succeeded sinking three ships at anchor in the harbour'. The five men whom Sidek Bin Safar observed leaving Mustika shortly before it sank and the two on Subar formed the raiding party. Lyon and Ross were killed on Soreh; Davidson and Campbell were found dead on Tapai; Stewart was captured; Warne, who did not succeed in his mission owing to the tide, escaped to Merapas with Huston who, with Ross, had been collected from Subar. Although this signal states September of 1944 instead of October, there is no question that the Japanese have confused Rimau with the Jaywick raid of September 1943, which used six men, blew up seven ships and was conducted while Lyon was a major.

38) Pritchard's Report; Sidek interview; Arafi and Mahat interview; Judicial Department account, p. 31-9; Furuta's Interrogation Appendix A; Military Court translation, p. 13-3.

39) Opinion of A.H. Taylor, N.I.D.(Q) for DNI, in minute of February 19 1945, XC/B 3197 ADM 199/511 (PRO).

40) Judicial Department account, p. 31-11; Furuta, Harimu, p. 13 (C).

41) There was a total of eleven folboats. With two folboats at Merapas there were nine left on Mustika plus one recce kayak at Subar (see Stores List, September 8 1944, Plan Rimau Folio 2, A 3269 Item E 4 AA ACT). Six were used by the first group, leaving three plus the recce kayak for the remaining seven men. A rubber raft was found by the Japanese on October 18 at Tapai (see Fugita's statement). As a five-man rubber raft (see stores list)

is incapable of carrying five men, Bren guns, three folboats, stores, ordinance material, limpets and other supplies, the folding engineer's boat, described by Sidek as being 'launched' off *Mustika* must have been used for the Kasu to Soreh leg.

42) Japanese 48 Division Staff Message No. 4024; Japanese Oka Staff 2 signal No. 62, January 25 1945, Box 39 J 21468 A to H serial numbers SR 30295-30298 (USNA); Report on Interrogation of Shizuo Tachino, December 28-31 1947 by Captain J. Sylvester, p. 2, MP 742/1 File 336/ 1/1939 Pt 1 (AA VIC). Note: The Admiralty charts for Singapore area list three wrecks, off Samboe and in the Singapore Roads, for which the Port of Singapore Authority is unable to account. Documentation from — the Japanese Research Division, US Forces August 29 1956; the Information Room, Historical Section, Admiralty, Royal Navy, August 3 1956 and the Cabinet Office, UK Foreign Office Historical Section, August 1 1956, (all THP) reveal that none of these authorities is able to offer any explanation as to why these ships were sunk.

43) Sidek's statement; Statement by eye-witness Private Roy Bliss, *The Grim Glory*, pp. 746-47.

44) Oka Staff 2 Signal No. 62. Note: Dongas was the only island known to them from which they could safely observe the harbour. Since the rubber raft and a great deal of material were later found at Tapai, the raft must have been taken from Subar and hidden during the day, probably at Dongas. The engineer's boat was most likely sunk at Subar as it had served its purpose.

45) Sidek's statement.

46) Ibid; Sidek interview.

47) No message was received until Friday October 13. In *Harimu*, Furuta is adamant that headquarters was informed on a Monday, three days after the news had been received. The actual dates are confused, but he is certain about the day of the week.

48) Arafi and Mahat interview. In his Jaywick report, Lyon noted that there was intense activity at Samboe day and night and from the sounds of machinery and use of arc lamps he was certain that there was a shipbuilding and repair yard on the island. See Operation Jaywick Collated Intelligence Report p. 6, Narrative Account p. 4, XC/B 3197 ADM 1/16678 (PRO). For this reason, Samboe was one of the targets for Operation Rimau.

49) Arafi and Mahat interview.

50) Sidek statement; Military Court translation, p. 13-3; Judicial Department account, p. 31-3; Furuta, *Harimu*, pp. 1-2(O), p. 2(C); Japanese signal from Commander Special Base Force 10 Singapore, October 15 1944 War Department Serial No. 15129, Box 73 Serial No. SRN 58234, RG 457 Records of NSA Japanese Naval Messages (USNA).

51) Statement by Sergeant Major Chizu Takeo, Tandjang Pinang Kempei Tai, ADM 1/18596 (PRO); Furuta, *Harimu*, p. 2(O), p. 3 (C); Base Force 10 Signal.

52) Sleeman and Silkin, Appendix II D, p. 297.

53) During the war, US submarines sank 8 000 000 tonnes of enemy merchant shipping, 5 000 000 of which was sunk in 1944 — *Report of Joint Army/ Navy Assessment Committee*, February 3 1947, Washington D.C.

54) 48 Division Staff Message No 4024; Memorandum on Operations, Organisations and Personnel Requirements of Services Reconnaissance Department April 6 1945, p. 1, A 3269/1 Item V 5. (AA ACT).

55) Statement by Bliss, *The Grim Glory*, pp. 746-47. Bliss, a prisoner of war housed at the River Road Camp which was a work camp for prisoners awaiting transhipment to Japan (see information from J.D. Flaherty who was also a River Road prisoner, THP), was a member of a party working on the Singapore wharves. According to his evidence, there is no doubt that the date is October/November 1944. Following a 'big stir' among the civilian population, heads of Chinese and Malays appeared on spikes all around the city. This occurred some time after *Rokuyu Maru*, carrying 700 Australian and 600 British prisoners-of-war to

Japan, was accidentally torpedoed by an American submarine, at 5.30 pm on September 12 1944, when six days out of Singapore (see statement by Mr Forde, Acting Australian Prime Minister, quoted in *Sydney Sun*, 17 November 1944). As Bliss was supposed to sail on this ill-fated ship, on which only ninety-two Australians survived, he remembers the sequence of events with utmost clarity. As he did not return from Thailand until late 1943 or early 1944, and the air raids in Singapore and his ultimate date of departure to Japan are supported by the evidence of others in his Battalion, there is no doubt of the accuracy of his statements. Likewise there is no question of his being confused with the Jaywick raid of 1943.

Chapter 11: For God, King and Country

1) Statement by Major Fugita CO Garrison Bintang [sic] Island to John J. Ellis, MP 742 Defence Army Correspondence Files (AA VIC); Report from HQ 'E' Group South File 40 Appendix B, ADM 1/18596 — 3231 (PRO); Kagayaki Staff 2 Message No. 227 January 25 1945, Box 38 J 21138 A/B/C Serial Numbers SR 29841-3 (USNA).

2) Maps of Riouw Archipelago; Taped observations, tape 1 1981, and photographs of Pangkil Island by Tom Hall 1981, 1989 (THP).

3) Taped interview by Tom Hall with Raja Muhammad, tape 1 1981, tape 5 1989 (THP); Naval Signal, Special Base Force Singapore October 15 1944, War Department Number 15129, Box 73 Serial Numbers SRN 58234, RG 457 Records NSA Japanese Naval Message (USNA).

4) Muhammad interviews 1981, 1989; Taped interview by Tom Hall with Abdul Rachman Achap, tape 3 1989(THP).

5) Observations, photographs and film footage of Tapai by Tom Hall 1981, 1989 (THP); Summary of Information, Food, SRD Intelligence Summaries, A 3269 Item H 9 (AA ACT); Muhammad interview, 1981, tapes 5, 6 1989;

Statement by Raja Mun to John J. Ellis, October 11 1945, MP 742 (AA VIC).

6) Muhammad interviews 1981, 1989.

7) Mun's statement.

8) Taped observations, photographs and film footage of Soreh Island 1981, 1989 by Tom Hall (THP).

9) Ibid; Muhammad interviews 1981, 1989; Fugita's statement. For identification of the personnel, see note 38 following.

10) Mun's statement; Statement by Yap Chin Yan [sic] to John J. Ellis, October 11 1945, MP 742 (AA VIC); Achap interview, tape 3 1989; Muhammad interview, tapes 5, 6 1989.

11) Statement by Sgt. Major Chizu Takeo, Kempei Tai Tandjung Pinang, to F/Lt. Gardner, MP 742 (AA VIC); Special Base Force Signal.

12) Taped interviews by Tom Hall with Abdul Latif, tape 3 1981 and tapes 1, 4 1989 (THP); Hall's observations of Soreh.

13) Ibid; Fugita's statement.

14) Latif interviews, 1981, 1989; Muhammad interviews, 1981, 1989. Note: Lanyards were supplied to SRD operatives — see Operational Adder storelist, SP 87/2574 [W10 SRD4], A 3269 (AA ACT).

15) Takeo's statement; Special Base Force Signal; Fugita's statement.

16) Summary of Information, Tactics.

17) Muhammad interviews 1981, 1989.

18) Ibid, 1981; Latif interviews 1981, 1989.

19) Latif interviews 1981, 1989; Takeo's statement.

20) Latif interviews 1981, 1989 and additional translation, tape 7 1989; Muhammad interview, 1981; Notes on Tom Hall's meetings with Raja Ibrahim, tape 7 1989 (THP). Note: After the war, Ibrahim escaped punishment by fleeing to Malaya, where he lived for the next fifteen years.

21) Latif's interview 1989 and additional translation, tape 7 1989.

22) Latif interviews 1981, 1989; Muhammad interviews 1981, 1989.

23) Written notes by Tom Hall on interview with Mrs Latif, 1981 (THP).

24) The battle started at 3 pm (Fugita), lasted two hours, and finished about 5 pm (Muhammad and Latif). Only

two men were wounded (Mrs Latif). The two bodies on Tapai, which had old wounds (Latif) were those of Campbell and Davidson — see Report by L.F.G. Pritchard, Missing Personnel of Clandestine Party from Australia, October 13 1945 ADM1/18596-3231 (PRO); Information on A.G.P. Campbell from Office of Australian War Graves, June 18 1981 (THP); SACSEA Naval office message 605/2D/1 to Admiralty February 1946, A 3269 (AA ACT); Investigations Regarding Missing Personnel of Clandestine Party Launched from Australia 11 Sept. 44, Appendix A, Interrogation of Interpreter Furuta October 21 1945, ADM 1/18596-3231 (PRO).

25) Muhammad interviews 1981, 1989; Fugita's statement; Kagayaki Staff 2 Message 227; Statement by Raja Ibrahim (THP).

26) Muhammad interview 1989. For troop numbers etc from Singapore, see Kempei Tai Documents, translation p. 4 (THP).

27) Nicholas Du Quesne Bird, *The Observer's Book of Firearms*, London 1978, p. 174; Latif interviews 1981, 1989, and additional information 1981; Muhammad interviews 1981, 1989; Maps drawn from information supplied by Latif 1989 and photographs and sketches of Ru tree, identified by Muhammad 1989 (THP). Note: As, in addition to the dead, over twenty were injured by hand grenades (Muhammad 1989), quite a number of grenades must have been thrown. Military experts are of the opinion that it is almost impossible to throw a hand grenade from a tree because of its instability and the proliferation of branches. Therefore most, if not all, of the grenades must have been thrown from the ditch. As Stewart was not detected, it is possible that he may not have fired his Sten gun.

28) Muhammad interview 1989.

29) Ibid.

30) Ibid. Note: The Japanese version of the 'six officers and men of one battalion [Daitai] were killed here', see Oka Staff 2 Message No 799 October 21 1944, Box 45 J 25021 A/B/D, Serial Numbers SR 35040-42 (USNA); and

Lieutenant Muraroka and seven other army personnels' [sic] (two of whom were killed on Merapas), see Translations of Proceedings of Military Court of 7th Area Army, MP 742, File No. 336-1-755 (AA VIC), is at great variance with the eyewitness accounts of Muhammad, who was present all the time, and Latif, who was there to see the first fight and to count at least twelve dead bodies on the barge at the end of the second fight. It appears that the Japanese only reported the deaths of Japanese nationals and did not bother to record the deaths of Hei Ho, who, according to Latif and Muhammad, formed the greater part of the search parties. This is also evidenced by the fact that the deaths of the Hei Ho in the first engagement on Soreh did not rate an official mention.

31) Ibid; Furuta's interrogation.

32) Latif interviews 1981, 1989; Muhammad interviews 1981, 1989; Fugita's statement; Kempei Tai Documents, translation p. 4. Note: Muraroka is identified in Translation of Military Court. The officer killed on Merapas was Captain Sungarno — see Achap interviews, 1981, 1989.

33) Latif interview 1981; Fugita's statement; Kagayaki Staff 2 Message No 227. Note: Had Warne and Huston been on Tapai when Davidson and Campbell arrived they would have either taken the wounded men with them or, failing that, left them in good defensive position with adequate weapons and ammunition.

34) Hall's observations of Tapai; Latif interviews 1981, 1989; Muhammad interview 1989.

35) Ibid; Mun's additional statement.

36) Furuta, *Harimu*, p. 3(O), p. 5(C). See also note 56, chapter 8 of the current work.

37 Instructions, Security, p.5, SRD Intelligence Summaries, A3269 Item H 9 (AA ACT); Furuta, *Harimu*, p.3 (O), p.5 (C); Additional statements by Furuta, Document F, p.4 (THP).

38) Stores List, Plan Rimau; Pritchard's Report; Fugita's statement. Note: The identification of the personnel has been established by examining various pieces of information. The seven men

on the raid went to the Riouw Archipelago. The two men who went directly to Tapai from Pangkil were not killed and escaped back to Merapas. They were Warne and Huston. Raja Mun saw three men on Pangkil, two of whom he identified as having died on Soreh. The two who were found dead at Tapai were unknown to Mun. The other man seen by Mun, who was not one of those found dead on Tapai, was Stewart. (He was later captured on Soreh). Two of the men seen by Raja Muhammad at Pangkil went to Soreh, where they joined the three whom Raja Mun had seen. (The other two men seen by Muhammad at Pangkil were Warne and Huston who went to Tapai). The four men whom Latif met on Soreh were all killed — two on Soreh and two on Tapai. The only combination which makes all of the above possible is for Lyon, Ross (killed at Soreh) and Stewart to meet Raja Mun; for Davidson, Campbell, (dead at Tapai) Huston and Warne to meet Raja Muhammad; and for Latif to meet Lyon, Ross, Davidson and Campbell. For references on which this deduction is based, see individual statements of the eye witnesses, note 24 above and War Graves Statement.

39) Furuta, *Harimu*, pp. 1,4,8(O), pp. 2,11(C).

40) Kagayaki Staff 2 Message No. 227.

41) Latif interview 1981, 1989; Muhammad's interview 1989.

42) Latif interview 1981.

43) Furuta, *Harimu*, p. 8(O), pp. 11,12(C) indicate that the patrol sent to check out Merapas Island was less than vigilant and was extremely lax in its search.

Chapter 12: Right Place, Wrong Time

1) Report on 28th War Patrol of HM Submarine *Porpoise*, October 15 1944, from the Commanding Officer *Porpoise*, p. 9 (Section L), ADM 199/511 (PRO); Minute by A.H. Taylor NID(Q) for DNI, February 19 1945, attached to Appendix 1, Report of Sixth War Patrol of HM Submarine *Tantalus* and Captain (s) Eight Submarine Flotilla HMS *Maidstone*, October 30 1944 to Commander-in-Chief Eastern Fleet p. 3, XC/ B3197 ADM 199/513 (PRO); Report of Interview by Tom Hall with Commander Hubert Marsham January 20 1981 p.1 (THP). Note: Marsham was replaced by Commander H.B. Turner. A few months later, in early 1945, *Porpoise* disappeared while laying a minefield in the Malacca Straits. Reports indicate that, after being forced to dive to evade Japanese aircraft, *Porpoise* was sunk by an anti-submarine vessel which tracked the submarine's oil leak, thereby making *Porpoise* the 74th and last British submarine sunk in WWII, see Alastair Mars, *Submarines at War*, London 1971, p.235.

2) Signals October 9, 12, 1944 regarding substitution of another submarine for *Porpoise* and Operation Vulture, A 3269/1 Items E 4, H 13 (AA ACT); A.J. Wilson to General Northcott, May 20 1944, SOA and SRD Policy A 3269 Item H 14 (AA ACT).

3) Annex D to Operational Order No 44, L.M. Shadwell Captain (s) Eighth Submarine Flotilla, A 3269 Item E 4 (AA ACT); Mars, pp. 109,154,170; L.M. Shadwell January 9 1945 to Commander-in-Chief East Indies Station, p. 4, XC/3197 ADM 199/511; Record of Interview by Tom Hall with Vice-Admiral Sir Hugh Mackenzie January 23 1981, p. 4 (THP).

4) Monthly Log of HM Submarine *Tantalus*, October 1944, ADM 173/18950 (PRO); Report of Sixth War Patrol of HM Submarine *Tantalus*, December 6 1944, pp. 1, 3, 8, 13 ADM 199/1862-3186 (PRO); Appendix 1 of *Tantalus* Patrol Report, pp. 1,2; Ian Trendowden, *The Hunting Submarine*, London n.d., pp. 7-8, 13-14; Specifications of T Class Submarine (THP); Order 44.

5) Report — Intelligence Gained by Major W. Chapman During the Sixth War Patrol of HM Submarine *Tantalus*, December 15 1944, pp. 2-3, A 3269 Item E 4 (AA ACT); *Tantalus* Patrol Report, pp. 3-5,8.

6) Order No. 44; Appendix 1 of *Tantalus* Patrol Report, p. 1; *Tantalus* Patrol Report, pp. 8-9; *Tantalus* Log No-

vember 7,8,9 1944, ADM 173/18952 (PRO); Note: Only two signals were sent from *Tantalus* — see Log entries for November 11 and December 2; *Tantalus* Patrol Report, p. 21 Section L and Shadwell to East Indies Station, January 9 1945, p. 3.

7) Order No. 44.

8) Trenowden, pp. 10-11, 13-14; Note: Mackenzie, having found no targets, proceeded to Merapas for the pickup with fifteen torpedoes still intact. On November 27, Mackenzie fired four torpedoes, worth £2500 each (Trenowden, p. 14), two of which fired prematurely and two of which missed — see *Tantalus Patrol Report*, pp. 14-15,20.

9) For comparison of US attacks and British attacks see *Report of Joint Army/Navy Assessment Committee*.

10) *Tantalus* Patrol Report, pp. 10,23; Chapman's Intelligence Report, pp. 5-6. Note: Chapman's version differs in detail from the report by Mackenzie. As Chapman was on the spot and has included greater detail, his version has been accepted as being more correct.

11) *Tantalus* Patrol Report, p. 10; Shadwell to East Indies Station, January 9 1945, p. 1; Chapman's Intelligence Report, p. 7; Order No. 44; Appendix 1 of *Tantalus* Patrol Report, p. 1; *Tantalus* Log, November 11 1944.

12) *Tantalus* Patrol Report, p. 10; Shadwell to Commander-in-Chief East Indies Station, January 3 1945, XC/3197 ADM 199/511 (PRO).

13) *Tantalus* Patrol Report, pp. 11-12; Chapman's Intelligence Report, pp. 7-8; Report on Attempted Pick Up of Rimau Party by HM Submarine *Tantalus* by Major W.W. Chapman, R.E., December 12 1944, p. 1, A 3269 Item E 4 (AA ACT); Appendix 1 of *Tantalus* Patrol Report, p. 1.

14) Pick Up Report, p. 2; Appendix 1 of *Tantalus* Patrol Report, p. 1.

15) SRD Intelligence Branch, Rimau Project, Lieutenant-Commander Davidson's Diary, September 11-September 30 1944, pp. 3-5 and sketch map, A 3269 Item E 4 (AA ACT); Appendix 1 of *Tantalus* Patrol Report, p. 1; Pick Up Report, p. 2.

16) Pick Up Report, p. 2; Taped Interview by Tom Hall with Ron Croton, January 1982 (THP).

17) Davidson's Sketch Map; Observations and photographs taken by Tom Hall at Merapas Island, September 1981, May 1989 (THP); Pick Up Report, pp. 2-3; Record of conversation between Ron Croton and Harry Browne, in interview by Tom Hall with Harry Browne, August 8 1981, p. 3 (THP).

18) Croton to Browne; Pick Up Report, p. 3; Croton Interview.

19) Additional statements by Chapman, recorded in Connell, p. 132-133; Croton interview; Pick Up Report, p. 3.

20) Davidson's Diary, pp. 3-5.

21) Pick Up Report, p. 3; Chapman's statements, p. 133; Croton interview.

22) Pick Up Report, p. 3; Croton interview. Note: Chapman's Pick Up Report mentions only the dog.

23) Croton interview.

24) Pick Up Report, p. 3; Chapman's statement, p. 134. The sudden decision to have Croton cover him must have resulted from the close encounter with the Japanese.

25) Croton interview; Pick Up Report, pp. 3-4; Report of Interrogation of Lance Corporal Croton (Rimau Rescue Sortie) December 11 1944, Rimau Report C, A 3269 Item E 4 (AA ACT).

26) Pick Up Report, pp. 4-5; Croton's interrogation.

27) Pick Up Report, p. 5. Note: Had Chapman traversed Kingfisher's Rest path he would have discovered the decomposing body of Cameron, killed on November 5 1944, lying beside a stone sangar. (See Report of Recovery of Rimau Remains on Merapas Island by Tom Hall, September 1981, THP).

28) Ibid, p. 6. Note: Had Chapman actually covered this area, as he claimed, he would have discovered that fires, noticed during the initial submarine reconnaissance, were still burning (see Appendix 1 of *Tantalus* Patrol Report, p. 2) and were not, as he stated, extinguished. He would also have seen the grave of Sub-Lieutenant Riggs, buried by Mr Achap, November 5 1944. (See Report on Discovery of Grave Site, May 1989 by Tom Hall,

THP).

29) Pick Up Report, p. 6; Croton interrogation; Croton interview.

30) Pick Up Report, pp. 11,12; Appendix 1 of *Tantalus* Patrol Report, p. 2.

31) Pick Up Report, p. 6; Investigation Regarding Missing Personnel of Clandestine Party launched from Australia 11 September 1944, Appendix H, Statement of Abdul Wahab, Headman of Mapur [sic] Island, to Major M.L. Shephard 10 Oct 45, ADM1/18596-3231 (PRO).

32) Croton interview; Pick Up Report, p. 7.

33) Appendix 1 of *Tantalus* Patrol Report, p. 2.

34) Ibid; *Tantalus* Log for November 22 1944; *Tantalus* Patrol Report, pp. 12-13.

35) *Tantalus* Patrol Report, pp. 13-16; Chapman's Intelligence Report, pp. 9-11; *Tantalus* Log, December 6 1944.

36) Chapman's Intelligence Report, p. 11; *Tantalus* Patrol Report, p. 23; Memos and Minutes from senior naval officers, annexed to Appendix 1 of *Tantalus* Patrol Report. Note: It is estimated that, in 1990 currency, the cost of fuel and torpedoes expended would have been in the region of one million Australian dollars.

37) Croton was interrogated for approximately half an hour on December 11 1944 — see Croton interview. The information he gave is in his Record of Interrogation; Chapman's reports covered a total of seventeen pages. Compare details of the attack on the native vessel with that recorded by Mackenzie.

38 Pick Up Report, written by Chapman, has no record of these incidents; Military Record of Lance Corporal R. Croton (THP).

39) The copy of Mackenzie's report is with the Pick Up Report, A 3269 Item E 4 (AA ACT); Appendix 1 of *Tantalus* Patrol Report, p. 2; Copy of Appendix 1 of *Tantalus* Patrol Report.

40) Pick Up Report.

41) Pick Up Sortie, Deductions and Remarks upon Facts and Evidence — Merapas Is., pp. 1-3 and Statement of Mohamed Juni January 9 1945 at Richmond N.S.W., A 3269 Item E 4 (AA ACT); Papers associated with Rimexit, A 3269 Item E 5 (AA ACT). Note: Rimexit was cancelled when intercepted messages revealed that the Rimau men had been captured.

42) Furuta, *Harimu*, p. 9(O), pp. 12-13(C) (THP). See also note 56, chapter 8 of the current work.

43) Notes of Evidence, Inquest on Walter William Chapman, May 8 1964, evidence of Police Constable Donald Whitehead and Doctor R.W. Harries and Post Mortem Report by Harries, at Amersham General Hospital, Amersham, England; Report of Chapman's suicide, *Daily Mail* (London), May 9 1964.

Chapter 13: Pursued

1) Furuta, *Harimu*, p. 8 (O) THP). See also note 56, chapter 8 of the current work.

2) Interview by Tom Hall with Abdul Rachman Achap, 1981, 1989 (THP).

3) Investigation Regarding Missing Personnel of Clandestine Party Launched from Australia 11 September 1944, Appendix H, Statement of Abdul Wahab, Headman of Mapur[sic] Island, to Major M.L. Shephard 10 Oct 45, ADM 1/18596 - 3231 (PRO); Achap interview 1981, 1989.

4) Report by Major W.W. Chapman on Attempted Pick Up of Rimau Party by HMS *Tantalus*, pp. 4,6, A 3269 Item E4 (AA ACT); Achap interview 1989; Umi San Message 228 February 3 1945, Information about Operation Rimau, A 3269 (AA ACT); Furuta, *Harimu*, pp. 2, 8-9 (O), pp. 3,11-12 (C).

5) Furuta, *Harimu*, p. 2 (O), p. 3 (C); Achap interview 1981; Investigation Regarding Missing Personnel, Appendix B, Statement by Major Fugita, C.O. Garrison Bintang [sic] Island; Statement by Sgt Major Chizu Takeo of Kempei Tai to F/Lt Gardner, MP 742, Defence, Army Correspondence Files, Multiple Number Series 1943-51 (AA VIC); Wahab's statement. Note: In Furuta, *Harimu*, the name given to the dead captain is fictitious.

6) Furuta, *Harimu*, p. 2 (O), p. 4 (C); Wahab statement; Achap interview

1989.

7) Six of the eight were those who fled with Sargent, to either die or become prisoners between Maja and Romang Islands. Riggs, identified by Achap, and Cameron, identified by the forensic analysis of the skull recovered by Tom Hall in 1981, were the two killed on Merapas.

8) Furuta, *Harimu*, p. 9 (O), p. 13 (C); Achap interview 1989; Interview by Tom Hall with Karta, a Merapas Islander, September 1981, Tape 7 (THP); Statement by Karta to Lt. R.W. Lowry, 'A Report on Exercise Jaywick', *Army Journal 1971*.

9) Achap interview 1989.

10) Karta interview; Lowry's report; Forensic report on remains found on Merapas Island (THP).

11) Photographs and Report on Merapas Island by Tom Hall, 1981, 1989 (THP); Achap interview 1989; Lowry's report; Karta interview; Forensic Report. Note: The bullet wound to Cameron's skull is consistent with the angle of a bullet fired from below, probably from the water.

12) Achap interview 1989; Map of Merapas Island; Sketch of the bracelet by Achap in notebook of Tom Hall, 1989 (THP).

13) Achap interview 1989.

14) Investigation Regarding Missing Personnel, Appendix A, Interrogation of Interpreter Furuta 21 Oct 1945. Note: As the bodies of Lyon, Ross, Davidson and Campbell were left unburied, (see Interview by Tom Hall with Abdul Latif 1981, 1989 THP, and Lieut. L.G. Palmer's Report on Investigations on Bintan Island 12th October 1945, AA 1981/155/1 Item 605/2D/1, AA ACT which gives an uncensored version of the same report filed at MP 742 AA VIC), the 'very fine graves' must refer to that of Riggs. A grave (believed at the time to be Japanese, which was impossible as Captain Sungarno's body was removed and cremated — see Wahab's statement and Achap interview 1981) was noted by the investigating team when it visited Merapas Island in October 1945 (see Report by Captain John Ellis on Search for Missing Personnel 13

Oct 45, MP 742, 336-1-755, AA VIC).

15) Karta interview; Hall's report on Merapas Island.

16) Achap interview 1981, 1989. Note: The radio was an A.W.A. — Amalgamated Wireless Australasia. One of the Japanese was probably Wata Nabe Take Hiro, the owner of the name tag found by Major Chapman (see Statement by Mohamed Juni, 9/1/45 A 3269 Item E 4).

17) Wahab statement; Chizu statement; Fugita statement. Note: The number of folboats seen after the Merapas battle varies but the Japanese state that they captured ten and sank one (I Staff Message 211 January 9 1945, Serial Numbers J 16625 A-I, L-O, USNA). As three were recovered in the Riouw Straits, four in the Lingga Archipelago, and one sunk, three must have been recovered at Merapas.

18) Translation of Proceedings of Military Court of 7th Area Army, p. 13-3 and Judicial Department's Full Account of Australian Special Overseas Operation Party, pp. 31-10,11,13, MP 742, 336-1-755 (AA VIC); Furuta *Harimu* p. 6 (O), p. 10 (C); Wahab's statement.

19) Wahab's statement; Achap interview 1989.

20) Furuta, *Harimu*, p. 3 (O), pp. 4,5 (C); Additional statements by Hiroyuki Furuta, Documents G, I p. 3 (THP); Translation of Kempei Tai Records, p. 5 (THP).

21) Sleeman and Silkin, Appendix II, p. 295; Investigation Regarding Missing Personnel, Appendix F and Exhumation Report by Captain R.S. Ross RAMC, 22 November 1945.

22) To have travelled from Merapas Island to Romang Island with such pinpoint accuracy (Umi San Message 228), Reymond's group must have had both charts and sextant. It seems likely that when the Japanese arrived they were doing some kind of work on the tents (Umi San Message 228), probably in the vicinity of Cache Swamp, which gave them access to their kit.

23) Report on the Re Interrogation of Ozaki Chikari, March 4-5 1948, p. 2, MP 742/1 File 336/1/1939 Pt 1 (AA VIC). In this report Sargent tells Ozaki that 'two or three' Australians were

killed at Merapas — information that he can only have obtained by observation. Page's party had no knowledge of anyone being killed (see Furuta's Interrogation 21 October 1945).

24) Ozaki interrogation, p. 2; Statement by Mr Ouvarow to Captain John Ellis 11 October 1945, MP 742 (AA VIC).

25) Furuta, *Harimu*, p. 9 (O), p. 13 (C).

26) There was never any suggestion that a submarine other than *Porpoise* would do the pickup. It was the submarine specifically assigned to Hornbill (see Colonel Chapman-Walker Director SRD to Colonel Roberts Controller AIB September 19 1944, A 3269/1 Item H 13, AA ACT).

27) Appendix I to Report of Sixth War Patrol of HM Submarine *Tantalus*, p. 1, XC/3197 ADM 199/511 (PRO).

28) Achap interview 1989; Ellis's Report on Missing Personnel, p. 3. Note: Chapman's sense of smell was so acute that he could detect the presence of *Tantalus* from the shore when the hatch opened. It was not until Hall discovered the remains of Cameron in 1981 and the burial site of Riggs in 1989 that their fate was established.

29) Investigation Regarding Missing Personnel, Appendix C, Statement by Amir of Senegang [sic]; Report by Lt. Col. Pritchard on Missing Personnel, Oct 13 1945, AA 1981/155/1 Item 605/2D/1 (AA ACT) and ADM 1/18596 (PRO); Karta interview. Note: After the war, information about the route taken came to light in Ouvarow's statement.

30) Kempei Tai pp. 7,12; Pritchard's report; Umi San Message 228 (For an explanation of the corrupt translation of this message, see note 1, chapter 14 of the current work). Note: By intensive cross referencing of clues found in the Dabo Police Book and statements by various people (ADM 1/18596 PRO and MP 742 AA VIC), translation of Kempei Tai Records and interviews with eyewitnesses (THP) and knowledge of the distances between Boeaja and Singkep Islands, it has been possible to reconstruct the movements and sequence of events that led to the capture of personnel. There has been great confusion in the

past as hearsay evidence had incorrectly stated that six men went to both Boeaja and Selajar. The matter was further complicated by post-war Kempei accounts which listed a total of fourteen men either killed or captured in the Lingga Archipelago. The discovery of the two bodies on Merapas by Tom Hall and the evidence obtained by eyewitness Engku Haji Said Nuh, which states that four men were on Selajar and that three small folboats were 'sunk' near Pompong (in reference to the fight which took place with Ingleton's group), has enabled the number of men in each group at Lingga to be fixed at four and six, thereby eliminating a great deal of erroneous information.

31) Kempei Tai p. 7; Investigation Regarding Missing Personnel, Appendix C, Statement by Soekarti and Extracts from Dabo Police Book; Interview by Tom Hall with Engku Haji Said Nuh, Tape 5 1981 (THP); I Staff Message 211; Interview by Tom Hall with aged eyewitness at Kidjang 1981, Tape 4 (THP).

32) Kempei Tai p. 7; Investigation Regarding Missing Personnel, Appendix C, statement by Amir of Serajang [sic]; Pritchard's Report October 13 1945.

33) Kempei Tai pp. 7-8; Dabo Police Book entry (Hardy, who was wounded in the shoulder, was the 'white man'); Statements by Furuta, Docs F, p. 4 and I, p. 1

34) Furuta's statements Docs F, p. 4 and I, p. 1.

35) Kempei Tai p. 8; Cyril Wild, 'Expedition to Singkep', *Blackwood's Magazine* October 1946, pp 220-21; Dabo Police Book entry; Observations and photographs of Dabo Police Station by Tom Hall September 1981 (THP); Soekarti statement; Investigation Regarding Missing Personnel, Appendix C, statement by Said Abdullah; Engku interview.

36) Statement by J.D. Flaherty, Australian Army NX 38745, an eyewitness standing on the wharf (THP).

37) Kempei Tai Diary p. 8; Dabo Police Book; Investigation Regarding Missing Personnel, Appendix C, Information by Boeang, a Malay Policeman (Hei

Ho), Pritchard's Report October 13 1945; Interview with aged Kidjang eyewitness.

38) Furuta, *Harimu*, p. 7 (C); Furuta statements, Docs. F, p. 3 and I, p. 2; Wild, p. 221.

39) Lord Russell of Liverpool, *The Knights of Bushido*, London 1958, pp. 174,201-02. Note: Sleeman and Silkin, John McGregor 'Blood on the Rising Sun', (privately published Perth 1978), and Information of C. Wyett THP, give numerous examples of doctors being summoned when it was far too late.

40) Furuta, *Harimu*, p. 4 (O), pp. 5-6 (C); Achap interview 1989; Statement by Office of Australian War Graves, June 18 1981 (THP); Pritchard's Report October 13 1945. Note: According to statements of H. Shinozaki (THP), by the time the Rimau men were captured, the Water Kempei Tai Headquarters, formerly housed in the Tandjung Pagar Police Station, had been moved to the Chinese YMCA building off Palmer Street. This should not be confused with the Kempei Tai HQ at the European YMCA in Stamford Road, the place where many, including the victims of the 'Double Tenth', were tortured. Furuta's loose references to the building being the YMCA has led to some confusion.

41) Memo, Securities — Prisoners of War, A 3269 Item H 9 ((A ACT); Furuta, *Harimu*, pp. 4,5 (O), pp. 6,7 (C).

42) Furuta, *Harimu*, pp. 4,5 (O), pp. 6,7 (C). From the personal details revealed to Furuta it seems that Hinomoto, with Furuta interpreting, interrogated Page, Carey and Stewart, while Noguchi interrogated Ingleton's group, p. 7 (C).

43) Cover — Rimau Plan, 14 July 1944, A 3269 Item E 4; Furuta, *Harimu*, p. 9, (O), p. 13 (C).

44) Furuta, *Harimu*, p. 9 (O), pp. 13,14 (C). Note: The original version, which was written as an entry in a competition, was altered for dramatic effect.

45) McGregor and Information from Chris Neilson (THP) give excellent accounts of the 'cigarettes and lolly racket'.

46) Report marked 'Top Secret', February 13 1945, Enemy Information on Inter-Allied Services Dept, Z Special Unit and Services Reconnaissance Depart-

ment [collated from intercepted messages and other intelligence], A 3269/1, Item H 10 Pt 3 (AA ACT). Note: This twelve-page report contains only a fraction of the information which was in enemy hands.

47) I Staff 2 Message 211.

Chapter 14: Dark Days at Soerabaya

The sources on which this chapter is based are investigation reports etc, contained in MP 742/1 File 336/1/1939 Pt 1 (AA VIC) and trial papers in A 471/1 Items 81961, 81966 (AA ACT). Because of the fragmented nature of the evidence in both sources, which cover thousands of pages, the notes below have been arranged under the subject matter and the names of individuals. In order to assess this evidence it is imperative to study the entire contents of all files.

1) Information on Lieutenant Albert Sargent: Judge Advocate W.E. Van Beek, June 18 1947; Appendix A Sheet 2, Report on Fate of Sachs and Perske, Soerabaya Java; Appendix A Sheet 2, War Crimes Soerabaya, Java; Statements, interrogations or reports of Akari, November 3 1947; Tatsuzaki, December 24-28 1947; Tachino, 28-31 December 1947, March 17-18, September 14, November 16 1948; Ozaki, January 15, March 4-5, September 13 1948; Tanaka, February 16-17 1948; Tawara, (undated); Yasuda, March 22 1948; Nakuno, June 22 1948; Yoshimoto (undated); Sylvester, December 3 1948; Shibata, February 24 1949; Hase, February 24 1949; Furuno, March 4 1949; Sannomiya, May 3 1949 (All in MP 742/1); Nomaguchi, August 30 1948; Saito, August 1 1949. (All in A 471/1, Item 81966). Japanese Umi San Message 228, February 3 1945, appearing in SRD Summary, Information about Operation Rimau, A 3269 (AA ACT). Note: The translation from the Japanese, which was itself originally translated from the English, is rather corrupted in this summary and the location of Tandjung Dato, assumed in 1945 to be the Tandjung Datu on the NW tip of Borneo, is misleading. It appears that the tendency for the Japanese to

pronounce 'L' as 'R', as in Lyon and Ryon, has caused Lima Island to be transmitted as Riam, a place which does not exist. Because of poor typeface in the summary, the surname of Goking could be either Riaz, Fiaz or Kiaz. Similarly T. (Tandjung) Goroh, has been interpreted phonetically as Igaru.

2) Information on Sargent; SRD Project Summaries September 1945 by Lt Col J.E.B. Finlay, A 3269 (AA ACT); Umi San Message 228; I Staff 2 Message 238, January 13 1945. Box No 37, J 20187 A-F, Serial Nos. SR 28578-82 (USNA).

3) Staff Message 238.

4) Information on Sargent; Atis Bulletin No. 730, copy of Japanese PW Examination Report, Document 3/6643 2156.9 (AWM).

5) Information on Sargent; Staff Message 238.

6) Information on Sargent.

7) Information on Warne and Sargent: Statements, interrogations or reports of Sylvester (undated) pp. 3-4; Sasaki, November 12 1947; Araki, November 12 1947, March 22 1948. (MP 742/1).

8) Information on Douglas Warne: Statements, interrogations or reports of Sylvester (undated), December 3 1948; Appendix A, Sheet 2 War Crimes Soerabaya; Akari, November 3 1947; Sasaki, November 12 1947; Tatsuzaki, December 24-28 1947; Tachino, December 28-31 1947, March 17-18 1948; Tawara (undated); Yoshimoto (undated); Ozaki, September 13 1948; Furuno, March 4 1949; Sannomiya, May 3 1949; Noguchi, June 2 1949 (all in MP 742/1); Saito, August 1 1949 (A 471/1 Item 81966).

9) Ibid; Information on Warne and Sargent.

10) Information on the mission and capture of Lieutenants John Sachs and Clifford Perske: W.L. Jinkins, 31 August 1945; L. Talbot, Summary of Information re Missing Personnel of 'Politician' Project, October 10 1945; Witsell (USA) to Commanding General US Armed Forces Western Pacific (undated); copy of letter from L. Bakker of Royal Netherlands Marines to Mr Schow, August 21 1946; Rear Admiral James Fife to Adjutant-General, AMF Melbourne, November 22 1946; Extract from 2nd Echelon Letter No. 030, January 6 1947; Telegram PA.103 from RAAF HQ to CG AFWESPAC MANILA, 28 Feb; Director of Prisoners of War and Internees to 1 Australian War Crimes Section Hong Kong, October 23 1947; Telegram from Army Melbourne to 2 Aust War Crimes Sec (SCAP) March 11 1948; Director of Prisoners of War and Internees to Detachment Commander, Royal Netherlands Indies Army, Melbourne, May 4 1948; Statements, interrogations or reports of Goslett June 5, November 12 1948; Tatsuzaki, December 24-28 1947; Tachino, March 18, August 31, September 14 1948; Sylvester, December 3 1948; Kinoshita, December 3 1948; Masuda, April 28 1949; Sannomiya, May 1 1949; Nakayama, May 17 1949; Saito, August 1 1949 (all in MP 742/1); Tachino, August 31 1948; Mike, June 17 1949; Saito, August 1 1949 (all in A 471/1 Item 81966); Information of Peter and Thomas Sachs and Sachs Family Papers, particularly John Sachs's battle diary, papers, press reports and personal letters. Note: For information on Greek Campaign see Gavin Long, *Australia in the War of 1939-1945. Greece, Crete and Syria,* Canberra 1953, chapter 7.

11) R.W. Christie to Commander Seventh Fleet, November 12 1944, A 3269/1 Item E 3 Copy 1 (AA ACT).

12) Memo dated January 6 1945, A 3269/1 Item E 3 Copy 2 (AA ACT); An account of Operation Optician-Politician, pp. 19,20 A 3269/1 Item 08 Vol 2., (AA ACT); Information on Capture of Sachs and Perske. Note: Lieutenant Barnes was replaced by Sachs on this operation. For verification see statements by Hawkins and others in Sachs Family Papers.

13) Information on mission and capture of Sachs and Perske.

14) Saito August 2, 1949 (MP 742/1). For information on Shinohara, see Nomaguchi March 8 1948; Kai, April 1-7 1948; Saito, August 2 1949 (all in MP

742/1); Yoshino, September 30 1948; Nomaguchi, January 19 1949 (all in A 471/.1 Item 81966).

15) Information on Sargent and Warne; Information on Executions without Trial: Summary of facts governing the decision by Fleet Headquarters and Base Units to execute POWs and spies without benefit of trial by court martial in the Soerabaya-Borneo-Celebes Area; Statements, interrogations or reports of Kishi, October 22 1947; Hirai, March 17 1948; Nomaguchi, March 8 1948. For information on what was supposed to occur when spies and prisoners were captured, see Kanai, a Japanese lawyer, August 13 1948 (all in MP 742/1); Nomaguchi, August 30 1948; Saito, August 8 1949; Kurisu, November 3 1949 (A 471/1 Item 81966).

16) Information on Injections administered to Prisoners: Statements, interrogations or reports by Noguchi, March 31 1947, January 22 1948; Tatsuzaki, 24-28 December 1947 and addendum, undated; Okamoto, December 23 1948; Shibata, February 18 1949; Nakamura, April 14, 19 1949; Mike, June 10 1949; Saito, August 1 1949 (all in MP 742/1); Nakamura at his trial at Manus Island, 1951, *Sydney Morning Herald*, March 22 1951; Saito, August 1 1949; Kurisu, November 11 1949. (all in A 471/1) (Note: Although Nakamura did not admit to injecting white prisoners of war, there is sufficient evidence in the statements of eyewitnesses to establish that he did so. The same applies to Yoshio Edakobo who, in his interrogation of November 24 1947, denies that any white men were ever admitted to hospital). For information on tetanus and its treatments, see medical texts such as Burrow's 16th edition of *Textbook of Microbiology*, Philadelphia and London, 1954, and Harrison's 5th edition of *Principals of Internal Medicine*.

17) Information on Warne; Statements of Iwamura, March 17 1949, (MP 742/1); Kurusu, November 3 1949 (A 471/1).

18) Information on Soemba Castaways: Statements, interrogations or reports

of Sylvester (undated); Goslett, December 2 1947; Appendix A Sheet 1, Fate of Sachs and Perske Soerabaya Java; Appendix A Sheets 1 and 9 Addendum, War Crimes Soerabaya Java; Noguchi, March 31 1947, January 21 (1948?), 22 1948; Hayashi, November 7 1947; Okomoto, November 17 1947; Ozaki, November 28 1947, March 4-5, 16-17, September 13 1948; Tatsuzaki, December 24-28 1947; Tachino, December 28-31 1947, November 16 1948; Kobayashi, December 30 1947; Nomaguchi, January 15 1948; Yoshimoto, translated August 19 1948; Goslett, November 12 1948; Okamoto, December 23 1948; Shibata, February 18 1949; Bunyu, May 31 1949, addendum June 2 1949, June 21 1949; Nakatsu, June 30 1949; Saito, August 1 1949 (all in MP 742/1); Nakayama, May 17 1949; Nakatsu, June 30 1949; Kurisu, November 3 1949 (A 471/1 Item 81966); Information on Warne.

19) Nakamura's trial statements.

20) Information on the Executions of Sachs, Perske, Schow, Palmer and the Indonesians: Telegram from 2 Aust War Crimes to Army Melbourne, March 17 1948; Goslett to 2 Aust War Crimes Tokyo, June 5, November 12 1948; Statements, interrogations or reports of Tatsuzaki, addendum to December 24-28 1947; Tawara (undated); Hamada (undated); Tachino, March 18, August 31, September 14 1948; Nakamura, May 21 1948; Konishi, September 3 1948; Yoshino, September 30 1948; Iwamoto, October 12 1948; Furuno, October 21 1948; Nomaguchi, November 6 1948; Sylvester, December 3 1948; Shibata, February 18 1949; Nakauchi, March 7 1949; Hashimoto, April 19 1949; Shiragiko; April 19 1949; Masuda, April 28 1949; Sannomiya, May 3 1949; Nakayama, May 17, 1949 and letter July 27 1949; Tanaka (presumed) June 2, document 48520-B, June 3, 1949; Bunyu, June 2 1949; Mike, June 5, 10, 17 and undated 1949; Nakatsu, June 30 1949; Yamashita, July 12 1949; Hamada, July 22 1949; Ikeda, June 17 1949, addendum of March 31 1949; Saito, August 1 1949; Yamamoto,

October 20 1949 (all in MP 742/1); Tachino, August 31 1948; Konishi, September 3, 5, 9, 1948; Yoshino, September 30 1948; Shiragiku, April 18 1949; Hashimoto, April 19 1949; Nakayama, May 17 1949; Tamara, June 30 1949; Hanada, July 21 1949; Saito, August 1 1949; Kurisu, November 3 1949 (all in A 471/1 Item 81966); Precis of Evidence; Statement by Judge Advocate General W.B. Simpson (all in A 471/1 Item 81961).

21) Information on Mission and Capture of Flight Officer Mason Schow and Sergeant Donald Palmer: Memorandum Mix-X Section APO 500, October 23 1945; Major James Callender to Adjutant General, Washington 25 February 1946; Witsell (USA) to Commanding General US Armed Forces, Western Pacific, undated; copy of a letter from L. Bakker, Royal Netherlands Marines to Mr Schow, August 21 1946; Statements, interrogations or reports of Noguchi, January 22 1948; Iwamoto, October 12 1948; Goslett, November 12 1948; Bunyu, June 2 1949; Mike, June 5, 10 1949; Hironaka, June 28 1949; Saito, August 1 1949. For authority to execute Schow and Palmer and the general attitude to captured airmen, see Nomaguchi, November 6 1948 (all in MP 742/1); Information on the executions of Sachs, Perske etc.

22) Information on the executions of Sachs, Perske etc. Note: The time has been calculated from the facts that the order to execute was issued at 11.30; that the prisoners were taken from their cells, handcuffed and blindfolded; that the drive took thirty minutes, and that there was a one-hour wait at the execution site. Other witnesses attest that the executions took place in the afternoon and that the actual decapitations took about thirty minutes. By the time Sachs was executed it would have been between 1.00 and 1.30 Tokyo time, which was 2.30 Sydney time.

23) Handwritten statement recorded shortly after 2.30 pm March 30 1945 by Fritz Sachs, who died in September 1945, without ever knowing the fate of his son (Sachs Family Papers).

24) Information on the execution of Sachs, Perske etc; Information on the Dissection of one American airman and one Indonesian: Statements, interrogations or reports of Goslett, November 12 1948; Tawara, undated; Konishi, September 3, 10 1948; Yoshino, September 30 1948; Furuno, October 21 1948; Okamoto, December 23 1948; Shibata, February 18 1949; Nakauchi, March 7 1949; Shiragiki, April 19 1949; Masuda, April 28 1949; Bunyu, June 2 1949; Mike, undated day in June 1949; Ikeda, June 17 1949; Nakatsu, June 30 1949; Yamashita, July 12 1949; Hamada, July 22 1949; Yamamoto, October 20 1949. The information regarding Shinohara's intention to eat the gall bladder is in Goslett, November 12 1948 (all in MP 742/1); Konishi, 3, 5, 9 November 1948; Shiragiki, April 18 1949; Hishimoto, April 19 1949; Mike, June 17 1949; Tamara, June 30 1949; Hirada, July 21 1949; Yoshino, September 30 1949; Kurusu, November 3 1949 (all in A 471/1 Item 81966).

25) Information on Executions without Trial. For reactions to Shinohara's intention to eat the gall bladders, see Kinoshi, September 10 1948 (A 471/1 Item 81966).

26) Seventh Area Army Message, February 10 1945, Box 4, Magic Far East Summaries, SRS 339 of February 22 1945 (USNA); Information concerning execution of prisoners involved in Singapore Incident: Facts governing decisions to execute POWs and spies without benefit of trial; Statements, interrogations or reports of Tachino, September 14, 18 1948; Nomaguchi, November 6 1948; Shibata, February 24 1949; Furuno, March 4 1949. Note: In trial LN5, A 47181945 (AA ACT), expert witness General Imomura admitted that most subordinates would interpret 'genju shobun' (punish strictly and firmly) as 'punish by death'.

27) Statements of Nomoguchi, November 6 1948; Tachino, September 14, 18 1948 (all in MP 742/1).

Chapter 15: A Death Fit for Heroes?

1) Interrogation of Interpreter Furuta by Lt-Col. L.F.G. Pritchard and Major C.H.D. Wild, Appendix E, ADM 1/18596 (PRO); Furuta, *Harimu*, pp. 4,5,10,11 (O), pp. 6,7,14-17 (C) (THP) — see also note 56, chapter 8 of the current work; Additional statements of Hiroyuki Furuta, Documents B and I (THP); Lieut L.G. Palmer to POW Liaison Officer, November 21 1945 and Commander Long to SRD October 22 1945, AA 1981/155/1 Item 605/2D/1 (AA ACT).

2) SRD Intelligence Summaries, Part III Security, A 3269 Item H9 (AA ACT); Furuta statements, Docs B, J. For examples of Kempei Tai treatment see Chapter 8 of the current work; McGregor, pp. 114-117; Information of C. Nielson, copies of Depositions and Sworn Statements of Penrod Dean April 29 1946 and February 1946, Sworn Statements of Alexander Weynton November 27 1945 and numerous other Sworn Statements made to the Board of Enquiry into War Crimes, DWP and I Files (THP).

3) See Chapter 17 of the current work; Umi San Staff Message 228, 3 February 1945 (USNA).

4) Furuta, *Harimu*, p. 11 (O), p. 17 (C); Furuta statements, Docs H,J; Testimony of John A. MacDonald, p. 2, WO 235/975 034863 (PRO).

5) Russell, pp. 70-81; Statements by Furuno and Iwamura, March 4, 17 1949, MP 742/1 File 336/1/1939 Pt 1 (AA VIC).

6) Furuta, *Harimu*, p. 13 (O), pp. 20-22 (C). Note: Furuta, in 1945, only refers to the date as being 'last year'. As all other Jaywick suspects had long been executed, it is almost certain that the Malays awaiting execution must have been those rounded up after Rimau.

7) Staff Area Message February 10 1945, Box 4 Magic Far East Summaries SRS 339 of February 22 1945 (USNA); Judicial Department, 7th Area Army, Full Account of Australian Special Overseas Operation Party, p. 31-1, MP 742 File 336-1-755 (AA VIC); Furuta, *Harimu*, p. 11 (O), p. 17 (C); Furuta

statements, Doc B. Note: See also note 26, chapter 14 of the current work.

8) Furuta, *Harimu*, pp. 1,4,12 (O), pp. 2,4,5,18 (C); Furuta statements, Docs B, I.

9) Page is particularly mentioned by Furuta, whom he describes as a 'slender-faced, handsome youth with a fine mustache' [sic]. A photograph of Furuta, aged 37 in 1945, is in THP.

10) Furuta, *Harimu*, pp. 6,10,11 (O), pp. 9, 14, 16 (C); Furuta statements, Docs F, I.

11) Furuta, *Harimu*, p. 12 (O), p. 18 (C); Furuta's interrogation, Appendix E.

12) Statement by Nomaguchi November 6 1948, MP 742/1 File 336/1/1939 Pt 1 (AA VIC); Furuta statements, Docs F, I. Note: Furuta only knows what the prisoners in Singapore had told him. Although Willersdorf and Pace had mentioned Jaywick in their interrogations in Timor (Umi San Staff Message 228) and Warne had revealed that he had been on the Rimau raid, (Report on Interrogation of Tachino, December 28-31 1947, p. 2, MP 742/1 File 336/1/1939 Pt 1, (AA VIC), this information was available only to the top echelon. Furuta did not know about Jaywick until told by Page. In common with all but a select few, he did not know anything about the fighting at Tapei or Soreh either. He had no idea that Lyon had been killed and in 1957 believed that he was the author of a book about the Jaywick raid written after the war.

13) Furuta, *Harimu*, pp. 13-14 (O), pp. 20-21 (C); see also explanatory note in note 6 above.

14) Ibid, pp. 10,12 (O), pp. 14,19,21-22 (C); Furuta statements, Docs F, J. That *Harimu* version (O) is incorrect in stating that the Malays were reprieved is confirmed in Doc F, and, the fact that the Japanese were anxious to obtain information for propaganda purposes is confirmed in SRD Intelligence Summaries.

15) Furuta statements, Doc B; Wild, 'Expedition to Singkep', p. 222.

16) McGregor, pp. 5, 132-92, biographical notes; Information of J.W.C. Wyett

and Bert Rollason (THP); Board of Enquiry testimonies; Nielson's information; numerous other depositions, see note 2 above; Furuta statements, Document J; MacDonald's tesitmony; Information of anonymous former Australian POW, sent from Sandakan in Borneo to Outram Road Gaol (THP).

17 Furuta statments, Docs F, J. Note: Furuta statements, *Harimu* and Interrogation Appendix E, contain many references to good treatment at Tandjung Pagar. The conditions at Outram Road, where the Rimau men were interned for five months, are never mentioned, apart from the good treatment from July 3-6 1945.

18) MacDonald's testimony; Nielson's information; Information of Frank Martin (THP).

19) Furuta, *Harimu*, p. 11 (O), pp. 14-15,17 (C); Furuta statements, Docs B, I; MacDonald's testimony, p. 13.

20) Furuta statements, Doc B.

21) Judicial Account, p. 31-1; Furuta statements, Doc G.

22) Statement of Tachino, September 14 1948, MP 742/1 File 336-1-1939 Pt 1 (AA VIC); Judicial Account, p. 31-1.

23) Judicial Account, pp. 31-1, 31-2; Extract from Report on Interrogation of Major General Ohtsuka [sic] and Major Kamiya (Judicial Dept. Jap. G.H.Q. Singapore) by Major C.H.D. Wild 'E' Group 19 Oct 1945, Appendix D, ADM 1/18596 (PRO); Hague Convention of 1907, Law and Usages, Section II Spies, Article 29.

24) Furuta, *Harimu*, pp. 22-23 (C); Furuta statements, Docs B, G; Munemija Shinji, *The Account of the Legal Proceedings of the Court for War Criminal Suspects*, translated by Yoshioka Kazuo, Japan 1946, pp. 37-38.

25) Judicial Account, p. 31-2, 31-3.

26) For examples of executions without trial see: MP 742/1 File 336-1-1939 (AA VIC), ADM 116/5665/044233 (PRO); Execution of Nine New Zealand Pilots without trial, ADM 116/5665/044233 (PRO); various reports of the trials of war criminals at Manus Island, *Sydney Morning Herald*, 1950-51. For examples of trials which occurred but were rudimentary, see

McGregor, pp. 143-44; James Bradley, *Towards the Setting Sun*, Wellington NSW 1982, pp. 115-16; Information of Blee, Martin and Rollason.

27) Translations of Proceedings of Military Court of 7th Area Army, pp. 13-3, MP 742 File 336-1-755 (AA VIC); Judicial Account, p. 31-3; Furuta, *Harimu*, p. 12 (O), pp. 18-19 (C); Decisions Passed at the 7th Area Army Court Martials [sic] During 1944 and 1945, Appendix F, ADM 1/18596 (PRO).

28) Furuta, *Harimu*, p. 14 (O), pp. 22,23 (C); Furuta statements, Docs F, G, I, J; Judicial Account, p. 31-4, 31-5; Military Court Translation, pp. 13-1 to 13-3.

29) Military Court Translation, p. 13-3; Furuta, *Harimu*, p. 12 (O), pp. 18-19,23 (C). Note: According to Furuta's Interrogation, Appendix E, both the Administration flag and the Japanese national flag were produced in court as evidence.

30) Judicial Account, pp. 31-5 to 31-11.

31) Brooke, *Dunkirk*, p. 237; Bradley, p. 115.

32) Statement by Mohamed Juni, Tue 9 Jan 1945 at Richmond N.S.W., Rimau Report Copy II, A 3269 Item E 4 (AA ACT).

33) Judicial Account, pp. 31-5 to 31-15; Hague Convention of 1907, Regulations Respecting the Laws and Customs of War on Land, Article 23; Wild, p. 233; Furuta's interrogation, Appendix E.

34) Judicial Account, pp. 31-15 to 31-18; Hague Convention, Law on Land, Article 23; Australian Manual of Military Law 1941, Chapter XIV paragraphs 144, 152, 443; Furuta, *Harimu*, p. 12 (O), p. 19 (C); Hague Rules, Rule 23. Note: According to the trial documentation, some of which is believed to be highly suspect, Ingleton stated that the decision to adopt a disguise was on their own volition. The inclusion of this 'statement' in the documents allowed Kamiya to ignore the Hague Rule which indemnifies from punishment those obeying an order to use disguise in a battle situation

35) Athol Moffitt, *Project Kingfisher*, Sydney 1989, p. 170.

36) Judicial Account, p. 31-18, 31-19; Hague Convention, Spies, Article 29; Hague Rule 24.

37) Furuta statements, Docs G, J; Furuta, *Harimu*, pp. 23-24 (C). Note: Furuta statements, coupled with the corrected version, give the most comprehensive account. His original version is similar but shorter and the account in the Judicial Account is quite brief by comparison. As Furuta's corrected *Harimu* has proven to be the most reliable account overall, this version was selected over the other two.

38) Judicial Account, pp. 31-20,31-21; Military Court Translation, p. 13-1.

39) Furuta statements, Doc I; Furuta, *Harimu*, both versions.

40) Judicial Account, p. 31-21; Rollason's information; Nielson's information; Report on Interrogation of Noh Bok Kun and Kim Hyong Soon, Oct 14 1945, Appendix G, ADM 1/18596 (PRO); Interrogation of Interpreter Furuta, 21 Oct 45, Lt. Col. Pritchard interrogating, Appendix A, ADM 1/18596 (PRO); Furuta, *Harimu*, p. 15 (O), p. 25 (C); Furuta statements, Doc J. Note: Bob Page's father, Major H.H. Page, DSO, MC (1st AIF: Major 25th Battalion), Government Secretary of New Guinea 1923-42, Acting Administrator September 1941-42, born in Grafton, NSW 8 August 1888, died when the *Montevideo Maru*, carrying 849 Allied [Australian] military prisoners and 200 civilian prisoners was torpedoed and sunk by an American submarine off Luzon in the South China Sea. All prisoners were lost. Wigmore, pp. 663n, 674).

41) Furuta, *Harimu*, p. 24 (C); Furuta statements, Doc J.

42) Judicial Account, 31-21; Furuta statements, Doc J.

43) Rollason's information; Blee's information; Interrogation of Noh and Kim.

44) Wild, p. 219; Furuta statements, Docs F, J; Judicial Account, p. 31-21; Interrogation of Noh and Kim; List of Japanese War Criminals Implicated in War Crimes Against Australians, DOC 422/7/8 (AWM). Note: Nibara was known as Woof Woof, Okamura as Boofhead or Horsehead and Shimoi as Cookhouse; Furuta, *Harimu*, p. 15 (O),

p. 25 (C).

45) Judicial Account, p. 31-21; Furuta, *Harimu*, pp. 1, 15 (O), pp. 2,25 (C). Note: In both versions, for dramatic effect, Furuta changed the identity of the speaker from Ingleton to Page; Furuta statements, Doc F.

46) Interrogation of Noh and Kim; Exhumation Report of Captain R.S. Ross, RAMC, Nov 22 1945, ADM 1/18596 (PRO); Rollason's information.

47) Kempei Tai Documents, translation p. 7 (THP).

Chapter 16: Only Partial Retribution

1) Document 2701, Journal of Taiwan POW Headquarters, August 1 1944[?], translated and quoted in Jack Edwards, *Banzai You Bastards* (privately published, n.d.), p. 260; Statement by Ian Duncan, *Sydney Morning Herald* (Magazine), August 26, 1989, and to Lynette Silver, March 1990.

2) Wigmore, Appendix 6, 'Central Army Records Office and the Prisoners of the Japanese', p. 682; Report on Activities of 2 Aust Contact and Enquiry Unit (SEAC) by Maj. A.N.H. Mackinnon, November 15 1945, AWM 52, 2nd AIF and CMF Unit War Diaries, 1939-45 War 25/1/9, 2 Prisoners of War Contact and Enquiry Unit, July-Nov 1945. (AWM).

3) Photograph of the Surrender at Singapore (LFP); Report from E Group Singapore to HQ 15 Indian Corps 11 Sept 1945, ADM 1161/566/044233 (PRO); Wild, 'Expedition to Singkep'; Information Regarding Missing Australians, report dated Oct 10 1945, MP 742 File 336-1-755 (AA VIC) and ADM 1/18596 (PRO). Note: It is normal for Malays to place the surname first. As the Australians had all supplied two given names, it seems that the surname was ignored by the gaol recorder.

4) Reports of Mackinnon, Sweeney, Burnett, War Diary, Lloyd October 25 1945, Capt. John Ellis on Aerial Reconnaissance Bintan Island 26 Sept. 1945 and Search for Allied Personnel in Riow [sic] Archipelago 13 Oct 45, Lieut. L.G. Palmer on Investigations on

Bintan Island, all in 2 Aust. Contact and Enquiry Unit.

5) Palmer's report; Interview by Tom Hall with Abdul Rachman Achap, September 4 1981, Tape 1 (THP).

6) Palmer's Report; Statement of Mr Ouvarow 11 Oct 1945, 2 Aust. Contact and Enquiry Unit; Statement of Headman of Mapur [sic] Island, Abdul Wahab, 10 Oct 45, Appendix H of Report from E Group South, ADM 1/18596 (PRO).

7) Ellis's Report of 13 October; Palmer's Report; Statements of Sgt Major Chizu Takeo of Kempei Tai at Tandjoengpinang [sic] to F/Lt Gardner (undated), Yap Chin Yan [sic] 11 Oct 1945, Roger Dol [Raja Rool] 11 Oct 1945, Raja Mun of Penegad [sic] 11 Oct 1945, 2 Aust. and Enquiry Unit War Diaries; Achap Interview Tape 4; Statement by Major Fugita, CO Garrison Bintang [sic] Is., Appendix B of E Group South Report. (This statement has been censored. For full version see MP 742, Defence, Army Correspondence Files, Multiple Number Series 1943-1951 AA VIC). Note: No post-war recovery units visited Soreh or Tapai until about February 1946, when Abdul Latif escorted a Dutch War Graves team to recover the skeletons of Ross, Lyon, Davidson and Campbell, see Interview by Tom Hall with Abdul Latif, September 7 1981, Tape 3 (THP).

8) Report on Interrogation of Noh Bok Kun and Kim Hyong Soon by Lt. Col. L.F.G. Pritchard and Major C.H.D. Wild, 14 Oct 45, Appendix G, E Group South Report; Wild, 'Expedition to Singkep'; Interrogations of Interpreter Furuta by Lt. Col. L.F.G. Pritchard and Major C.H.D. Wild, 21 Oct 45, Appendices A and E, E Group South Report; Colin Sleeman (ed), *Trial of Gozawa Sadaichi and Nine Others*, London 1948, pp. xiii-xiv.

9) Furuta, *Harimu*, p. 26(C) — see also note 56, chapter 8 of the current work; Furuta's Interrogation, Appendix A.

10) These messages were not delivered until 1981, when Tom Hall found them in the files and passed them on to the relevant families.

11) Compare the Rimau trial with that of Captain Matthews, a prisoner at Sandakan, Borneo, who was executed, A 471 File 81597, Trial LN 17, Exhibit M (AA ACT). Note: The intercepted message appeared as part of an SRD Magic Far East Summary 25 January-23 February 1945, RG 457 Records of the National Security Agency (USNA).

12) William Stevenson, *A Man Called Intrepid*, London 1976, pp. 16, 184, 319-20; Extracts from the diary of Eric Nave, reprinted in *Sydney Morning Herald* March 11 1989, originally to be published in *Codebreaker Extraordinary* until the intervention of the British Ministry of Defence, which resulted in the publication being withdrawn. See also, in the same article, extracts of the diary of Captain Malcolm Kennedy.

13) Full Account of Australian Special Overseas Operation Party, Judicial Department 7th Area Army, MP 742 File 336-1-755, entitled War Crimes Singapore, Execution of 10 Members of Lt. Col. Lyon's party, (AA VIC); Furuta, *Harimu*, p. 15(O).

14) Russell; Statement by Richard Haynes, who knew Wild well (THP). For examples of cover-ups see Executions of Australian and American Airmen at Matupi, Rabaul, A 703 File 614/1/7 (AA ACT) and the Kavieng Massacre, AWM Document 1010/6/134 (AWM).

15) Extract from Report on Interrogation of Major General Ohtsuka [sic] and Major Kamiya by Major C.H.D. Wild E Group, 19 Oct. 45, Appendix D, E Group South Report; Exhumation Report of Capt. R.S. Ross, RAMC, 22-11-45, ADM 1/18596 (PRO). Note: No investigation was ever carried out on any of the islands. When Tom Hall arrived at Kasu, Soreh, Pangkil and Merapas in 1981, apart from at Merapas, he was the first person to ask any questions of the native people. In 1945 the only island where fighting took place that was searched was Merapas. Although Pritchard's information differed from that of Ellis, and Lloyd wanted further investigations carried out, see Report of Lieut. Palmer 21 November 1945 AA 1981/155/1 Item 605/2D/1 (AA ACT), there were no further enquiries made.

16) Signal of January 18 1946, MP 742 File 336-1-755 (AA VIC); 1 Aust War Crimes to HQ AMF January 29 1946 and signal of January 27 1946, MP 742 File 336-1-755 (AA VIC).

17) Sleeman, *Trial*, pp. xiii-xiv.

18) Director of Prisoners of War and Internees, 7 June 1946 to 1 Aust War Crimes, Singapore, MP 742 File 336-1-755 (AA VIC); Minute Paper, 27 Feb 46, by Colonel Allaway MP 742 File 336-1-755 (AA VIC).

19) Memorandum by Director DPW and I, 7 June 1946, MP 742 File 336-1-755 (AA VIC).

20) Papers relating to Fleet Air Arm personnel missing from Operation Meridian, ADM 116/5665/044233 (PRO).

21) Interrogation of Noh and Soon; Collated Report on Fate of Japanese Personnel involved in Rimau case (THP).

22) Statements by Hiroyuki Furuta, Doc J (THP).

23) Statement by General Finlay, June 13 1984, PC 84/5353 (DODA ACT); For censorship of Ingleton's information compare Information about Operation Rimau, p. 3 A 3269 (AA ACT), with original I Staff 2 Message 211, part 9-15, January 9 1945, J 11625 I-L, M, N, O (USNA); Telegram 7/12/45, 32 2nd Echelon — Missing Personnel, A3269 Item V 16 (AA ACT).

24) Cyril Chambers to Mrs J.S. Hardy, March 27, 1947, MP 742 File 336-1-755 (AA VIC).

25) Mackinnon's Report; Report by Captain J. Sylvester (undated) referring to evidence given by Nomaguchi that all remaining were executed after the cessation of hostilities, MP 742/1 File 336-1-1939 Pt 1 (AA VIC); *Sydney Morning Herald*, May 1, 23 1946. Note: There are various statements by Japanese in MP 742/1 336-1-1939, which refer to the cremations, carried out on sheets of corrugated iron. War Graves uncovered the site of the mass graves in 1948, to find that the only evidence remaining were small finger, rib and arm bones and a lower jaw, which appeared from dental charts, to be that of Clifford Perske — see MP 742/1 336-1-1547.

26) Witsell to Commanding General US Armed Forces, California (undated); G.L. Bakker to Mr Schow, August 21 1946, Soerabaya; Extract from 2nd Echelon Letter No 030, 6 Jan 47; Signal of 28 February 1948 from RAAF HQ to Manila — all in MP 742/1 File 336-1-1939 Pt 1 (AA VIC).

27) W.L. Jinkins to SRD August 31 1945; Report by L. Talbot, October 10 1945; Memorandum MIS-X Section, October 23 1945; Rear Admiral James Fife to Adjutant General, AMF Headquarters, November 22 1946; DPW and I Memorandum January 1947; Report by Judge W.C. Van Beek, June 18 1947 — all in MP 742/1 File 336-1-1939 Pt 1 (AA VIC).

28) MP 742/1 File 336-1-1939 Pt 1 (AA VIC) contains over eight hundreds pages of interrogations, statements and reports collated by Sylvester and others 1947-49.

29) See note 2, chapter 9, and notes 7, 8, chapter 14 of the current work; Chapman, p. 416; BBC Television Documentary, *Arms and The Dragon* (THP); various summary reports in Fate of Sachs and Perske, MP 742/1 File 336-1-1939 Pt 1 (AA VIC).

30) Report by J. Sylvester relating to Facts governing the decision by Fleet Headquarters and Base Units to execute PsOW and Spies without benefit of trial by court Martial in the Soerabaya-Borneo-Celebes Area, (undated); Statements by Tachino, September 9, November 16 1948; Nomaguchi, November 6 1948; Furuno, March 3 1949; Shibata February 2 1949; Fujimoto, July 13 1949 and Lt. Col. Evans to Australian War Crimes Tokyo, 8 April 1949, all in MP 742/1 File 336-1-1939 Pt 1 (AA VIC); *Sydney Morning Herald*, September 27 1946. Note: In November 1943, *Suez Maru* was sunk between Ambon and Soerabaya by an Allied submarine. The 250 POWs who survived the sinking were machine gunned to death by the crew of *Minesweeper No. 12*, which was later sunk by USS *Besugio* on April 12 1945 — see statement of Fujimoto and *Report of Joint Army/Navy Assessment Committee*.

31) Documents from the Trial of Yaichiro Shibata and Fourteen Others, and the Trial of Tamao Shinohara and Two Others, A 471/1 Items 81961, 81966 (AA ACT); *Sydney Morning Herald*, February 15, March 13, 22, April 3, June 1 1951.

32) Shibata and Shinohara Trials; *Sydney Morning Herald*, February 15, March 13, April 3, June 1 1951; Statement by Prime Minister Chifley regarding Sturdee's 'absolute powers' reported in *Sydney Morning Herald*, February 22 1946.

33) Shibata and Shinohara Trials; *Sydney Morning Herald*, June 1, 11, 12 1951. Because of extremely wet weather the dying wishes of the condemned men that their bodies should be cremated and returned to Japan were not carried out. They were buried at sea instead.

34) It was not until 1989, when Tom Hall located the families of Bill Reynolds and Clifford Perske, and Lynette Silver found the family of John Sachs, that their fate was disclosed to their relatives.

Chapter 17: The Timor Conspiracy

1) Notes on SRD Operations Part 1, (Partizan Phase, Lizard I,II,III, Portolizard, Lagarto), pp. 10-29, Services Reconnaissance Department, Special Operations Australia, Organization Copy No. 1, A 3270, Item SOA Vol. 2, Q 8 (AA ACT); Directive to Lieut. M.de J. Pires, Timor Mission, June 12 1943, A 3269 Item D4 (AA ACT).

2) Captain A.J. Ellwood's Operational Report on Lagarto, pp. 1-3, Relevant Maps and Miscellaneous Papers Associated with Jaywick, Rimau and Hornbill Operations, 1942-45, Tracing and Recovery SRD POWs, A 3269 Item V17 (AA ACT); Lagarto Signals, July 2 1943-September 28 1943, A 3269/1 Item D4 (AA ACT).

3) SRD Lagarto, pp. 29-30; Lagarto Op. Report, pp. 3-6; Captain A.J. Ellwood's Report on Treatment while Prisoner of War in Timor, October 26 1945, Exhibit 7, Trial of Captain Saiki and Others, Attorney-General's Department, Courts Martial File 1901- A

471/1 Item 80708 (AA ACT); Sworn Statement of Alfred James Ellwood, April 5 1946, Document 1010/4/48 (AWM); Summary of Examination of Antonio Augusto dos Santos, June 28 1946, MP 742/1 File 336/1/1724 (AA VIC).

4) SRD Lagarto, p. 30; Lagarto Report, pp. 4-6; Ellwood's POW Report, p. 1; Ellwood's sworn statement; Lagarto Signals, October 6 1943; Statement of Chung Hai Cheng, MP 742/1 File 336/1/1724 (AA VIC).

5) SRD Lagarto, pp. 31, 33; Lagarto Signals, October 5,6,7 1943, March 3 1944; Lagarto Report, pp. 5-7.

6) Lagarto Report, pp. 6-7; For examples of other information being transmitted, see Lagarto Signals.

7) SP 87/2574 [WIO SRD 3], A 3269 (AA ACT); Lagarto Signals December 24 1943, January 5, 11, 16 1944.

8) Lagarto Report, pp. 7-8; Ellwood's sworn statement; Lagarto Signals, October 29 1943 - January 1944; SRD Lagarto, p. 32.

9) SRD Operations, pp. 35-6 (Cobra); Captain J.R. Cashman's Report on Cobra Party, October 23 1945, pp. 1-2, Tracing and Recovery SRD POWs, A 3269 Item V7 (AA ACT); Examination of dos Santos; Examination of Sancha Da Silva, June 27 1946 MP 742/1 File 336/1/1724; Statement by S. Kamimoto, The Case of Capt Cashman, MP 742/1 File 336/1/1213 (AA VIC) and A 471 Item 80708, Exhibit 5 of Saiki Trial (AA ACT); Statement by Captain J.R. Cashman, General Treatment whilst Prisoner of Japanese Jan 44 - Sept 45, Exhibit 2 of Saiki Trial.

10) SRD Cobra, pp. 36,37; Cobra Report, p. 3; Cobra Signals, February 8-26 1944, A 3269/1 Item D 3 (AA ACT); SRD Lagarto, p. 33; Lagarto Signals, March 2 1944.

11) SRD Lagarto, p. 33, Cobra, pp. 36-37; Lagarto Signals, March 3 1944; Cobra Report, pp. 1,4; H.J. Giskes, *London Calling North Pole*, London 1953, statement by H.M.G. Lauwers, p. 184; E.H. Cookridge, *Inside SOE*, London 1966, pp. 407-09, 419-22; Statement by Leo Marks, SOE coding expert, BBC Television Documentary

on SOE Operation 'England Spiel' (THP); Cobra Signals, February 28 1944.

12) Kamimoto Statement; Cobra Report, p. 4; SRD Lagarto, p. 33, Cobra p. 37; Lagarto Signals, March 2,3 1944; Cobra Signals, March 2,7 1944.

13) Cobra Signals, March 2,6,7 1944; Cobra Report, p. 4; SRD Cobra, pp. 27-8, 37; SRD Lagarto, p. 33; Lagarto Signals, March 16 1944.

14) Lagarto Signals, March 23 1944 and various; Lagarto Report, p. 7; Sworn statement of Minoru Tada, December 11 1947, MP 742/1 File 336/1/2073 (AA VIC).

15) Cobra Report, p. 4; Kamimoto Statement; Various Cobra messages and Intelligence Information Reports by Brigadier K.A. Wills, Controller AIB, Cobra Signals; SP 87/2574 [W10 SRD 9], A 3269 (AA ACT). Note: The reference in telegram from Hollandia to SRD Melbourne, May 6 1945 (Cobra Signals), which notes the navigational irregularities, places the Cobra relief insertion point in the ocean.

16) SRD Operations, pp. 41 (Adder); Cobra Signals; Cobra Report, p. 5; Lagarto Report, p. 9; Telegram from Captain Goto (Japanese Intelligence) November 10 1945, A 3269 Item D 26, Groper Copy II (AA ACT).

17) Various Lagarto and Cobra Signals, May-October 1944.

18) Cobra Signals, April 30, October 5,9,11 1944.

19) Cobra Signals, March 10 1945; memorandum on Lagarto and Cobra Security by Major Bingham, February 19 1945, Cobra Signals; SRD Lagarto, p. 33; SRD Personnel — index of Officers and senior NCOs, A 3269 Item H 17; Appendix 2, current work.

20) Cobra Signals, March 10,15 1945. On March 10 Bingham was informed that new ciphers were not to be included in the next drop to Cobra and Lagarto. Note: SRD Operations, p. 34, states that the date Lagarto was reported captured was April 1945. As a summary of missing personnel in 32 2nd Echelon Missing Personnel, A 3269 Item V16, states that Lagarto was reported captured on January 29 (after

'the chaps in hiding captured' intercept and after the memo was dropped, see note 21 below), the April date is incorrect.

21) Top Secret SRD Intelligence Branch Report, February 13 1945, p. 6, A 3269/1 Item H10 Pt 3 (AA ACT); Lagarto signals, January 18,23 1945; Messages to and from Leanyer and Melbourne, March 15-19 1945, A 3269 Item D3 Cobra Field (AA ACT); Cobra Signals, March 21,24,28,29 and April 2 1945; Instructions, 'not to be Divulged', carrying handwritten notation 'Dropped in March', A 3269 Item D4 (AA ACT). Note: Evidently no one in SRD realised that 'chaps in hiding captured' (stated by SRD as having occurred on 19 January) and the 'memo captured' (dropped on January 19) were almost certainly one and the same incident. It is probably indicative of the general inefficiency at SRD that, in answer to a question from the SRD advance base at Hollandia, Darwin replied that Cobra's quite definite answer of April 2 (that it still had all its memo papers) had not been received — see Cobra signals May 18 1945.

22) SRD Index of Personnel shows Bingham replaced by Lieutenant-Colonel Holland and Chapman-Walker replaced by Campbell; Chapman-Walker to Blamey, July 4 1945, 3 DRL 6643, Papers of Field Marshall Sir Thomas Blamey, WW 1914-18, 1939-45, Document 56.4. (AWM).

23) Final Report by OC Groper Party 29 Nov 45, pp. 2-3, A 3269, Groper Copy I Item D 26 (AA ACT); Report and Amplifying Report by Sgt. J.R. White 20 Oct 45, Report by Sgt. J.A. Shand 20 Oct 45, A 3269 Item V 17 (AA ACT).

24) SRD Operations, pp. 57-59 (Sunlag) and pp. 60-62 (Lagatout and Brim); Lagarto Signals, June 30 1945.

25) Operation Suncob, SP 87/2574 [W10 SRD 1], A 3269 (AA ACT); Report on Suncob Operation by Capt. P. Wynne 22 Oct 45 and Corporal B. Lawrence 19 Oct 45, A 3269 Item V 17 (AA ACT); Groper Final Report, pp. 3-4; Original Statement of Cpl. J.B. Lawrence extracted from Aust. War

Crimes Questionnaire, Statements of Capt. Mori 1 Dec 45, Sgt. Maj. Haraguchi 1 Dec 45, Sgt.-Maj. Eigi Naruta 15 November 45, all in Trial Documents of Saiki and Others. (For another copy of Japanese statements see MP 742/1 file 336/1/1213 AA VIC); Report by Captain P. Wynne, (undated) of Treatment of SRD Prisoner while in Japanese Hands and Statements of Kasukane Saiki 25 November 1945, MP 742/1 File 336/1/1213 (AA VIC).

26) Cobra Signals, July 14,16,17,18 1945.

27) Cobra Report, p. 5; Casualty Reports for Lieut. Liversidge, Paulo Da Silva, and Appendix A, A 3269 Item V 17 (AA ACT); Signals on Missing Personnel, A 3269 Item V 16 (AA ACT); Report on Investigations of War Crimes made at Dilli [sic], Portuguese Timor by Capt. A.D. Stevenson, Oct 2 45, Document 1010/2/29 (AWM); Timforce Report on Investigations into War Crimes, Atrocities and Missing Allied Personnel 8 Oct 45, Document 571A/4/3 (AWM); SRD Lagarto, pp. 23,34A; SRD Cobra, pp. 35, 40; SRD Adder, p.42; Da Silva's statement; Ellwood's POW Report; Ellwood's sworn statement.

28) Operation Sunbaker, SP 87/2574 [W10 SRD 1], A 3269 (AA ACT); Timforce Report, p. 3. Note: Those who died were seven members of the Lagarto party (which should have been evacuated by SRD), three from Cobra, five from Adder, one from Sunable and all fifteen on board Sunbaker's Liberator — a total of thirty-one. There does not appear to be any figure on the death toll among the Timorese. However, as whole villages were wiped out, the number must run into thousands.

29) Cobra and Lagarto Signals, August 12 1945; Lagarto Report, p. 10. For debate which surrounded what the answers to Cobra and Lagarto should be, see all signals August 12,13 between Morotai, Darwin, SRD and Timor, Cobra and Lagarto Signals.

30) SRD Operations, pp. 74-75 (Groper); Lagarto report, pp. 11-12; Ellwood's sworn statement; Cobra Report, p. 6.

31) SRD Groper, p. 75; Stevenson's War Crimes Report, pp. 1-2; Weekly Progress Report by Stevenson, 9 Oct 45, A 3269 Item V 16 (AA ACT); Casualty reports of Grimson, Gregg from interrogation of Da Silva by Ellwood, October 4,9 1945, A 3269 Item V 17 (AA ACT); Lagarto Report, p. 11; Cobra Report, p. 5,6.

32) Umi San Staff Message 171, January 23 1945, Box 43 J 23826 A,B,C, Serial Numbers SR 33451/2/3 (USNA), translated February 7 and March 14 1945; Umi San Messages 158 and 228 (continuation of message 171), in SRD intercept summary, Information About Operation Rimau, A 3269 (AA ACT); Project summary by J.E.B. Finlay, A 3269 Item E 4 (AA ACT); SRD Groper, p. 74; NEFIS Interrogation Report, quoted in Groper summary of missing personnel, A 3269 D 26 (AA ACT); LMS to Rimau Plans, September [?] 5 1944, A 3269 Item E 4 (AA ACT); Letter from C.H. Finlay to 2nd Echelon, November 13 1945, A 3269 Item V 16 (AA ACT); Captain Goto's telegram.

33) Note at foot of Casualty Report for Gregg (actually Pace).

34) Lagarto Report; Cobra Report. Note: SRD, being part of AIB, was under Blamey's control.

35) Stevenson's Final Groper Report; Signal from Landops to Landforces, December 6 1945, MP 742/1 File 336/1/1213 (AA VIC).

36) Ibid; Signal from Timforce to Landops Z Special Unit, December 27 1945, MP 742/1 File 336/1/1213 (AA VIC); Charter of the International Military Tribunal for the Far East, Article 13.

37) Sylvester's investigation is in MP 742/1 File 336/1/1939 (AA VIC). The trial papers are in A 471/1 Items 81961, 81966 (AA ACT).

38) Examination of dos Santos, Sworn Statement of Minoru Tada; Sworn Statement of Alfred James Ellwood, examination of Patricio Luz June 28 1946 and Sancha D Silva June 27 1946, MP 742/1 File 336/1/1724 (AA VIC).

39) Minute Paper by Director of Legal Services, 28 Mar 46, Trial of Capt. Saiki and Others, A 471/1 Item 80708

(AA ACT); International Charter, Article 13; Exhibits 2 and 7, Statements by Cashman and Ellwood, Saiki Trial; Record of Military Court (Sentences and Date), First Schedule Records, Minute Paper, all in Saiki Trial; Newspaper reports of trial, March 16 1946, in *Argus*, *The Age* and *Sydney Morning Herald*.

40) *Argus*, *The Age*, *Sydney Morning Herald*, March 1-18 1946.

41) Military Records of A.J. Ellwood and J.R. Cashman, Central Army Records.

42) *Argus*, *The Age*, *Sydney Morning Herald*, see July 1946-March 1947 for Cousens publicity, January-February 1946 for Murphy and Calwell. For Additional details on Murphy see Suzy Baldwin (ed) *Unsung Heroes and Heroines of Australia*, Melbourne 1988, pp. 270-73. Dick Horton, *Ring of Fire*, Melbourne 1983, pp. 141-45 states that Ellwood went to the beach and lit the fires that lured Cobra to its doom.

43) John Hetherington, *Blamey Controversial Soldier*, Canberra 1973, pp. 53-56, 64-69, 78.

44) Ibid, pp. 389-91; David McKnight, 'A Very Australian Coup', *Sydney Morning Herald*, November 11 1989.

45) Hetherington, pp. 393-96.

46) Umi San Messages 158,171,228; NEFIS Interrogation Report, No. 2055/III, by Ibrahim, p. 10, A 3269 Item D 30; Summary of Examination of Sebastiao Graca, June 25 1946, MP 742/1 File 336/1/1724 (AA VIC); Examinations of Da Silva, Luz; Casualty reports of Grimson and Gregg (actually Willersdorf and Pace). Note: Da Silva's evidence is corroborated in part by the hearsay evidence of Luz, who unfortunately muddles Adder, Cobra, Willersdorf and Pace. The men of whom Luz speaks must be Rimau as no Australians in Cobra were tortured in this manner and both Adder men died on insertion.

47) Taped interviews by Tom Hall with Abdul Latif, 1981, 1989 (THP); Exhumation Report of Captain R.S. Ross, RAMC, nov 22 1945, ADM 1/18596 (PRO).

48) Graves Registration Record of Personnel Buried at Kranji Military Cemetery, Set 9/32 Sheet 26, which gives the reburial dates of Lyon and Ross as December 28 1946, in Row A Plot 27 Graves 14 and 15, and Ingleton's group as August 2 1946, Row A Plot 28 Graves 1-10 (Common grave), ADM 1161/5665/044233 (PRO); Observations made by Lynette Silver at Kranji War Cemetery, June 1989. Note: In cases where the identity of the victims was known but where individual identification of the remains was impossible, headstones were erected alphabetically, from left to right. For this reason, upon the common grave which holds the remains of the ten executed men, Carey's headstone is first in the line, while Warren's is the last. The bodies of Lyon and Ross, who were positively identified by their disks (called 'necklaces' by Raja Muhammed and Latif), are buried beneath the headstones on which their names are inscribed.

Appendix I

1) Letters, Percival to Secretary, Military Board, March 8 1943 and Percival to Berryman, September 4 1945, Exhibits D, E, and H, 'Report and Copy of Transcript of the Proceedings of the Court of Inquiry, held at Victoria Barracks, Sydney on 26-30 October 1945 into the Circumstances in which Lt Gen H.G. Bennett, CB, CMG, DSO, VD left Singapore in February 1942', MP742, Item B/3/2265 (AA VIC); Letters, Blamey to Minister for the Army, September 6 1945 MP 742/1, Item B/3/2265 (AA VIC). For information on the escape of Spooner and Pulford, see Percival, pp. 287-88 and Air Vice-Marshall Sir Paul Maltby, Despatches to the Security of State for Air, published in the Third Supplement to *The London Gazette*, February 26 1948, p. 1383. According to Percival and Maltby, Pulford was free to leave at any time after February 5.

2) Wigmore, Appendix 3, General Bennett's Escape, p. 651.

3) Bennett, pp. 216-219; Frank Legg, *The Gordon Bennett Story*, Sydney 1965, pp. 263-301. For details of some of Bennett's outspoken comments see F.M. Budden, *The Chocos*, Sydney

1987, pp. 7-8.

4) T.P. Fry, 'Legal Aspects of the Departure of Major-General Gordon Bennett from Singapore', *University of Queensland Law Journal*, Vol. 1, No. 1, December 1948, pp. 34-57.

5) These publications were Percival, Despatches to the Secretary of State for War, April 25 1946, published in *The London Gazette*, Second Supplement, February 26 1948, and *The War in Malaya*.

Appendix II

1) Giskes, pp. 64-86,184,188-94; Cookridge, pp. 406-22, 425-28, 431-32,436; BBC Television Documentary on SOE Operation England Spiel (THP).

2) SOE Documentary; Giskes, p. 203; Pieter Dourlein, *Inside North Pole*, London 1953, p. 170. Note: Giskes, who had guaranteed their safety, had matters taken out of his hands when the SS removed forty-eight prisoners to Mauthausen.

3) SOE Documentary.

4) Giskes, pp. 123-26; Cookridge, pp. 475-76; Dourlein, pp. 104-168.

5) SOE Documentary. The date of winter 1943 is at variance with that of Giskes, who states that airdrops were suspended in mid 1943.

6) Giskes, pp. 134-35; Cookridge, p. 477.

7) SOE Documentary; Cookridge, p. 476.

8) Netherlands Parliamentary Commission of Inquiry, Cookridge, pp. 487-97; Dourlein, pp. 169-203; Appendix B, Statement by L.A. Donker (Dutch Inquiry) for the Foreign Office quoted in Cookridge, pp. 607-09; SOE Documentary.

9) Giskes, Dourlein, SOE Documentary and Cookridge, p. 495. Note: In 1941 Giskes, by engineering the marriage of ace spy Alfred 'Freddy' Kraus to Churchill's cousin Jacqueline Princess de Broglie (a prominent member of the resistance), had penetrated the French underground movement. Although Kraus was detained by MI-5 after the war, he was not brought to trial. In what appears to have been a deal, Kraus returned to Austria a free man, Jacqueline was given a divorce and custody of their child and Churchill no longer had a spy in the family — see Ladislas Farago, *The Game of the Foxes*, London 1972, pp. 683-93.

10) Such subterfuge was not uncommon. The secret intelligence agencies often employed great cunning to convince Germany that their plans were quite different from what was intended, e.g. dummy planes on airfields to indicate that the D-Day landings would be at Calais. See also statement by Churchill, quoted in Farago, p. 666.

11) SOE documentary; Cookridge, p. 432.

12) Cookridge, p. 494.

13) Statements by Marks, SOE Documentary.

14) SOE Documentary; Giskes, p. 109, 113-14; Cookridge, pp., 446-7, 450-2.

15) Farago, p. 666.

16) Statements by Marks; SOE Documentary; Dourlein, pp. 170-71.

Bibliography

For works other than published books — pamphlets, magazines, special collections and private papers — see individual chapter notes.

Allen Louis, *The Politics and Strategy of the Second World War, Singapore 1941-1942*, London 1977.
Arniel Stan, *One Man's War*, Melbourne 1988.
Austin Victor, *To Kokoda and Beyond. The Story of the 39th Battalion 1941-1943*, Melbourne 1988.
Baldwin Suzy (ed), *Unsung Heroes and Heroines of Australia*, Melbourne 1988.
Barker A.J., *Japanese Army Handbook 1939-1945*, New York 1979.
Bennett Lieut.-Gen. H. Gordon. *Why Singapore Fell*, Sydney 1944.
Bostock John, *Australian Ships at War*, Sydney 1975.
Braddon Russell, *The Naked Island*, London 1952.
Bradley James, *Towards the Setting Sun*, NSW 1982.
Brooke Geoffrey, *Alarm Starboard*, Cambridge 1982.
Brooke Geoffrey, *Singapore's Dunkirk*, London 1989.
Browne Courtney, *Tojo The Last Banzai*, London 1967.
Budden, F.M., *The Chocos*, Sydney 1987.
Caffrey Kate, *Out in the Midday Sun*, London 1973.
Callahan Raymond, *The Worst Disaster*, London 1977.
Chapman F. Spencer, *The Jungle is Neutral*, London 1949.
Churchill Winston S., *The Second World War Vol. 7, The Onslaught of Japan*, London 1951.
Coaldrake Maida S., *Japan in the Twentieth Century, Modernisation and Militarism*, Sydney 1971.
Connell Brian, *Return of the Tiger*, London 1965.
Cookridge E.H., *Inside SOE*, London 1966.
Cruikshank Charles, *SOE in the Far East*, Oxford 1983.
Davis Sir Robert H., *Deep Diving and Submarine Operations*, London n.d.
Day David, *The Great Betrayal*, Sydney 1988.
Day David, *Menzies and Churchill at War*, London 1986.
Dourlein Pieter, *Inside North Pole*, London 1953.
Du Quesne Bird Nicholas, *The Observer's Book of Firearms*, London 1978.
Edwards Jack, *Banzai You Bastards*, privately published, n.d.

Falk Stanley L., *Seventy Days to Singapore*, London 1975.
Farago Ladislas, *The Game of the Foxes*, London 1972.
Fergusson Bernard, *Wavell Portrait of a Soldier*, London 1971.
Firkins Peter, *From Hell to Eternity*, Perth 1979.
Foot M.R.D., *SOE*, London 1984.
Gibson Walter, *The Boat*, London 1974.
Gillison Douglas, *Australia in the War of 1939-1945. The Royal Australian Air Force 1939-1942*, Canberra 1962.
Giskes H.J., *London Calling North Pole*, London 1953.
Gough Richard, *SOE Singapore 1941-42*, London 1985.
Gough Richard, *The Escape from Singapore*, London 1987.
Hall, Richard, *The Secret State*, Sydney 1978.
Hall Timothy, *The Fall of Singapore*, Sydney 1983.
Hampshire Cecil A., *The Secret Navies*, London 1978.
Harrison Kenneth, *The Brave Japanese*, Sydney 1966.
Hetherington John, *Blamey Controversial Soldier*, Canberra 1973.
Horner D.M., (ed) *The Commanders*, Sydney 1984.
Horner D.M., *High Command*, Sydney 1982.
Horton Dick, *Ring of Fire*, London 1983.
Howard Frederick, *Kent Hughes*, Melbourne 1972.
Ind Allison, *Spy Ring Pacific*, London 1958.
Ismay, *The Memoirs of Lord Ismay*, London 1960.
Kahn David, *The Codebreakers*, London 1973.
Kirby Major-General S. Woodburn, *Singapore: The Chain of Disaster*, London 1971.
Kirby Major-General S. Woodburn, *History of the Second World War Vol. 1, The War Against Japan*, London 1957.
Ladd James J., *SBS The Invisible Raiders*, Glasgow 1983.
Leasor James, *Singapore*, London 1968.
Legg Frank, *The Gordon Bennett Story*, Sydney 1965.
Lodge A.B., *The Fall of General Gordon Bennett*, Sydney 1986.
Long Gavin, *Australia in the War of 1939-1945. Greece, Crete and Syria*, Canberra 1953.
Long Gavin, *The Six Years' War*, Canberra 1972.
McGregor John, *Blood on the Rising Sun*, Perth 1978.
MacIntyre Donald, *The Thunder of the Guns*, London 1959.
McIntyre W. David, *The Rise and Fall of the Singapore Naval Base*, London 1979.
McKie Ronald, *This Was Singapore*, Sydney 1942.
Manchester William, *American Caesar. Douglas MacArthur 1880-1964*, London 1979.
Manual of Military Law, 1941.
Mars Alastair, *Submarines at War*, London 1971.
Moffitt Athol, *Project Kingfisher*, Sydney 1989.
Montgomery Brian, *Shenton of Singapore*, London 1984.

Morrison Ian, *Malayan Postscript*, London 1942.
Moyes John F., *Mighty Midgets*, Sydney 1946.
Muggenthaler Karl August, *German Raiders of WW II*, London 1978.
Nelson Hank, *Prisoners of War*, Sydney 1985.
Owen Frank, *The Fall of Singapore*, London 1960.
Percival Lieut.-Gen. A.E., *The War in Malaya*, London 1949.
Prance Gordon W. and Others, *Pearl Harbour*, New York 1986.
Report of Joint Army/Navy Assessment Committee, Washington 1947.
Richardson H., *One Man War, The Jock McLaren Story*, Sydney 1957.
Robertson John, *Australia Goes to War*, Sydney 1981.
Robertson John and McCarthy John, *Australian War Strategy 1939-1945*, Brisbane 1985.
Russell Lord of Liverpool, *The Knights of Bushido*, London 1958.
Russell-Roberts Denis, *Spotlight on Singapore*, London 1965.
Shinozaki Mamoru, *Syonan — My Story, The Japanese Occupation of Singapore*, Singapore 1975.
Shinji Menemija, *The Account of the Legal Proceedings of the Court for War Criminal Suspects*, translated by Yoshioko Kazuo, Japan 1946.
Simons Jessie Elizabeth, *In Japanese Hands*, Melbourne 1954.
Simson Ivan, *Singapore Too Little Too Late*, London 1970.
Skidmore Ian, *Escape from the Rising Sun*, London 1973.
Sleeman Colin, *Trial of Gozawa Sadaichi and Nine Others*, London 1948.
Sleeman Colin and Silkin S.C., *The Trial of Sumida Haruzo and Twenty Others*, London 1951.
Smyth Sir John, *Percival and the Tragedy of Singapore*, London 1971.
Stevenson William, *A Man Called Intrepid*, London 1976.
Swinson Arthur, *Defeat in Malaya; the Fall of Singapore*, London 1970.
Taylor Phil and Cupper Pam, *Gallipoli*, Sydney 1989.
Trenowden Ian, *The Hunting Submarine*, London n.d.
Tsuji Colonel Masanobu, *Singapore the Japanese Version*, Sydney 1960.
2/19 Association, *The Grim Glory, The History of the 2/19 Battalion AIF*, Sydney 1975.
Waldron Tom and Gleeson James, *The Frogmen*, London 1950.
Walker Richard and Helen, *Curtin's Cowboys, Australia's Secret Bush Commandos*, Sydney 1986.
Wall Don, *Singapore and Beyond. The Story of the 2/20 Battalion AIF*, Sydney 1985.
Whitecross Roy, *Slaves of the Son of Heaven*, Sydney 1951.
Wigmore Lionel, *Australia in the War of 1939-1945. The Japanese Thrust*, Canberra 1957.
Williamson Kristin, The Last Bastion, Sydney 1984.
Wynyard Noel, *Winning Hazard*, London c. 1948.
Young Edwward, *One of Our Submarines*, London 1952.
Ziegler Oswald L. (ed), *Men May Smoke, Final Edition of 2/18 Battalion Magazine*, Sydney 1948.

Index

Grimson, Capt J. 236-7, 241-2.
Grumber, Flt-Lt Harry 15.
Gubbins, General Colin 260-1.

Hall, Maj Tom 1-4, 251-4.
Hague Convention 209-11, 221.
Hardy, L-Cpl Jack 118, 179, 180, 205, 226, 250.
Hasler, Maj (Blondie) 108.
Hatfield, Douglas 224.
Hei Ho 142, 143, 144, 146, 148, 151, 152, 156, 177, 180, 198, 200.
Hidaka, Maj-Gen 203.
Hinomoto, Lt Norio 183, 184.
Hirata, Cpl 214, 225.
Hirohito, Emperor 197, 217.
Hisada, Maj M. 205.
'Hill 120' 94, 96.
Hin Leong 45, 48, 49, 54, 56.
Holmes, Lt 113.
Holwell, Lt (Holly) 56.
Hong Chuan 43-44.
Hornbill, Operation
    alterations to 111.
    cancelled 111.
    becomes Rimau 111.
    planning stage 107-10.
Hughes, Col W. Kent 29.
Huston, AB Andrew 86, 89, 92, 96, 97, 99, 110, 112-3, 122, 131, 145, 149, 154, 156, 160, 179, 180, 250.

Ide, Cmdr Natase 193, 194.
Ikeda, WO 125, 228.
Indo-China 6, 40, 41.
Indragiri R 5, 42, 43, 44, 49, 50, 57, 63, 65, 77, 218.
Ingleton, Maj R.G. (Otto) 111, 112, 130, 133, 134, 137, 177, 179, 180, 185, 198, 199, 205-8, 211, 212, 215, 219, 225, 249, 281 n30.
intercepted signals 221-2.
ISD (see also SRD) 69, 70, 76, 78, 80.
Itagaki, Gen 202, 213, 225.
Iyer Molek 52.

Jamal Bin Diam 48, 49, 56, 60, 89.
Japanese (see also Kempei Tai)
    attitude to torture 221.
    executions by 124-6, 177-8, 194-5, 200, 215-16, 220, 224, 227, 228.
    invasion of Malaya 7, 13-14, 16, 17-19.
    invasion of Singapore 24-8, 29, 31-2.
    training methods and tactics 12, 18-19, 24, 25-7.

Java 30, 48, 53, 54, 124, 180, 197, 228, 248.
Jaywick, Operation
    awards for 110.
    consequences of 104, 105-6, 200.
    contingency plan 89-90.
    kept secret 104.
    postponed 79.
    preliminary plan 67, 69, 70.
    operation 88-104.
    operational plan 83, 88.
    raid 97-8.
    re-instated 83.
    rejection by US 70, 107.
J containers 108, 114-15, 128, 130.
Jifuku, Maj M. 203, 205, 206.
Joel, Lt Asher 82.
Johnson, Seaman 83.
Johore Bahru 19, 24, 25, 41.
Johore Str 19, 24.
Jones, AB Arthur (Joe) 87, 89, 92, 93, 97, 98, 101, 110.

Kamiya, Maj 202-14, 215, 221, 225.
Kangean I 90, 104, 123.
Kapala Djernith 116, 140, 141, 273 n5.
Karas I 149, 155, 156.
Karta 139-40, 252.
Kasu I 141-5, 146, 148, 158, 160, 204, 206, 207, 208, 220, 253.
Katapongan I 189, 193, 243, 248.
Kempei Tai 105, 106, 142-59 passim, 177-85 passim, 188, 197, 198, 201, 204, 207, 208, 209, 216, 218, 220, 221, 231.
Kidjang 171, 173, 177, 182, 219.
Kim Hyong Soon 216, 220, 223.
Kobayashi, Maj S. 214, 216, 220, 225.
Kofuku Maru (see also Suey Sin Fah, Krait) 33-4, 45, 50-1, 64, 65, 268 n73.
Kokoda Track 53, 74, 117, 270 n11.
Konishi, Medical Officer 228.
Kookaburra, Operation 111.
Koshida, Col Nagayaki 200.
Kota Bharu 7, 14, 15, 38.
Krain, SS 44.
Krait (see also Kofuku Maru, Suey Sin Fah) 68, 73, 75, 76, 77-9, 83, 84, 87, 89, 91, 92, 93, 99, 100, 101, 102, 103, 104, 107, 110, 207, 251.
Kranji 27, 28.
Kranji War Cemetery 248, 303 n48.
Kraus A. (Freddie) 304 n9.
Kuala 45, 91.
Kung Wo 45, 56.
Kwai, Looi Lam 65.